S0-EYP-763

Serials Cataloging: Modern Perspectives and International Developments

ALL HAWORTH BOOKS & JOURNALS
ARE PRINTED ON CERTIFIED
ACID-FREE PAPER

Serials Cataloging: Modern Perspectives and International Developments

Jim E. Cole
James W. Williams
Editors

The Haworth Press, Inc.
New York • London • Norwood (Australia)

Serials Cataloging: Modern Perspectives and International Developments has also been published as *The Serials Librarian*, Volume 22, Numbers 1/2 and 3/4 1992.

The Haworth Press, Inc., 10 Alice Street, Binghamton, NY 13904-1580, USA

Library of Congress Cataloging-in-Publication Data

Serials cataloging: modern perspectives and international developments / Jim E. Cole, James W. Williams, editors.
p. cm.
"Has also been published as The Serials Librarian, Volume 22, Numbers 1/2 and 3/4, 1992"–T.p. verso.
Includes bibliographical references and index.
ISBN 1-56024-281-7 (acid-free paper)
1. Cataloging of serial publications. I. Cole, Jim E. II. Williams, James W.
Z695.7.S45 1992
025.3'432–dc20 92-18492
CIP

To

DOROTHY J. GLASBY

Assistant Chief, Serial Record Division
Library of Congress

who through her efforts has greatly shaped
American serials cataloging

ABOUT THE EDITORS

Jim E. Cole, MA, Associate Professor at Iowa State University, Ames, has been involved in serials cataloging for over twenty years. He is Co-Author of *Notes Worth Noting: Notes Used in AACR2 Serials Cataloging* (Pierian Press, 1984) and Co-Editor of *Serials Cataloging: The State of the Art* (The Haworth Press, Inc., 1987), as well as the author of several articles on various aspects of serials cataloging. Mr. Cole is a member of the American Library Association, currently serving on the Serials Section's Committee to Study Serials Cataloging. He is also a member of the *Verein Deutscher Bibliothekare*.

James W. Williams, MLS, is Cataloging Coordinator for the Social Science Council libraries at the University of Illinois Library at Urbana-Champaign. He is the author of numerous technical services related articles and has written an annual review of serials cataloging for *The Serials Librarian* since 1986. A member of the American Library Association, Mr. Williams presently serves as the Serials Sections's liaison to the Catalog Form and Function Committee.

Serials Cataloging: Modern Perspectives and International Developments

CONTENTS

INTERNATIONAL ASPECTS

OPTIONS FOR CHANGE

Introduction

Serials Cataloging: Modern Perspectives and International Developments is an attempt to document the major issues of concern to serials catalogers in the early 1990s and is intended to complement and update–rather than replace–the 1987 volume *Serials Cataloging: The State of the Art*. Together the two works record the advances made in the cataloging of serials since the implementation of the second edition of the *Anglo-American Cataloguing Rules* more than a decade ago. It is anticipated that *Serials Cataloging: Modern Perspectives and International Developments* will itself be succeeded by other volumes as warranted by future developments.

The present collection is arranged in several sections: Education and Training; Cataloging Practice, Theory, and Current Developments; International Aspects; and Options for Change. As stated in the introduction to the previous volume, however, any classification scheme is to some extent arbitrary, and other groupings of the papers would have indeed been possible. The editors therefore once again beg the indulgence of the reader in this matter.

Two articles comprise the initial section, "Education and Training." In the first, Kathryn Luther Henderson sets forth her thoughts on the training of serials catalogers. Next, Boydston discusses continuing education and staff development of practicing catalogers.

The second section, "Cataloging Practice, Theory, and Current Developments," opens with Williams' survey of the issues and developments in serials cataloging in the last five years. Next, Engel discusses the copy cataloging of serials at the University of Illinois at Urbana-Champaign. This is followed by Osmus' examination of the decision-making process in the recataloging of serials and Riemer's presentation of the work of the CONSER Subject and Classification Task Force. Bross, in turn, deals with the need for uniform titles in AACR2 serials cataloging, where title entry predominates, and Turitz looks somewhat at both uniform titles and the multiple versions question. Monson discusses serials records in online public access catalogs, looking particularly at NOTIS. Two articles on newspaper cataloging are found next: the first, by Todd Butler, examines the *Newspaper Cataloging and Union Listing Manual*, of which he is the author; the second, by Beverley Geer-Butler, discusses the cataloging and inventory phase of the Maryland Newspaper Project. Following these are two articles relating to the cataloging of microform reproductions–a description by Clark and Jones of the cataloging of such materials at the National Library of Canada, and a discussion by Graham of U.S. cataloging policy and proposed changes as related to microform reproductions and the multiple versions question. The section concludes with an analysis by Osmus and Morris of serials cataloging costs at Iowa State University.

"International Aspects," the third section, consists of six articles. In the first of these, Callahan compares the 1988 revision of AACR2 to the revised edition of ISBD(S). Mullis then discusses the *ISDS Manual* and its relationship to ISBD(S) and compares the *Manual* further to AACR2. Next come three articles focusing on serials cataloging in specific countries. Mullis and Cameron discuss serials cataloging in the United Kingdom and Australia, respectively, and Dini details the history and current state of serials cataloging in Italy. The final article, by Zotova, is a well reasoned, convincing argument favoring the complete registration of serials in the current national bibliography.

Three articles are found in the last section, "Options for Change." First, Case and Randall present the results of surveys dealing with latest entry cataloging of serials. Next, Sheble and Havens explore both the currently operative and projected applications of the Linked Systems Project and their relationship to serials cataloging. In the concluding article, Madison examines the concept of the name main-entry heading and its role in the environment of the online public access catalog.

The editors wish to express their sincere gratitude to these authors who through their time and talent have made possible this collection detailing the current state of the art of serials cataloging.

Jim E. Cole
James W. Williams

Personalities of Their Own: Some Informal Thoughts on Serials and Teaching About How to Catalog Them

Kathryn Luther Henderson

SUMMARY. One cataloging teacher's approach to the preparation of serials catalogers is detailed. Emphasis is placed on the goals, objectives, philosophy and methods employed in teaching. Serials do have unique characteristics, consequently, the areas where serials cataloging differ from the cataloging of other materials are cited. Stress is placed on the importance of relating serials cataloging to other bibliographic control measures for serials.

INTRODUCTION

The results of literature searches are somewhat sparse in regard to education for the preparation of serials catalogers. Surveys have been made regarding the coverage of serials in the curricula of schools of library and information science. Practitioners tell of their education and

Kathryn Luther Henderson is Professor of the Graduate School of Library and Information Science at the University of Illinois at Urbana-Champaign, 410 David Kinley Hall, 1407 W. Gregory Drive, Urbana, IL 61801.

their training. Also there are general articles on cataloging and on serials which touch upon the subject. This article has made no survey among schools or teachers. It does not purport to tell the "correct" or "only" way to approach the teaching of serials cataloging. Rather, it is the approach, developed over a quarter of century, by one teacher who has had the privilege of working with a number of talented students and reflects her personal approach to the goals, objectives, methods, and philosophy of teaching about a subject she enjoys very much. To this teacher it does not seem an unusual approach; rather it seems a very natural approach.

THE CRUX OF TEACHING ABOUT SERIALS

Not long ago, a former student from almost a dozen years past telephoned me about a matter totally unrelated to serials. As we finished the business that precipitated the phone call, she noted that just that morning she had related to her staff something that she had learned in her cataloging courses. A teacher is always grateful when students remember something for a dozen years so I was anxious to hear what had been remembered. She related how her staff were complaining about the difficulty of serials cataloging. Then she told them that her cataloging teacher had made plain to her how exciting serials are to work with because serials have "personalities" of their own. After a long teaching career, I have learned that what one may think is a great "pearl of wisdom" is not really what students may, in the future, consider to be the "pearl." This was not the "pearl" I had expected.

The fact that someone remembered that serials are exciting to work with and that they have personalities of their own among library materials may really be the crux of teaching about serials. Basic tenets of all teaching are that a teacher must know the subject, enjoy it, demonstrate excitement for the subject, show enthusiasm for it, and possess the ability to convey all of this to the student. Genuine excitement and enthusiasm have converted more than one student who came to a cataloging class with a negative attitude. But, of course, much more than excitement and enthusiasm must go into the teaching of any subject. What, then, are some of the elements that teach not only the excitement of working with serials but also the solid theory and practical work that pertain to serials cataloging for the preparation of those who will make and use catalogs?

GOALS AND OBJECTIVES

Any teaching experience makes use of goals (translated into objectives), whether or not the teacher identifies and states them. But it is prudent to both identify and state one's goals. An important goal in a graduate professional school is to prepare students for their initial professional positions while realizing that not everything can be learned in school; training in particulars, procedures, and practices will have to come in the individual libraries. Much in the particular training will depend on whether manual or automated systems are used; what specific systems are used; the size of the library; what auxiliary files are used for serials operations, etc. So from the beginning, students must realize that not every aspect of serials cataloging can be covered in courses in school. Education does not end with the completion of a course so the students also learn that another goal in a dynamic field is to foster the idea of continuing education for these changing times. Yet another goal of graduate level education is to encourage, identify, produce, and evaluate research. A rich area for research certainly exists in serials work and one always hopes that at least some of the students in any one class will be engaged, in the future, in that research.

Goals must be translated into objectives for the specific learning experience. By the end of the serials unit, the student should be able to:

1. Define terms related to serials cataloging such as: serials, series, monographic series, periodicals, successive entry cataloging, latest entry (full bibliographic) cataloging, earliest entry cataloging.
2. Identify International Serials Data System (ISDS), International Serials Bibliographic Description (Serials) (ISBD(S)), National Serials Data Program (NSDP), International Standard Serials Number (ISSN), CONSER.
3. State how the systems and elements mentioned in 2. above relate to serials cataloging.
4. Compare monographic cataloging with serials cataloging by citing ways in which the cataloging data differs in serials cataloging records because of the nature of serials.
5. Catalog serials publications at an intermediate level.
6. Illustrate different methods of serials cataloging for changes in entry and/or title. Cite advantages and disadvantages of the different methods for users of card and/or online catalogs including the advantages and disadvantages for different library staff members.

7. Relate serials cataloging to bibliographic control in general and to serials bibliographic control in particular.
8. Identify important sources in the literature to enhance the present learning experience and to carry with him/her for continuing education in serials management.

At this point it is important to stress that most librarians work with serials. As much of the budget in many libraries is increasingly spent on serials, every librarian should have a basic foundation in serials bibliographic control measures that are achieved through cataloging; therefore these objectives have meaning for more than would-be catalogers.

PHILOSOPHY AND METHODS

How does one begin to accomplish these objectives? Principles of bibliographic control will last a lifetime while rules, codes, subject headings, and classifications will change. So theory is of first importance, and each student needs to learn the underlying fundamental theory of bibliographic control. But theory without the test of application is bare.

Timing is an important factor in any learning situation; therefore, it is obvious that the fundamentals of bibliographic control in general and basic mastery of tools should precede the introduction to the more difficult aspects of cataloging. Since current descriptive cataloging rules for all formats are based on the same basic principles and the same rules in Chapter 1 in the *Anglo-American Cataloguing Rules* 2d edition, 1988 revision (AACR2),[1] a mastery of the general rules is of first importance. In introductory cataloging courses, the students learn that serials, although requiring the use of general chapters, also have a chapter of their own (Chapter 12, "Serials") which is consulted in conjunction with the chapter dealing with the physical form in which the serial is published since serials are not limited to any one format of material. For example, in describing a serial motion picture, both Chapters 12 and 7 are used. But knowing that Chapter 12 exists does not necessarily mean that the student should apply it at an early point in the learning process.

In dealing with choice of access points, where there are no specific rules for serials, the instructor should not be so cautious about introducing a serials problem. In fact, the more one can play down differences at this stage, the more easily the student will master the concept that all types of items are on the same footing for this part of cataloging.

Since corporate headings are so closely aligned with serials, a good foundation in the construction of corporate headings is of considerable importance to the would-be serials cataloger. It soon becomes obvious that the timing for teaching about some parts of cataloging in regard to serials will be in the latter stages of cataloging courses.

Teaching about any aspect of cataloging is really teaching students to think by teaching them how to analyze a problem. It is that simple–if one doesn't know what the problem is, how can one solve it? The answer is clear–one can't. So, first of all, it is helpful if the student can begin to identify the types of problems that result from the "personalities" of serials. The whole range of problems associated with the cataloging of serials can not be covered within the time constraints of any cataloging course. It is well known that even experienced serials catalogers will, from time to time, encounter a new type of problem that the codes don't cover. Then, the cataloger must retreat to basic principles so early on students will benefit from learning to consider solutions to problems, to weighing alternatives, and to making and evaluating decisions.

At this point, the teacher is ready to consider methods. If one needs to know *about* serials to catalog them, how better can a teacher do this than to collect a number of serials for a "show and tell" introductory session where there is an actual viewing of physical items? For the teachers who have been serials catalogers, this approach may seem too obvious or too rudimentary, but a teacher must remember that not all of the students have been checking in serials since the sophomore year in college! Almost any serial illustrates some point important to serials cataloging that may not be known to library school students; therefore the instructor need not search for really "weird" examples.

Readiness is another important factor in teaching. One of the biggest mistakes a teacher can make is to early on choose exceptionally difficult problems that would tax the talents of even experienced catalogers. To introduce problems that are too difficult too early does not excite–it frightens. Students should be challenged, but not frightened.

DEFINITION TIME

As a group, serials really do have "personalities of their own"–they are not monographs which one catalogs once and, usually, for all. But what is a serial? Armed with definitions from reading and study, students come to a session to discuss this question and to engage in decision making and testing of definitions. "Is it or is it not a serial" can be an interesting game as students test the definition against a variety of real serials–periodicals, annual reports, newspapers, newsletters, house organs, proceedings, etc.,–contrasting them with multiple volumes in a set or items in a monographic series. Together the students begin to sort out what constitutes a serial at least by definition. One important criterion of most definitions of serials is that a true serial is *intended* to be continued indefinitely. But how can a cataloger determine a publisher's intent? Guidelines such as those used by the Library of Congress Rule Interpretations may be a start to at least the interpretation of Library of Congress catalog records. But is a serial really "set in stone"? Is there a "well maybe" category in our game? Are there administrative decisions which local libraries make in the interest of expediency for local handling? Do some items such as conferences which *seem* as if they will continue over time have personalities of their own which may call for their being locally handled as serials even though not technically serials? Does ownership of only one issue of a serial purchased for a specific purpose call for its being cataloged as a monograph rather than a serial?

DESCRIPTIVE CATALOGING

In monographic cataloging, students know the sanctity of the title page. With many serials there is no title page to begin the cataloging process especially when cataloging from the first issue as is the prescribed pattern in AACR2. Learning the substitute sources and the prescribed priority of sources becomes necessary in serials cataloging. Selecting a title for monographic works is usually a rather straightforward process. Certainly there are times when it is difficult to distinguish a monographic "title proper" from an "other" title but these occasions are not numerous in the totality of monographic cataloging experiences. But in serials cataloging, the cataloger is frequently faced with a number of words modifying the noun "title" such as masthead, cover, caption, and running. Knowing the definitions of these titles is important as is recognizing their usual locations in serials. Viewing an example where there are several such titles in the same item is evidence that some serials have dual or even triple personalities. Some parts of monographic cataloging need to be "unlearned" in cataloging serials such as recording "other" titles which, except in a few instances, the Library of Congress Rule Interpretations (LCRIs) generally exclude from the body of the entry in serials cataloging. One such instance where the "other" title is retained illustrates another personality of serials: the use of initialisms or acronyms as title propers or "other" titles, where AACR2 prescribes use of the full form as the title proper (e.g., Monthly labor review : MLR). Another aspect of the personality of serials is that statements of responsibility are not infrequently embedded in titles. Here is another instance where seeing examples such as *Field Museum Natural History Bulletin* or *Journal of the Federal Home Loan Board* contrasted with *Science*/American Association for the Advancement of Science makes an explicit point that is helpful in identifying a cataloging problem calling for decision making.

One data element that students have difficulty attributing to serials publications is the edition statement, yet in the time of electronic publishing this feature is likely to become more common as computers can easily spew out different editions for diverse clientele. These new edition statements will join those editions already prepared for different geographic areas, for special interest groups, for special formats, for variant language groups, or for revisions or reissues. Showing examples such as the now deceased serial *A.D.* in its Presbyterian and United Church of Christ editions opens up the possibility of the student's becoming much more aware of varied editions in serials.

An important part of the personality of serials is their numeric and/or alphabetic or chronological designations. One of the requirements of many definitions of serials is that a true serial must carry numeric and/or chronological designations, but it is not clear to many students the wide range of such designations that may occur in serials. Showing serials with a variety of such designations awakens the student to variant patterns. Particularly important to point out is the fact that the same serial can have several sets of numbering, for example, volume numbering, numbering within the volume, and whole numbering. The latter type seems to be somewhat of a mystery to most beginning catalogers until they see examples that illustrate this phenomenon such as *Science* with whole numbers half the way to ten thousand. As students may not have previously encountered Area 3 in their cataloging courses, this is the appropriate time to explain its role in serial catalog records or to contrast Area 3 in Chapter 12 with Area 3 in map, computer file, and music catalog records. Also this is a good opportunity to indicate the purpose of open entry records.

Certainly one of the most important parts of serials cataloging is learning to formulate clear, concise, and effective notes, but it is not always easy to express oneself in the economy expected in a bibliographic record. Writing notes is something of an art and one treasures examples that meet all the above criteria. I can still remember the little file of "good notes" that I began on my first day as a serials cataloger. A "good note'' became almost like a poem or a symphony. Fortunately, examples in the codes as well as in some published collections made by serials librarians are useful aids.[2]

Much of the necessity for notes relates to the propensity for serials to express their personalities in a variety of ways related to their changing nature. In many ways, the lives of serials parallel those of the humans who use them. Each serial is ''born'' after a period of preparation and waiting. (Some serials even have ''prenatal'' existences such as the several ''Premier'' issues that preceded the original *Ms.* magazine and the ''Premier issue 1990'' that preceded the rebirth of Ms..) As in human life, longevity is not a ''given.'' Wars, economic conditions, and changes in society bring their toll to serials as to humans. Postal increases may limit the size of a person's or an institution's budget for other essentials; for serials it may limit their physical size both in number of pages or in height and/or in width. (How many publications are available today in the size of the old *Life* or *Saturday Evening Post* magazines?) Like persons, some serials die in ''infancy'' while others flourish until ''middle age'' or well beyond the span of ''three score years and ten.'' For some few serials, real longevity can be a fact of life, as they far exceed the life span of any human except perhaps Methuselah. (Serials as a form of communication are not known to have existed for over 900 years!) Between ''life'' and ''death'' many things can happen to serials as to humans–some live calm, consistent, orderly lives; others find life to be turbulent, inconsistent, changeable; some ''marry'' (merge); some ''divorce'' (split). Some even have ''offspring.'' Some are ''resurrected'' or ''born again.'' A favorite example used to illustrate the resurrection of a serial is *Vanity Fair* which grew from its January 1914 beginning into ''young adulthood.'' But its demise at the age of twenty-two (volume 45, number 6) occurred in February 1936. In the following month, it was absorbed by *Vogue.* Some forty-seven years later (March 1983), *Vanity Fair* resumed publication with no word of explanation about its ''rebirth'' except what could be garnered through a lamenting letter to the editor in which the letter writer complained because he had not been selected by the publisher to subscribe to the new journal. As only a seasoned cataloger would expect, *Vanity Fair* began its new life with volume 46, number 1 as if the forty-seven intervening years had not occurred. Even *Life* found a new life for itself. The notes required to show the continuing life cycle of a serial, its absorption by, its merger with, or its split into another serial are keys to retrieval of the ''work'' whether manual or online systems are in use. Without these linkages, important retrieval elements will be missed. Introducing a few choice, but not unusual, examples of these points makes notes seem much more real and important.

Frequency is part of the personality of serials that requires a unique type of note. But students often are unaware of the different types of frequencies that can exist even within the life space of any one serial let alone how to frame these statements into a viable note–for example, do the terms "semimonthly," "biweekly," "fortnightly," "twice a month," "every two weeks" really mean the same time span and, if so, which should be used? Not all serials carry open statements of responsibility, yet there are often indicators that the serials are the official (or other) publications of issuing bodies for which access points are made calling for their identification in the catalog record. The association of these bodies with the publication often adds "authority" to the publication. Again, notes are vital conveyors of information. Important at this point is the recognition that editors are *not* recorded in responsibility statements for serials; however, depending upon the longevity of the editors with the serial or if their names are likely to be better known than the title of a serial, the names of editors may be cited in a note. Numbering changes over time for some serials; complexities or irregularities must be explained to users. The presence of cumulative indexes is another type of important note.

Because change is a constant in serials cataloging, it is another part of the personality of serials. Change is also part of the challenge, the excitement, and the fun of serials cataloging that have previously been conveyed to the student. In teaching cataloging, one also finds it necessary to show the changes that have taken place because of changes in codes and in technology. And if one teaches long enough, one should never be surprised if some things come "full circle." This can be illustrated by the different methods which have been used over time to take care of the seemingly endless recataloging that is necessitated by changes in serial titles or issuing bodies. There are three basic ways to handle this: (1) enter each serial under its earliest entry, (2) enter each serial under its latest entry, or (3) enter each serial under successive entries. When I first began to teach, latest entry cataloging was still the accepted form in the codes. But as a consultant to the code revision committee for the *Anglo-American Cataloging Rules* (AACRl),[3] I knew about the impending changes that AACRl would bring to serials records when title or other entry elements changed, so I also introduced that pattern to my first class. Although successive entry cataloging (even at the Library of Congress) soon became firmly established, it has always seemed important to me that students know about the other methods. After all, most catalogs have a history. Because catalogs reflect earlier methods of entry and because changes in serials always call for some degree of recataloging, librarians, whether users or makers of catalogs, need to be aware of why different methods are reflected in catalogs. With retrospective conversion projects, knowing variant methods is important for those who supervise and participate in such projects.

The recent revival of interest, with online catalogs, of having all of a serial's history portrayed on one record (either earliest or latest entry) has proven the worth of not throwing out teaching about older methods when newer ones appear on the scene. (To those without a sense of history, the old methods seem like the new methods!) The examples (updated over time by ISBD punctuation, etc.) seen by scores of my students over the years showing the same serial cataloged by latest and by successive entry cataloging have, in recent years, been joined by an earliest entry record (a method suggested by Charles A. Cutter). In a role playing session, "serials librarians," "reference librarians," "acquisitions librarians," "catalogers," "users," etc., speak to the advantages and disadvantages of the different methods in trying to decide what to use in "their library." The students don't solve the problem for every (or maybe any) library but they do read from the growing literature on the subject and do think through the merits of each method.

Students will soon be librarians and become the next generation of catalog makers and users as well as code revisers. They need to know where our codes are inadequate or in need of improvement. Aside from the fact that they may decide that present codes are inappropriate for a new generation of online catalogs, the students should be aware of the weaknesses in present codes. In AACR2, as far as choice of entries is concerned, serials follow the same rules as other types of materials and the close tie of serials to corporate bodies has already been mentioned. Current rules reduce the possibility of corporate main entries; therefore, many serials are left with bare generic titles as access points. (Here one might hope for a little *more* personality!) Chapter 25 (Uniform titles) continues to fall short in providing unique identification for such items and misses the opportunity to provide a formalized title in a standard predictable way. But the Library of Congress Rule Interpretations for 25.3B are the beginning of an answer to that problem and are an important part of the student's learning.

MARC FORMAT

The MARC format was not in existence when I first began to teach but changing the format of the catalog has resulted in this added dimension to teaching. Since students have applied the MARC formats to books, audiovisual materials, music, and maps prior to the study of serials cataloging, the MARC concept is already known. Of course, there are some differences among the formats for books, audiovisual materials, music, maps, and serials. Particularly in the linking notes area for serials are the differences apparent. On the whole, the translation of serial cataloging into the MARC format seems to cause little difficulty except in the linking note areas. As we move nearer the time of an integrated MARC format, the students should be prepared for that event.

SUBJECT CATALOGING

The difficulty of assigning subject headings and classification notations for a potentially long history of a serial is a constant area of concern for the student, especially when the subject control devices must be determined from only the first issue of the serial. Title or corporate name changes may herald also *content* changes, yet few librarians may take the time to show such changes in their catalogs. Why subject control devices may have seemed ineffective to the student as a catalog user becomes quite clear to the student as a cataloger, especially if the cataloging has gone unrevised for a particular item over a number of years. Subject control, particularly with earliest or latest cataloging, may not seem very truthful if it gives the impression of reflecting the content of the whole span of the serial. This point can be made in evaluating the various methods for handling change of entry.

BEYOND INVENTORY CONTROL

As the student ponders the ineffectiveness of subject control for serials, the instructor might raise the question of the ineffectiveness of the *inventory* type of control that we continue to give to serials as a whole in most libraries. In a paper I delivered in 1969 at a conference on serials,[4] I put forth what to the conferees appeared then to be a "radical" suggestion when I proposed that some day we should bring back into our catalogs what we abandoned to commercial indexing firms in the late nineteenth century. We should consider giving control to the individual parts of serials. At that time, many conferees approached me with the question: "You don't really mean that, do you?" In 1969, MARC was an infant. We had not yet entered the online catalog era. But technology brings changes and sometimes even a revival of older ideas which have been dropped from consideration. Studies of even early online catalogs indicated that users expected to find indexes to periodicals included in the new format of the catalog. Over a decade later we are seeing the mounting of reference databases in online catalogs, raising questions of incompatibility of forms of entry with those of catalog entries and the possible need for gateway systems. In an age when serial pricing is an issue of grave concern, each serial must pay for itself in optimal use. Whether to go beyond inventory control, whether to rely only on reference databases if we do go beyond inventory control, whether to cover the content of serials not included in reference databases, whether cooperative efforts could be mounted to give additional coverage, or whether in the age of austerity we fail to even dream about wider service are just the beginning of issues that seem ripe for discussion in a cataloging course. Several recent articles by Sheila S. Intner may start the discussion.[5]

RELATING SERIALS CATALOGING TO OTHER SERIAL CONTROL MEASURES

In the last several decades, serials cataloging conventions have become closely aligned with other bibliographic standards. The alphabetical array of standards and programs such as ISSN, ISDS, NSDP, CONSER, ISBD(S) must be understood for the role that they have played and will play in influencing our current codes and practices in the total picture of bibliographic control. The relationship of a key title and the ISSN to the decision of whether a serial needs a new entry should be part of the fund of information that the student takes away from the cataloging course.

Serials cataloging is also closely aligned to other parts of the total serials control picture. If no other courses in the program present general serials management issues, the cataloging course can introduce related topics of serials acquisition and control. (It is useful to learn, for example, that helpful information for the cataloging process may originate in the records and files assembled in the acquisitions process.) As integrated systems become more prevalent, an understanding of all aspects of serials control becomes more important to each librarian.

CONCLUDING THOUGHTS

Once again, it should be stressed that no cataloging course can teach everything. The purpose of professional education is to present a body of knowledge: to introduce history, development, and theory, to teach about identifying and solving problems. A grounding in what bibliographic control purports to do can carry through in whatever way serials cataloging may be utilized in the student's future. That grounding is probably much more important than remembering a specific rule or a method that was used to teach a precept. Problem solving, weighing alternatives, making decisions, are components of every librarian's day. Thinking through problems leading to solutions should be part of the educational experience as should an acquaintance with the cataloging and auxiliary tools that will be used. Practical application is also part of the process, but the mastery of *specific* routines should come with the new position.

Instilling the confidence for serials work is part of the process that began with instilling an excitement about serials. I have found that most students who want to be catalogers feel, as they leave school, that they are capable of monographic and even nonbook cataloging; fewer feel as confident that they are ready to be serials catalogers. Yet many have become serials catalogers and have apparently succeeded under the guidance of librarians ready to help in the transition. Since serials are no longer separated from monographs in many libraries, beginning catalogers need to be ready to handle both monographs and serials.

The work of the teacher is not quite completed. The realization that change is inevitable not only in the serials, but also in the tools, and the catalog fosters the need for continuing education. Sending the student off with a bibliography of sources to begin that continuing study has proven to be an important link between school and the first job.

Now the cataloging-student-about-to-be-a-catalog-librarian is ready for the training and further education that begins on the job. I often tell my students that they will probably learn more in their first month on the job than they learned in a semester. They will find that to be true if the profession has recognized the need for training. Knowing that librarians are waiting to provide "a helping hand" is an important link in the total educational process.

REFERENCES

1. *Anglo-American Cataloguing Rules.* 2nd edition, 1988 revision. (Chicago: American Library Association, 1988).

2. Useful tools are: Jim E. Cole and David E. Griffin, *Notes Worth Noting: Notes Used in AACR2 Serials Cataloging.* (Ann Arbor, MI: Pierian Press, 1984); Nancy G. Thomas and Rosanna O'Neil, *Notes for Serials Cataloging* (Littleton, CO: Libraries Unlimited, 1986); Carol L. H. Leong, *Serials Cataloging Handbook: an Illustrative Guide to the Use of AACR2 and LC Rule Interpretations.* (Chicago: American Library Association, 1989).

3. *Anglo-American Cataloging Rules.* North American Text. (Chicago: American Library Association, 1988).

4. The conference was the Allerton Park Institute, number 16, entitled "Serial Publications in Large Libraries." It was published as *Serials Publications in Large Libraries,* edited by Walter C. Allen. (Urbana, IL: Graduate School of Library Science, University of Illinois, 1970).

5. Articles by Sheila S. Intner include: "Access to Serials–Part l. A Look at the Bibliographic Unit," *Technicalities,* 10, 1 (January 1990), p. 3-5; "Serials Catalog Records: Image and Reality," *Technicalities,* 10, 3 (March 1990), p. 5-7; "Modern Serials Cataloging," *Technicalities,* 10, 5 (May 1990), p. 4-6; and her contribution to "The Future of Serials Librarianship: Part 2" *Serials Review,* 16, 3 (fall 1990), p. 65-67, 80.

Continuing Education and Staff Development Among Serials Catalogers

Jeanne M. K. Boydston

SUMMARY. A survey was conducted to examine the professional involvement of serials catalogers in continuing education and staff development activities in several relevant areas. Analysis of the survey found that the respondents are involved with a wide variety of professional organizations, but tend to attend local conferences rather than those on the national level. Furthermore, the respondents are keeping abreast of current trends in serials librarianship by reading a variety of professional journals and using both basic and auxiliary cataloging tools. In most cases, there is administrative support for these activities; however, the level of support varies from library to library.

INTRODUCTION

Keeping up with a constantly changing profession is one of the most challenging aspects of being a serials cataloger today. While in library school, the student is exposed to the most recent information and thought within the profession. Yet, what happens once the student leaves the nurturing collegiate world of library school and enters the "real" world of librarianship? The increased reliance on automation, the never ending revisions and interpretations of cataloging codes, and other such issues all tax the cataloger's ability to keep current. How does one keep up with the changes?

To cope with the changing world of serials librarianship, an ongoing

Jeanne M. K. Boydston, MSLIS 1985 (Illinois), is employed as an Assistant Professor and Serials Cataloger at Iowa State University Library, Ames, IA 50011-2140.

program of staff development and continuing education is needed. Staff development is training and knowledge made available by the institution that directly impacts one's specific job within the library. Continuing education, on the other hand, is a broader concept that involves acquiring information relevant to the profession.[1]

Continuing education has a number of forms. Contact with other librarians provides an excellent source for both formal and informal education.[2] Likewise, professional journals can be a rich resource for librarians who wish to remain knowledgeable in their profession.[3]

There have been several studies that focus on continuing education and staff development among academic librarians. For examples, see the NCLIS sponsored study conducted in the 1970's,[4] and Neal.[5] Also, Hegg has studied continuing education and job satisfaction in four Midwestern states.[6] The Hegg study focuses on formal continuing education, such as attendance at workshops and conferences and writing for publication. In a related article, Hegg specifically focuses on faculty status as correlated with continuing education and job satisfaction.[7]

OBJECTIVE

This project is intended to examine professional development and involvement among serials catalogers working in college and university libraries. Professional development may be achieved by several methods, such as involvement in professional organizations, attendance at conferences and meetings, and reading literature related to the field of librarianship. The project is designed to examine whether these methods are used by serials catalogers.

METHODOLOGY

The sample population for this survey consists of 200 serials librarians working at university or college libraries. This group is large enough to yield meaningful statistics, yet is also manageable, given the scope and time frame of the project. The first source used to collect a list of potential respondents is the *Directory of Library and Information Science Professionals*.[8] Every individual who listed "serials cataloging" as a specialty and is employed in an academic library has been included in the survey. This source yielded fifty-seven individuals. Additional librarians were chosen from the *American Library Directory 1990-91*[9] using the following method. The first academic library listed on every fifteenth page was chosen for inclusion in the survey. If the first library listed was not an academic library, then each successive entry for the page was considered until an academic library was encountered. As a result, libraries located in the United States, Canada, and the Virgin Islands were included. In order to minimize redundancy, libraries that were already included in the first group of respondents were omitted from consideration in the second group; rather, the next academic library listed was chosen instead. The second source, used in this manner, provided 143 potential respondents.

Once the survey population was assembled, the survey and a cover letter were sent to all the potential respondents. Since the project was designed to study professional involvement among serials catalogers, it was desirable whenever possible to send the surveys directly to individuals who were actually cataloging serials. The sources used, however, do not identify individual librarians as serials catalogers. For example, in the *Directory of Library and Information Science Professionals* the listing of "serials cataloging" as a specialty does not necessarily mean that an individual actually catalogs serials. This problem is magnified in the *American Library Directory*, where in general only individuals in middle and upper level administration are listed. In an attempt to alleviate this problem, the cover letter encouraged the recipient to redirect the survey to another individual in their library if the other individual was more directly involved in the actual cataloging of serials. The cover letter also named a specific deadline for the return of the survey, and in approximately three weeks, a follow-up letter was sent urging the return of the survey.

The survey itself begins with an introductory section which concerns the educational and professional background of the respondent. The next sections focus on various aspects of professional involvement: membership in professional associations, attendance at meetings and workshops, and reading professional literature. The last section contains questions regarding the status of librarians within their institutions. For the text of the survey, see Appendix I.

RESPONDENTS

Of the 200 surveys that were mailed, 143 have been returned. Twelve of the returned surveys are unusable. The usable surveys total 131, or a 66% return rate. Since many of these surveys contain one or more unanswered questions, the calculations in this study are based upon the total responses to each question.

Most of the respondents have similar educational backgrounds. Of the 131 individuals that answered the question, 89% (116 cases) have an MLS (or similar) degree from an ALA-accredited library school program, while 11% (15 cases) do not. The time that has passed since the receipt of this degree ranges from six months to forty years. The mode (11 out of 105 cases) is ten years. The mean time elapsed since the receipt of this degree is fifteen years.

Far fewer of the respondents have an advanced degree in library science such as a Certificate of Advanced Study (CAS) or PhD. Only 4% (5 cases) of the respondents have advanced degrees. Of the five cases, four indicate the type of degree (3 PhD, 1 CAS). Obviously, the respondents have overwhelmingly declined to pursue a CAS or PhD degree.

MEMBERSHIPS IN PROFESSIONAL ORGANIZATIONS

One possible avenue of professional development and involvement for a librarian is membership in a professional organization, such as the American Library Association (ALA). A majority of the respondents (57%, 73 cases) are members of the association, while 43% (55 cases) are not members. ALA subgroups such as divisions, round tables, and discussion groups also afford the possibility of professional involvement. Only 43% (55 cases) of those polled are members of these groups. The majority (57%, 73 cases) do not belong to any subgroup of ALA. While the survey does not ask, possible reasons for this relative lack of participation may include, among other things, the membership costs and a lack of relevancy to the personal work situation.

The Association for Library Collections and Technical Services (ALCTS) is the most frequently named subdivision (57%, 30 cases). Since the survey is aimed at serials catalogers, this should be expected. The next most commonly listed groups are the Association of College and Research Libraries (55%, 29 cases) and the Library Information and Technology Association (28%, 15 cases). The North American Serials Interest Group (NASIG) is a relatively new professional organization; however, it is the only group dedicated solely to serials. Yet, the overwhelming majority (84%, 107 cases) of the respondents reply that they are not members of this group. Just 16% (21 cases) of the respondents are members of NASIG. ALA and NASIG are just two of the many associations to which librarians may belong. The majority of the respondents report, however, that they do not belong to any other national association (60%, 76 cases). Only 40% (50 cases) of the respondents hold membership in another professional library association. The Canadian Library Association is the most commonly listed group (16%, 8 cases). This obviously reflects the Canadian librarians included in the survey. The American Association of Law Librarians is the second most frequently listed group (14%, 7 cases).

Professional library associations exist at different levels, including state associations. The frequency of membership in a state library association closely mirrors that observed at the national level. Out of 130 respondents, 58% (75 cases) belong to a state library association, while 42% (55 cases) are not members of such organizations. There are, of course, many other professional library associations that do not fit into the categories just outlined. For example, there are regional library associations and various user groups of bibliographic utilities. Nevertheless, 56% (71 cases) of the respondents are not members of any other professional library group, while 44% (55 cases) belong to some other library association. Of these associations membership in regional groups tends to dominate (53%, 29 cases). Collectively, other national library groups are the next most mentioned category (22%, 12 cases). These national groups include the American Society of Information Science, Beta Phi Mu, Association of Seventh-Day Adventist Librarians, and Chinese-American Librarians Association.

ATTENDANCE AT PROFESSIONAL MEETINGS

Contact with other librarians is an important way to foster professional development. Professional meetings are an excellent medium for this contact. The majority of respondents (58%, 76 cases), however, report that they do not attend the annual meeting of the ALA. Fifty-four respondents (42%) do attend this conference. Of those that indicated how often they have attended in the last five years, the most common reply is once (36%, 16 cases). Even fewer respondents attend the Midwinter Meeting of the ALA. Just 26% (32 cases) of the respondents have attended this meeting in the last five years. Most individuals do not attend the Midwinter Meeting (74%, 93 cases).

Attendance of the annual conference of the North American Serials Interest Group is even lower than that of the ALA meetings. Just 13% (17 cases) of the respondents regularly attend this conference, while 87% (111 cases) do not attend. Perhaps this figure reflects the low rate of membership in this group among the respondents, as reported before.

Furthermore, the overwhelming majority of the respondents (72%, 91 cases) reply that they do not attend the conferences or meetings of any other national library association. Of the thirty-six (28%) respondents that attend the meeting of such a group, the Association of College and Research Libraries (21%, 7 cases), the American Association of Law Librarians (18%, 6 cases), and the Canadian Library Association (15%, 5 cases) are mentioned most frequently.

In contrast, the majority of respondents (68%, 88 cases) attend the meetings of a state or regional library association. Most of the other respondents (29%, 37 cases) are not involved with such groups. Only 3% (4 cases) report that this question is not applicable to their situations. Seventy-seven different associations are listed by the seventy-five respondents that name the specific meetings they attend. State library associations are the most frequently listed (64%, 48 cases). Less frequently listed are various regional groups (23%, 17 cases), groups that focus on only part of a state (8%, 6 cases), and city wide groups (4%, 3 cases). The remainder (12%, 9 cases) consists of a group of enigmatic acronyms which the author is unfamiliar with and unable to identify.

Workshops given on various library-related topics also may provide professional contact and development. Most of the respondents (89%, 113 cases) take advantage of these opportunities. Only 6% (8 cases) reply in the negative, while 5% (6 cases) indicate that such workshops are unavailable in their areas.

Workshops given within the library can afford a convenient means for expanding professional knowledge and expertise. The majority of respondents (61%, 80 cases) report that they take advantage of these workshops, while only 2% (2 cases) indicate that they do not attend such sessions. A sizeable group (37%, 49 cases), however, reports that such in-house workshops are not available in their libraries.

PROFESSIONAL READING

Scholarly journals have long been a mainstay for the dissemination of information in many professions. Library science has its body of professional journals, with several of them focused on serials or cataloging. They include *Serials Librarian*, *Serials Review*, *Cataloging & Classification Quarterly*, *ALCTS Newsletter*, *NASIG Newsletter*, and *Library Resources & Technical Services.*

Among respondents who maintain personal subscriptions, the *ALCTS Newsletter* is most frequently listed (34%, 43 cases). *Library Resources*

& Technical Services is the next most frequently listed personal subscription (32%, 40 cases). The high personal subscription frequencies for these two journals undoubtedly reflects the frequency of membership in ALCTS which has already been noted. Sixteen percent (20 cases) have a personal subscription to *NASIG Newsletter*. The other three journals listed in this section are subscribed to by 1 or 2 percent of the respondents. In contrast, the library subscription frequencies for these three journals tend to be the highest reported by the respondents. The frequencies are: *Serials Librarian* (49%, 61 cases), *Cataloging & Classification Quarterly* (44%, 55 cases), and *Serials Review* (37%, 46 cases). *Library Resources & Technical Services* also is reported to have a high library subscription frequency (41%, 52 cases). This is compared to the relatively low number of library subscriptions for *ALCTS Newsletter* (14%, 17 cases) and *NASIG Newsletter* (10%, 12 cases).

A sizeable percentage of the respondents report that they do not have access to the journals just listed. For example, *Serials Librarian* is inaccessible for 42% (52 cases) of the respondents, *Serials Review* for 54% (66 cases), *Cataloging & Classification Quarterly* for 49% (62 cases), *ALCTS Newsletter* for 49% (61 cases), and *NASIG Newsletter* for 71% (87 cases). The respondents report that the most accessible journal is *Library Resources & Technical Services*; but it is inaccessible in thirty cases (24%).

Although given the opportunity, very few respondents report that they have access to, but do not read, the journals listed in this section. Therefore, it is assumed that if they have access to a personal or library subscription, then they use it. Of course, the survey cannot determine whether the respondents actually read these journals, or if they simply feel uncomfortable reporting that they do not read professional journals. Table 1 summarizes the information concerning subscriptions and access to journals.

Twenty-five respondents listed twenty-seven other titles they are reading that deal primarily with serials or cataloging. The most frequently listed are *Technical Services Law Librarian*, *International Cataloguing and Bibliographic Control*, *Newsletter on Serials Pricing Issues*, and *Cataloging Services Bulletin*. A complete list of these journals may be found in Table 2.

AVAILABILITY OF CATALOGING TOOLS

One of the basic tenets of career development is the concept of keeping current with cataloging practices. While this can be accomplished by

Table 1

Access to Journals

Journal	Personal Subscription		Library Subscription		No Access		Does Not Read	
	N	Percent	N	Percent	N	Percent	N	Percent
Serials Librarian	2	2	61	49	52	42	10	8
Serials Review	1	1	46	37	66	54	10	8
Cataloging & Classification Quarterly	2	2	55	44	62	49	7	6
ALCTS Newsletter	43	34	17	14	61	49	4	3
NASIG Newsletter	20	16	12	10	87	71	4	3
Library Resources & Technical Services	40	32	52	41	30	24	4	3

many means, there are several cataloging tools that are basic to this task. It is assumed that most catalogers have access to certain tools that are essential to the practice of cataloging such as *AACR2 Revised*, some form of the *Library of Congress Subject Headings*, and a basic copy of the appropriate classification scheme. Additionally, there are many auxiliary tools designed to update these basic works.

The *Cataloging Service Bulletin* is one such work. Fifty-three respon-

Table 2

Journals Read by Serials Catalogers

Journal	Numbers of Respondents
Library Resources & Technical Services	92
Serials Librarian	63
ALCTS Newsletter	60
Cataloging & Classification Quarterly	57
Serials Review	47
NASIG Newsletter	32
Technical Services Law Librarian	4
International Cataloguing and Bibliographic Control	3
Newsletter on Serials Pricing Issues	3
Cataloging Service Bulletin	3
Conser	2
OCLC Micro	2
OLAC Newsletter	2
OCLC Publications (Exact publication specified)	2
Technical Services Quarterly	2

Table 2 (continued)

Journal	Numbers of Respondents
Acquisitions Theory & Practice	1
Against the Grain	1
Amigos Agenda	1
Information Technology and Libraries	1
Judaica Librarianship	1
LC Bulletin	1
Library Hi Tech	1
National Library News (National Library of Canada)	1
Newsletter of the IFLA Section on Serials Publications	1
Newsletter of the Serials Interest Group of the Canadian Library Association	1
OCLC Connection	1
OCLC Technical Bulletin	1
RQ	1
Technicalities	1

dents (42%) have their own desk copy. Another forty-two respondents (33%) report that they have access to a copy of this work. However, thirty respondents (24%) report that their library does not provide this tool. Two respondents (2%) volunteer that their libraries use the Oberlin Updates in lieu of the *Cataloging Service Bulletin*.

Turning to tools used for subject analysis, the *Library of Congress Subject Headings–Weekly Lists* details the constant revision of subject headings. About half of the respondents (49%, 60 cases) report that they share a copy of this work with colleagues. Only ten respondents (8%) are fortunate enough to have their own desk copy. In fifty-two cases (43%) the library does not provide this tool for the cataloger's use. The information gathered in the survey does not explain why such a high percentage of libraries choose not to make this tool available. Some libraries may not use the Library of Congress subject headings, or may have an alternative source for providing this information, such as the OCLC Authority Files.

The Library of Congress and Dewey schemes are the two major classification schemes currently in use. The majority of respondents (60%, 73 cases) whose libraries use the LC Classification report that they share a copy of the *Library of Congress Schedules Cumulations of Additions and Changes*. Only twenty-two (18%) of the respondents have their own desk copy. Presumably, the high cost of the work is reason enough for its shared status in many cases. Twenty-seven respondents (22%) report that their libraries do not use the Library of Congress classification scheme.

Dewey Decimal classification is the other common classification scheme. Seventeen respondents (14%) report that they share a copy of its updating medium, *Dewey Decimal Classification Additions, Notes and Decisions*, while ten respondents (8%) have their own desk copy. Eighty-seven respondents (74%) report that their library does not use the Dewey Decimal system.

STATUS OF LIBRARIANS

The relative status of librarians and the encouragement they receive from their libraries for professional activities and growth may influence involvement in these activities. Arguably, membership in the faculty may be considered a mark of status. The majority (57%, 73 cases) of respondents have faculty status, while 43% (54 cases) do not. Half of those who have faculty status (50%, 31 cases) report that their institution has a system for librarians that is similar to that used for teaching faculty, 37% (23 cases) have systems exactly like that of teaching faculty, and 13% (8 cases) are evaluated in a system that is completely different from teaching faculty. The most commonly reported difference is that the librarians are not tenure track faculty. Instead, most have a continuing appointment status. More emphasis also seems to be placed on the librarian's job performance and less on publications, although several respondents comment that publications are necessary to achieve continuing appointment.

One might speculate that faculty status with its requirements for professional development would be significantly correlated with involvement in national professional organizations, such as ALA. In order to test this as a hypothesis, the presence or absence of faculty status is cross tabulated with membership in ALA. Also, when it is possible through written comments to determine that the respondent is non-tenure track faculty, this can be tabulated as a separate third category. Finally, if it is possible through written comments in other parts of the survey to identify respondents from Canadian libraries, these individuals were not included in the tabulation. The tabulated results appear in Table 3. A chi-square test (χ^2 = 1.213, df = 2) quantifies what is obvious from Table 3–there is no significant relationship between faculty status and ALA membership. This outcome may be due to the broad based interests of the various ALA divisions and perhaps to a widespread attitude of professionalism among librarians.

The presence of administrative support for professional activities is beneficial to individuals committed to professional development. The overwhelming majority of respondents (90%, 114 cases) report that the administration at their library encourages attendance at professional meetings. Only a small minority (9%, 11 cases) indicates that they are not supported in such activities. One respondent (1%) reports that this question is not applicable to her/his situation. Administrative support usually takes the form of release time (91%, 99 cases) or financial support (88%, 96 cases). The written comments accompanying this question indicate that the financial support generally covers only part of one's expenses. This practice of partial funding probably reflects the limited budgets of most libraries, rather than an administrative evaluation of attendance at professional meetings.

The majority of respondents (57%, 67 cases) indicate that they are encouraged by their library administration to conduct library-related research. Encouragement usually takes the form of release time to work on research and verbal support. Financial support is also mentioned by a small number of respondents. As with limited travel funds, the lack of financial support may reflect the budgetary situation in libraries rather than an evaluation of the activity. Many respondents (42%, 50 cases), however, are not administratively encouraged to conduct such research.

Table 3

ALA Membership and Faculty Status

ALA Membership	Tenure Track Faculty	Non-Tenure Track Faculty	Non-Faculty
Yes	30	11	23
No	25	5	20

This lack of support apparently reflects a preferential emphasis on job-related performance over research activities.

Among respondents that are employed in a tenure system, 21% (25 cases) report that research is not required for tenure, while 19% (22 cases) reply that it is required. The question is not applicable for 60% (70 cases) of the respondents. As reported above, release time is the most common form of administrative support given for research. Most respondents, however, indicate that they spend very little time on research during the working day. This suggests that while release time may be available, few respondents are able to take advantage of it.

Institutional criteria for tenure change constantly. For a plurality of respondents (47%, 28 cases) these criteria have become more stringent over the last five years. The criteria have become less stringent for 5% (3 cases) and have not changed significantly for 41% (24 cases) of the respondents. A small group (7%, 4 cases) are not sure how the criteria have changed. Some respondents (14 cases) comment that the criteria are becoming more stringent because of an increased emphasis on research and other activities that are not related to one's job performance.

SUMMATION

The survey indicates that the average serials cataloger received an MLS degree about fifteen years ago. Usually their formal education stopped there. Approximately equal numbers belong to a state or regional library association as belong to a national group. When it comes to meeting attendance, however, the respondents clearly prefer to attend local, state, or regional conferences. Possible explanations for this preference include the affordability of local conferences, their relative convenience, and the relevancy of materials presented on the local level. It also may be easier for an individual to become integrated and involved in a local association.

The typical respondent is reading the relevant professional literature and has access either through a personal or library subscription to such journals. Unfortunately, a fairly sizable group of respondents also report that they do not have access to professional journals.

In order to keep current with cataloging practices, most respondents report that they have access to the *Cataloging Service Bulletin*, *Library of Congress Subject Headings–Weekly Lists*, and the updating medium for the appropriate classification system.

The majority of respondents have faculty status within their institutions. Of this group, most are evaluated in a system that is similar to that used to evaluate the teaching faculty. The librarians in these systems generally hold continuing appointment status rather than tenure track positions. While publication may be an important activity for their employment evaluation, more emphasis is placed on job performance.

It is common to have administrative support for such professional activities as attendance at conferences and, to a lesser extent, conducting library-related research. Support for attendance at conferences frequently takes the form of release time and partial financial support. Release time and verbal support are the chief forms of support for conducting research. For about half of the respondents in tenure systems, such research is required for tenure. A plurality of respondents also report that the tenure requirements at their institutions have become more stringent over the last five years.

CONCLUSION

This study demonstrates a serious commitment among many of the respondents to professional development and involvement. This development is achieved by membership in national, regional, and state professional organizations. Attendance at conferences is another method in which this interest is manifested. Attendance is most common at the more easily accessible local level rather than at the national level.

The respondents are also reading a variety of library journals and keep abreast of changes in cataloging practices by using both basic and auxiliary cataloging tools.

The administration of most of the libraries surveyed support library related travel and research, although the funding for such activities may be limited.

The survey did not address why serials catalogers choose to become involved in continuing education and staff development. Certainly some individuals feel a pressure to do so due to job requirements; however, the lack of correlation between faculty status and membership in national organizations suggests that this is not the sole reason for involvement. Perhaps individuals who involve themselves in these activities do so as a matter of personal commitment. Continuing education and staff development may be one possible variable in increased job satisfaction.[10] The satisfaction derived from the learning experience itself may be another.

NOTES

1. Sheila D. Creth, "Continuing Staff Development and Continuing Education," *Personnel Administration in Libraries*, 2nd edition, (New York: Neal-Schuman Publishers, 1989):118-151.

2. Elaine K. Rast, "Formal Continuing Education for Serials," *Illinois Libraries* 67, no. 5 (May 1985): 453-462.

3. Susan Matson, "Informal Continuing Education for Serials: Keeping Up With the Journal Literature," *Illinois Libraries* 67, no. 5 (May 1985): 458-462.

4. Continuing Library and Information Science Education Project, *Final Report to the National Commission on Libraries and Information Science* (Washington, D. C.: Catholic University of America, May 1974).

5. James G. Neal, "Continuing Education: Attitudes and Experiences of the Academic Librarian," *College and Research Libraries* 41, no. 2 (March 1980):128-133.

6. Judith L. Hegg, "Continuing Education: A Profile of the Academic Librarian Participant," *Journal of Library Administration* 6, no. 1 (Spring 1985): 45-63.

7. Judith L. Hegg, "Faculty Status: Some Expected and Some Not-So-Expected Findings," *Journal of Library Administration* 64, no. 4 (Winter 1985/86): 67-79.

8. *Directory of Library and Information Professionals* 1st Edition (Woodbridge, Conn.: Research Publications, 1988).

9. *American Library Directory 1990-91*, 43rd edition (New York: Bowker, 1990).

10. Hegg, "Continuing Education: A Profile of the Academic Librarian Participant."

APPENDIX I

Serials Cataloging Interests Survey

A. Introduction

1. Do you have a degree from an ALA-accredited library school in library science (such as an MLS, MSLIS, etc.)?

   __Yes
   __No

   If yes, how many years has it been since the receipt of your degree?
2. Do you have a CAS or PhD in library science?

   __Yes
   __No

   If yes, how many years has it been since the receipt of this degree?

3. How many individuals at your library catalog serials?

   How many of these individuals have a degree in library science?

B. Membership in Professional Associations

4. Are you a member of the American Library Association?

   __Yes
   __No

5. Are you a member of any ALA divisions, roundtables, discussion groups, task forces, etc.?

   __Yes
   __No

   If yes, please specify.

6. Are you a member of the North American Serials Interest Group?

__Yes
__No

7. Are you a member of any other national library association?

__Yes
__No

If yes, please specify.

8. Are you a member of a state library association or society?

__Yes
__No

9. Are you a member of some other professional library group?

__Yes
__No

If yes, please specify.

C. Attendance at Meetings

10. Do you attend the Annual Conference of the American Library Association?

__Yes
__No

If yes, how often have you attended in the last five years?

11. Do you attend the Midwinter Meeting of the American Library Association?

__Yes
__No

If yes, how often have you attended in the last five years?

12. Do you attend the Annual Conference of the North American Serials Interest Group?

 __Yes
 __No

 If yes, how often have you attended in the last five years?

13. Do you attend the meetings of some other national library association (such as, the Association of College and Research Libraries).

 __Yes
 __No

 If yes, please specify the association and how often you have attended in the last five years.

14. If there is a regional or state library association in your area, do you attend its meetings?

 __Yes
 __No
 __Not applicable

 If yes, please specify the group and how often you have attended in the last five years.

15. If available, do you attend local workshops on library topics that are given in your geographic area?

 __Yes
 __No
 __Not available in my area

16. If available, do you attend in-house workshops given by your library?

 __Yes
 __No
 __Not available in my library

D. Subscriptions to Professional Journals Dealing Primarily with Cataloging or Serials.

17. Do you have a personal subscription or have access to a library subscription for the following journals?

Serials Librarian

__Personal subscription
__Library subscription
__Do not have access to this journal
__Have access, but do not read this journal

Serials Review

__Personal subscription
__Library subscription
__Do not have access to this journal
__Have access, but do not read this journal

Cataloging & Classification Quarterly

__Personal subscription
__Library subscription
__Do not have access to this journal
__Have access, but do not read this journal

ALCTS Newsletter

__Personal subscription
__Library subscription
__Do not have access to this journal
__Have access, but do not read this journal

NASIG Newsletter

__Personal subscription
__Library subscription
__Do not have access to this journal
__Have access, but do not read this journal

Library Resources & Technical Services

__Personal subscription
__Library subscription
__Do not have access to this journal
__Have access, but do not read this journal

Are there other professional journals dealing primarily with cataloging or serials that you read regularly?

__Yes
__No

If yes, please specify.

E. Serials Cataloging Tools

18. Which of the following cataloging tools does your library provide? Is it a single copy shared among co-workers or your own desk copy?

Cataloging Service Bulletin

__Shared copy
__Own desk copy
__Library does not provide this tool

Library of Congress Subject Headings – Weekly Lists

__Shared copy
__Own desk copy
__Library does not provide this tool

Library of Congress classification schedules cumulations of additions and changes

__Shared copy
__Own desk copy
__Not applicable (Library does not use Library of Congress classification scheme)

Dewey Decimal Classification Additions, Notes and Decisions

__Shared copy
__Own desk copy
__Not applicable (Library does not use Dewey Decimal classification scheme)

F. Status of Librarians

19. Do the librarians at your institution have faculty status?

__Yes
__No

If yes, are they evaluated for promotion and tenure in a system that is:
__Exactly like the system used to evaluate teaching faculty?
__Similar to the system used to evaluate teaching faculty?
__Completely different than the system used to evaluate teaching faculty?

If similar or completely different, briefly explain the differences.

20. Are you encouraged by the administration of your library to attend professional library meetings?

__Yes
__No

If yes, what form does that encouragement take (for example, release time to attend meetings, financial assistance to cover costs of attendance)?

21. Are you encouraged by the administration of your library to do library related research, such as writing articles?
__Yes
__No

If yes, what form does that encouragement take (for example, release time to work on research, monetary aid for research)?

22. If you are in a tenure system, is library-related research required to receive tenure at your library?
    __Yes
    __No
    __Not applicable

    If yes, approximately how many hours a week do you spend on library-related research?

23. If you are in a tenure system, do you feel that over the last five years your institution's criteria for tenure have

    __become *more* stringent
    __become *less* stringent
    __not changed significantly
    __Not sure

    If more or less stringent, please explain briefly.

Serials Cataloging, 1985-1990: An Overview of a Half-Decade

James W. Williams

SUMMARY. A new approach whereby serials cataloging is becoming more simplified, efficient, and user-oriented was apparent. The rules defining title changes were revised and the number of needless successive entry catalog records has appreciably declined. Guidelines for the expeditious cataloging of microform masters were devised and adopted. Format integration was finished and its implementation is being planned. Major changes were made in CONSER. The component recommendations of a proposed solution to the multiple versions dilemma are being given concentrated and serious study. A fine-tuning of cataloging practices was continued by LCRIs. Uniform titles continued to be the most controversial aspect of serials cataloging. Serials catalogers proved themselves to be prolific writers. The subjects given substantive exploration in the literature were many and diverse.

An assessment of trends and developments in serials cataloging for the years 1985-1990 was made by (1) an examination of the Library of Con-

James W. Williams, is an Assistant Education and Social Science Librarian and Cataloging Coordinator, Social Science Council Libraries at the University of Illinois at Urbana-Champaign.

gress rule interpretations (LCRIs) published in the quarterly issues of *Cataloging Service Bulletin* (*CSB*); (2) the work of the American Library Association (ALA) Association for Library Collections and Technical Services (ALCTS) Serials Section (SS) Committee to Study Serials Cataloging; and (3) the published literature specific to serials cataloging. Excluded from discussion in the following review are a number of important matters elsewhere covered in this state-of-the-art volume, most specifically the United States Newspaper Program, the proposed changes in the cataloging of serial reproductions, and the implications of the Linked Systems Project for serials cataloging. Also omitted are the essays collected in *Serials Cataloging: The State-of-the-Art*, published in 1987 under the editorship of Jim E. Cole and Jackie Zajanc.[1]

A trend toward a common sense, simplified approach to serials cataloging was manifested during the period. The traditional concern for access remained paramount; if anything, many new practices are more user-friendly than those which they replaced. Major advancements were made and the processes were begun for other beneficial changes. A revision of the rule defining title changes decreased much needless successive entry cataloging. Guidelines for an expeditious means by which to catalog microform masters were devised within the Association of Research Libraries (ARL) and given ALA endorsement. An LCRI eliminated much of the prior need to bracket data in serials description and another LCRI solved the problem of access for serials issued in hardcover reprint. Integration of the seven MARC formats into one was completed. CONSER was restructured, shifted focus to current serial publications, and began moves by which to strengthen the database.

A solution to the multiple versions problem was proposed and its component recommendations are receiving serious study. LC counted the backlog and has begun to develop a plan for its eradication. Whether or not successive entry cataloging is the most efficient and user-oriented option for handling title changes in online systems was debated. The controversy surrounding uniform titles showed no signs of abatement and a multitude of suggestions were forthcoming concerning this area of serials cataloging. The LCRIs for serials treatment of conference and loose-leaf publications were refined and were a topic of discourse in the literature. Several technical services aspects of serials in relation to public services were also discussed. A number of institutional reports on retrospective conversion projects appeared. The placement of serials and serials cataloging within administrative structures was given attention. Diverse other serials cataloging related subjects also received coverage in the literature.

REVISED CRITERIA FOR CHANGES IN TITLES PROPER

Taking impetus from the work done by the Committee to Study Serials Cataloging, LC drafted a revision for the rule defining changes in titles proper (21.2A)[2] which was given approval by the Joint Steering Committee for Revision of AACR (JSC) near the end of 1986. The basic tenets of the new rule and various LCRIs concerning its application first appeared in *CSB* 36 (Spring 1987)[3] and implementation was immediate. The rule itself was subsequently stated in the AACR2 1988 Revision.[4] The revision has not only lessened the number of title changes for which successive entry cataloging was required, but has also brought the code into closer conformity with both the 1983 *Guidelines* of the International Serials Data System and the second edition of the *ISBD(S): International Standard Bibliographic Description for Serials.*

The new definition begins with the words "In general,"[5] recognizing a need to provide for possible exceptions and to allow for cataloger judgment. While both versions of the rule instructed that a title change had occurred if any important word was added, deleted, or changed, the revised text's use of the phrase "any word other than an article, preposition, or conjunction"[6] is an improvement over the earlier wording "any important words (nouns, proper names or initials standing for proper names, adjectives, etc.)"[7] The current rule also specifies that a title has changed "if the order of the first five words (the first six words if the title begins with an article) is changed"[8] while the previous rule stipulated a title change when "there is a change in the order of words."[9]

Following a simple definition of changes in titles proper, the new rule states:

> However, in general do not consider a title proper to have changed if:
>
> a. the change is in the representation of a word or words . . .
> b. the addition, deletion, or change comes after the first five words . . . and does not change the meaning of the title or indicate a different subject matter
> c. the only change is the addition or deletion of the name of the issuing body (and any grammatical connection) at the end of the title
> d. the only change is in the addition, deletion, or change of punctuation.[10]

With the exception of changes in punctuation, the earlier rule made no provision for the minor and unimportant changes covered by the foregoing and changes in spelling (covered by category a) were among those explicitly stated to constitute a title change. The original rule also allowed for no margin of uncertainty, but directed: "All other changes . . . do not constitute a change in the title proper."[11] The revised text carries the more realistic statement: "In case of doubt, consider the title proper to have changed."[12]

The guidelines published in *CSB* 36 brought welcome changes, although several components of the revision had been previously instituted by LC and, therefore, had already become the *de facto* national policy. The LCRIs as first stated have undergone several modifications and have been expanded to cover two sources of unimportant title changes not originally addressed. Not to be treated as title changes by the subsequent mandates are instances in which ". . . words that link the title to the chronologic or numeric designation . . . are added, changed, or dropped" and those in which ". . . the name of the issuing body or an element of its hierarchy at the end of the title changes from one form to another . . ."[13]

AACR2 rule 21.3B requires the construction of a new catalog record even when the title proper remains the same ". . . if the heading for a corporate body under which a serial is entered changes *or*. . . if the main entry for a serial is under a personal or corporate heading and the person or body named in that heading is no longer responsible for the serial."[14] LCRIs have added another two conditions:

> . . . if the main entry for a serial is under a uniform title heading and that uniform title heading changes because
>
> 1. the corporate body used as a qualifier changes . . .
> 2. the title of a serial used as the uniform title heading on an entry for a translation changes.
>
> . . . when the physical format in which the serial is issued changes (not a reproduction of the same serial in another manifestation . . .)[15]

The stipulation concerning changes in physical format was issued shortly before the 1991 ALA Midwinter Meeting and was discussed in a session of the Committee to Study Serials Cataloging. Some feeling was expressed that the implementation of this policy seemed questionable in light of the recommendations for changes in the treatment of serials appearing in multiple versions. The LC liaison to the committee correctly stated that the LCRI did not involve a case of multiple versions but one in which two distinct serials were represented, with a title in one format having ceased and a title in a different format having begun. In previous sessions the committee to Study Serials Cataloging has discussed a need to discontinue the use of uniform titles for English translations of serials because the English title often remains the same when the foreign title undergoes change. The presence of the foreign title as uniform title (and, therefore, main entry) requires a successive entry catalog record.

OPTIONS TO SUCCESSIVE ENTRY CATALOGING AND RELATED CONSIDERATIONS

Glasby[16] provided a historical overview of the rules for serials main entry and the treatment of title changes. Zajanc[17] advocated a return to latest entry cataloging and Lim[18] expanded upon Zajanc's position. Flaspeter and Lomker[19] and Cole[20] presented cases for the earliest entry technique. Earliest entry cataloging was implemented by LC for U.S. state session laws in *CSB* 36 (Spring 1987) as a part of the LCRI for uniform titles for general collections of laws. Chapman[21] reviewed the LCRI and urged its extension to include U.S. territories, U.S. jurisdictions below the state level, and foreign jurisdictions.

In this state-of-the-art volume, Mary Case provides a current status report on Northwestern University's experiment with selective latest entry cataloging. Mering[22] reported that Louisiana State University gave consideration to following the lead of Northwestern when plans were underway to implement the NOTIS system. A sample of serials in the LSU catalog suggested that 55.14 per cent had never changed title, 16.26 per cent had undergone changes of a rather complex nature, and "almost thirty percent, a sizeable portion, . . . had undergone straightforward title changes."[23] Mering noted that possible changes in numbering systems were not examined and no effort was made to determine whether or not LSU held all of the variant titles. LSU elected to remain with successive entry cataloging. Among Mering's concluding remarks were: "Without national support, OCLC libraries choosing to follow Northwestern's lead are faced with the time consuming editing of records which are already in the OCLC database in order to match local procedures. With original input, they face double cataloging."[24]

Bernhardt[25] suggested that certain problems encountered with title changes in online catalogs could be corrected by computer programs to guide and instruct clientele. She wrote, "A programmer can easily take the existing bibliographic fields in the MARC serials format and manipulate them so that certain subfields and codes present in the searchable

780 or 785 title fields will trigger appropriate helping responses by the online searching system."[26] As an example, Bernhardt outlined a program which would display a summary history of a serial title, with directives instructing the user to request more information about the variant title form which matched his/her query.

Dorothy Glasby, LC liaison to the Committee to Study Serials Cataloging, has several times stated a conviction that it makes no substantive difference whether successive or latest entry cataloging is done as long as appropriate access is given and staff and clientele are apprised of policy. While it is important to remain open to change, Callahan cautioned against the abandonment of successive entry cataloging "until a realistic cost/benefit analysis of the alternatives demonstrates compelling logic for change."[27] Callahan stated that latest entry records have been converted into successive entry records for approximately twenty years. "The cost of changing back will be large and we should be sure that the benefits accrued are worth such a cost."[28]

THE MULTIPLE VERSIONS CONCEPT AND SERIAL REPRODUCTIONS

To avoid having redundant records in the online catalog, Nadeski[29] reported that Pennsylvania State University added notes describing all secondary versions onto the bibliographic record for the original publication when conversion was done. Elsewhere in this volume Graham gives thorough coverage to the recommendations concerning the use of a single bibliographic record to account for all physical manifestations of the same serial title. Therefore, this writer does not discuss the implications of those recommendations in the sections which presently follow on the cataloging serial reproductions.

PRESENTATION OF HOLDINGS DATA

Bryant stated that holdings data should be presented in a more detailed manner with the coming of online catalogs. He wrote, "Our users want *one source of information* that tells them whether the library takes, or has taken, the periodical title, and *the necessary details* to tell them which parts and volumes it stocks, and whether the volume they want is available, missing, mutilated, at binding, etc."[30] Automation has made this possible provided ". . . the necessary investment is made in recording the details required."[31]

The adoption of the aforementioned recommended changes in the treatment of multiple versions is contingent upon the implementation of the *USMARC Format for Holdings and Locations* at the national level. Both OCLC and RLIN have begun to study its integration into their networks. An excellent introduction to the format was written by Litchfield and Norstedt.[32] Because many libraries computerized holdings data prior to the development of the format, the discussion of a free-text field is of interest: "A library's holdings that are already in any kind of machine-readable form can be loaded into the MARC format using the 666 fields. The holdings will not be coded . . . but at least the standard format can be put in place and holdings need not be reentered."[33]

The writers reviewed as well the format in conjunction with the SISAC (Serials Industry Systems Advisory Committee) code project. SISAC is promoting the printing of issue-specific bar codes on periodicals. "When the information from the bar code is linked with coded holdings records, which can anticipate expected issues and automatically update public holdings screens, the potential for very sophisticated serials control is tremendous."[34] Such a development would be a major advancement toward the provision of holdings information on the scale urged by Bryant. Litchfield and Norstedt and Heush[35] stressed the importance of implementation at the local level. Through user experience problem areas will be identified and refinements can be made accordingly.

The USMARC Format for Holdings and Locations: Development, Implementation, and Use,[36] an essay collection edited by Barry B. Baker, featured papers on SISAC, the ANSI display standards, the development of the format, and descriptions of its implementation by Harvard, the University of Kansas, the University of Florida, VTLS, Faxon, and NOTIS. Elsewhere Kim[37] discussed the coding of serials holdings data into the format at the University of Tennessee, Knoxville and described the numerous problems encountered in supplying the information retrospectively. That the format has not yet been widely integrated into local networks undoubtedly accounts for the fact that very little has appeared concerning its use to share data between dissimilar systems, the purpose for which it was designed.

HARDCOPY REPRINTS

The application of AACR2 rule 1.11 (facsimiles, photocopies, and other reproductions) to reprinted serials was a source of ire to serials catalogers during the first years of the code's use. The emphasis on the publication in its reprinted form was seen as a barrier to access because users are far more likely to seek the original serial. In *CSB* 32 (Spring 1986) the LCRIs for 12.0A (scope) and 12.0B1 (sources of information for printed serials) were expanded to encompass serials issued in hardcopy reprints.[38] LC stated that most hardcopy serial reproductions would be treated as serials to provide necessary access. Exceptions to the general policy would be reprints of single issues or a limited number of issues and collections of bibliographically unrelated serials. When doubt existed as to whether or not the criteria for monograph cataloging was fulfilled, LC prescribed serial cataloging.

While minor modifications were made in the wording of the LCRI for 12.0B1 in *CSB* 38 (Fall 1987), the essence of the policy remained unchanged. The directive reads in part:

> In order that the description of the reprint resemble and file with the description of the original, the earliest *issue* reprinted is used as the chief source for the first three areas of the description. . . . In area four the place of publication, publisher, and date of the reprint are recorded . . . The physical description area gives the physical description of the reprint, not the original. . . . Usually a single note . . . gives important details about the original while other notes give necessary information about the reprint.[39]

Since Chapter 11 (Microforms) of AACR2 was never implemented, the LCRI serves to treat hardcopy reprints in a manner more comparable to that of microform reprints. While the resultant record is a strange mixture of elements from both the original and the reprinted publication, the crucial issue of access has been resolved. The "single note" mandate for details about the original publication remains less than popular, but "usually" gives latitude for judgment.

MICROFORM MASTERS FOR SERIALS

Near the end of the 1980s, ARL and ALCTS each had a group at work on "guidelines for the bibliographic control of master microform catalog records toward the building of a national database of preservation master microform records."[40] The ARL Committee on Bibliographic Control concluded its assignment first and its guidelines were approved by the ALCTS Task Force on the Bibliographic Control of Microform Masters.

The second preliminary draft of the ARL *Guidelines for Bibliographic*

Records for Preservation Microform Masters (Serials) was finished immediately after the December 1989 Multiple Versions Forum and included the statement: "The ARL Committee on Bibliographic Control supports the recommendation of the recent LC-sponsored Multiple Versions Forum to use the *USMARC Format for Holdings Data* for communication of data describing microform reproductions."[41] The final guidelines were therefore completed with the recognition that they would in likelihood be used as nothing more than an interim measure.

In a discussion of the guidelines, Graham mentioned the present impossibility of using a single catalog record, but stated:

> The guidelines suggest another method of employing existing bibliographic records, which is the application of "retrospective conversion standards" in the creation of new records for microform masters. Existing MARC records for original items are "cloned" to form the framework of new records . . . Data elements describing the microform are added to the record. RLIN network standards approve this practice . . .[42]

OCLC subsequently allowed microform masters to be an exception to its strict requirement for adherence to AACR2 and the LCRIs. The ARL guidelines allow for the input of access points in the form found on an extant record if no authority record is located and permit as well the use of latest entry catalog copy if successive entry copy is unavailable. The assignment of topical subject headings is encouraged but not mandatory, although it is requested that inputting institutions retain any subjects present on an existing record. The guidelines are emphasized to constitute an absolute minimum.

SOURCES OF INFORMATION FOR PRINTED SERIALS

An important advancement in cataloging simplification was made with the revised LCRI for rule 12.0B1 which appeared in *CSB* 47 (Winter 1990). Use of the "whole publication as the prescribed source of information"[43] was directed for all areas of the description with the exception of title/statement of responsibility and edition. The new policy not only eliminates much bracketing, but also brings U.S. practice into conformity with the guidelines of the second edition of the *ISBD(S)*. The Committee to Study Serials Cataloging had advocated on the behalf of this change during 1987 and 1988. As an alternative, the members of the committee urged an expansion of prescribed information sources.

The Committee to Study Serials Cataloging also discussed the addition of the contents page to the list of prescribed title page substitutes at the 1988 ALA Midwinter Meeting. "The Library of Congress indicated that they would not support the proposal because they contend that the definition of a masthead encompasses the title on the contents page."[44] The proposal was abandoned. Some feeling was expressed, however, that LC's definition of neither title page nor masthead was entirely clear. Roberts, Vidor, and Bailey urged change in the literature. In a proposition that would extend the concept of the LCRI which allows use of a less preferred title page substitute when the less preferred source is known to carry the stable title, they stated: "Perhaps the best solution would be the adoption of a new definition of title page for periodicals that allows the cataloger to base the choice of title on the fullest information available."[45]

Uniform Titles

The LCRIs governing uniform titles underwent some expansion and had various refinements introduced between 1985 and 1991, but the tenets of their application and construction remained essentially unchanged. Elsewhere in this volume Bross states that some device was needed to distinguish between serials with identical titles proper when AACR2 was implemented in 1981. Uniform titles became an immediate issue of controversy and the debate showed no signs of quieting during the latter half of the 1980s. Pro and con arguments have been presented in several open forums of the Committee to Study Serials Cataloging. The following paragraph presents in a summarized manner a number of the contrary views that have been expressed.

Uniform titles were created by LC as a filing device. Are they needed or useful in online catalogs? The purpose of the catalog record is to describe a serial and the record itself should be adequate to distinguish between two or more serial publications having identical titles. The catalog record should not attempt to meet the requirements of union listing. When necessary, an adaptive record could be created for union lists by computer manipulation. Serials can usually be located in online systems through corporate body added entries, if a title search is unsuccessful. However, corporate access points are often not provided when a body's sole affiliation with a monograph lies with the series. Therefore, series having uniform title entries are lost both to library users and to a large number of library staff who do not understand their awkward form. Finally, the change to place of publication as the generally preferred qualifier served to render uniform titles largely meaningless.

As the LCRIs stand, a change in the name of a corporate body used as a uniform title qualifier requires a successive entry record while a change in a place of publication used as a uniform title qualifier requires no action. Corporate body was initially designated as the generally preferred qualifier in recognition of its meaningfulness. The change to place of publication was made by LC to lessen the number of title changes for which a successive entry record was mandated and the decrease proved substantive. For that reason the Committee to Study Serials Cataloging rejected a proposal to recommend a return to corporate body as preferred qualifier when the issue was given consideration at the 1988 ALA Midwinter Meeting.

Turitz[46] suggested a return to corporate body in the literature and offered a solution to the problem of successive entry cataloging by a policy change. Under the terms of this unique and thoughtful proposal, a serial would continue to be treated as one title when the name of a corporate body used as the uniform title qualifier underwent change. The information concerning the name change would be recorded in a 550 note, a new uniform title would be generated for the 130 field, and the prior uniform title would be moved to a 730 field.

Havens[47] urged the abandonment of uniform titles, suggesting that the information presently given in the parenthetical qualifier be stated either (1) as a part of the title proper or, better (2) author/title entry be reinstated for serials with generic titles. Havens expressed the aforementioned concern for series and series analytics becoming lost. Shelton[48] seconded Havens' proposal for the reinstatement of author/title entry for serials having generic titles. She stated, however, that a means would continue to be needed to distinguish between identical non-generic titles. In a discussion of CONSER, Barron mentioned a possible solution that is not unlike Havens' first proposition. "There is . . . interest in linking the title and publication fields when necessary, eliminating the need for uniform titles."[49]

At the 1989 ALA Midwinter Meeting a proposal to incorporate into AACR2 a statement on the use of uniform titles for serials was presented by the Library Association/British Library representative to the ALCTS Committee on Cataloging: Description and Access (CC:DA), the ALA group which must endorse proposed rule revisions. CC:DA referred the proposal to the Committee to Study Serials Cataloging whose members drafted the appropriate rule revisions during 1989. While acknowledging the problems that exist both with the concept and the application, members concurred that inasmuch as uniform titles are the national practice the cataloging code should include a statement on their use.

Action on the proposed rule revisions by CC:DA was delayed because of the work underway on like revisions within the Canadian Library Association (CLA). A copy of the committee's proposal was sent to CLA with the hope that compatible documents could be developed. The final CLA proposal proved very prescriptive and quite detailed. The U.S. proposal was very general, by contrast, in recognition that the practices of each AACR2 nation differ somewhat; the actual guidelines for application would continue to be stated by the LCRIs. CC:DA examined both statements in 1990 and gave approval to the one prepared by the Committee to Study Serials Cataloging. The proposal has passed from CC:DA to JSC.

MONOGRAPH VERSUS SERIAL TREATMENT

In keeping with its predecessors, AACR2 provides no guidance for serials versus monograph treatment of library materials. The policies which were evolved by LC before and subsequent to the publication of the code were reiterated, with some revisions, in *CSB* 29 (Summer 1985).[50] The categories of publications upon which the LCRIs have impacted most greatly for serials cataloging are loose-leaf materials, conference proceedings, and items emanating from exhibitions. Serials cataloging of these materials was a traditional practice in many libraries. However, the LCRIs serials treatment had become quite restricted by the mid-1980s. While certain requirements were subsequently relaxed, new restrictions were also imposed. Sanders[51] reviewed the LCRIs and stated a good case for serial treatment in the online environment for publications of a quasi-serial nature. He suggested a general policy change: "Library of Congress policy has been to give the benefit of the doubt to monographic treatment; pragmatically, it might be better to favor initial serial treatment . . ."[52]

Tallman, Scott, and Russell[53] described a loose-leaf recataloging project done at the University of Arizona to bring material into accord with the current practices. They stated, "Historically, the approach to the treatment of looseleaf publications in large academic libraries has been to consider them serials . . . primarily for practical considerations rather than because specific rules dictate cataloging practice."[54] Whether cataloged as a serial or as a monograph, Bluh[55] wrote, the procedures designed for serial check-in must be used to control and monitor updates to a loose-leaf title. The monitoring becomes more difficult with a computerized system because extraneous items frequently accompany revised pages. Cole suggested that a loose-leaf service be defined "as a distinct class of publication possessing qualities of both serials and monographs but separate from each"[56] and, in recognition of this dual nature, they be cataloged as monographs in accord with the LCRIs but coded by the serials format so "a serial record would exist for control purposes and for use by the National Serial Data Program."[57]

Berman[58] discussed a policy change at Pennsylvania State University where an attempt was made in the past to unite all proceedings from the same conference by classification even when monographic cataloging was done. An examination on a case by case basis determined that this policy was unnecessary for all subject disciplines. "While scientists rely heavily on conference proceedings as such, find references to them in published indexes, and expect to be able to find the volumes together on the shelves, in other fields conference proceedings are regarded as one source among many, and not as a special place to look but rather as a complement to other sources."[59] Elsewhere Ahtola discussed the difficulty of retrieving certain conference publications in online catalogs and stated, "To a large extent, the inconsistent forms of conference names used by publishers constitute an excuse for cataloging shortcomings."[60]

FORMAT INTEGRATION

The work of the ALA MARBI (Machine-Readable Bibliographic Information) Committee toward the integration of the seven MARC formats into a single format was completed in 1988 and was subsequently approved by the USMARC advisory group and LC. LC is working with OCLC, RLIN, and WLN to coordinate the implementation which is planned for late-1993 or 1994. Bales[61] discussed each network file and stated that the impact on systems will vary because of the differences present in technology and current search capabilities.

Evans noted the reasons for integration "include the seriality of non-textual materials, the potential archival nature of all material types, inconsistencies between the fields of different formats, and a need to adequately describe multi-format materials with accompanying items for a different format.[62] And McCallum stated, "Increasingly, nonconventional material will be entering libraries, and the format should accommodate the same standard of bibliographic description and access that is now possible for conventional material.''[63] The changes made in the current formats to develop the integrated format are of four varieties: deletions, obsoletes, expansions, and additions.

Deleted fields were ones which were either undefined or only partially defined and, whichever, were never used. Deletions from the serials format were 320 (Current frequency control information), 330 (Publication pattern), and 331 (Former publication pattern) which McCallum stated ". . . were three tags that had been reserved long ago for information that is now essentially a part of the *USMARC Format for Holdings Data*.''[64] The fields rendered obsolete had been defined but were either never used or used only with great inconsistency. While these fields continue to appear in the integrated format, their obsolescence is noted and the instruction is given that they are not to be assigned. From the serials format 008/30 (Title page availability), 008/31 (Index availability), and 008/32 (Cumulative index availability) became obsolete ". . . because they were so poorly maintained they had ceased to be used.''[65] Other fields made obsolete included 212 (Variant access to title), 265 (Source of acquisition/Subscription address), 350 (Subscription price), and 570 (Editor's note). The information previously contained in 265 and 350 will go into a redefined 037 field while 212 was absorbed into the 246 field. Editor information will be placed in the 500 (General note) field.

McCallum wrote "the most pervasive and obvious changes are the extensions. Every field and element in the format was extended to be valid for all forms of material except Leader/6 Type of Record *values* and character positions 18-34 of the 008 field.''[66] For example, the 246 field has additions by which to note title variations for monographs and all other materials categories. The number of additions made in the integration process were fewer than either the expansions or the obsoletes. Evans wrote:

> Many of the additions are new subfields that will have limited use and impact. At the other extreme, however, is the addition of the 006 Fixed-Length Data Elements–Additional Material Characteristics. This field duplicates many of the data elements in the 008 field, but will be applied to describe the secondary nature of an item which falls into two formats.[67]

Davis stated:

> If an item is basically textual, the seriality aspects will always be carried in the 008 field as is done presently . . . In addition, non-

> textual media aspects . . . can be recorded in one or more 006 fields. For basically nontextual items . . . any serial aspects or secondary media aspects may be coded in one or more 006 fields.[68]

Gibbs[69] reported on UCLA's experience with cataloging some material by both the current and the integrated formats as a test case for the MARBI Committee. Near the end of this article, he wrote:

> Looking ahead to the impact of format integration on cataloging operations, I believe that serials cataloging would be affected more than other areas. The majority of samples . . . are usually for a serial plus another format.[70]

DEVELOPMENTS IN CONSER

An LC contracted study provided the impetus for a late-1986 management retreat of CONSER participants which, in turn, started the process for substantive changes. The acronym CONSER, formerly representing *Con*version of *Ser*ials Project, was given the new meaning Cooperative *On*line *Ser*ials Program and, while retrospective input remains an important component, the emphasis has moved to current serials. Bartley and Reynolds[71] provided a historical review of CONSER and described the changes with restructuring, which included the formulation of a new mission statement:

> To build and to maintain cooperatively a comprehensive machine-readable database of authoritative bibliographic information for serial publications; to uphold standards and to exercise leadership in the serials information community. The five goals that support this mission all address the major program areas, namely: the database, membership, operations, standards, and leadership.[72]

"To identify language and subject weaknesses . . . so that new participants possessing expertise in these areas could be recruited, the CONSER database was analyzed using the RLG conspectus codes."[73] The sciences were identified as a generally weak area and the Massachusetts Institute of Technology was subsequently brought into the program as a step toward the correction of this deficiency. Law was a second discipline found to be underrepresented. Barron wrote: "Records for rare serials were also identified as a weak point . . . In the near future, new fields currently valid in rare book cataloging will be added to the *CONSER Editing Guide*, allowing rare serials to be cataloged within CONSER guidelines.''[74] The consultants report to LC included the recommendation that a greater emphasis be given to subject analysis. The Subject and Classification Task Force was formed in response. John Riemer reports on the work of this group in another essay in *Serials Cataloging II*. Another task force was appointed to study the creation of vernacular records, with an initial concentration on Chinese, Japanese, and Korean.

The accuracy of data in catalog records remains important. LC's role continues to be the provision of documentation, rigorous training and revision for new participants, and database sampling for quality assurance. The primary responsibility for cataloging excellence lies with other CONSER members as individual institutions. A certain level of maintenance is encouraged, but capricious changes are not acceptable. Barron stated, ''A CONSER participant accepts the cataloging of other CONSER members unless that participant has information to the contrary.[75] According to Bartley and Reynolds, ''a basic assumption of the maintenance objective is to concentrate efforts on those changes resulting from changes in the publication itself.''[76] CONSER sets no standards, but adheres to those set by other groups in the serials community. Bartley and Reynolds wrote, ''Even when the same standards are in use, differing practices can exist in their application. One task . . . is to identify areas where practices differ and to 'harmonize' them.''[77] Discussing standards a number of years later, Barron alluded to LC's effort to simplify cataloging and stated, ''More attention is being paid to a serial's identification rather than to its description.''[78]

Four membership categories were established to carry out the mission of the restructured CONSER.

> National Membership is characterized by institutions with mandates for acquiring items appropriate for the national bibliography and for organizing and disseminating information about the items. These institutions have national and international constituencies; they are responsible parties for classification schedules and subject heading lists. Members . . . include the Library of Congress, the National Library of Canada, the National Library of Medicine, and the National Agricultural Library.[79]

In the Full Membership category are ''. . . research institutions that have collections at the university level and a high volume of serial record creation/conversion.''[80] These libraries possess diverse, in depth collections in many disciplines and in a broad array of languages. The Associate Membership division is comprised of institutions with smaller, very specialized collections, either in a subject discipline or in a specific format. Associate institutions are also productive with original cataloging and/or actively involved in serials conversion projects. Affiliate Membership is made up of agencies, such as publishers or A and P services, which hold the most current information about titles and supply this information to specific fields of authenticated records.

ACTIVITIES AT THE LIBRARY OF CONGRESS

Dorothy Glasby, LC liaison to the Committee to Study Serials Cataloging, discussed the moves by LC to simplify cataloging at the 1990 ALA Annual Conference. Ms. Glasby stated the LCRIs concerning the application of AACR2 are themselves a means of simplification. The earlier mentioned LCRI by which the entire publication is used for Areas 3-6 of serials description was cited as an example. Ms. Glasby discussed other proposed LCRIs under consideration in the Serial Record Division.

LC counted the backlog in 1989 and announced it to total 38,069,000 constituted by ''. . . 1,178,000 books (3.1% of the total); 2,543,000 serials (6.7%); 34,348,000 in other formats (90.2%).''[81] The final category includes serial publications in formats other than print. The hiring of 164 new staff members was begun in January 1991 to carry out a mandate from the U.S. Congress to catalog the backlogged material.[82] A plan has been devised with the general goal of cataloging around 30 per cent of the unprocessed items by the end of fiscal 1993.[83] ''The Librarian [of Congress] told Congress that the plan emphasizes 12 pilot programs and four areas where 'per item processing costs are relatively low and the importance of the unprocessed materials justifies prompt attention: manuscripts, serials, music, and pictorial materials.'''[84]

The LC ''Arrearage Reduction Goals for 1991-93'' listed eighteen areas, two of which described serial backlogs and stated goals for their reduction:

. . . Arrearage:	Uncataloged serials
Description:	Current and retrospective materials
Quantity:	125,000
Goal:	Reduce to 65,000 or below
. . . Arrearage:	Unbound periodical issues

Description:	Issues waiting to be assembled and sent for binding
Quantity:	675,000 items (est. 56,250 volumes)
Goal:	Catalog all items[85]

Another category, "University and monograph series," will also involve serials cataloging somewhat. Described as "Serial publications in English and other Western languages," the goal is to bring the unprocessed items from 10,000 to 1,000.[86] The "Microforms" category would also have the potential to include serials as would certain specialized areas such as "NAACP Archives," the "Yudin Collection," and "Pre-1801 imprints."

Minimum level cataloging (MLC) for serials was officially begun in 1985 when the CONSER Minimum Level Cataloging Section (CMLC) was established in LC's Serial Record Division. *CSB* 38 (Fall 1987)[87] described the MLC program. "Included in MLC are (1) serials in the subject areas of sports and recreation, applied arts and crafts, and genealogy; (2) reprints and foreign language publications judged to have little research value; (3) microform sets; and (4) publications in the 'LC serials cataloging arrearage' (which contains titles added prior to 1971, primarily in English and European languages, for which full level cataloging seems unlikely because of time and cost constraints) with the exception of earlier or later titles, supplements, and indexes to titles which have full level cataloging; printed materials that would classify in law and music; and publications originally issued in microform."[88] Hirons[89] reported that in 1989, under a program administered through LC's Preservation Microfilming Office, CMLC began a project to catalog more than 8,000 serial titles microfilmed at LC between 1968 and 1987. The majority of the publications are U.S. and British imprints and most come within the disciplines of the humanities and the social sciences. "The cataloging of titles filmed . . . will alert others to the existence of a microform master, avoiding duplication of microfilming, while also making these resources . . . accessible . . ."[90] CMLC staff have begun as well to authenticate records for serial titles in large microform sets.

CSB 51[91] (Winter 1991) outlined the first significant revision of LC's cataloging priorities since 1981. "The revised set of priorities continues to put primary emphasis on the content of or the need for a particular work, that is, its need and/or research value rather than its source, its language, or the Library's internal procedural or processing requirements."[92] A former emphasis on English language publications has been dropped. The new guidelines apply to monographs, serials, and microforms. It is planned that separate guidelines will be developed for other categories of materials.

LC's experiment with whole book cataloging was declared successful and plans are underway for its implementation. Although at least one of the experimental groups included serials cataloging and while some LC personnel favored the inclusion of serials in the major reorganization, serials are to be kept separate for the present and the Serial Record Division will remain intact.

SERIALS CATALOGING AND PUBLIC SERVICE FUNCTIONS

Serials use in the provision of reference services was the subject of a double issue of *The Reference Librarian*, with one section focused on technical services matters. Rast[93] provided a historical review of the professional literature concerned with cataloger/reference interaction, discussed the benefits of automation in making readily available certain information previously found only in technical services files, and stressed the importance of good communication. Benson[94] examined "(1) the results of studies on serials catalog use; (2) the reasons for serial search failures; (3) the cataloging rules and practices researchers need to understand in order to effectively use a serials catalog; and (4) the local in-house modifications which often complicate the search process."[95]

Soper[96] reported on a study which suggested that online systems do not necessarily provide more current information than the card catalogs which they are replacing. Recent issues of nearly 300 social sciences and humanities periodicals were compared against their OCLC records.

> Attention was directed primarily to data concerning place of publication, publisher/sponsoring body, and editor. Over 18% of the records contained information that was no longer correct according to later issues.
>
> These discrepancies are not catalog errors; they are errors in currency. Once a serial record is created it is usual that it be ignored until the title and/or main entry changes . . . When other elements in the record change, they are rarely noted, even if existing access points such as added entries . . . are affected.[97]

Soper acknowledged that complete record maintenance was likely to remain impossible in the foreseeable future. "All librarians can do is be aware of the problem and instruct their users that it exists."[98]

Decker[99] discussed, element by element, the meaning of the serials catalog record. Mueller and Whittaker[100] examined the MARC serials format. Bross[101] discussed the benefits of the classification of periodicals. Reporting elsewhere on a questionnaire survey concerned with periodical arrangement in U.S. academic libraries, Segesta and Hyslop[102] stated that the arrangement of bound volumes by a classification scheme went upward in proportion to the number of serial subscriptions. Unbound issues, however, were very often arranged alphabetically by title, in a separate area, in institutions of all sizes. While 79 per cent of the libraries having current serials subscriptions in excess of 10,000 shelved the bound volumes by a classification number, a full 50 per cent nonetheless kept unbound issues in an alphabetical sequence by title.

The provision of access to journal articles in online catalogs was the subject chosen for the ALCTS Serials Section's 1990 ALA Annual Conference Program. A prolific volume of literature has begun to appear on catalog expansion and many writers make the reminder that in-house indexing of journals and other collected works was a common practice until around the turn of the century when commercial indexes began to be produced and library collections began to reach the size that made the task too onerous. Wilson[103] argued that the second objective of the catalog, as defined by the Paris Agreement of 1961, was open to interpretation. He urged the adoption of the concept of an "index-catalog" which would include extensive analysis of collected works and serials.

Intner[104,105] and Tyckoson[106] are among the writers who have discussed the need for library catalogs to provide access to journal literature at the article level. Tyckoson studied access to the collection by catalog use at Iowa State University and stated his conclusions quite dramatically. With each journal article treated as a separate intellectual entity and with other uncataloged materials (such as the individual microfiche which comprise the ERIC document collection) taken into account, he estimated that catalogs in medium-sized research libraries represent only about two per cent of the actual resources available. Tyckoson projected that in larger institutions the percentage of the collection accessible by the catalog would be even smaller.

RETROSPECTIVE CONVERSION REPORTS

The difficulty of procuring funding for retrospective conversion projects has been discussed in meetings of the Committee to Study Serials Cataloging. Grants, it has been stated, are usually available only if the conversion will be of value beyond the parameters of the institution itself. Possession of specialized collections or collections that are particularly strong in certain subject disciplines are means by which to obtain outside money. Copeland[107] described the conversion at Colorado State University of 2,790 serials in the disciplines of agriculture and the social sciences which was done as a part of an RLG grant for the retrospective conversion of materials in these areas of the RLG conspectus. RLIN was used and retrospective conversion standards were applied.

Regional resource sharing by cooperative networking is another means by which monies are sometimes procured. Kottcamp[108] described a project at the University of North Carolina at Chapel-Hill and Millican[109] described a project at Louisiana State University which were funded by Higher Education Act Title II-C grants to promote resource sharing. OCLC was the utility used by both institutions. OCLC is also the utility in use for the ongoing, in-house conversion of a previously uncataloged periodicals collection at Memphis State University. Broadway and Qualls[110] discussed the project for which neither additional money nor staff were provided.

Banach and Spell[111] described the serials conversion project done for the University of Massachusetts of Amherst by OCLC. This was the largest completed project identified by the author and its statistics are of interest because of the substantive size of the converted collection. OCLC staff worked from UMA shelflist cards and over 27,000 titles were fully converted. While around 2,000 more titles were also converted, verification of one or more areas of the records was requested. A final 1,376 titles were not converted due to problems. This group included cases where not all of the titles (or, in a few instances, none of the titles) represented in latest entry cataloging had copy in OCLC. While under the terms of the contract OCLC was required to create new successive entry records, the shelflist cards for the problem titles lacked a sufficient quantity of information to make this possible. the unconverted serials also included titles for which only monograph cataloging was available in OCLC. While Banach and Spell cautioned that a final evaluation could not be made until the records had more use, the initial response at UMA has been very favorable. Unfortunately, the source of funding and the cost of the project were not stated.

Van Avery[112] studied the records for 357 serials recataloged at the University of Albany, State University of New York and found that more than 50 per cent of OCLC copy required adjustments to meet current standards, a percentage comparable to those disclosed by earlier studies done elsewhere. Unlike RLIN where users may see the records of each RLIN member and benefit from the modifications made for local records, only the master record is visible in OCLC and changes made by OCLC member institutions for their own catalogs are unknown to one another. Van Avery stated that retrospective conversion would become an easier process if records were maintained for currency as various changes occurred in the publications. She suggested that such maintenance could be made possible through the development of a reporting technique. Procedures would be somewhat comparable to those governing error reports at present and, to encourage maintenance, reporting libraries would receive some kind of credit. Documentation would be required and a quality screening by OCLC would be mandatory. Van Avery stated that a second screening by holding libraries would also seem desirable. Soper[113] elsewhere discussed the lack of maintenance in OCLC records in relation to public services.

Van Avery stated, however, "if the goal is adequate access rather than perfect cataloging, the situation is not so bad. Although fewer than 50% of the hits were AACR2, many of those pre-AACR2 records were perfectly adequate and usable."[114] She also expressed the belief that the record with the most complete information should be chosen for use.

> The difference between latest entry and successive entry cataloging will not affect patrons so much in an online catalog, and therefore should perhaps not be the main basis of choice of which record to use. Obsolete corporate headings are also not an important problem, since they can be corrected later using an authority control service. If one has a choice of several records . . . the library . . . may choose the record which has the most desirable elements . . .[115]

ADMINISTRATIVE PLACEMENT OF SERIALS CATALOGING

The inaugural volume of *Advances in Serials Management* appeared in 1986 and featured three discussions on the placement of serials in the organizational structure of libraries. Cook[116] provided a superb historical perspective which reviewed the literature from the 1930s through the 1950s and covered as well serials activity within ALA. While Carter[117] discussed functions from the angle of decentralization, her remarks included "within either a single library or libraries in general . . . there is not one best approach"[118] and "it seems clear that there is not strong trend either toward or away from decentralizing serials activities in large or medium size libraries."[119]

Ezzell[120] focused on integrated serials functions. She reviewed previous surveys and reported the results of her 1984 survey of the 117 ARL member libraries to which 107 institutions responded with usable returns. Selected findings from the survey follow. Centralized serials departments existed in 64 (60 per cent) of the libraries while 43 (40 per cent) had no serials department. "Two-thirds of the serials departments include the cataloging of serials among their activities."[121] Among the 43 institutions wherein functions were dispersed, four had plans to establish a serials department in the future and 22 other libraries had formerly had a serials department. Two respondents whose institutions had abolished their departments indicated, "One purpose . . .was to promote greater consistency between monographic and serials cataloging practices by placing all cataloging activities in one department, and to standardize the philosophy of cataloging."[122]

Published as a special issue of *The Serials Librarian* in 1990, *The Good Serials Department*[123] gave descriptions of serials management in thirteen academic libraries. Centralized and decentralized operations were discussed. Most writers provided some historical background on serials treatment in their institutions and discussed as well the philosophical and practical reasons underlying the present arrangements. As indicated by Ezzell's ARL survey, centralized departments were more likely than not to include serials cataloging. Peter Gellatly, editor of *The Serials Librarian*, acted as the editor for *The Good Serials Department* and justly stated ". . . if the serials department has outlived its usefulness and is on the way out, more evidence is needed to support this view than is at present available."[124]

OTHER TOPICS IN BRIEF

A review article of journal length cannot do full justice to the dynamic activity and the prolific volume of literature that characterized serials cataloging during the second half of the 1980s. The lead article in the volume in hand is a vibrant discussion on the teaching of serials cataloging by Henderson and a survey report on continuing education and staff development follows by Boydston. The professional literature from 1985 through 1990 included numerous other discussions on education and training. Library school education was described by Stine.[125] Rast [126] discussed formal continuing education. Matson[127] reviewed the journal literature as a means of current awareness. Peters[128] conducted a survey examination of the content of cataloging courses and found that serials and other non-book materials tended to be taught in depth only at the advanced level. Soper[129] described the teaching of serials cataloging at the University of Washington's Graduate School of Library and Information Science. Gorman[130] proposed a course for serials librarianship, in which a cataloging component was featured, for Australian library schools. Fitzgerald[131] described the training of catalogers at Harvard University and noted the differences between monographic and serials training. Serials catalogers must learn to interpret the related acquisitions records and also be taught the use of the several card catalogs to deal with title changes.

Serials Librarianship in Transition: Issues and Developments[132] was the title of a special issue of *The Serials Librarian* when the journal entered its tenth year of publication in 1986. Cole and Madison,[133] McIver,[134] Sadowski,[135] and Cummins[136] each explored an aspect of serials cataloging, reminding the reader of the almost kaleidoscopic change that transpired between 1975 and 1985. Elsewhere in the literature Hood[137] provided an unsurpassed examination of the catalog record in relation to union listing and Scott[138] reviewed union listing from the serials cataloging perspective. Jasco[139] discussed the potential for using the *Bibliofile* database on CD-ROM as a serials cataloging tool. Wang[140,141] examined the serials cataloging of CD-ROM products and stated what was really important. In a survey of academic libraries concerned with production standards, Smith[142] found that serials were considered comparable to audiovisual media and music scores where cataloging norms existed. Full-time original catalogers of each format were expected to complete about 50 titles per month.

Mueller[143] provided a historical assessment of the impact of AACR2 on serials management and concluded with a discussion of current concerns such as the implementation of revised rules and LCRIs. Several writers described procedural and/or managerial changes which came as a result of institutional computerization. "Access to a fixed number of computer terminals and relieving congestion in the Serial Record file were the primary reasons . . ."[144] for the LC Serial Record Division to schedule some employees for evening work. Havens[145] described the changes which occurred in serials acquisitions and cataloging with the implementation of the NOTIS system at Auburn University. NOTIS was also implemented by the University of Louisville and Niles[146] reported on the consequent reorganization of technical services. Bedner[147] discussed the changes in staff utilization at Pennsylvania State University after cataloging operations were automated.

CONCLUSION

The years that constituted the latter half of the 1980s were an exciting time to have involvement with serials cataloging. The literature was prolific. Authors reported the results of research studies, described various institutional changes which came with computerization, questioned certain practices and proposed alternatives, and suggested solutions to the prevalent problems. Through the diligent efforts of the Committee to Study Serials Cataloging, the Library of Congress, and appropriate groups within ALCTS, substantive changes were made to improve access and efficiency. With the processes for other changes firmly entrenched, the 1990s are likely to prove an equally challenging and eventful time.

REFERENCES

1. *Serials Cataloging: The State of the Art*, ed. Jim E. Cole and Jackie Zajanc, The Serials Librarian 12, no. 1/2 (New York: The Haworth Press, Inc., 1987).
2. *Anglo-American Cataloguing Rules*. 2nd ed. (Chicago: American Library Association, 1978): 286.
3. *Cataloging Service Bulletin* 36 (Spring 1987): 12-14.
4. *Anglo-American Cataloguing Rules*. 2nd ed., rev. (Chicago: American Library Association, 1988): 314-315.
5. Ibid., p. 314.
6. Ibid.
7. *Anglo-American Cataloguing Rules*. 2nd ed., p. 286.
8. *Anglo-American Cataloguing Rules*. 2nd ed., rev., p. 314.
9. *Anglo-American Cataloguing Rules*. 2nd ed., p. 286.
10. *Anglo-American Cataloguing Rules*. 2nd ed., rev., p. 314-315.
11. *Anglo-American Cataloguing Rules*. 2nd ed., p. 286.
12. *Anglo-American Cataloguing Rules*. 2nd ed., rev., p. 315.
13. *Cataloging Service Bulletin* 48 (Spring 1990): 12.
14. *Anglo-American Cataloguing Rules*. 2nd ed., rev., p. 316.
15. *Cataloging Service Bulletin* 50 (Fall 1990): 34-35.
16. Dorothy J. Glasby, "Historical Background and Review of Serials Cataloging Rules," *Library Resources & Technical Services* 34, no. 1 (January 1990): 80-87.
17. Jackie Zajanc, "Title Changes in an Automated Environment: The Last Shall Be First," *The Serials Librarian* 11, no. 1 (September 1986): 15-21.
18. Sue C. Lim, "Successive Entry Serials Cataloging: An Evaluation," *The Serials Librarian* 14, no. 1/2 (1988): 59-69.

19. Marjorie Flaspeter and Linda Lomker, "Earliest Online," *Serials Review* 11, no. 2 (Summer 1985): 63-70.

20. Jim E. Cole, "The First Shall Be Last: Earliest Entry Cataloging," *The Serials Librarian* 11, no. 1 (September 1986): 5-14.

21. Renee D. Chapman, "Laws, Etc.," *Serials Review* 15, no. 1 (Spring 1989): 35-39.

22. Margaret V. Mering, "Would the Reintroduction of Latest Entry Cataloging Create More Problems Than It Would Resolve?," *Cataloging & Classification Quarterly* 10, no. 3 (1990): 35-44.

23. Ibid., p. 40.

24. Ibid., p. 41.

25. Melissa M. Bernhardt, "Dealing with Serial Title Changes: Some Theoretical and Practical Consideration," *Cataloging & Classification Quarterly* 9, no. 2 (1988): 25-39.

26. Ibid., p. 31.

27. Patrick F. Callahan, "Cataloging Forum," *Arkansas Libraries* 44, no. 4 (December 1987): 39.

28. Ibid., p. 38.

29. Karen Nadeski, "The Retrospective Conversion of Microforms at Penn State," *Microform Review* 18, no. 2 (Spring 1989): 84-92.

30. Philip Bryant, "What Is That Hyphen Doing, Anyway? Cataloguing and Classification of Serials and the New Technologies," *International Cataloguing & Bibliographic Control* 18, no. 2 (April/June 1989): 29.

31. Ibid.

32. Charles A. Litchfield and Marilyn L. Norstedt, "Coded Holdings: A Primer for New Users," *Serials Review* 14, no. 1/2 (1988): 81-88.

33. Ibid., p. 85-86.

34. Ibid., p. 88.

35. Daphne Heush, "Getting Started with the USMARC Format for Holdings and Locations," *The Serials Librarian* 15, no. 3/4 (1988): 147.

36. *The USMARC Format for Holdings and Locations: Development, Implementation, and Use*, ed. Barry B. Baker, Technical Services Quarterly Monograph Supplement #2 (New York: The Haworth Press, Inc., 1988).

37. Sook-Hyum Kim, "Application of the USMARC Format for Holdings and Locations," *The Serials Librarian* 16, no. 3/4 (1989): 21-31.

38. *Cataloging Service Bulletin* 32 (Spring 1986): 21.

39. *Cataloging Service Bulletin* 38 (Fall 1987): 33.

40. *ALA Handbook of Organization 1989/1990.* (Chicago: American Library Association, 1989): 45.

41. Crystal Graham, *Guidelines for Bibliographic Records for Preservation Microform Masters (Serials).* 2nd draft. (Washington, D.C.: Association of Research Libraries, Committee on Bibliographic Control, 1989): 2.

42. Crystal Graham, "Guidelines for Cataloging Microform Masters (Serials)," *RTSD Newsletter* 14, no. 6 (1989): 2.

43. *Cataloging Service Bulletin* 47 (Winter 1990): 41.

44. Ellen Siegel Kovacic, "Report of the Meeting of the Serials Section Committee to Study Serials Cataloging, ALA Midwinter, January 1988," *Serials Review* 14, no. 3 (1988): 87.

45. Constance F. Roberts, Ann B. Vidor, and Dorothy C. Bailey, "Time and Cost Analysis of Title Changes in Serials," *The Serials Librarian* 11, no. 3/4 (1987): 141.

46. Mitch L. Turitz, "Uniform Titles for Serials: The Controversy Continues," *Serials Review* 16, no. 1 (Spring 1990): 85-89, 98.

47. Carolyn Havens, "Proposed Changes in the Cataloging of Serials with Generic and Uniform Titles," *The Serials Librarian* 13, no. 4 (December 1987): 59-68.

48. Judith M. Shelton, "Proposed Changes in the Cataloging of Serials: Another View," *The Serials Librarian* 16, no. 1/2 (1989): 101-108.

49. Lucy A. Barron, "Concerning CONSER: Accomplishments and Aspirations," *The Serials Librarian* 19, no. 3/4 (1991): 180.

50. *Cataloging Service Bulletin* 29 (Summer 1985): 12-14.

51. Thomas R. Sanders, "Monographs of a Regular Frequency," *Cataloging & Classification Quarterly* 9, no. 1 (1988): 37-57.

52. Ibid., p. 54.

53. Karen Dalziel Tallman, Sharon K. Scott, and Carrie Russell, "Looseleaf Publications in Large Academic Libraries: The Looseleaf Recataloging Project at the University of Arizona," *The Serials Librarian* 16, no. 3/4 (1989): 33-47.

54. Ibid., p. 34.

55. Pamela Bluh, "Legal Looseleafs: No Grounds for Intimidation," *Serials Review* 15, no. 3 (Fall 1989): 65.

56. Jim E. Cole, "Caught in a Bind: The Cataloging of Looseleaf Publications," *The Serials Librarian* 16, no. 1/2 (1989): 80.

57. Ibid., p. 81.

58. Barbara L. Berman, "Coping with Conference Proceedings," *Cataloging & Classification Quarterly* 10, no. 3 (1990): 19-34.

59. Ibid., p. 32.

60. A. Anneli Ahtola, "Online Cataloging and Quality of Service: A Case of Conference Proceedings," *Technicalities* 8, no. 3 (March 1988): 11.

61. Kathleen Bales, "Format Integration: Coordinating the Implementation," *Information Technology and Libraries* 9, no. 2 (June 1990): 167-173.

62. Katherine G. Evans, "MARC Format Integration and Seriality: Implications for Serials Cataloging," *The Serials Librarian* 18, no. 1/2 (1990): 38.

63. Sally H. McCallum, "Format Integration: Handling the Additions and Subtractions," *Information Technology and Libraries* 9, no. 2 (June 1990): 161.

64. Ibid., p. 157.

65. Ibid., p. 158.

66. Ibid., p. 160.

67. Evans, "MARC Format Integration and Seriality," p. 40.

68. Stephen P. Davis, "Format Integration: Handling Serials and Mixed Media," *Information Technology and Libraries* 9, no. 2 (June 1990): 165.

69. George Gibbs, "Applying Format Integration: An Operational Test," *Information Technology and Libraries* 9, no. 2 (June 1990): 173-178.
70. Ibid., p. 178.
71. Linda K. Bartley and Regina R. Reynolds, "CONSER: Revolution and Evolution," *Cataloging & Classification Quarterly* 8, no. 3/4 (1988): 47-66.
72. Ibid., p. 57-58.
73. Barron, "Concerning CONSER," p. 178.
74. Ibid., p. 179.
75. Ibid., p. 178.
76. Bartley and Reynolds, "CONSER," p. 59.
77. Ibid., p. 63.
78. Barron, "Concerning CONSER," p. 180.
79. Bartley and Reynolds, "CONSER," p. 60-61.
80. Ibid., p. 61.
81. "LC's Arrearage," *in* "AL Asides," *American Libraries* 21, no. 10 (October 1990): 841.
82. "Challenge for LC: Hire 164 New Staff," *in* "News Fronts," *American Libraries* 22, no. 1 (January 1991): 7.
83. "Library Develops Plan to Cut Arrearages," *LC Information Bulletin* 49, no. 10 (May 7, 1990): 170, 174.
84. Ibid., p. 170.
85. Ibid., p. 174.
86. Ibid.
87. *Cataloging Service Bulletin* 38 (Fall 1987): 52-57.
88. James W. Williams, "Serials Cataloging in 1987," *The Serials Librarian* 15, no. 1/2 (1988): 73-74.
89. Jean Hirons, "Report on Serial Microform Cataloging Activities," *LC Information Bulletin* 49, no. 7 (March 26, 1990): 124-125.
90. Ibid., p. 125.
91. *Cataloging Service Bulletin* 51 (Winter 1991): 3-7.
92. Ibid., p. 3.
93. Elaine K. Rast, "Narrowing the Gap: Serials Service Improved by Cooperation Between Technical and Public Services," *The Reference Librarian* 27/28 (1990): 105-122.
94. Larry D. Benson, "The Serials Catalog: A View from the Reference Desk," *The Reference Librarian* 27/28 (1990): 123-139.
95. Ibid., p. 123.
96. Mary Ellen Soper, "What You See May Not Be What You Get: Errors in Online Bibliographic Records for Serials," *The Reference Librarian* 27/28 (1990): 185-213.
97. Ibid., p. 201.
98. Ibid., p. 212.
99. Jean S. Decker, "Is This a Serial?," *The Reference Librarian* 27/28 (1990): 141-160.

100. Carolyn J. Mueller and Martha A. Whittaker, "What Is This Thing Called MARC(S)?," *The Reference Librarian* 27/28 (1990): 161-175.

101. Rex Bross, "Classification of Periodicals," *The Reference Librarian* 27/28 (1990): 177-183.

102. Jim Segesta and Gary Hyslop, "The Arrangement of Periodicals in American Academic Libraries," *Serials Review* 17, no. 1 (Spring 1991): 21-28, 40.

103. Patrick Wilson, "Interpreting the Second Objective of the Catalog," *Library Quarterly* 59, no. 4 (1989): 339-353.

104. Sheila S. Intner, "Modern Serials Cataloging," *Technicalities* 10, no. 5 (May 1990): 4-6.

105. Sheila S. Intner, "A New Paradigm for Access to Serials," *The Serial Librarian* 19, no. 3/4 (1991): 151-172.

106. David Tyckoson, "The 98% Solution: The Failure of the Catalog and the Role of Electronic Databases," *Technicalities* 9, no. 2 (February 1989): 8-12.

107. Nora S. Copeland, "Retrospective Conversion of Serials: The RLIN Experience," *Serials Review* 14, no. 3 (1988): 23-28.

108. Christina Kottcamp, "Defining Standards for Serials Retrospective Conversion Projects," *Advances in Serials Management* 2 (1988): 159-171.

109. Rita Millican, "Serials Conversion: LSU's Experience," *The Serials Librarian* 9, no. 4 (Summer 1985): 45-51.

110. Rita Broadway and Jane Qualls, "Retrospective Conversion of Periodicals: A Shoestring Experience," *The Serials Librarian* 15, no. 1/2 (1988): 99-111.

111. Patricia Banach and Cynthia Spell, "Serials Conversion at the University of Massachusetts at Amherst," *Information Technology and Libraries* 7, no. 2 (June 1988): 124-130.

112. Annalisa R. Van Avery, "Recat vs. Recon of Serials: A Problem for Shared Cataloging," *Cataloging & Classification Quarterly* 10, no. 4 (1990): 51-67.

113. Soper, "What You See May Not Be What You Get," p. 185-213.

114. Van Avery, "Recat vs. Recon of Serials," p. 59.

115. Ibid., p. 66-67.

116. Jean G. Cook, "Serials' Place on the Organization Chart: A Historical Perspective," *Advances in Serials Management* 1 (1986): 53-66.

117. Ruth C. Carter, "Decentralization of Serials Functions," *Advances in Serials Management* 1 (1986): 83-99.

118. Ibid., p. 83.

119. Ibid., p. 98.

120. Joline R. Ezzell, "The Integrated Serials Department," *Advances in Serials Management* 1 (1986): 67-82.

121. Ibid., p. 76.

122. Ibid., p. 78.

123. *The Good Serials Department*, ed. Peter Gellatly, The Serials Librarian 19, no. 1/2 (New York: The Haworth Press, Inc., 1990).

124. Peter Gellatly, "The Serials Department Revealed," in *The Good Serials*

Department, ed. Peter Gellatly, The Serials Librarian 19, no. 1/2 (New York: The Haworth Press, Inc., 1990): 1.

125. Diane Stine, "The Adequacy of Library School Education for Serials Librarianship," *Illinois Libraries* 67, no. 5 (May 1985): 448-452.

126. Elaine K. Rast, "Formal Continuing Education for Serials" *Illinois Libraries* 67, no. 5 (May 1985): 453-458.

127. Susan Matson, "Informal Continuing Education for Serials: Keeping Up With the Journal Literature," *Illinois Libraries* 67, no. 5 (May 1985): 458-462.

128. Stephen H. Peters, "Time Devoted to Topics in Cataloging Courses," *Journal of Education for Library and Information Science* 29, no. 3 (Winter 1989): 209-219.

129. Mary Ellen Soper, "Descriptive Cataloging Education in Library Schools, Using the University of Washington as a Specific Example," *Cataloging & Classification Quarterly* 7, no. 4 (1987): 47-56.

130. G.E. Gorman, "The Education of Serials Librarians in Australia: A Proposed Course in Serials Librarianship," *The Serials Librarian* 17, no. 1/2 (1989): 45-67.

131. Michael Fitzgerald, "Training the Cataloger: A Harvard Experience," *in Recruiting, Educating, and Training Catalog Librarians: Solving the Problems*, ed. Sheila S. Intner and Janet Swan Hill (New York: Greenwood Press, 1989): 341-353.

132. *Serials Librarianship in Transition: Issues and Developments*, The Serials Librarian 10, no. 1/2 (New York: The Haworth Press, Inc., 1986).

133. Jim E. Cole and Olivia M.A. Madison, "A Decade of Serials Cataloging," *in Serials Librarianship in Transition: Issues and Developments*, The Serials Librarian 10, no. 1/2 (New York: The Haworth Press, Inc., 1986): 103-116.

134. Carole R. McIver, "The AACRs and Serials Cataloging," *in Serials Librarianship in Transition: Issues and Developments*, The Serials Librarian 10, no. 1/2 (New York: The Haworth Press, Inc., 1986): 117-127.

135. Frank E. Sadowski, Jr., "Serials Cataloging Developments, 1975-1985: A Personal View of Some Highlights," *in Serials Librarianship in Transition: Issues and Developments*, The Serials Librarian 10, no. 1/2 (New York: The Haworth Press, Inc., 1986): 133-140.

136. Lynn Mealer Cummins, "Serials Cataloging in Transition," *in Serials Librarianship in Transition: Issues and Developments*, The Serials Librarian 10, no. 1/2 (New York: The Haworth Press, Inc., 1986): 129-131.

137. Elizabeth Hood, "The Catalog Record and Automated Union Listing," *Serials Review* 14, no. 1/2 (1988): 31-42.

138. Sharon K. Scott, "OCLC Union Listing and the Serials Cataloger," *in* "The Balance Point," *Serials Review* 15, no. 1 (Spring 1989): 84-85.

139. Peter Jacso, "*Bibliofile* for Serials Cataloging," *The Serials Librarian* 18, no. 1/2 (1990): 47-80.

140. Anna Wang, "Cataloging CD-ROMs at the Ohio State University," *Serials Review* 14, no. 3 (1988): 11-21.

141. Anna Wang, "The Challenge of Cataloging Computer Files," *The Serials Librarian* 15, no. 3/4 (1988): 99-115.

142. Philip M. Smith, "Cataloging Production Standards of Academic Libraries," *Technical Services Quarterly* 6, no. 1 (1988): 3-14.
143. Carolyn J. Mueller, "AACR2 and Serials Management," *Advances in Serials Management* 2 (1988): 47-61.
144. Jean L. Hirons, "Working Evenings in the Serial Record Division," *LC Information Bulletin* 47, no. 16 (April 18, 1988): 162.
145. Carolyn Havens, "Adaptation of Serials Practices to NOTIS at Auburn University," *The Serials Librarian* 13, no. 4 (December 1987): 21-38.
146. Judith Niles, "Technical Services Reorganization for an Online Integrated Environment," *Cataloging & Classification Quarterly* 9, no. 1 (1988): 11-17.
147. Marie Bedner, "Automation of Cataloging: Effects on Use of Staff, Efficiency, and Service to Patrons," *Journal of Academic Librarianship* 14, no. 3 (July 1988): 145-149.

Copy Cataloging of Serials: UIUC

Rhoda R. Engel

SUMMARY. Copy cataloging of serials at the University of Illinois at Urbana-Champaign is done in the OCLC cataloging unit of the Automated Services department. Matching OCLC records were found for just over 81 per cent of the serial titles searched from July 1989 through June 1990. One full-time paraprofessional is responsible for copy editing and classification A professional librarian spends approximately two hours a week in consultation with the paraprofessional to resolve complex problems. The UIUC computerized catalog, search searching routines, and serial copy editing procedures are described.

Copy cataloging of serials at the University of Illinois at Urbana-Champaign (UIUC) is done in the Automated Services department of the Library. Three units of the department are involved: Support Services, OCLC Cataloging, and FBR Maintenance. Searching and updating of OCLC records is done by Support Services; updating of the local UIUC catalog record is done by FBR Maintenance through the Illinet Online database; editing OCLC records and classification is done by OCLC Cataloging. Serials received for searching come from two sources: the Acquisitions department or direct from departmental (subject) libraries. They may be titles newly purchased, titles received as gifts, or title changes discovered during routine check-in procedures. Serials processed in Automated Services include titles covering all subject fields, those issued in Roman alphabet languages and Greek, and ones issued in all formats except maps.

Some information about the UIUC online catalog is useful for an understanding of copy cataloging at UIUC. The local catalog is part of

---

Rhoda R. Engel is OCLC Cataloging Librarian at the University of Illinois at Urbana-Champaign.

a statewide online union catalog called Illinet Online (IO). IO has two linked components: the Full Bibliographic Record (FBR) and the Library Computer System (LCS). FBR is a union catalog that contains one complete bibliographic record for each title entered in the database. LCS is a short record circulation system for each member library's holdings. The LCS record consists of author, title, edition, place and date of publication plus local call number, local holdings, and other library specific information. The FBR record is linked to as many LCS records as there are holding libraries for each title. For example, ten libraries in the state own the same title; there will be one record in FBR; the FBR record will be linked to ten separate LCS records (one for each library). Records are entered into IO from OCLC archival tapes of the individual member libraries. When an OCLC tape is loaded into IO, an FBR record is created or the library's holding symbol is added to an existing, matching FBR record; an individual LCS record is created containing that library's local circulation record; and finally, the link from FBR to LCS is made.

Various levels of personnel are involved in the processing of serials in Automated Services. Searching for copy in OCLC is done by two persons: a Library Clerk 3 who spends 2.5 hours a day on serials searching and a Chief Clerk (with 13 years of serials experience) who spends about 6 hours a week on serials searching. In OCLC Cataloging a full time Library Technical Assistant 3 (with some 13 years of experience with serials) is responsible for editing printouts of the OCLC catalog record and classifying serial titles, a half-time Library Clerk 2 does the routine clerical chores for serials, and a professional librarian spends approximately 2 hours a week in consultation with the LTA3 concerning complex problems. The actual OCLC updating is done by a Secretary 3 who spends 20 hours a week on serials with some assistance, amounting to approximately 5 hours a month, from another Secretary 3. A Library Technical Assistant 1 in FBR Maintenance spends about 10 hours a week on serials updating in Illinet Online.

From July 1989 through June 1990 a total of 2,563 serial titles were received for searching in Automated Services. Of those titles, matching OCLC records were found for 2,077 titles (just over 81%). During the same time period, the LTA3 recorded 3,045 titles cataloged. This larger figure included titles from a small backlog of problem items, recataloging of titles that holding units discovered as problems (e.g., titles changes not caught at check-in), and retrospective conversion of local latest entry card records to successive entry records online.

Serials received for searching in Automated Services are searched first by an LC3. Searching is done at a dedicated OCLC terminal making use of the ISSN or coden, if available, for the initial search. Title, corporate author, and author/title searches are done as necessary. The "ser" qualifier is used routinely for non-numerical searches; other qualifiers such as beginning date when known, "mf," etc., are used as appropriate. A printout is made of matching records. If a matching record includes 780 and/or 785 fields, records for titles indicated in those fields are called up and printed out also. All entries for corporate bodies and conferences (1xx, 6xx, 7xx fields) are searched in the OCLC authority file. Printouts are made of any relevant records.

The Illinet Online (IO) database is then searched for copy corresponding to the OCLC records already found. For OCLC records that indicate UIUC holdings (title in hand or titles from 780/785 fields), the clerk searches the LCS (circulation system) component of IO to find the local call number. If the record and call number are for the title in hand, a printout of the LCS record is made, inserted in the piece along with all OCLC printouts, and given to the added copy area for processing. LCS printouts are also made for related titles for use in classifying the new title. OCLC records not having UIUC holdings are searched in the FBR (full bibliographic record) component of IO. If an OCLC record has been entered in the IO database, any bibliographic editing of that record must be done through IO by the FBR Maintenance unit. Printouts are made of any matching records found in FBR. All printouts (OCLC, LCS, FBR) are inserted in the serial and it is forwarded to OCLC Cataloging.

Serial titles which the LC3 has not found in OCLC are researched by a Chief Clerk with greater experience and knowledge of serial publications. Additional authority work making use of the LSP capability is done if judged useful. If copy is found, IO is searched before forwarding to OCLC Cataloging. Serials for which copy has not been found are sent to the Office of the Principal Cataloger where original cataloging of serials is performed. Serials for the Law Library, including those for which copy is found, are sent to the Law Library for cataloging.

The LTA3 in OCLC Cataloging is responsible for editing OCLC records and for assigning classification numbers to serial titles received by the unit. If there is an FBR record, editing is done on that printout, otherwise on the OCLC printout. Editing the copy entails checking the accuracy of information and updating headings to AACR2 form as necessary.

Changes made are substantive, not cosmetic (i.e., punctuation is not changed, format of the information given is generally not changed). For serials, choice of entry is routinely changed to reflect AACR2 rules. That is, if a title is entered under corporate body according to pre-AACR2 cataloging rules and AACR2 calls for entry under title, the 110 is changed to a 710 added entry and the title is made the main entry. The first indicator in the 245 is then changed to a zero. Unless upgrading the OCLC copy, the rest of the record is not changed to reflect AACR2. OCLC copy used includes all levels of cataloging from minimal level to full cataloging records. Some records require little or no editing; others require what amounts to original cataloging. If the LTA finds significant variations between the OCLC copy and piece in hand, the title will be returned for further searching or sent for original cataloging.

Following are the areas of the records given the most attention at UIUC: LC card number, ISBN, and ISSN are added to the record if missing and the piece in hand gives one or more of these numbers.

The title is checked for accuracy of transcription. If a uniform title is needed, but is not present in the record, it is added. Subfield delimiters "n" and "p" are deleted. The deletion is necessary because the local circulation system reads only the subfield "a" portion of the title field when adding records from OCLC tape. If the piece in hand has other title information not recorded on the OCLC copy, an appropriate note is added. Likewise a variant title may be added in an appropriate 246 field.

The statement of responsibility is checked and corrected if necessary. For pre-AACR2 copy that uses a space hyphen space between title and statement of responsibility, the hyphen is changed to a slash and a subfield "c" delimiter is inserted. If the piece in hand indicates that the responsible body has changed (either a name change or a different body), an appropriate 550 note and added entry are made.

Any edition statement is verified.

The serial numbering information is checked; if the copy gives numbering for the first issue, it is not changed. If the copy gives numbering based on other than the first issue and the first issue is in hand, the information in the 362 field is changed and the "description based on" note is deleted. Lacking the first issue, the "description based on" note is not changed unless the issue in hand is substantially earlier than that indicated in the copy. If information that the serial has ceased is available; the 362 field, the 260 subfield "c," and fixed field ("pub stat" and "dates") are closed.

Information regarding changes in numbering system is added to the copy when necessary. The format of the 362 field is changed only when information in the field is changed; the format is not changed as long as the information is correct.

Place of publication, publisher, and date will be changed if the first issue is in hand and the copy differs. If the date is changed, it is changed in the fixed field also. If place and publisher are lacking, they are routinely added to pre-AACR2 copy. Appropriate notes relating to publishing information are added as necessary; e.g., Publisher varies. If the serial has ceased, the date of publication is closed in both the 260 field and in the fixed field "dates."

In the physical description area the number of bibliographic volumes is added when the serial has ceased and the information is available. The size is changed to incorporate the actual size of the piece in hand; this number determines the need for an oversize prefix to the call number.

If the serial title is issued as part of a series, the 4xx field is checked for accuracy of transcription. If needed, corrections are made. If an ISSN for the series is found on the piece but is not on the copy, it is added. 440 and 8xx fields are checked for proper AACR2 form.

Notes are checked for accuracy of information. They are changed or added as necessary to reflect changes or additional information concerning frequency, languages, titles, responsible bodies, relationship with other serials, numbering, etc. Citation notes are not added or changed. If an OCLC serial record runs to three or more screens, all 510 notes are routinely deleted. This is necessary because the bibliographic component of IO has a record limitation that is shorter than OCLC's.

Subject entries (using LCSH) are added if missing from the copy or if only non-LC subjects are present. Entries coded as being from LCSH are generally accepted as they appear. Added entries for persons and corporate bodies are checked to ensure correct AACR2 form; entries are added to reflect new information added to the cataloging description. The 780 and 785 fields for related titles are carefully checked (the serial cited is changed to AACR2 form if it does not appear that way); ISSN and subfield "w" are added if missing and the information is available. Entries for related titles are added as necessary.

In the fixed field area, only these codes are routinely checked and changed as necessary: "lang," "ser tp," "frequn," "pub stat," "regulr," and "dates." If "S/L ent" is coded 1 for latest entry cataloging, the record is not used. The title is researched for successive entry cataloging. If "enc lvl" is other than "ƀ", "1," "I," or "L," the record is upgraded to complete level cataloging. In this case all codes in the fixed field are checked for accuracy, "desc" is coded "a," and the complete record is upgraded for AACR2 form and content.

After editing the OCLC record, the LTA3 assigns a classification number to the title. The latest edition of the DDC is used for the majority of titles; an in-house adaptation of Dewey is used for literature and LC is used for items housed in the Music Library. A half-time Library Clerk 2 does the Cuttering, shelflisting, marking of pieces, preparation of temporary records, and other housekeeping chores involved in distributing the cataloged serials. Edited printouts with call number, location, and holdings information are passed on to a Secretary 3 in the Support Services area who does the actual updating of the OCLC records at a dedicated terminal. If an FBR record has been edited, the OCLC record will have only UIUC's call number, location, and holdings added. This will create UIUC's LCS record and link it to the existing FBR record. The edited FBR printout will then be given to FBR Maintenance for updating in IO. Normally within two weeks, the archival tape from OCLC will have been received and added to the Illinet Online database. At that point UIUC's catalog and circulation records are available online.

Decision Making in the Recataloging of Serials

Lori L. Osmus

SUMMARY. Catalogers make decisions constantly, especially when recataloging serials. This article explores the decisions that need to be made when recataloging serials, within the framework of a decision-making model used in business. For catalogers, this model consists of becoming aware that a recataloging problem exists, defining what the problem is, analyzing the alternatives for handling it, selecting the best solution based on the library's goals and resources, implementing it, and obtaining feedback. Then the cycle begins again with new problems.

Catalogers make decisions constantly, especially when recataloging serials. Has the title really changed? Are additional access points needed? Is it worthwhile to make a note about a particular numbering irregularity?

Steps for making decisions have been described in business literature[1] and these can also be applied to the recataloging of serials:

1. Become aware of the problem.
2. Define the problem.
3. Analyze potential alternatives and consequences.
4. Select the best solution.
5. Implement the decision.
6. Provide or obtain feedback.
7. Become aware of new problems (the cycle begins again).

In this article, these steps will be used to organize the discussion about recataloging serials, as well as to suggest a method for making recataloging decisions.

Lori L. Osmus is Head, Serials Cataloging Section at Iowa State University Library.

BECOMING AWARE OF THE PROBLEM

The first decision to be made is: is the recataloging of serials necessary? There are so many fewer serial titles than monograph titles in a typical library collection that one might argue that recataloging serials is a minor concern. However, "it has often been estimated that, at least in some types of libraries, 75 percent or more of the library use centers around serials."[2] This is because "scholars and researchers want to know the latest developments in a great variety of fields long before they appear in book form"[3] and serials fill this need. Serials also absorb large portions of libraries' acquisitions budgets, and over time a complete run of one journal title may cost thousands of dollars, enormous compared to the cost of an average book. Considering a library's substantial investment in serials, and the heavy use they receive, complete and current cataloging is essential in larger libraries to obtain benefits from a serials collection comparable to its costs. Smaller libraries may be able to avoid the cost of recataloging if they can facilitate use of serials without cataloging them, such as arranging them in a display that can be browsed easily.

Why can't the best possible cataloging record be created for a serial title, and then be left alone? Unlike a monograph, which is a fixed, complete item when it is cataloged, a serial continues and changes, so eventually its catalog record becomes obsolete. In addition, cataloging done according to previous cataloging codes, even though it may have been high quality work, must be reconciled with current practices. The changes in existing serials provide perpetual work for serials catalogers, but the amount of work actually done depends upon how much recataloging a library believes is necessary to meet the needs of its users.

How does a library become aware of the need to recatalog a serial? Staff who check-in incoming issues will notice changes in title and frequency, and their work also will be affected by numbering irregularities and receipt of supplements, special issues, and separate indexes. They can then report these to the catalogers. However, unless check-in staff have the cataloging record in front of them and can spend time comparing it with each issue, it would be expecting a great deal of them to notice changes in issuing bodies or editors, place of publication, publisher, and slight changes in size. Changes missed at this stage might be caught by staff who prepare issues for binding, or by staff shelving the issues. Otherwise changes might not be found unless noticed by public services staff or a patron, or if a cataloger needed to examine the serial for other recataloging.

When one considers that the same work on a problem title is repeated in many other libraries in the United States and around the world, the total cost and time involved is overwhelming. Yet, few statistics have been published about recataloging in general, much less about serials recataloging. Recataloging has surpassed new title cataloging of serials at Iowa State University for each of the last thirteen years. In 1989/90, Iowa State University recataloged 2,276 serial titles, compared to 1,052 serial titles cataloged for the first time. A time and cost study that has been in progress in the Technical Services Division of the Iowa State University Library since 1987 reveals that 46.53% of the cataloging tasks of the Serials Cataloging Section are devoted to recataloging, compared to only 22.00% on new title cataloging, copy and original combined. On the average, recataloging of serials accounts for 71.37 hours per week and costs Iowa State University $991 per week in staff time.[4]

Despite the time and cost involved in recataloging, the only serials recataloging that has made it into the limelight is the title change, with a serial, *Title Varies*, devoted to this topic in the 1970's, and the establishment of the American Library Association's Worst Serial Title Change of the Year Committee. There seems to be widespread acknowledgment that a library must do something when a title changes, but not as much concern about the impact of less obvious changes, such as in issuing bodies or numbering. Gary Charbonneau's research found that "the chance that a serial will change title in any given year is approximately 1.3%"[5] Although the percentage seems small, it means that a medium-sized academic library with 18,000 current serials could expect to deal with 234 title changes a year, and this is only the tip of the recataloging iceberg.

DEFINING THE PROBLEM

What different libraries define as recataloging may vary greatly, making it difficult to compare any available recataloging statistics. In a study of cataloging statistics for fiscal year 1955, Joan Warren and Walter Barnard defined recataloging as "any correction, revision, or change which involves a 'cataloging' judgement as opposed to mechanical correction of errors."[6] The United States Department of Agriculture Library kept recataloging statistics under "old titles," which referred to "new work done on titles which are already cataloged in the collection,"[7] a much broader definition. Still other libraries look at whether or not extensive alterations to the catalog record are required, or what level of staff performs the work, in deciding whether it is regarded as recataloging or catalog maintenance.

In the index *Library Literature*, the heading "Cataloging–Recataloging" disappeared in 1988, and users are now referred to "Retrospective conversion"[8] which has some similarities but is not the same thing. Karla Petersen defines retrospective conversion as "the process of creating machine-readable records from already existing manual records. By definition, it does not involve cataloging or recataloging of materials, although some recataloging is usually necessary."[9] Patrick Callahan adds, "it deals primarily with existing catalog records as opposed to cataloging directly from the material."[10] However, articles on retrospective conversion are instructive in how to deal efficiently with recataloging problems, and this article will refer to them as appropriate.

Title changes are just one example of the kinds of recataloging. In addition to title changes, recataloging may result from:

- Changes in cataloging rules, which affect choice of entry, form of entry, format of the description, and how to deal with title changes;
- Local holdings changes, such as missing issues, transfers, or retention changes;
- Changes in medium, such as paper to microform or CD-ROM;
- Changes in almost any aspect of the serial that is recorded in a bibliographic record, from fixed field data to series added entries.

Let's not forget that recataloging also may be needed for the reason that springs to mind for most non-catalogers: cataloging that was incorrect or inadequate to begin with. In trying to find the items to match their citations, patrons suffer as much from the irregularities of serials as do librarians. Catalogers have the power to help by providing complete and current explanations of the problems through their cataloging.

ANALYZING POTENTIAL ALTERNATIVES AND CONSEQUENCES

Cataloging rules have been an effort to organize what were considered the best alternatives for handling various bibliographic situations, and have changed as other alternatives have become more attractive. All of the alternatives tried during the past one hundred years, from Cutter's 1876 *Rules for a Dictionary Catalog* to the 1988 revision of the *Anglo-American Cataloguing Rules*, second edition, (AACR2) will probably be encountered by some serials cataloger in the course of recataloging, and decisions will need to be made about how to reconcile past and current practices. The many choices leave serials catalogers with the moral dilemma of whether to use a time-consuming solution that is most correct according to the current rules, or an easy method which mixes current with past practice but still provides satisfactory access to users. Decisions need to be made about choice and form of entry as well as about the source, content and format of descriptive information.

To the users of the catalog, the most important cataloging decisions are those which affect access points. To determine the main entry, cataloging codes prior to AACR2 had different rules for different types of publications, but the current rules treat serials the same as any other library material. There are now three alternatives for main entry of a serial: title, corporate body, or personal author. Some librarians have questioned the need to differentiate between main and added entries in an online environment,[11] while others have pointed out the importance of having one way to cite an item.[12]

The title is an important access point for serials whether or not it is the main entry. "Something as basic as defining the title of a particular serial can be a dilemma."[13] This is because often serials do not have a title page, so the cataloger must determine the chief source, and then interpret the typography and layout of that page to choose the title. In the case of recataloging, the cataloger must decide whether a change has taken place in the title. AACR2 rule 21.2A provides some guidance as to what to regard as a title change, but considerable judgement is still involved. If the cataloging was done under old rules the form of the existing title may be set up differently than it appeared on the item itself. The cataloger risks discovering other title changes which had been overlooked if he or she diligently goes to the stacks and examines older issues to resolve discrepancies.

Once the cataloger determines that the title has really changed, historically there have been three options: keep the serial under its earliest title with a note about the change (earliest entry); recatalog the serial under its latest title with a note about the change (latest entry); or create a separate cataloging record for each title, with linking notes to earlier or later titles (successive entry). Since 1967, the cataloging rules (AACR and AACR2) have required successive entry, but latest entry was previously the accepted practice in the United States, and earliest entry in Great Britain. This means existing cataloging records may have been prepared using any of these methods, according to the rules in use at the time. If a cataloger doing a title change encounters a serial not cataloged according to successive entry, some libraries require that all the earlier title changes be recataloged with successive entry, while other libraries allow the option of closing the record as it is and only cataloging the new title successively. Some libraries, such as Northwestern University, are also taking a second look at latest entry as an option.

The main advantage of both earliest and latest entry cataloging was that the whole history of a serial was available in one record. However, it also meant catalogers had to search for this information, and gathering the full history was especially difficult if the library did not have a complete run. Latest entry cataloging required that the entry be continuously revised to the latest form, with notes about earlier information. In a manual environment, this resulted in labor-intensive re-typing of cards with long history statements. Under pressure from the library community to have one library provide complete bibliographic histories of serials, Library of Congress continued latest entry cataloging until 1971, when the burden became too great.[14] At least earliest entry cataloging did not require changing the descriptive paragraph, or the title. Variations were simply added in notes, although this could have obscured the most current data.[15]

Successive entry cataloging has several advantages. "The virtue of successive entry is the simplicity it offers for description of complicated materials . . . successive entry is ideal for cataloging a newly acquired title that has had a long and messy history of main entry changes, particularly if each was accompanied by other bibliographic variations."[16] It immediately satisfies a user who has a specific citation because it provides direct access to one title. Simple records are also easier to manipulate for machine applications and allow straightforward links to other records in integrated systems. In a manual environment, successive entry cataloging provides welcome relief from re-typing cards and searching through paper bibliographies for cataloging information.

As librarians have moved from a manual to an online environment, they have become more aware of the disadvantages of successive entry cataloging, and wonder if latest entry would be better, at least in some cases. Successive entry means having to work on two records when a title changes, rather than one. Access to the run is fragmented, especially when titles change back to a former title, and when titles are of short duration.[17] The resulting records can be difficult for users to understand. If the library doesn't have all of the titles involved, the continuity of the linking notes could be lost without references from the titles not held. Volumes or microfilm which had been kept together under latest entry cataloging may need to be split apart and relabeled, and supplements and indexes may need linking notes to several titles. Multiple records from successive entry cataloging also have a "ripple effect" resulting in the creation of more check-in and binding records as well as producing more access points in the online catalog, which could be confusing to users.[18]

To avoid the scattering of bibliographic, acquisitions, holdings, and circulation data among two or more records in its online integrated system, Northwestern University resumed using "latest entry whenever a serial title or corporate body main entry changes, the numbering continues, and the title is classified. Cataloger's judgement whether to apply latest entry is invoked when the title history is very complex."[19] Various authors have pointed out that "in an online environment, it becomes increasingly more expensive to create new records when existing ones can be modified fairly easily."[20] Annalisa Van Avery suggests that in retrospective conversion projects, "it makes little difference whether the newly loaded records are successive or latest entry records" as long as the earlier titles are properly formatted to generate added entries.[21] However, many libraries want to recatalog all of their serials to successive entry to follow national standards, as well as for the sake of uniformity in their own databases. Libraries which do not follow national standards have difficulty sharing their bibliographic information with others, and are less likely to receive full benefit from copy available on the utilities if they must modify it to match local practices.

Corporate issuing bodies, whether used as main or added entries, are almost as likely to change as are titles. "It is reported that the average corporate issuing body undergoes a change of name every 15 to 20 years."[22] As with titles, rules prior to AACR required a corporate body to be entered under its latest name, so current catalogers will encounter serials entered under the latest name of a body which had earlier names while it issued the serial. Bringing the record up to AACR2 standards will require noting when the name changed on the issues and making added entries for all the names, or processing a title change if the corporate body was the main entry, even if the title was stable. The same work is necessary on titles already cataloged according to current standards, when a body changes its name or a new body becomes involved. Unfortunately, all the other ongoing serials issued by a body which has changed its name will also need to be examined and updated to provide access to the new name, since users could reasonably expect to find any serial under later issuing body names as well as under earlier names. This kind of authority work normally does not occur for monographs.

Both monographs and serials are affected by changes in the cataloging rules which result in changes in the accepted form of entry for bodies even if they have not changed their identities. The rules since 1967 differ from their predecessors in that more bodies are entered under their names as they appear in their works, more subordinate bodies are entered directly under their own names, and very few bodies are entered under place names. Since in pre-automation days it would have been a monumental task to change all existing headings to conform to the new rules, from 1967 to the implementation of AACR2 in 1981, Library of Congress followed a policy of "superimposition." "This means that the rules for choice of entry will be applied only to works that are new to the Library and that the rules for headings will be applied only to persons and corporate bodies that are being established for the first time."[23] In the desuperimposition which followed AACR2, libraries had to choose whether to change all headings to conform to the new rules, or to accept split files and link old and new forms with cross-references. The choices libraries made in implementing AACR2 impact how those libraries handle their authority work today, especially when recataloging serials with old records. If all headings have not been changed to AACR2 forms, the cataloger or authorities staff must determine how to deal with them within the library's policies.

Another access point to consider for serials is subject. Some authors feel subject headings for serials are not very useful; "either they are too obvious to do much good or they are too vague and (over the years) too inconsistent to be of much help."[24] Others point out that "studies show that the majority of patrons' online catalog use is subject searching. Those patrons who search primarily in the online catalog will not have adequate access to serials if they are not fully cataloged with subject headings."[25] However, if one believes users seeking serials do so because they have a citation to a specific article, then subject headings for serials are less important. At Iowa State University, librarians have noticed that patrons who are unfamiliar with indexes request help in searching for serials by subject, saying they want to page through the issues to find articles of interest (certainly an inefficient technique). What users really seem to want is access by subject at the article level in the online catalog.

If subject headings are used for serials, they will need continued revision as nomenclature changes. Since subject headings for serials tend to be very general, however, it is likely they will require fewer changes than those used for monographs. Serial records available in OCLC often lack subject headings, since many libraries do not use subject headings for serials, subject headings used by member libraries were stripped from OCLC records at one point, and in-process records created by the Library of Congress do not have subject headings. Ruth McBride verified that prior to AACR2, adding or changing subject heading fields required the most modifications to serial OCLC copy.[26]

There is even more divergence of opinion over whether to classify serials than there is over whether to assign them subject headings. A 1989 survey by Jim Segesta and Gary Hyslop found that 59% of the libraries surveyed arranged their bound periodicals alphabetically by title, but the more subscriptions a library had, the more likely it was to classify its bound periodicals.[27] If serials are classified, they may need to be reclassified if their subject emphasis changes, or if changes are made in the classification system used. However, if they are unclassified, and the title changes, they may need to be shifted to the new title, or the run split up under different titles. In the interest of keeping a serial run together, libraries that classify serials want to keep the old call number when the title changes "even though the Cutter number reflects the old main entry."[28] The usually large number of serial volumes to be moved and relabeled in the case of any change causes libraries to try to avoid reclassifying them unless they feel strongly patrons are being ill-served.

Access points are only part of the serials cataloging record; description is the other part, and just as susceptible to changes in the serial as well as in the cataloging rules. Decisions need to be made on what parts of the description are worthwhile to keep up to date, and what changes can be ignored or just noted in general rather than specifically. The cataloger should consider how important the information is and how it will be used, and possible consequences if it is not added or updated. The value and purposes of each field in the description should be evaluated according to the library's needs. The more information provided in the cataloging description, the more must be kept up to date.

Some specific areas of the description to consider are imprint, collation, and frequency, as well as the numerical and/or chronological designation. The value of each of these areas has been questioned by some librarians, but affirmed as important by others. A general "imprint varies" note provides little information if a library uses the imprint for acquisitions purposes. If a library doesn't need this kind of specific imprint information, Arnold Trotier proposed that "the publisher statement may be omitted unless it is necessary to distinguish publications with the same title or to characterize indefinite titles."[29] Collation is of most interest when there is something unusual about the number of volumes, kinds of illustrations, or size, and staff may use the size information to determine appropriate shelving. If a library's online integrated system predicts when to expect the next issue based on the frequency in the bibliographic record, maintenance of the current frequency is essential. However, researching past frequencies can be very time-consuming, and one wonders how worthwhile when once more than three are known, the cataloger may simply note "frequency varies." Numerical and/or chronological designations differentiate issues from each other, enable a library to tell if it has all issues, and help library users request the issue they want,[30] but the area in which the first and last designations are recorded is sometimes mistaken by users for the library's holdings. Some staff or users are also confused when a chronological designation is lacking or differs from the imprint, because they don't understand the difference between the two.

Catalogers diligently make notes about numbering irregularities, such as "Chronological designation dropped with v. 6," but any notes are only helpful if library users or other staff read and understand them. Beatrice Simon thought that "elaborate notes concerning editors and changes in commercial publishers, are, in my opinion, a complete waste of time. The rare person who needs this information finds it by going to the journal itself . . . he will not take *your* note as his authority."[31] Andrew Osborn said that only three kinds of notes are generally used: continued by, merged with, etc.; cumulative indexes; and "bound with" notes, and the other notes "should be omitted in catalog copy for almost any organization."[32] Linking notes are important because they are the means of tracking the title's bibliographic history, but great care is needed to assure that the entry in the note matches the entry of the related title exactly. Correcting the entry on a record for a serial linked to many other titles can create an avalanche of work in correcting all the linking notes to match.

Once a library user finds the record for the serial he seeks, the next thing he will want to know is if the library has the issue he wants. Online integrated systems allow a return to the ideals of the turn of the century, in which libraries tried to record the most current issue received on every record for the item in the catalog. In a manual environment, libraries have tried to save time and money by referring the patron to the main entry card or to a separate serial record file for holdings. Libraries may use the "one-plus" system, simply giving the data relating to the first issue the library has, followed by a plus, a hyphen, or the words "to date," until the publication ceases and the entry is closed. Libraries must decide how or if to indicate issues are missing. Serials which are not ongoing but for which scattered issues are occasionally received are expensive to maintain, since each issue must be added to the holdings.

As these holdings are added, other needed recataloging may be discovered.

Even libraries with online catalogs are unlikely to be able to revise the cataloging as well as the holdings each time a new issue is received. Some changes may not be discovered until in the course of other recataloging, a cataloger consults a record in a bibliographic utility and discovers other discrepancies to be resolved through verification against the library's own issues. Even online records cannot change fast enough to reflect all the changes in a serial, and Mary Grace Fleeman noted that only 3.9-9.1 percent of OCLC serial records were accepted without modification.[33] In dealing with OCLC copy, "often the most difficult problems arise due to changes in cataloging rules or differences in interpretation, rather than actual errors."[34] Because online records are constantly changing, a cataloger may resolve all the discrepancies at one point and then need to deal with new ones the next time the library uses the record. "Chances are good that a printout two weeks old no longer matches the online record."[35]

"The continuing nature of serials, in combination with the span of years over which serials are cataloged, requires serials catalogers 'to learn the new but remember the old.'"[36] Librarians involved in recataloging or retrospective conversion have debated whether it is necessary to completely upgrade records to match the latest cataloging rules. Since most old titles were cataloged from the latest issue, AACR2's change to cataloging from the earliest issues means that it is often necessary to look at those issues in order to create an accurate AACR2 record. While recataloging to AACR2 standards is very expensive, it does have advantages. "It brings cataloging performed within the library itself prior to 1981 into conformity with current cataloging, and brings consistency in the individual library's own catalog. It also means that new records entered into OCLC are useable by other libraries for shared cataloging without extensive editing."[37]

C. Sumner Spalding advised:

> The urge to change the information already in the catalog should be repressed in favor of simply providing necessary additional information. It should be recognized that when a serial changes its title, for instance, the cards in the catalog do not thereby become erroneous. They are still correct as far as they go–they only become incomplete.[38]

SELECTING THE BEST SOLUTION

Once the cataloger has examined all the alternatives, it is time to select the best solution. The cataloger needs to weigh all factors against the library's goals, user needs, efficiency, completeness and correctness, and finally, use judgement to make the decision. Care must be taken that what is done is sufficient for all the library's purposes for the record, which may be not only part of an online catalog, but also may be used for resource sharing, union listing, cooperative collection development, an online circulation system, and automated serials check-in.

If the library's goal is delivery of information, then the goal of cataloging is providing efficient access to that information through the catalog. Mary K. Bolin says keeping cataloging goals in mind will help catalogers make decisions more quickly. "Along with confidence and competence, catalogers need to have internalized the principles underlying any cataloging code: identify the item, house it with like materials, make appropriate and plentiful access points, and exert authority control to integrate the individual record with its fellows."[39]

What do users need where serials are concerned? "In very simple terms, the user wants to (1) find an article on a given topic; (2) find the location of the periodical containing the article; (3) find the issue and find it immediately,"[40] and prefers to find all of this information by consulting only one source.[41] Apparently a simple finding entry would satisfy the needs of many serial users. Michael Gorman points out that all serials do not need to be treated alike. There are high-culture serials and mass-culture serials, and "processing, accessibility needs, life span, and value to an institution of these two classes of publication are very different."[42]

Recataloging can be kept to a minimum by following the policy the New York Public Library applied to books in 1934: recatalog only if "existing records fail to locate the book or enable the reader to decide whether he wants to see it."[43] However, in seeking efficiency catalogers must be careful not to inadvertently transfer "the cost in time and money to another department of the library or to one's clientele . . . Cataloging should be so done that there is a reasonable degree of assurance that it need not be redone in the foreseeable future, with the resulting transfer of cost from the present to the future."[44] With inflation, the cost of cleaning up records is likely to be higher later.

Even if "upward of half the serials published do not warrant more than simplified cataloging in virtually any library,"[45] libraries using bibliographic utilities are tied to research-oriented records. Libraries also have less freedom than in the past to solve cataloging problems creatively because of the need to follow national standards in the bibliographic utilities.

> In the spirit of cooperation, a library may need to put more effort into cataloging serials, including periodical publications, than it would care to for its own purposes. However, presumably, there will be more benefits than disadvantages to the library because of the opportunity to use the cataloging already done at another institution.[46]

Some libraries have put considerable effort and expense into bringing their records up to current national standards, such as doing retrospective conversion to put all their records into the full MARC format, with all possible access points in correct AACR2 form, and separating latest entry records into successive entry records. Catalogers take pride in the quality and accuracy of their records, but this should be "not because a high-quality record shows our great virtuosity as catalogers, but because accurate and complete cataloging information serves the users of the library."[47]

Serials catalogers constantly feel pulled between the desire to create a "perfect" record and the knowledge that someday they or someone else will have to recatalog it due to changes in the serial. Libraries used to wait until the first complete volume of a serial was received before cataloging it, to be more certain that the characteristics of the serial evident in the first issue were stable. However, it really isn't possible to catalog a serial for all time until it ceases, and to wait that long to first catalog a serial would deny access to it when it is likely to be most in demand. Even then, the great number of issues and multitude of changes which occur during the life of a serial would make it impractical to catalog in as much detail as a monograph.

If there were only one correct solution to every cataloging problem, there would be no decision-making. Judgement is needed. When cataloging lacked a statement of principles, there was a proliferation of rules to cover specific situations.[48] Even now, with a cataloging code based on principles,

> . . . it is disheartening to watch cataloging slide from the terseness of the *Paris Principles* to the attempts of AACR2 to generalize and

> standardize through the dense and, at times, indecipherable advice of the *Cataloging Service Bulletin* and the Library of Congress rule interpretations.
>
> But this plunge from the lofty and general to prescriptions for dotting i's and crossing t's is probably inevitable. It is what always happens when the general principles created by people with vision are applied in daily life and routine tasks by more limited people.[49]

We should expect new catalogers to know what the rules are, then help them develop judgement and flexibility in dealing with ambiguous situations not covered by the rules. "Confidence is essential to productivity. To be productive, we must develop confidence in our ability to make judgements, and to make them without agonizing."[50] If it was possible for every cataloging decision to be written down for us to consult, cataloging would be entirely mechanical and repetitive; instead, it is often demanding and intellectual.

IMPLEMENTING THE DECISION

Often recataloging decisions are made by the individual cataloger, using his or her best judgement, so implementing the decision is simply a matter of action by that person. However, this action needs to take into account other factors, such as cataloging policies and procedures, workflow, quantity of work, time, cost, other staff who will be affected, and the role of automation and the bibliographic utilities. On a larger scale, decisions need to consider the staffing available to recatalog serials.

There is a wide range of opinion on what level of staff is needed for serials cataloging, including recataloging, or even whether someone with a special knowledge of serials is needed. In general, cataloging "modifications which require use of the LC classification schedules and subject headings lists, or interpretation of the *Anglo-American Cataloging Rules*, are considered to be professional, while mechanical modifications can usually be handled by the nonprofessional."[51] At the State University of New York at Buffalo, teams consisting of a professional cataloger and a clerk are "responsible for cataloging or recataloging all periodicals and serials for those library locations assigned to them."[52] With successive entry cataloging, Duke's copy catalogers "close out the old entry on the appropriate catalog cards and add linking notes to the printouts. They also handle material that needs recataloging and materials that are transferred. A professional cataloger reviews the work of each copy cataloger."[53]

The time and cost of recataloging serials varies according to the standards the catalogers follow, as well as the level of staff employed and the difficulty of individual titles. The four-year time and cost study at Iowa State University found that the average cost of recataloging a serial was $16.53, and that it required 1.19 hours.[54] Two professionals and 4.25 paraprofessionals recatalog an average of 252 serials a month, out of a serials collection of 48,000 titles. Retrospective conversion projects usually follow different standards than recataloging, due to time limits. "Cataloging time averaged 30-40 minutes per title during the CRL project. This figure includes time devoted to error reporting, checking reference sources, and recataloging."[55]

Workflow and cataloging procedures also play a role in implementing recataloging decisions. The cataloger will need to consider what records will need to be changed due to the recataloging. Cards may need to be pulled, data added or new cards produced, and then refiled. If records in a machine-readable database need to be changed, the cataloger may do the work directly online, or obtain a printout and edit it for input by other staff. When major editing is required, as was the experience during the Center for Research Libraries' serials retrospective conversion,

> . . . it is actually more efficient to print out the records and edit offline . . . Conflicts between data on the local bibliographic record and the matching OCLC record were so frequent that a substantial amount of time was spent verifying information in reference sources. It is obviously an inefficient use of terminal time to have the operator jumping up to consult a reference book.[56]

To establish consistency among the catalogers as to the degree of editing and the proper priorities for how to spend their time, it is useful to compile decisions regarding individual MARC fields,[57] or list elements in the bibliographic record that the cataloger is expected to examine and correct, the extent of searching permitted to verify data, and the amount of modification required to conform to AACR2.[58]

Annalisa Van Avery points out that bibliographic editing is only half of what is accomplished during recataloging; the other half involves periodicals management processes within the library: checking holdings, correcting binding and kardex records, updating the periodicals printout or a union list, and straightening out shelving of the item in the stacks or periodicals area.[59] In a library with an integrated automated system, all other records (check-in, binding, payments, circulation) may be tied to the bibliographic record. Staff in other areas need to be kept informed of changes to records which affect them. Even though serials catalogers "use many of the same tools as the rest of the catalogers, they are most tied in with the record keeping of the serials department."[60] They may help the serials acquisitions staff determine when a title has changed and what the new title is, as well as aid the binding staff with interpreting numbering variations.

In libraries in transition to fully automated systems, synchronization of manual and machine-readable files is a critical concern. An online integrated system is not efficient until all manual files are gone; otherwise there is duplication of effort. While updating records is easier in an online system than in a card catalog, minor spelling or punctuation errors can make a record inaccessible. Online systems require some different decisions than manual systems due to the inflexibility of automated filing and indexing. However, online catalogs free catalogers from decisions based on the cost of maintaining manual systems, allowing an increase in access points and the ability to provide the complete holdings on every record. There is hope that more sophisticated online catalogs will offer improvements such as searching by natural language, network access to area union lists, automatic links between indexing and location tools, access to journal contents, and remote user access and document delivery.[61]

Unfortunately, "the trend toward having individual systems within each library actually works against the updating of serial records on the utilities."[62] It is faster to change records directly in a local system than to edit a record in another system and transfer it, or to wait for it to be batch-loaded on tape. At least RLIN libraries can see and edit their own records, but modifications OCLC libraries have made to a record are visible only in their local systems, and must be done over again if recataloging is done on OCLC. Unless an OCLC library is also a CONSER participant, or the OCLC record is less than a full-level record, the changes a library makes to an OCLC record are not visible to the other OCLC libraries, who must cease the same title over and over until a CONSER library does it. Few OCLC libraries have time to send error reports with supporting documentation to OCLC for all the recataloging they find necessary.

PROVIDING OR OBTAINING FEEDBACK

Sending error reports to OCLC is one way of providing feedback to other libraries in the same network. Catalogers are also involved in providing feedback to co-workers, to makers of the rules, and sometimes even to publishers who seem to be the creators of some cataloging problems. Once a recataloging decision has been made and implemented, the effects of the decision can be observed and evaluated. Unfortunately, catalogers seldom receive feedback about what good their work has done, but they are likely to be told if a title is difficult to find, a note is unclear, or an error is made. User studies have attempted to find out how the public uses serials cataloging records, to help catalogers make better decisions about things that matter.

Quality control occurs at a local level when staff check the cataloging of others, either after a printout has been edited, after the online record is modified, or after cards have been received. Each library must make its own determination of how much quality control is enough. If quality control at a local level does not catch all errors, there are error reporting mechanisms for users of the national bibliographic utilities, and the shame of having other users find an error in one's record is incentive to keep quality high. Annalisa Van Avery proposed that another kind of feedback, in the form of reports or tapes of revised records, be available to libraries which wish to know about revisions occurring to records which they have used on a utility.[63]

Catalogers have also provided feedback on the cataloging rules themselves through committees in their national organizations and by writing to their national libraries, which influence how the rules are applied. As a result, we now have a cataloging code based on principles, with choice of entry the same for all kinds of materials, serials cataloged from the first issue, definitions of what constitutes a title change, and corporate bodies more likely to be entered under their own names. The Library of Congress responded to libraries' pleas to do something about the proliferation of serials main entries under nondistinctive titles by developing the uniform title for serials. The rules are constantly being re-evaluated and interpreted, as evidenced by the *Cataloging Service Bulletin*.

Librarians can also complain, as Huibert Paul did, about "the great waste in processing time caused by the present anarchy in serials."[64] Michael Gorman advocates that "the many inconsistencies and inefficiencies of modern serial publications need not be accepted in a passive way by librarians and libraries."[65] They can provide feedback to publishers. Librarians have been vocal about many serials problems, especially serials pricing; they have begun to meet with publishers in a positive way at meetings of the North American Serials Interest Group; and they vent some of their frustration with humor through the annual Worst Serial Title Change of the Year awards.

Of all the kinds of feedback, catalogers are probably most interested in feedback from users. In cataloging, we make certain assumptions about what users want. We like to believe that users will carefully ponder all the wonderful notes we make, but do they? How often do users even find what they want?

In studies of serials users, retrieval rates in unmediated searches have ranged from 43% to 84%, with lack of success attributed mainly to either collection failure, catalog failure, or user failure.[66] Of 445 patron searches studied by Gary Golden, Susan Golden, and Rebecca Lenzini, "49 percent of the failed searches were because of user failures. The primary type of patron failure was caused by the patron failing to locate a citation that had in fact an exact match in the serial catalog."[67] Users coming to the catalog with incomplete entries accounted for 9 percent of the searching failures.[68] Marjorie Murfin gave 155 citations to students, and only 55% were retrieved. "Of those not retrieved, 15 percent were not retrieved due to user error and 30 percent were not retrieved due to library problems." Making the serials directory easier to use and understand would have eliminated 43 percent of the user errors, Murfin estimated.[69]

What did patrons look for, and why was a search successful? Golden, Golden and Lenzini found that most of the publications sought were English language journals and magazines, with only 6 percent in other languages. They discovered that "most of the patrons who were successful used a title entry." Twenty searches would have been successful on the first try if there had been a title entry, instead of forcing the patron to look under a corporate body. However, only 3 percent of the users in the sample encountered a cross-reference. Sixty-three of the searchers came to the catalog with only an abbreviated form of entry, but were still successful.[70]

The results of these studies indicate that serials catalogers should be putting their time into making the catalog easy to use and understand, cataloging English language periodicals and journals, and providing access to titles and abbreviated titles. These studies investigated the usage of manual catalogs, and it is uncertain whether patrons now searching serials in an online environment achieve greater levels of satisfaction. The online catalog is one of several developments beginning to affect serials recataloging decisions, and there are more changes in progress or on the horizon.

BECOMING AWARE OF NEW PROBLEMS

"Since change and serials are practically synonymous words, serialists live on the cutting edge of the action."[71] Among the changes which may affect the recataloging of serials are electronic publishing, serials on CD-ROM, and providing access to articles through a library's local online catalog. Not so many years ago, serials were the only odd format in the library, and they were segregated and uncataloged, as are some of the new formats now. Ruth Carter predicts,

> Serials publications will continue to exist in the foreseeable future, and they will appear in more varied physical forms and formats than ever before . . . New technologies will augment, not replace, existing ones. Therefore, we are likely to have to cope with more forms of serial publications, not less.[72]

CD-ROMs have quickly gained ground in libraries because of their versatility, high data storage density, and user-friendliness, but they complement rather than supplant paper and microforms.[73] Recataloging is involved in linking existing paper and microformats to their CD-ROM counterparts, and vice versa. However, the main challenge of cataloging CD-ROMs is that, like the serials many of them are, they are constantly changing. "It requires an ongoing effort to keep abreast of the product's technical characteristics and specifications. The technology is developing so rapidly that some producers provide a new version of software with each quarterly cumulative disk."[74] In a large library system, different libraries may have different CD-ROM versions, cumulations, and equipment. The cataloging rules require a separate bibliographic record for each version, and these must be kept up to date as holdings and disk format specifications change. The cataloging rules and bibliographic input standards for computer files are also evolving. Libraries may also debate whether to catalog disks which are leased but not owned, and must be returned; and databases available only by remote access.

Serial CD-ROMs provide a preview of the effects of electronic publishing. Online journals may have frequently revised articles, and this may cause confusion if not controlled.[75] The basic unit of publication may become the article rather than the journal.

This would be a radical change from the present method of cataloging serials at the journal level. Serials have multidimensional relationships which are difficult to express adequately on one record without recataloging as the relationships change. Michael Gorman and Robert Burger point out that linkage of serials presents problems of chronology (successive title changes) and of hierarchy (subseries, parts, articles).[76] They propose a developed machine system which would allow one to catalog an item at the lowest level (such as an article), and then link these simple records to all related records. This would make it possible to integrate library catalogs with indexing systems.[77]

Such a system is likely to reduce recataloging as we know it, but massively increase new cataloging. Instead of a cataloger creating a record for a journal and adding general notes to deal with changes in the issues, each issue or article would be specifically described, like a monograph. "The net effect of adding journal article citations to an online catalog would be to intensify the use of information already *in* the library,"[78] getting more benefit from expensive serials.

While article-level access would be a great boon to users, most libraries don't have the staffing to catalog at that level, and that is why they purchase indexes and abstracts from commercial publishers. These tools also furnish access to articles in serials not owned by the library, but there are times when users would want to limit their searches only to articles in the library and immediately available. Some commercial indexes are now available in machine-readable form and can be loaded into online catalogs, as is planned with NOTIS's Multiple Database Access System. In NOTIS, the indexes will be accessible as separate databases in the online catalog, because the headings used in various commercial indexes do not match each other or the standard Library of Congress-established headings used in library catalogs. If the databases were not separate, catalogers would be faced with a massive authority clean-up of headings to match their local catalog's terminology.

Several ideas have been put forth on how to catalog serials more specifically without overwhelming catalogers. David Cohen proposed putting "standardized, bibliographic data for journal articles into a national database, perhaps tied to one of the existing bibliographic utilities, and to allow local libraries to include these records in their online catalogs."[79] Sheila Intner alternatively proposed the Theory of Physical Equivalence as a compromise to a separate record for each work. "If the physical unit of a title is larger than the average printed monograph, break it down into book-like units for cataloging purposes."[80] The result would be to separately catalog each issue of a serial, perhaps with contents notes to allow access to the individual articles. Any recataloging needed would then be similar to recataloging needed for monographs, usually due to subject heading changes, reclassification, or changes in the cataloging rules.

CONCLUSION

Unless the methods of cataloging serials change drastically in the future, so that cataloging at the piece or article level becomes common, the need to recatalog serials as they change will continue to call for decisions from catalogers. This article outlined a decision-making model borrowed from business, which could be applied to making cataloging decisions. Catalogers need to become aware that a problem exists, define what the problem is, analyze the alternatives for handling it, select the best solution based on the library's goals and resources, implement it, and obtain feedback, and then the cycle begins again with new problems. These decision-making skills are needed in a world where rules cannot be written to cover every situation, because the situations are constantly changing. "We hold to the notion of change as happening once and for all, after which we can breathe a sigh of relief that normalcy has returned. But . . . there is no foreseeable tomorrow when we will have mastered once and for all the appropriate skills for our jobs."[81] All we have to see us through is our good judgement; the choices are ours.

NOTES

1. Paul E. Moody, *Decision Making: Proven Methods for Better Decisions* (New York: McGraw-Hill, 1983), p. 1.

2. Kathryn Luther Henderson, "Serial Cataloging Revisited–A Long Search For a Little Theory And a Lot of Cooperation, in: Walter C. Allen, ed., *Serial Publications in Large Libraries* (Urbana, Ill.: University of Illinois, Graduate School of Library Science, 1970), p. 56.

3. Huibert Paul, "Serials: Chaos and Standardization," *Library Resources & Technical Services* 14, no. 1 (Winter 1970):19.

4. Lori L. Osmus and Dilys E. Morris, "Serials Cataloging Time and Costs: Results of an Ongoing Study at Iowa State University," *The Serials Librarian*, in this issue.

5. Gary Charbonneau, "Taylor's Constant," *The Serials Librarian* 7, no. 1 (Fall 1982):20.

6. Joan Patricia Warren and Walter M. Barnard, "Cataloging Statistics: Report on an Experiment," *Library Resources & Technical Services* 1, no. 2 (Spring 1957):77.

7. Bella E. Shachtman, "Cataloging Statistics and Standards," *Journal of Cataloging and Classification* 12, no. 3 (July 1956):161.

8. *Library Literature*, 1988 (New York: H.W. Wilson, 1989), p. 111.

9. Karla D. Petersen, "Planning for Serials Retrospective Conversion," *Serials Review* 10, no. 3 (Fall 1984):73.

10. Patrick F. Callahan, "Retrospective Conversion of Serials Using OCLC," in: Diane Stine, ed., *Projects and Procedures for Serials Administration* (Ann Arbor, Mich.: Pierian Press, 1985), p. 115.

11. Annalisa R. Van Avery, "Recat vs. Recon of Serials: A Problem for Shared Cataloging," *Cataloging & Classification Quarterly* 10, no. 4 (1990):59.

12. Henderson, "Serial Cataloging Revisited," p. 78.

13. Ellen Siegel Kovacic, "Serials Cataloging: What It Is, How It's Done, Why It's Done That Way," *Serials Review* 11, no. 1 (Spring 1985):78.

14. Dorothy J. Glasby, "Historical Background and Review of Serials Cataloging Rules, *Library Resources & Technical Services* 34, no. 1 (January 1990):85.

15. Jim E. Cole, "The First Shall Be the Last: Earliest Entry Cataloging," *The Serials Librarian* 12, no. 1/2 (1987):88.

16. Beth Reuland, "Successive Entry: Another Look," *Serials Review* 9, no. 3 (Fall 1983):92.

17. Ibid., p. 93.

18. Ibid.

19. Mary M. Case, et al., "Rules for Latest Entry Cataloging: Northwestern University Supplement to AACR2," *Cataloging & Classification Quarterly* 9, no. 2 (1988):42.

20. Melissa M. Bernhardt, "Dealing with Serial Title Changes: Some Theoretical and Practical Considerations," *Cataloging & Classification Quarterly* 9, no. 2 (1988):27.

21. Van Avery, "Recat vs. Recon of Serials," p. 62.

22. Cresap, McCormick and Paget, *Survey of Preparation Procedures, Reference Department, New York Public Library*, ([New York, 1951]), chapter 6, p. 11, cited in: Andrew D. Osborn, *Serial Publications: Their Place and Treatment in Libraries*, 3rd ed. (Chicago: American Library Association, 1980), p. 265.

23. *Cataloging Service* 79 (January 1967):1.

24. Osborn, *Serial Publications*, p. 248.

25. Van Avery, "Recat vs. Recon of Serials," p. 60.

26. Ruth B. McBride, "Copy Cataloguing of Serials According to AACR2 Using OCLC: the University of Illinois Experience," in: Peter Gellatly, ed., *The Management of Serials Automation* (New York: The Haworth Press, Inc., 1982), p. 144.

27. Jim Segesta and Gary Hyslop, "The Arrangement of Periodicals in American Academic Libraries," *Serials Review* 17, no. 1 (Spring 1991):23.

28. Alexander Bloss, "Coping with the Evolving Serial Record," *Serials Review* 8, no. 4 (Winter 1982):92.

29. Arnold H. Trotier, "Some Persistent Problems of Serials in Technical Processes," *Serial Slants* 1, no. 3 (January 1951):9-10.

30. Paul, "Serials: Chaos and Standardization," p. 23.

31. Beatrice V. Simon, "Cataloguing of Periodicals," *Ontario Library Review* 33 (1949):242.

32. Osborn, *Serial Publications*, p. 220.

33. Mary Grace Fleeman, "The Availability and Acceptability of Serial Records in the OCLC Data Base," in: Peter Gellatly, ed., *The Management of Serials Automation* (New York: The Haworth Press, Inc., 1982), p. 158.

34. Callahan, "Retrospective Conversion of Serials Using OCLC," p. 134.

35. Lynn Mealer Cummins, "Serials Cataloging in Transition," *The Serials Librarian* 10, no. 1/2 (Fall 1985-Winter 1985-86):130.

36. Carole R. McIver, "The AACRs and Serials Cataloging," *The Serials Librarian* 10, no. 1/2 (Fall 1985-Winter 1985-86):117.
37. Petersen, "Planning for Serials Retrospective Conversion," p. 75.
38. C. Sumner Spalding, "Keeping Serials Cataloging Costs in Check," *Library Resources & Technical Services* 1, no. 1 (Winter 1957):18.
39. Mary K. Bolin, "Make a Quick Decision in (Almost) All Cases: Our Perennial Crisis in Cataloging," *The Journal of Academic Librarianship* 16, no. 6 (January 1991):360.
40. Wilma Reid Cipolla, "Finding a Way Out of the Serial Maze," *Library Resources & Technical Services* 32, no. 2 (April 1988):151.
41. Ibid., p. 154.
42. Michael Gorman, "Dealing with Serials: A Sketch of Contextual/Organizational Response," *The Serials Librarian* 10, no. 1/2 (Fall 1985/Winter 1985-86):16-17.
43. Elizabeth H. Thompson, "Recent Cataloging Activities in American Libraries, 1934-39," *Catalogers' and Classifiers' Yearbook* 8 (1939):111.
44. Emily C. Schilpp, "Short-cuts in Serials Cataloging?" *Serial Slants* 1, no. 4 (April 1951):3.
45. Osborn, *Serial Publications*, pp. 222-223.
46. Ruth C. Carter, "Serials Management–Some Dilemmas and Prospects," *Canadian Library Journal* 43, no. 5 (October 1986):289.
47. Bolin, "Make a Quick Decision in (Almost) All Cases," p. 358.
48. Henderson, "Serial Cataloging Revisited," p. 62.
49. Bolin, "Make a Quick Decision in (Almost) All Cases," p. 360.
50. Ibid.
51. Fleeman, "The Availability and Acceptability of Serial Records in the OCLC Data Base," p. 159.
52. Ruth B. McBride, ed. "Copy Cataloging of Serials: Proceedings of the ALA/RTSD/CCS Copy Cataloging Discussion Group Meeting, July 10, 1982 in Philadelphia," *The Serials Librarian* 8, no. 2 (Winter 1983):28.
53. Ibid., p. 39.
54. Osmus and Morris, "Serials Cataloging Time and Costs," in this issue.
55. Callahan, "Retrospective Conversion of Serials Using OCLC," p. 117.
56. Ibid., p. 133.
57. Ibid., p. 140.
58. McBride, "Copy Cataloging of Serials," p. 31.
59. Van Avery, "Recat vs. Recon of Serials," p. 64.
60. Kovacic, "Serials Cataloging," p. 82.
61. Cipolla, "Finding a Way Out of the Serial Maze," pp. 152-154.
62. Van Avery, "Recat vs. Recon of Serials," p. 64.
63. Ibid., pp. 65-66.
64. Paul, "Serials: Chaos and Standardization," p. 20.
65. Gorman, "Dealing with Serials," p. 17.
66. Cipolla, "Finding a Way Out of the Serial Maze," p. 152.
67. Gary Golden, Susan U. Golden, and Rebecca T. Lenzini, "Patron Ap-

proaches to Serials: A User Study," *College & Research Libraries* 43, no. 1 (January 1982):27.

68. Ibid., p. 27.

69. Marjorie E. Murfin, "The Myth of Accessibility: Frustration & Failure in Retrieving Periodicals," *The Journal of Academic Librarianship* 6, no. 1 (March 1980):17-18.

70. Golden, Golden, and Lenzini, "Patron Approaches to Serials," pp. 24-25.

71. Mary Ellen Soper, "Cataloguing in a Time of Change," in: Peter Gellatly, ed., *The Management of Serials Automation* (New York: The Haworth Press, Inc., 1982), p. 117.

72. Carter, "Serials Management–Some Dilemmas and Prospects," pp. 289-290.

73. Anna M. Wang, "The Challenge of Cataloging Computer Files," *The Serials Librarian* 15, no. 3/4 (1988):105.

74. Anna Wang, "Cataloging CD-ROMs at The Ohio State University," *Serials Review* 14, no. 3 (1988):11.

75. James R. Dwyer, "Evolving Serials, Evolving Access: Bibliographic Control of Serial Literature," *Serials Review* 12, no. 2-3 (Summer-Fall 1986):61.

76. Michael Gorman and Robert H. Burger, "Serial Control in a Developed Machine System," *The Serials Librarian* 5, no. 1 (Fall 1980):17-21.

77. Ibid., p. 25.

78. David Cohen, "A National Networked Solution to Improving Access to Journal Articles," *The Journal of Academic Librarianship* 15, no. 2 (May 1989):79.

79. Ibid., p. 81.

80. Sheila S. Intner, "A New Paradigm for Access to Serials," *The Serials Librarian* 19, no. 3/4 (1991):156.

81. Joan Rapp, "Personnel Selection for Cataloging," *Library Resources & Technical Services* 34, no. 1 (January 1990):81-96.

The Work of the CONSER Subject and Classification Task Force

John J. Riemer

SUMMARY. After a consideration of the value of the subject analysis fields in serial bibliographic records, this article reports on the work of a recent CONSER task force on serial subject analysis. It presents findings of a detailed survey of the current subject analysis practices of all the Full Participants in the program, the policy issues the Task Force identified, and the recommendations it formulated. The group also anticipated what the resultant supporting documentation would look like in the *CONSER Editing Guide*.

INTRODUCTION

Inclusion of subject analysis fields in cataloging records for serials adds considerable value to them.

Current thinking views key word indexing as at best an adjunct to controlled vocabulary, not an alternative to it.[1-2] Subject headings should be added to serial records, if for no other reason than augmented "level one" descriptions[3-4] do not contain very much text on which to base natural language retrieval.

Bross builds the case for a shelf arrangement of serial publications based on classification.[5] Setting aside the particular shelving arrangements institutions may have committed themselves to in the past

---

John J. Riemer is Head of Serials Cataloging at the University of Georgia Libraries, Athens, GA 30602, and serves as its representative to the CONSER Operations Committee.

Address all correspondence to John J. Riemer, 1554 Pine Creek Way, N.E., Lawrenceville, GA 30243-2750.

and the degree of freedom they have to change them now, one can observe benefits for *all*, in the form of browsable classification indexes in online catalogs. This assumes a view of classification as an indexing language versus a mere location device. In such a catalog, users may learn of the existence of related materials whether or not they are designated oversize, currently on reserve, part of a reference collection, out for circulation, or otherwise absent from the shelf where logically expected.

Subject analysis extends beyond subject headings and classification to such things as Geographic Area Codes and coding of the nature of the entire work and/or its contents.[6] Certainly there is a burden of effort involved in adding these to bibliographic records in an age of cataloging simplification. This can be offset by the realization that online systems will only return this investment in added search capabilities if we have taken the time to tag and delimit the data at the outset.

Moreover, for all these subject analysis fields, the idea of onetime labor at the indexing stage obviating repetitive expenditures at the retrieval stage evinces an attractive efficiency.

The need for policy guidelines in the CONSER program in an area where there were none lay behind the creation of a task force.

BACKGROUND

The Subject Analysis and Classification Task Force was formed in the fall of 1988, and the membership and text of the initial charge appears in Appendix A. Communicating primarily by mail, the group interpreted subject analysis broadly and expanded its charge by brainstorming a list of the policy issues in subject analysis that needed to be addressed in the *CONSER Editing Guide*. This served as the agenda for the remainder of the Task Force's work.

To provide information for the deliberations of the Task Force, the group designed a questionnaire on the current subject analysis practices of Full Participants in CONSER. The survey was conducted in spring 1989 and returned with a 100% response rate. The results can be found in Appendix B.

Those results and the subsequent work of the Task Force, culminating in a special meeting at the April 1990 Operations Committee meeting, generated the recommendations outlined below.

RECOMMENDATIONS

1. A 3-level LC-class number assignment system in CONSER records:

   a. 050 for LC's use, as it is currently employed.
   b. 050, second indicator 4 for national-level class number assignment by other Full CONSER participants using that scheme. We recommend repeatable use of this field not only when the LC number is a non-classification number such as an MLC number or "IN PROCESS," but also when an alternative class number is needed, say, for a bibliography, or when the existing 050 is no longer based on the most current class schedules. If LC later inputs a call number on a record whose class portion is identical, the 050, second indicator 4 should be deleted or overwritten.
   c. 090 for use by all other OCLC members.

2. Adoption of 060, second indicator 4, in a similar vein, for those CONSER participants who might wish to apply NLM classification to serials in the same manner as for monographs (versus the customary W1 main entry arrangement).

3. Machine profiling of the CONSER database. Stemming from the questionnaire results, the group identified a number of further questions which it felt made sense to "ask" in programming a *machine profile* of the CONSER database subject analysis fields. The following general questions are designed to determine the extent of that subject analysis:

   a. What percentage of authenticated records contain LC-type classification?
   b. What percentage of authenticated records have a DDC number assigned?
   c. What percentage of authenticated records have either type of number assigned?
   d. What percentage of records contain at least one LCSH string?
   e. What percentage of records contain at least one MeSH string?
   f. What percentage of records contain at least one Canadian subject heading?
   g. What percentage of records contain a subject heading of any of these types?
   h. What percentage of records with geographic content in an LCSH string also contain a Geographic Area Code?

i. As a broad and general measure of the extent of subject analysis in the CONSER database, how many authenticated records have *either* a class number or a subject heading of the types cited above? (Not all CONSER members classify serials; serials classed in LC's A subclass generally do not receive subject headings; a number of serial records observed in other subclasses are not accompanied by any LCSH.)

j. Assuming the only subject field possible for newspaper records is the 752 field for hierarchical place name access, what percentage of authenticated newspaper records include this field?

For all of these questions, it is anticipated that both an arithmetic count will be made as well as a calculation of the percentage for the entire CONSER database. The group feels that performing the same inquiries on the rest of the serial records in the OCLC database (non-CONSER) may provide a useful comparison.

The following reiteration of the same questions is designed to provide a programmer with the specifications necessary to carry out the measures:

If the serial record contains an 042 field,

a. Does the record contain an 090 field
   OR
   an 070 field
   OR
   an 050 field (but not containing the strings IN PROCESS, LAW, Newspaper, PAR, REV PAR, UNC, NOT IN LC, Microfilm, Microfiche, DISCARD, CURRENT ISSUES ONLY, or a string beginning with the character W, e.g., WMLC)?
b. Does the record contain an 082 or an 092 field?
c. Does the record meet the criteria in either a or b above?
d. Does the record contain any 600-651 field with a second indicator of zero?
e. Does the record contain any 600-651 field with a second indicator of two?
f. Does the record contain any 600-651 field with a second indicator of five?
g. Does the record meet any of the conditions in d, e, or f?
h. In a record meeting the conditions of d, if there is any 651 field or if there is any subfield ≠z in 600-650, is an 043 field present in the record?
i. Does the record meet the criteria in either c or g above?

j. If the record contains value "n" in 008/21, does the record contain any 752 fields?

(A)-j could then be repeated on all records *without* an 042 field.)

To get at the *content* of CONSER records, the group recommends taking the records identified in 3c above and measuring the "collection strengths" of the CONSER database. The breakdown used could be the same 51 categories listed in the application form for full CONSER membership. So that each record in 3c is counted only once (some will contain multiple class numbers and schemes), the following "table of precedence" could be used:

050
090
070
082
092

If multiple occurrences of the same tag exist in a particular record, the first one could arbitrarily be used in the tally.

The group has not identified a person or institution to perform the programming.

4. Not to reflect the authoritativeness of subject analysis data in CONSER records either at record level or the field level. The problem with doing so at the *record* level is that, as the questionnaire confirms, there is sufficient variation in the use/nonuse Participants make of the schemes and subject heading systems to make something like "042 lcs" meaningless. The problem in attempting a *field* level reflection of the data's authoritativeness lies in the unduly complicated and unworkable nature of a 3-tiered MARC tagging for *each* subject heading system. (Even if all existing CONSER records' subject headings were updated, via second indicators or subfield ≠w's, to designate their origin, there will be nothing to signal out-of-date terminology, to say nothing of the prospect of updating the three sets of headings.)

Right now, the unclear assortment of partially redundant subject headings makes it difficult to direct serial records to copy catalogers. In the environment of cataloging simplification, it represents a better expenditure of effort to have everyone work with the same set of headings for a given vocabulary.

A third alternative for assessing the state of subject analysis in the CONSER database would be periodic running of the machine profile outlined above, if it is desired. (Cf. Objective 1.1 of the Summary CONSER Plan, distributed to the November 1989 Policy Committee meeting.)

5. Changes in Section B of the *CEG* to document subject analysis policies as outlined below. (B1.3 already states that subject analysis is done according to "standardized schemes" and "standardized lists," and B3.2.1 already refers to unauthenticated records being "brought into conformance with the principles outlined in B1.")

B4.1 <new final paragraph> **Obvious errors in 050 fields should not simply be corrected but instead should be reported to Section I-III of the Serial Record Division.**

Under B4.2 Changes in the Publication
B4.2.2 Changes affecting access points

add:

6) Subject fields (600-651, 043, 008/24-27) [O]

Expand or modify subject headings, geographic area codes, and fixed field contents codes to reflect obvious changes in the scope of a publication that has not changed title to indicate this.

Change the caption of B4.3 to:
B4.3 Changes in Cataloging Codes or RIs *or Subject Analysis* or CONSER practice.
and add:
B4.3.5. Revising subject analysis fields to reflect current practice.

Participants may make changes to subject analysis fields that clearly do not correlate with the subject matter of the publication. Data should be removed from records only when clearly incorrect, not just when a matter of judgment on predominant subject emphasis. When there is doubt, fields should not be changed.

B4.3.5.1. Subject headings. The Participant adds, changes, or deletes subject headings to reflect vocabulary changes in standard subject heading lists as well as heading and subdivision assignment practices in such source documents as *Subject Cataloging Manual: Subject Headings*, etc. Redundant, largely duplicative fields should be removed from a record.

B4.3.5.2. Classification. The Participant adds, changes, or deletes classification fields to reflect additions and changes to standard classification schemes. A clear exception to this is call number assignment by a national library; in this case, an updated class number

may be added to the record in a separate field according to the guidelines in Section E.

Change the caption of C4 from ''Name Authority Records'' to **''Authority Records,''**

and add:

C4.8. Optionally, CONSER Participants submit new subject headings and revisions to subject headings for LCSH per the invitation published in *Cataloging Service Bulletin* 41 (summer 1988).

Establishing Subject Headings for the Library of Congress

The Library of Congress realized long ago that it was unable to catalog all items and to establish all headings needed by libraries in the United States. As a result, the NACO operations and more recently the National Coordinated Cataloging Program were initiated. Now that Library of Congress subject headings can be input and updated online and tape distribution of subject authorities with updates has begun, the Library is experimenting with cooperative projects to establish subject headings similar to the projects to establish name headings.

The National Library of Australia, Harvard University Library, and several individuals on the ALA ALCTS CCS Subject Analysis Committee have recently submitted proposals to establish new headings for LCSH on an experimental basis. The success of these experiments has demonstrated that it is feasible for other persons to create subject headings for inclusion in LCSH.

Persons wishing to submit headings for LCSH should write to Mary K.D. Pietris, Chief, Office for Subject Cataloging Policy, Library of Congress, Washington, D.C. 20540, for an instruction sheet and blank subject authority worksheets. Participants are expected to follow all instructions and procedures in the *Subject Cataloging Manual: Subject Headings* and to propose headings that will fit into the LC structure.

Since the Library is staffed to establish headings needed only in its own cataloging, it welcomes the cooperative efforts of others in order to build a subject authority file that will be useful to other libraries receiving materials not acquired by LC or cataloging items at a depth not practiced by the Library of Congress. In particular the Library of Congress invites the participation of those persons who recently signed petitions recommending needed subject headings for new topics.

6. Updating of the *CEG* appendices relating to subject analysis:

a. Replacement of an Appendix I that has been superseded by DCM Z11 with a new one entitled **''Participant Responsibilities for**

Applying Subject Indexing Languages." (The Summary CONSER Plan (November 1989), in Task 1.1.1, includes in its charge to our Task Force, "... confirm or identify thesauri or classification systems falling within the purview of CONSER; identify who has responsibility for quality control in application of thesauri or schedules...") A compilation of which institution uses each class scheme/heading list could be drawn from the questionnaire results.

b. The caption to Appendix J can be altered to reflect that its scope is limited to LCSH.

7. Not to employ the 653 field in CONSER. While there is some interest in strictly local use of uncontrolled index terms, no one on the Task Force wanted to see them enshrined in the national record. During first time authentication of an existing record, any 653 fields present would be removed. If this recommendation is adopted, a future update to the *CEG* would need to include a page stating CONSER nonusage of 653.

8. A change in the programming for the new OCLC system which would permit non-CONSER institutions to add call numbers or subject headings to authenticated records lacking such. We recommend this change, feeling that "a (responsible) something is better than nothing." In other words, a CONSER record lacking full subject analysis should not go wanting until a CONSER institution happens to perform maintenance on it. We envision OCLC member institutions being able to add call numbers and subject headings based on the class schemes and the subject heading authorities they have been "profiled" for.

9. Not to alter the CONSER statistical record keeping practices in any special way for subject analysis-related modifications to serial records. While constituting a major enhancement to a record, the addition of subject analysis fields considered in isolation cannot be readily recognized or tallied, given the recommendations in 4 above. Whether they are considered anything more than maintenance will depend on what other editing occurs on the record.

10. To underscore the importance of including in serial records other title information which provides a good indication of the publication's subject scope. Such information is quite valuable in online catalogs capable of providing keyword access to it. The group welcomes the recently revised RI 12.1E1 to permit giving other title information whenever the cataloger determines it useful. So long as the data *can* be included in the bibliographic record, the task force does not have a strong preference *where*–in 245 subfield ≠ b or in a 500 note.

11. Clarification of the necessity for separate 6XX fields with second

indicator 3 in serial records if they in fact contain LCSH. Upon consultation with the National Agricultural Library the Task Force learned there is no problem with Participants simply changing the second indicator to zero instead of inputting virtually duplicate fields. The group believes at one point in the past there had been a batch job proposed to OCLC to accomlish this.

12. Reduction in the number of authentication requests merely involving a Participant's desire to see subject analysis fields added to the record for a Canadian title but which had to be sent to the National Library of Canada. (Recent documentation on Canadian/NLC records, in section C12, will do a great deal to expedite work in this area and alleviate the concern. It specifies that CONSER Participants can add, delete, or change LCSH on NLC-authenticated records followed by notification without surrogates to NLC; revision of geographic area codes or subject contents codes in the fixed field does not require any notification.)

13. The Task Force noted the lack of generally available access to LC's shelflist data. Such data would aid the verification of LC class number selection, give concrete examples of new classification numbers listed in *Additions and Changes*, and illustrate correlations between class numbers and LCSH vocabulary. Collection development, acquisitions, and public services staff could also benefit. The most current publicly available product providing such access is over 10 years old. If an up-to-date microfiche tool is not the answer, the group hopes that CD-ROM or online access to the LC MARC database with shelflist indexing becomes available soon.

CONCLUSION

The CONSER Policy Committee, at its November 1990 meeting, approved the large majority of the Task Force's recommendations. As of this writing, discussion continues on items 7, 8, and 10. The final disposition of these recommendations will be reflected in future updates to the *CONSER Editing Guide*.

NOTES

1. Hildreth, Charles R. "To Boolean or Not To Boolean," *Information Technology and Libraries* 2, no. 3 (Sept. 1983):235-237.

2. Fugmann, Robert. "The Complementarity of Natural and Indexing Languages." In *Theory of Subject Analysis: a Sourcebook*, edited by Lois Mai Chan,

Phyllis A. Richmond, Elaine Svenonius. Littleton, Colo.: Libraries Unlimited, 1985, p. 390-402. (First published in *International Classification* 9, no. 3 (1982):140-144.)

3. *Anglo-American Cataloguing Rules.* 2nd ed., 1988 rev. Chicago: American Library Association, 1988, rule 1.0D, p. 14-15.

4. *Cataloging Service Bulletin* 13 (Summer 1981):3-4.

5. Bross, Rex. "Classification of Periodicals," In *Serials and Reference Services*, edited by Robin Kinder and Bill Katz. Reference Librarian, no. 27/28. New York: The Haworth Press, Inc., 1990, p. 177-183.

6. MARC fields 043 and 008, bytes 24-27, respectively. (Cf. *CONSER Editing Guide*, Washington, D.C.: Serial Record Division, Library of Congress, 1986-).

APPENDIX A

Task Force Membership

John Riemer, Chair, University of Georgia
Leighann Ayers, University of Michigan
Linda Bartley, ex officio, Library of Congress
Carol Davis, OCLC
Kathleen Dougherty, National Agricultural Library
Marianne Kasica, University of Pittsburgh
Kevin McShane, National Library of Medicine
Mary Pietris, Library of Congress
Christina Yuen, National Library of Canada

Original Work Statement

Charge

Suggest guidelines pertaining to subject analysis in support of Objective 1.1 in the CONSER Plan: Build a database providing identification and bibliographic access, subject analysis, description, and bibliographic history of serials.

Method and Assumptions

1. The task force should first survey the
   - -- extent of subject analysis and classification data available in CONSER records,
   - -- level of subject treatment,
   - -- thesauri and schedules used, and
   - -- effort employed to maintain data.

2. The task force should then consider
   - -- the desirability of expanding subject and classification coverage in CONSER and extending authentication to include subject and classification data, and
   - -- the resources and level of effort required of participants and centers of responsibility.

3. Finally, the task force should prepare a set of recommendations for the Policy Committee which includes a model of the cooperative contribution and authentication of subject and classification data.

Documents to be considered by task force

- -- Guidelines for Cooperative Subject Cataloging (1/22/88)
- -- NCCP Subject Cataloging Quality Review (2/19/88)
- -- Subject Headings Checklist (2/19/88)
- -- Classification Numbers Checklist (2/19/88)

APPENDIX B
COMPILATION OF RESPONSES TO CONSER MEMBER SUBJECT ANALYSIS PRACTICE QUESTIONNAIRE

100% response rate: 19 of 19 surveys returned.

Sources of comments are indicated by NUC symbols as follows:

CLU - UCLA
CaOONL - National Library of Canada
CtY - Yale
DGPO - U.S. Government Printing Office
DLC - Library of Congress
DNAL - National Agricultural Library
DNLM - National Library of Medicine
FU - University of Florida
GU - University of Georgia
ICRL - Center for Research Libraries
InU - Indiana
MCM - Massachusetts Institute of Technology
MH - Harvard
MiU - University of Michigan
N - New York State Library
NIC - Cornell
PPiU - University of Pittsburgh
TxU - University of Texas
WaU - University of Washington

Subject Headings

1. What is the basis for the headings you add to original records? (Check all that apply.)

a. LCSH 17 Weekly list 8 Subj. Cat. Manual 13

b. Other thesauri, e.g. MESH (specify) 4 thesauri @ 6 insts.
MeSH (DNAL, MH, CLU, WaU)
CAB Thesaurus (DNAL)
Canadian Subject Headings [CSH] (CaOONL)
Repertoire des vedettes-matières [RVM] (CaOONL)
(One institution explicitly cited AACR2r)

c. Local or non-controlled vocabulary terms of any type (please specify and provide situation(s) used)

none

2. Do you assign subject headings to everything you catalog?

a. Yes 15 (6 cited the obvious exceptions of LC subclass AP and newspapers; if a response of "no" listed only these, it was tallied as a "yes")
b. No 4
(If no, what categories of serials do not receive subject headings?)
DLC: form card serials
CaOONL: government document serials (except some from Statistics Canada)
ICRL: all but those from which subject headings can be copied from an earlier title
CLU: some minimal cataloging

3. When authenticating existing records, do you routinely verify the authoritativeness of the headings found in the record?

a. Always 14
b. Sometimes (explain) 4
DLC: only if a cataloger notices an obsolete heading or obsolete or incorrect formulation of heading
ICRL: do most often for geographic headings; sometimes for other headings
NIC: not applicable, since only original records are contributed to CONSER
TxU: only if the headings look questionable

c. Never 1 (CtY)

... the currency of the headings?

a. Always 14
b. Sometimes (explain) 4
DLC, ICRL & NIC: same as above
TxU: only if the cataloger suspects the heading to be out-of-date

c. Never 1 (CtY)

... the appropriateness and specificity level of the headings?

a. Always 14
PPiU: add and correct existing headings but do not normally delete any; delete only when heading is obviously wrong
b. Sometimes (explain) 4
DLC: with 780/785 relationships, catalogers may adjust headings for appropriateness and specificity. (050 ≠a for 780/785 with second indicator 0 will generally not change)
ICRL, NIC: same as above
TxU: only if the cataloger suspects the heading to be inappropriate
c. Never 1 (CtY)

APPENDIX B (continued)

4. In your updating or maintenance of authenticated records, do you modify or add subject headings as needed?

a. Always 11
(2 institutions pointed out that this assumes exclusion of record modifications in which one is merely adding a linking field, i.e. an unowned title which cannot be examined.)

b. Sometimes (explain) 5
DLC: 1. 6XX fields are adjusted when a change to a subject heading is made or if a new subject heading is added to LCSH. 2. if a cataloger notices obsolete headings or obsolete practice.
CaOONL: on a case-by-case basis, e.g. wrong heading
ICRL: headings not added; occasionally modify geographic headings, if need is obvious
TxU: usually add, especially to LC partial records

c. Never 3 (N, FU, CtY)

Classification

5. What classification scheme(s) is (are) used in your institution? (Check all that apply.)

a. LC 16
DNLM: a few non-medical serials on reference are classed in LC; even these are entered in 060

b. Dewey - TOTAL of 7:
3 [currently being assigned] (DLC, CaOONL, N);
1 [assigning modified Dewey] (MiU);
& 3 additional institutions report Dewey-classed serials exclusively from past practice (MCM (1850-1964), TxU, WaU)

c. Other(s) (specify)
As PRIMARY scheme used:
DGPO: SuDOCs classification
DNLM: NLM classification
As SECONDARY, supplemental scheme used:
DNAL: U.S. Dept. of Agriculture Library scheme (past practice only; used in serial recon)
MH: various local schemes
MCM: abbreviated LC classification
MCM: SuDOCs classification
N: N.Y. State Documents classification
WaU: NLM classification--in place of LC's R schedule)
NO scheme used, i.e. serials not classified: ICRL

6. Do you assign the form of class number in 5 above to every title cataloged?

a. Yes 6 Scheme involved: LC-5; Dewey-1;
(=InU, FU, GU, PPiU, CtY; CaOONL)
Comments: PPiU assigns LC class to periodicals, microfilm, & microfiche despite not using as a location device.
CaOONL does not shelve by the Dewey no.; its use of LC is limited to non-government serials (class no. only, in 055 field) and govt. serials either shelved in reference or published also by a non-govt. publisher (full call no.); for shelving arrangements, see below.

b. No 12
(If no, what categories of serials do not receive classification?)
DLC: MLC serials, microforms, LAW serials; Dewey applied only to selected serials (NSDP applies Dewey to 90% of US imprints it authenticates)
DNAL: microforms, AV, MRDF
DNLM: medical serials (NLM scheme in W1-W3+ does not reflect any of the serial subject matter as is done for monographs)
NIC: most microforms
MH: various categories
MCM: periodicals
N: most law publications
DGPO: U.S. government serials (SuDOCs scheme does not reflect any of the serial subject matter)
CLU: "current year only" titles
MiU: medical library titles
TxU: microforms
WaU: microforms and CD-ROMs

(How are they shelved?)
DLC: accession number; microform serials are filed by microform reading room numbers with LC class assigned as an alternative number; for law serials, Law Library adds 050 ≠u for shelf location
DNAL: accession number
CaOONL: various methods:
govt. serial:
Statistics Canada--by special C.S. no.
pre-'85: federal--by DSS no.
provincial--by prov., subarr. by m.e.
post-'84: by blocks of acc#s, reflecting jurisdict.
non-govt. serial:
annual or less freq.--by class no.
periodicals--by "location no." reflecting bldg., room & shelf; based upon title's freq., format & shelf availability
In all the above, title changes are kept together.

APPENDIX B (continued)

DNLM: form, subarranged by main entry/title
NIC: accession number
MH: various methods
MCM: most shelved by main entry; some by abbreviated class + Cutter-Sanborn number
N: alphabetically by title or category, depending on type of publication
DGPO: issuing agency/subagency, subarranged by title
CLU: alphabetically in folders by corporate body, subarranged by title
MiU: title
TxU: accession number
WaU: accession number

SUMMARY: Of the 18 institutions who classify at least some of their serials, 7 assign a class number to all serials cataloged.

NOTE: The 4 national library institutions provide maintenance for the class numbers in the unique MARC fields they are exclusively responsible for. They do not assess the classification present in other fields in the record.

The data in questions 7-9 reflect only the responses of the 15 full member institutions of CONSER. Among this group, it is assumed that the verification issue is confined to the class scheme actually used in cataloging a given title locally. In other words, if an institution was using NLM or some local scheme, it would not consider verifying an LC-based class number found in the record.

It is also assumed that verification is limited to the cataloging of new titles, since it is impractical to reclassify a full run at the time of a cessation.

7. When authenticating existing records, do you routinely verify the authoritativeness of the class number found in the record?

a. Always __9__
  NIC: call#s do not appear on printouts sent to NST
b. Sometimes (explain) _2_
  MCM: rarely verify; edit in case of obvious error
  TxU: only if cataloger suspects call# is invalid

c. Never __3__ (ICRL, MiU, CtY)

... the currency of the class number?

a. Always __11__
b. Sometimes (explain) _1_
  TxU: only if the cataloger suspects the number to be outdated

c. Never __3__ (ICRL, MiU, CtY)

... the appropriateness of the class number?

a. Always __11__
b. Sometimes (explain) 1
TxU: only if the cataloger suspects the number to be inappropriate

c. Never __3__ (ICRL, MiU, CtY)

8. In your updating or maintenance of authenticated records, do you modify or add class numbers to the master record when the existing ones are not usable as is?

a. Always __9__
b. Sometimes (explain) 2
MCM: situations not specified; generally edit numbers for local use
TxU: usually add, especially to LC partial records
c. Never __4__ (ICRL, MH, FU, CtY)

9. If you use LC classification, do you add a workmark, such as a zero or an "x," to cutters to differentiate LC-assigned numbers from locally assigned or older call numbers?

a. Yes __1__ (MH)
b. No __11__
[not applicable for 3 institutions]

Geographic Access Code (GAC/043)

10. When authenticating original and existing records, do you routinely add applicable GACs?

a. Always __14__
b. Sometimes (explain) 1
DLC: systematically done on original records; seldom for existing records

c. Never __4__ (DNAL, DNLM, N, TxU)

11. In your updating or maintenance of authenticated records, do you ever add or make applicable modifications to GACs?

a. Always __9__
b. Sometimes (explain) 5
DLC: 1) when a new GAC is created (rare situation), 043 is updated throughout MARC database 2) when a subject heading is changed to add or change a ≠z subfield, 043 data is sometimes updated
CaOONL: occasionally, if modification readily apparent
NIC: not applicable, since only original records are contributed to CONSER
FU: when codes are changed

APPENDIX B (continued)

PPiU: have not done so in past for records being closed, but will do so in future, in anticipation of local applications based on GAC

c. Never __5__ (DNAL, DNLM, N, TxU, CtY)

Fixed Field Nature of Contents Code
(008/24 & 25-27)

12. When authenticating original and existing records, do you routinely add (edit) applicable coding to the fixed field?

a. Always __16__
b. Sometimes (explain) _2_
DLC: systematically done on original records; seldom for existing records
TxU: only when cataloger chooses to do so
c. Never __1__ (FU)

13. In your updating or maintenance of authenticated records, do you ever add or make applicable modifications to the coding?

a. Always __9__
b. Sometimes (explain) _7_
DLC: not usually
DNAL: if errors or changes are noted during the cataloging process
CaOONL: if readily apparent
NIC: not applicable, since only original records are contributed to CONSER
MCM: modify obvious errors; add if lacking
CLU: if needed _and_ we have same issue description was based on
TxU: only when cataloger chooses to do so

c. Never __3__ (DNLM, MH, FU)

Use of Subject Analysis Data
for Retrieval
In an Online Environment

14. Do you have an online catalog available for public use at this time?

a. Yes __15__ (since __________)

1970s (DLC)	1985 (FU)
1978 (CaOONL)	1986 (MCM)
1980 (N)	1987 (PPiU)
1982 (CLU)	1988 (NIC, MH, MiU, TxU, WaU)
1983 (DNLM)	1989 (CtY)
1984 (GU)	

b. Anticipate one by (date) __________ 2
Oct. 1989 (DNAL)
Jan. 1990 (InU)

c. None in foreseeable future __2__ (ICRL, DGPO)

(NOTE: If you do not currently have an online catalog, please answer the last part of each of the remaining questions.)

15. Does your online catalog provide classification browsing?

a. Yes __10__ (DLC, DNAL, CaOONL, DNLM, MH, MCM, N, GU, TxU, WaU)
DLC: through SCORPIO, browse is only up to first decimal point; new release of SCORPIO may extend browsing further into call number; serials currently excluded from SCORPIO.
GU: browse is based on piece-level vs. bibliographic record, as is customary in card shelflist; thus one work could appear undesirably dozens of times in such a browse.
WaU: browsing may be done in online call number index; index screen displays only the call no.
b. No, but we anticipate this capability sometime in the future __6__ (NIC, CLU, FU, MiU, PPiU, CtY)
CLU: a test file is available for staff use.
c. No, and we do not ever expect to have it __0__
d. When we have an online catalog, we
do __1__ (InU)
do not __1__ (ICRL)
anticipate implementing such a feature.
Unsure/no answer: DGPO
Comments:

16. Does your online catalog provide subject searching by keyword?

a. Yes __10__ (DLC, DNAL, DNLM, MH, MCM, N, CLU, GU, MiU, CtY)
b. No, but we anticipate this capability sometime in the future __6__ (CaOONL, NIC, FU, PPiU, TxU, WaU)
WaU: to be avail. in late fall 1989.
c. No, and we do not ever expect to have it __0__

d. When we have an online catalog, we
do __1__ (InU)
do not __1__ (ICRL)
anticipate implementing such a feature.
Unsure/no answer: DGPO

Comments:

APPENDIX B (continued)

17. Does your online catalog provide subject searching by exact phrase (e.g. the ability to retrieve items by the heading "Birds" without subdivisions)?

a. Yes __15__ (DNAL, CaOONL, DNLM, NIC, MH, MCM, N, CLU, FU, GU, MiU, PPiU, TxU, WaU, CtY)
MH: ability indirectly available through online cat. guide screen (see sample at end)
CLU: has browse capability which allows exact term searching from left to right.
GU: situation very similar to MH, except that keyword/phrase can will come from anywhere in the LCSH string, not just left end.
b. No, but we anticipate this capability sometime in the future __1__ (DLC)
c. No, and we do not ever expect to have it __0__
d. When we have an online catalog, we
do __0__
do not __2__ (ICRL, InU)
anticipate implementing such a feature.
Unsure/no answer: DGPO

Comments:

18. Does your online catalog provide search limitation by GAC?

a. Yes __1__ (DLC)
DLC: in MUMS via JANUS retriever run; in SCORPIO via a GAC limit command.
b. No, but we anticipate this capability sometime in the future __4__ (CaOONL, MH, MCM, GU)
c. No, and we do not ever expect to have it __9__ (DNAL, DNLM, NIC, N, CLU, FU, PPiU, WaU, CtY)
PPiU: expect to be able to produce offline products by GAC at some future date.
d. When we have an online catalog, we
do __0__
do not __2__ (ICRL, InU)
anticipate implementing such a feature.
Unsure/no answer: DGPO, MiU, TxU

Comments:

19. Does your online catalog provide search limitation by fixed field contents code?

a. Yes __2__ (DNLM, CtY)
DNLM: available through separate field(s) in the MEDLARS format, equivalent to MARC format's fixed fields.
b. No, but we anticipate this capability sometime in the future __8__ (DNAL, CaOONL, MH, MCM, N, CLU, GU, WaU)

c. No, and we do not ever expect to have it __4__ (DLC, NIC, FU, PPiU)
   DLC: in MUMS via a JANUS retriever run.
   PPiU: expect to be able to produce offline products by fixed field contents code at some future date.

d. When we have an online catalog, we
   do __0__
   do not __2__ (ICRL, InU)
   anticipate implementing such a feature.
   Unsure/no answer: DGPO, MiU, TxU

Comments:

20. For those institutions which are not national libraries, please indicate if you use any of the following subject related fields. Consider "use" to mean locally adding them to bibliographic records, modifying them during the editing process, or indexing or otherwise utilizing them in the catalog. (Check all that apply.)

	MARC Field	Please specify how used
1	045 Time period of content	(ICRL)
1	052 Geographic classification code	(ICRL--possibly for some microform publications
	055 Call#/class# assigned in Canada	
	070 NAL call#	
	072 NAL subject category code	
	080 UDC number	
	096 Locally assigned NLM-type call# [if not covered in 5.-8. above]	
	098 Other classification schemes (please specify)	
	653 Uncontrolled subject heading	
	654 Subject added entry - faceted topical	
1	655 Genre heading	(TxU--added in rare books cataloging, but probably not to serials)
	68X PRECIS system	
1	690 Local subject vocabulary - topical	(CLU--a very few subject headings are assigned, continuing past library practice)
1	691 Local subject vocabulary - geographic	(CLU--same as 690)

APPENDIX B (continued)

MARC Field | Please specify how used

_____ 699 Added class numbers for classified catalogs

Comments:

GENERAL COMMENT RECEIVED:

CONSER concerns:

Present lack of policy or guidelines in the CEG for call numbers and subject headings re modification of fields, addition of fields (e.g., adding a 2nd 090), retention of unedited existing fields.

Since 69X fields have been eliminated for locally assigned LCSH-based subject headings, it has become more complicated and more time-consuming for copy cataloguing assistants to select appropriate subject headings for serials titles. Inappropriate, invalid, and near-duplicate subject headings are significant problems in the training of copy cataloguers.

Designation of CONSER verified LC subject headings and CONSER verified call numbers will enable cataloguers and cataloguing assistants to work more efficiently.

(--MCM)

Institution Name ______________________

Name of individual(s) filling out questionnaire

____

Date ______________

Saved by the Uniform Title: Would AACR2 Have Worked for Serials Without It?

Rex Bross

SUMMARY. AACR2 would not have worked for serials without the development of the serial uniform title. AACR2 serials entries are used in many single access point files, e.g., in check-in and holdings lists and as monographic series tracings in catalogs. Most serials are entered by title under AACR2, and generic titles are a problem in single access point files. While some authors suggested alternative methods, others suggested fine tuning the system developed by the Library of Congress.

Would AACR2 have worked as written without the development by the Library of Congress of the use of unique serial identifiers a.k.a. serial uniform titles? In answering this question, one definition is crucial. What do we mean by "work"? I can go fishing with a safety pin tied to a piece of string tied to one end of a golf club and say that this will "work" to catch fish. However, other options of equipment would be preferable.

As many of us remember from the introduction of AACR2 to the American cataloging community, there would be "No Special Rules For Serials." In carrying out this program, the production of AACR2 ignored some situations and assumed others. The situation most crucially ignored was that the serials catalog entry is used in libraries in several files besides the catalog (be it card or OPAC). The assumption was that we would have online catalogs and other automated systems in most libraries soon after AACR2 was adopted. I deduced this assumption from the

Rex Bross is Head, Monographs Department, University of Toledo Libraries, 2801 W. Bancroft St., Toledo, OH 43606. He was a member of the ALA RTSD Serials Section Committee to Study Serials Cataloging from 1978 to 1982.

frequent arguments that the concept of main entry was dead and access by any entry point was equally relevant.

What other files should have been considered? In many libraries the serials catalog entry matches the check-in record, the spine title for bound volumes, the binding record, and any printed holdings lists (either internal or multi-insitutional). Most of these files are single access point files. With single access point files, a title that is not unique can quickly become impossible to find among similar titles. Flipping through the kardex files for a check-in record or trying to find the holdings in a union list are dependent on having a unique title to look for. While many automated check-in systems do give multiple access points, ten years after the introduction of AACR2, there are still libraries that do not have one. Nor can these problems be sluffed off as ones that trained staff can deal with by interpretation. In many libraries holdings lists or kardex files have been used by the public without any more training than a page of instructions posted nearby.

While it may appear that if we all had OPACs and automated check-in systems there would be less need for uniform title entries for serials, there is one reason that is more relevant with an OPAC than without one. That reason is monographic series. Monographic series are a specific type of serial, and regardless of whether you collect them under a catalog record (as at least one library does) or only trace them and control them through your series authority file record, they need a unique access point. At least with the three online catalogs that I am familiar with, searching series without the title being unique would be a disaster. In the 1980s and continuing into the 1990s, monographic series have proliferated so that any problem with accessing them should be a major concern to librarians. Without a uniform title, would you like to find out if you have a specific item in a series with the title "Research paper" or "Monographic series" in your OPAC? Figure 1 shows an OPAC display with the first two titles not having a qualifier while items nine through eighteen are obviously uniform title entries. Consider the difficulty of finding a single item in the series if all of them showed only the generic series title.

In this article I have not been arguing that the scheme worked out by the Library of Congress was the best one that could have been adopted but that some scheme was necessary. It would have been greatly preferable to have the scheme worked out before AACR2 was published and debated as were other aspects of AACR2. As it occurred, there were changes issued by LC as to what to use as a qualifier in the uniform title. These changes were made after libraries had started to use the directions

FIGURE 1

```
UTMOST SEARCH REQUEST:  T=RESEARCH PAPER
 AUTHOR/TITLE INDEX -- 164 ENTRIES FOUND, 1 - 18 DISPLAYED
  1 LL:RESEARCH PAPER +REFERENCE ON ABORIGINAL CUSTOMARY LAW RESEARCH PAP <SYDN
  2 LL:RESEARCH PAPER +RESEARCH PAPER AUSTRALIA LAW REFORM COMMISSION <SYDN
  3 LL:RESEARCH PAPER AUSTRALIA LAW REFORM COMMISSION +RESEARCH PAPER <SYDN
  4 CA:RESEARCH PAPER FORM AND CONTENT *ROTH AUDREY J <1978
  5 CA:RESEARCH PAPER GATHERING LIBRARY MATERIAL ORGANIZING *HOOK LUCYLE <1962
  6 CA:RESEARCH PAPER MANUAL *SKOBLE MARTIN H <1977
  7 SP:RESEARCH PAPER PROCESS FORM AND CONTENT *ROTH AUDREY J <1982
  8 SP:RESEARCH PAPER PROCESS FORM AND CONTENT *ROTH AUDREY J <1986
  9 CA:RESEARCH PAPER SOUTHERN ILLINOIS UNIVERSITY AT +ARCHAEOLOGICAL EX <1986
 10 CA:RESEARCH PAPER SOUTHERN ILLINOIS UNIVERSITY AT +ARCHAEOLOGICAL IN <1987
 11 CA:RESEARCH PAPER SOUTHERN ILLINOIS UNIVERSITY AT +ARCHAEOLOGICAL SU <1984
 12 CA:RESEARCH PAPER SOUTHERN ILLINOIS UNIVERSITY AT +BRIDGES SITE 11 M <1983
 13 CA:RESEARCH PAPER SOUTHERN ILLINOIS UNIVERSITY AT +CARRIER MILLS ARC <1982
 14 CA:RESEARCH PAPER SOUTHERN ILLINOIS UNIVERSITY AT +CULTURAL FRONTIER <1984
 15 CA:RESEARCH PAPER SOUTHERN ILLINOIS UNIVERSITY AT +EXCAVATIONS AT TH <1987
 16 CA:RESEARCH PAPER SOUTHERN ILLINOIS UNIVERSITY AT +EXCAVATIONS ON BL <1983
 17 CA:RESEARCH PAPER SOUTHERN ILLINOIS UNIVERSITY AT +FINAL REPORT ON A <1978
 18 CA:RESEARCH PAPER SOUTHERN ILLINOIS UNIVERSITY AT +SEARCHING FOR A S <1989

TYPE m FOR MORE ENTRIES.  TYPE LINE NO. FOR BIBLIOGRAPHIC RECORD WITH CALL NO.
 TYPE g FOR GUIDE.  TYPE r TO REVISE, h FOR HELP, e FOR INTRODUCTION TO UTMOST
TYPE SEARCH and PRESS ENTER or RETURN==>
```

for determining qualifiers and resulted in at least some recataloging or inconsistencies in databases, catalogs, etc.

Several authors have suggested different alternatives to the basic problems that serials uniform titles are dealing with. Günter Franzmeier proposes the reintroduction of corporate main entry for any serial whose title consists of a generic term or a generic term and the name of the issuing body. If an LC uniform title is assigned to a serial whose title proper is solely a generic term, the heading for the issuing body is used as the qualifier. He says that the ISDS key-title is itself a de facto uniform title and that for serials with generic titles, the use of a corporate main entry would remove the need for the additional LC uniform title, which may differ from the key-title only in punctuation, or may differ significantly.[1] Certainly, as Carolyn Haven states, "the average library user would much more likely search under the issuing body of a generic serial rather than under a title that is obviously generic." Havens suggests adding information such as the issuing body to the 245 field rather than creating the 130 field as another possibility.[2]

The use of the corporate author main entry or adding information in the title area are both remedies that are contrary to AACR2 as it was adopted in 1981. These suggestions, while interesting, imply that AACR2 wouldn't work as written for serials. Other authors, such as Jim Cole, have written articles on suggested changes to the guidelines on how to construct the qualifier for uniform titles.[3] While tinkering with the guidelines would cover some problems of application, it does not imply that the uniform title or some other solution was not needed. No one is suggesting that the type of situation we now use serial uniform titles for does not need to be addressed. Many of the possibilities suggested would have worked equally as well as the uniform title but were even further from the text of AACR2 as we faced it in 1981.

REFERENCES

1. Franzmeier, G. "Multiplication of Serial Titles Forever." *Serials Librarian*, 12, nos. 1/2 (1987):63-72.

2. Havens, C. "Proposed Changes in the Cataloging of Serials with Generic and Uniform Titles." *Serials Librarian*, 13, no. 4 (1987): 59-68.

3. Cole, J. E. "Corporate Names as Qualifiers in Uniform Titles." *Serials Librarian*, 12, nos. 1/2 (1987):73-82

Presentation of Holdings Data in Union Lists and Uniform Titles: A View of Two Problem Areas of Serials Cataloging

Mitch L. Turitz

SUMMARY. Whether or not uniform titles serve any useful purpose has been debated almost since their implementation in 1981 with the adoption of AACR2 (Anglo-American Cataloguing Rules, Second Edition). The problems posed by a separate bibliographic record for each physical manifestation of the same intellectual work (e.g., original, reprint, microfilm) apply to some extent to all categories of material, but present special problems for union lists of serials. This article discusses these two problem areas of serials cataloging. A proposed solution to the multiple versions dilemma is also briefly discussed.

Whether or not uniform titles serve any useful purpose has been debated almost since their implementation in 1981 with the adoption of AACR2 (Anglo-American Cataloguing Rules, Second Edition). The problems posed by a separate bibliographic record for each physical manifestation of the same intellectual work (e.g., original, reprint, microfllm) apply to some extent to all categories of material, but present special problems for union lists of serials. This article discusses these two problem areas of serials cataloging.

Mitch L. Turitz is the Serials Librarian/Serials Cataloger at the J. Paul Leonard Library, San Francisco State University, 1630 Holloway Ave., San Francisco, CA 94132-1785. He is currently on the ALA/ALCTS Committee to Study Serials Cataloging and is also the Serials Section representative to the Committee on Cataloging: Description and Access of ALA.

UNIFORM TITLES

Uniform titles for serials have existed since their implementation at the Library of Congress almost a decade ago. Uniform titles for serials are used to differentiate unrelated publications with identical titles proper, e.g.:

Arrow (Montréal, Québec)
Arrow (Castlegar, B.C.).

Uniform titles for monographs are used to collocate different titles proper which are manifestations of a work, e.g.:

Dickens, Charles.
[Martin Chuzzlewit]
The life and adventures of Martin Chuzzlewit . . . 1868.

Dickens, Charles.
[Martin Chuzzlewit]
Martin Chuzzlewit's life and adventures . . . 1910.

Both are called uniform titles although they perform different functions. Use of uniform titles for serials was not limited to the Library of Congress but was necessitated by the adoption of AACR2. Recent developments giving consideration to the use of a single bibliographic record for all physical manifestations of the same intellectual work may necessitate changes in the rules or rule interpretations for uniform titles and serials cataloging. The changes in cataloging rules for serials have confused patrons and made bibliographic retrieval difficult.

BACKGROUND

Glasby cites the 1908 *Catalog Rules, Author and Title Entries* as recommending latest entry cataloging for serials.[1] In 1904 the American Library Association (ALA) was approached by the Library Association (formerly the Library Association of the United Kingdom) proposing a preparation of a joint code of rules. Although it was later decided that separate American and British versions would be published, each noted how the practices of the other differed.[2]

Both the 1908 and the 1949 cataloging rules entered periodicals under title main entry and required "latest entry" cataloging. ALA rule 5C1 stated:

> Enter a periodical . . . under its latest title. Make a reference or an added entry for any earlier title or titles under which the periodical might have been issued. In the case of a periodical which has ceased publication, make exception in favor of entry under an earlier title used for a much longer period than the later title. A publication which does not continue the volume numbering of an earlier publication is usually considered a new periodical, and should have separate entry.
>
> A periodical issued by a society, institution, or government body is ordinarily to be entered under its title (especially if this is distinctive in character) with added entry for the issuing body.[3]

In 1967, Anglo-American Cataloging Rules (AACR) rule 6D1 stated: "If the title of a serial changes, if the corporate body under which it is entered changes or undergoes a change of name, or if the person under whom it is entered ceases to be its author, *make a separate entry* [successive entry] for the issues appearing after the change."[4]

The Library of Congress did not adopt this policy until 1971 and, when the policy was implemented, a serial title cataloged under the earlier rules was not recataloged. Although the policy of successive entry cataloging reduced the constant removing, modification, and refiling of existing serial catalog cards, the amount of successive entry cataloging required soon became apparent. With governmental bodies as main entries, there was a greater need for successive entry when the governmental body changed, even if the title was distinct and did not change.

AACR was also published as separate North American and British texts. Appendix VI of AACR listed rules that differed materially from the British text.[5] With the implementation of AACR2, almost all series and serials are cataloged under title main entry.[6] Although not stated in the rules for AACR2, the Library of Congress rule interpretations (RIs) for 25.5B called for creation of a "uniform title heading" for a serial entered under title, whenever the title proper of the serial was identical to the title proper of another serial in the catalog.[7] This was a change in cataloging policy from AACR and the earlier A.L.A. Cataloging Rules for Author and Title Entries. The publication of AACR2 In 1978 was the first joint text prepared by representatives of ALA, the British Library, the Canadian Committee on Cataloguing, the Library Association and the Library of Congress. Although all participating libraries follow the rules of AACR2, each country has its own rule interpretations. The Library of Congress issues its rule interpretations through its *Cataloging Service Bulletin* and also as a separate publication. The British Library issues its *British Library Bibliographic Services Division Newsletter*. The National Library of Australia issues its *ABN Cataloguing Manual*. The National Library of Canada issues *Biblio-Tech*.

The publication of the 1988 revision of the Anglo-American Cataloguing Rules, second edition (AACR2R) included incorporation of the rules revised since the publication of AACR2 but did not include the rule interpretations. Generally, the National Library of Australia's interpretations of AACR2 follow those of the Library of Congress. Its policy is to use Library of Congress rule interpretations as published in LC's *Cataloging Service Bulletin* unless it has reason to make a conscious decision to do otherwise. The National Library of Australia does not vary from Library of Congress practice regarding chapters 12 and 25 as they concern serials.[8] The other libraries did not have significant variation regarding serials generally, and uniform titles for serials specifically.

Recently, however, the Canadian Committee on Cataloguing and the ALA Committee to Study Serials Cataloging each presented proposals to revise rules 25.1A, 25.5B, and others, to incorporate into the rules themselves provisions for the use of uniform titles for serials with identical titles proper.[9] This would make the AACR2 rules *explicitly* state the use of uniform titles for serials.

Other countries which do not follow AACR2 have their own cataloging rules and, therefore, may not use or need uniform titles for serials. For example, in Sweden the current cataloging rules are called *Katalogiseringsregler för svenska bibliotek*, or KRS for short, published in 1985. These rules are a modified translation of AACR2. Among the changes was the decision to make the key title the main entry for serials in all cases.[10] Since the rule interpretation regarding uniform titles for serials is not currently a part of the AACR2 rules themselves, this would be permitted under AACR2 by anyone not desiring to follow the Library of Congress rule interpretations.

The use of key title as main entry is similar to an idea originally proposed by Dorothy Glasby when the concept of uniform titles was first introduced. Glasby proposed using the ISSN as the uniform title qualifier, but this idea was rejected for a more "meaningful" qualifier.[11]

Originally, the LCRI for 25.5B stated that the uniform title was to consist of the title proper of the serial plus qualifying information, with preference given to corporate body as the qualifier.[12] After about three years of AACR2 cataloging, serials catalogers from the Library of Congress and elsewhere proposed changing this LCRI. The reason for this change was that although a corporate body was preferred over place of publication as a more "meaningful" uniform title qualifier, this resulted in more successive entry cataloging because of the following provision in LCRI 25.5B:

> When the name of a corporate body used as a qualifying term in the uniform title changes or the body's responsibilities for the publication are assumed by another body, create a new record (successive entry) . . .[13]

However, LC directs that a new record should not be created when the place of publication changes.[14] Thus, the use of a "meaningful" qualifier for patrons was dropped to reduce successive entry cataloging.[15] Stine reported on the effect of implementing AACR2 in medium-sized research libraries: "The choice of main entry was irrelevant to the catalog user. The rules for description were also only of interest to the cataloger."[16]

Revising the rules and rule interpretations of AACR2 signaled a change in serials cataloging trends. Gradually the rules and rule interpretations started to reduce "unnecessary" successive entry cataloging, especially when the title proper did not change. The revised rule 21.2A (changes in titles proper) now explicitly states,". . . in general, do not consider a title proper to have changed if . . ."[17] [Emphasis added by author.] Earlier the rule only stated, "Consider a title proper to have changed if . . ."[18] This was a substantial improvement for serials catalogers to clarify what are unnecessary title changes. Unfortunately, recent LCRIs have also added new conditions for making new successive entries for serials even if the title proper remains the same. Originally, AACR2 stated only two conditions for successive entry cataloging when the title proper remained the same (rule 21.3B):

1. if the name of a person or corporate body under which a serial is entered changes or
2. if the main entry for a serial is under a personal or corporate heading and the person or corporate body responsible for the serial changes.[19]

Recently, the Library of Congress in LCRI 21.3B added two other conditions (the above conditions were re-labeled as "a" and "b"):

> (c) if the main entry for a serial is under a uniform title heading and that uniform title heading changes because

1. the corporate body used as a qualifier changes (see also LCRI 25.5B) . . .
2. the title of a serial used as the uniform title heading on an entry for a translation changes . . .

(d) when the physical format in which the serial is issued changes (not a reproduction or the same serial in another manifestation, e.g, a braille edition)

New Zealand national bibliography
(Issued only in paper copy through Nov. 1983)
New Zealand national bibliography (Microfiche)
(Issued Dec. 1983- only in microfiche: not a microfiche edition of paper copy issues)''[20] [Italics added for emphasis by author]

Although condition "c" is merely a restatement of an earlier rule interpretation and follows already existing LC practice, condition "d" is a new problem. This situation applies to the physical format of the item, even if the title and subject coverage remains identical to the earlier physical format. This condition is consistent with AACR2 rule 0.24 which states:

> It is a cardinal principle of the use of part 1 that the description of a physical item should be based in the first instance on the chapter dealing with the class of materials to which that item belongs. For example, describe a printed monograph in microform as a microform . . . In short, the starting point for description is the physical form of the item in hand, not the original or any previous form in which the work has been published.[21]

This LCRI requires the generation of a successive entry record when absolutely nothing about the serial has changed except the physical format in which it appears. While strict adherence to AACR2 requires a separate catalog record for every physical version in which a title is issued, many union lists do not follow the mandate.

UNION LISTING

A union list of serials is a listing of serials held by two or more libraries. Aside from and equally important with the bibliographic data are the holdings information (enumeration and chronology) of each participating library. Most union lists of serials produced in paper form or in computer output microform (COM) contain only one entry per bibliographic record instead of the full range of access points found in a catalog record. Bloss points out that the content of the bibliographic record as viewed In AACR2 might or might not be used to define the framework of a union list. Given our ability to manipulate bibliographic data by computer, union list editors and participants can select for each edition and supplement of the list those data elements that they find are important for their needs. If the bibliographic record that resides in the data base is of good quality librarians can use it for a variety of purposes, such as cataloging, serials control and union listing.[22] Of the union lists of serials Bloss reviewed, "Bibliographic description for a microreproduction is based on the original format which, in almost all cases, is a printed version of the title . . . This one entry represents any and all [versions] of that title. The actual physical format of the title held by any one library appears as a function of the holdings statement and not the bibliographic description."[23]

For the individual library, it may be necessary to maintain separate bibliographic records for each format, as implied in AACR2 rule 0.24. This could be the case with serials check-in. However, in union listing, separate bibliographic records for each version of a title are confusing at best and can lead to a very large and unwieldy list. Bibliographic records for the same title might exist for the original and microfilm, microfiche, paper reprints, and so on.[24]

To add to this confusion the recent LCRI 21.3B1 type D adds yet another bibliographic record to the union list when the difference could be distinguished in the holdings statements. A union list of serials which is generated from the CONSER file or based on AACR2 and the Library of Congress' rule interpretations could easily confuse the user. These incidents of creating separate bibliographic records when there is no true "title change" or when it could be otherwise distinguished through holdings statements are not user-friendly. This is another case of catalogers not seeing the forest because of the trees.

Union list editors also have the difficult job of trying to have different libraries with varying cataloging practices agree on the selection of which bibliographic records to use. While most union lists only use one bibliographic record for multiple formats of serials, the individual libraries may actually be maintaining separate bibliographic records. These libraries need to agree on which bibliographic record to use and how to format holdings statements for multiple versions.

MULTIPLE VERSIONS

In recent years the issues concerning multiple versions have become the major topic of discussion in cataloging circles. Elsewhere in this volume Graham discusses the problems caused by the current policy of separate bibliographic records and the proposed change by which a single catalog record would represent all physical versions of an otherwise identical work.

A solution to the multiple versions question will, in some form, necessitate changes in current cataloging rules. Uniform titles that specify format, as in LCRI 21.3B1 type D, may need to be changed. Uniform titles might be used less for variations where the title proper remains unchanged. The current trend in cataloging to reduce successive entry cataloging, the use of one bibliographic record in union lists, and a resolution to the multiple versions problem are all signs that serials cataloging may become less complex and more user-friendly.

NOTES

1. Dorothy J. Glasby, "Historical Background and Review of Serials Cataloging Rules." *Library Resources & Technical Services* 34, no.1 (January 1990): 82-83.

2. Ibid.

3. American Library Association. Division of Cataloging and Classification. A.L.A. *Cataloging Rules for Author and Title Entries.* 2nd ed. Chicago: American Library Association, 1949. 5C1 p.10-11.

4. *Anglo-American Cataloging Rules.* North American Text. Chicago: American Library Association, 1967. 6D1 p.22-23.

5. Ibid. Appendix VI p.371.

6. Michael Gorman, and Paul W. Winkler, eds. *Anglo-American Cataloguing Rules.* 2nd ed., 1988 revision. Chicago: American Library Association, 1988. Rule 21.lC p.286.

7. *Library of Congress Rule Interpretations.* Washington, D.C.: Library of Congress, 1988. 25.5B p 1.

8. Diana B. Dack, Letter to author, 29th August 1990.

9. Canadian Committee on Cataloguing, Letter to Joint Steering Committee March 7, 1890.

10. Sten Hedberg, "Serials Cataloguing in Sweden," *Serials Librarian* 12, nos.1/2 (1987): 12.

11. Dorothy J. Glasby, Discussion on the relationship of serial check-in records to the bibliographic record. Discussion presented at the annual meeting of

the American Library Association's RTSD Committee to Study Serials Cataloging June 26, 1989 at Dallas, Texas.

12. Dorothy J. Glasby, "The Descriptive Cataloging of Serials: Library of Congress' Application of AACR2," *Serials Librarian* 12, nos.1/2 (1987): 45.

13. *Cataloging Service Bulletin.* no.14 (Fall 1981): 52.

14. Ibid.

15. Frank E. Sadowski, Jr., 'Serials Cataloging Developments, 1975-1985: a Personal View of Some Highlights," *Serials Librarian* 10, no. 1/2 (Fall 1985/Winter 1986): 135.

16. Diane Stine, "The Effect of AACR2 and Serials Cataloging on Medium-Sized Research Libraries" *Cataloging and Classification Quarterly* 3, nos. 2/3 (winter 1982/spring 1983): 74.

17. Michael Gorman, and Paul W. Winkler, eds. *Anglo-American Cataloguing Rules.* 2nd ed., 1988 revision. Chicago: American Library Association, 1988. Rule 21.2A p.314-15.

18. Michael Gorman, and Paul W. Winkler, eds. *Anglo-American Cataloguing Rules.* 2nd ed. Chicago: American Library Association, 1978. Rule 21.2A p.286.

19. Ibid. Rule 21.3B p.287.

20. *Cataloging Service Bulletin.* no.50 (Fall 1990): 34-35.

21. Michael Gorman, and Paul W. Winkler, eds. *Anglo-American Cataloguing Rules.* 2nd ed., 1988 revision. Chicago: American Library Association, 1988. Rule 0.24 p.8.

22. Marjorie E. Bloss, "The Impact of AACR2 on Union Lists of Serials" *Cataloging and Classification Quarterly* 3, nos. 2/3 (winter 1982/spring 1983): 100.

23. Ibid. p. 101-102.

24. Ibid.

The NOTIS Opac and Serials: The University of Iowa Experience

Mary H. Monson

SUMMARY. A look at the University of Iowa Libraries' OASIS system provides one perspective on the treatment of serials in an online public access catalog. This article describes "standard NOTIS" as well as local features which are the result of customization of the NOTIS software and local decisions on the use of fields in bibliographic and holdings records. Specific serial indexing and display problems are identified and local solutions to these problems are discussed.

At the University of Iowa Libraries our journey down the path that would eventually lead to a local integrated library system and an online public access catalog was begun at a relatively late date. Our first step, joining the Research Libraries Group, Inc., occurred in mid-1979; our first machine-readable record was created in RLIN (the Research Libraries Information Network) in early 1980.

With the availability of RLIN, machine-readable records were created for all newly cataloged serials and most recataloged serials. After an initial period of adjustment, catalogers became familiar with the intricacies of the MARC format and cataloging output increased; in a good year, over 2,000 serials were cataloged on RLIN.

In 1986 NOTIS was chosen as the local integrated system to be shared by the two independent library units at the University of Iowa: the University Libraries and the Law Library. In preparation for loading the RLIN-produced machine readable records into the local system, independent data conversion projects were undertaken at each unit and preparations were made for authority processing of all existing records.

A former Serials Cataloger, Mary H. Monson is now Coordinator, Central Technical Services and Database Manager at the University of Iowa Libraries, Iowa City, IA 52242.

The greatest challenges encountered during conversion of the University Libraries' data were found in holdings fields; the main reason for this was the lack of national standards for holdings information. Bibliographic fields, on the one hand, are highly standardized and, therefore, are consistently used in the same way in all systems. There are relatively few variations to consider when mapping bibliographic fields from one system to another.

Holdings fields, on the other hand, were typically independently defined for each system prior to the advent of the USMARC Format for Holdings Data. In RLIN, for example, holdings are entered into a location-specific structure; in NOTIS, the holdings structure is copy specific. The lack of a consistent relationship between RLIN holdings fields and NOTIS holdings fields created something of a data mapping nightmare (especially for serials) but, after the expenditure of considerable effort to write the data conversion specifications and significant machine resources to carry out the processing, the finished product was deemed worth the effort.

In preparation for the implementation of NOTIS, authority processing of all records was done by Utlas, a Canadian vendor. During processing at Utlas, copies of all LC authority records matching headings in our bibliographic records were "claimed" to be sent to us on tape and headings in bibliographic records that matched old forms of headings in authority records were "flipped" to current forms. At the University of Iowa Libraries, where most periodicals are unclassified, "flipping" of headings used as main entries caused some problems, which will be described later in this article.

In the summer of 1987, our NOTIS system went into production with close to 100,000 Law Library records and a name of its own: OASIS (Online Access System for Information Sources). Over 650,000 University Libraries bibliographic records and their matching authority records were loaded in June 1988 to complete implementation of the OASIS opac and cataloging and authority modules.

SERIALS PROCESSING AT IOWA

Until 1984 all serials processing at the University of Iowa Libraries was done within the structure of a traditional, separate Serials Department. In 1984 the acquisitions and cataloging functions were administratively split, with serials acquisitions personnel assigned to the Acquisitions Department and serials cataloging personnel assigned to the Cataloging

Department. As the result of a library-wide reorganization in 1990, the Cataloging Department was disbanded and serials catalogers now belong to a Serials Cataloging Unit, one of two units in the newly created Central Technical Services department. Throughout each of these administrative changes, however, all portions of the serials processing operation have remained physically together, just as they were when a separate Serials Department existed.

While all new title cataloging and most recataloging had been done on RLIN since 1980, serials retrospective conversion was not begun until 1988. In a pilot project on RLIN, the bibliographic records for approximately 1,000 serial titles were converted; in a follow-up project, another 10,000 serial bibliographic records were converted on OASIS, completing recon of all titles for which current issues were received. In a second pass, holdings information for all converted bibliographic records was added.

OPAC DISPLAY OF SERIALS

Opac display conventions for the bibliographic portion of serial and nonserial records are basically the same in OASIS. Example 1 shows the MARC tagged version of the cataloging for the title ''Medical anthropology quarterly"; Example 2 shows the corresponding OASIS opac display. You will note that some displayable fields, such as 022 (ISSN) and 710 (added entry-corporate name) do not appear in the opac. In some cases we have chosen to suppress display of a field, in others the NOTIS software automatically suppresses a field. You may also note that we have chosen to display both Library of Congress subject headings and MESH (medical) subject headings and that each type is clearly labeled in the opac display.

Examples 1 and 2 also illustrate some basic OASIS holdings display conventions. For all titles, location and call number information is provided. If a title has no call number, as is the case with unclassified serials, the text ''No call number.'' is displayed. Each NOTIS library can define publicly displaying coded notes to be input in copy specific notes fields in the holdings record. The note ''Library has a current subscription/order'' displays in the opac because the corresponding code (so:) was provided in the appropriate copy specific NOTES field in the OASIS holdings record. The University of Iowa has defined twenty-seven such publicly displaying coded notes; each contains a colon to serve as a simple visual device to identify the note as one that ''explodes'' into a

EXAMPLE 1. MARC record for "Medical anthropology quarterly."

```
LTUL MORE                                                        ADD9169
                                                       NOTIS CATALOGING          TKJO
UL# ADD9169 FMT S RT a BL s DT 06/23/88 R/DT none      STAT mc E/L   DCF a D/S D
SRC d PLACE dcu LANG eng MOD   OA a REPRO   S/STAT c DT/1 1983 DT/2 9999
CONT        S/T p FREQ q REG r MED   GOVT   TPA u IA u CIA u ISDS 1 CONF 0 SLE 0

010:   : .a    84643999 .z sc839219 .z sn833172 .z sn831995
022/1:0 : .a 0745-5194
032/1:  : .a 509870 .b USPS
035/1:  : .a (CStRLIN)IAUG87S1834
035/2:  : .a (CaOTULAS)159398112
040:   : .a DSI .c DSI .d NSDP .d MH .d DLC .d NST .d RCS .d NST .d DLC .d NST
.d DNLM .d NST .d AIP .d DLC .d NST .d OCoLC .d NST .d m/c .d MH .d IaU
042:   : .a nsdp .a lc
050/1:0 : .a GN296 .b .M44
060/1:  : .a W1 .b ME206D
082/1:0 : .a 306/.45 .2 19
210/1:0 : .a Med. anthropol. q.
222/1:00: .a Medical anthropology quarterly
245:00: .a Medical anthropology quarterly.
260:01: .a Washington, D.C. : .b Society for Medical Anthropology, .c c1983-
```

```
LTUL DONE                                                   ADD9169
                                                   NOTIS CATALOGING          TKJO

 265:  : .a Circulation Dept., Society for Medical Anthropology, 1703 New
Hampshire Ave., N.W., Washington, DC 20009
 300/1:  : .a v. ; .c 28 cm.
 310:  : .a Quarterly
 350:  : .a $40.00 (institutions) .a $12.00 (members)
 362/1:0 : .a Vol. 14, no. 2 (Feb. 1983)-v. 17, no. 5 (Nov. 1986); new ser., v.
1, no. 1 (Mar. 1987)-    .
 500/1:  : .a Title from cover.
 510/2:2 : .a Sociological abstracts .x 0038-0202
 650: 2: .a Anthropology .x Periodicals.
 650/1: 0: .a Medical anthropology .x Periodicals.
 710/1:20: .a Society for Medical Anthropology.
 780/1:00: .t Medical anthropology newsletter .x 0543-2499
 998:  : .a 11/06/87 .t c .s 9110 .n IaU .w DCLCSN8331728 .d 11/06/87 .c CL  .b
CM  .i 871106 .l IAUG
```

EXAMPLE 1. (continued)

```
LTUL DONE                                                             ADD9169
                                                       NOTIS COPY HOLDINGS       TKJO
UL SERL LC    84643999 sc839219 sn833172 sn831995  ISSN 0745-5194
S/STAT c FREQ q S/T p
Medical anthropology quarterly. Vol. 14, no. 2 (Feb. 1983)-v. 17, no. 5 (Nov.
 1986); new ser., v. 1, no. 1 (Mar. 1987)-     . -- Washington, D.C. : Society
 for Medical Anthropology, c1983- Circulation Dept., Society for Medical
 Anthropology, 1703 New Hampshire Ave., N.W., Washington, DC 20009
STATUS h DT 11/06/87 AD none
NOTES .a CL /CM
001 2X CN .a hsl/1 .b none                                          .d 06/23/88
    NOTES .a VH .a so:
    BN-001-001

LTUL DONE
                                                                      ADD9169
                                                       NOTIS VOLUME HOLDINGS     TKJO
UL SERL LC    84643999 sc839219 sn833172 sn831995  ISSN 0745-5194
S/STAT c FREQ q S/T p
Medical anthropology quarterly. Vol. 14, no. 2 (Feb. 1983)-v. 17, no. 5 (Nov.
 1986); new ser., v. 1, no. 1 (Mar. 1987)-     . -- Washington, D.C. : Society
 for Medical Anthropology, c1983- Circulation Dept., Society for Medical
 Anthropology, 1703 New Hampshire Ave., N.W., Washington, DC 20009
=>001 2X CN .a hsl/1 .b none .d 06/23/88
   VH 001 .a n.s.:v.1 (1987)-n.s.:v.3 (1989)                        .d 12/17/90
```

```
LTUL MORE                                                        ADD9169
                                                     OASIS ACQUISITIONS      TKJO
UL SERL LC    84643999 sc839219 sn833172 sn831995  ISSN 0745-5194
S/STAT c FREQ q S/T p
Medical anthropology quarterly. Vol. 14, no. 2 (Feb. 1983)-v. 17, no. 5 (Nov.
 1986); new ser., v. 1, no. 1 (Mar. 1987)-     . -- Washington, D.C. : Society
 for Medical Anthropology, c1983- Circulation Dept., Society for Medical
 Anthropology, 1703 New Hampshire Ave., N.W., Washington, DC 20009
PO#: 001ADD9169  11/03/88 ORDUNIT: SA RECUNIT: SA SCOPE: 2
VENDOR: FAXON/S    ACTINT: 0150 POP: x L1: us   L2:
VA:

NV: ORD 02/19/87
NO:
SOURCE: T.H. Charlton.                         REF:
DIV 001 CCN 001 NOTE: ==1222==;**207581**;
                                                              MED:    PCS:
001 BN v.18 (1987)-               E$         0.00 E# 00  AD none     MD 11/03/88
    FC MED        90/91 CUR usd AMT        40.00 C# 01 XPM a L3/4       ps
009 N  n.s.:v.3:no.4 (1989:Dec.)                      MD 12/18/90  AD none
010 R  n.s.:v.4:no.1 (1990:Mar.)                      MD 03/14/90  AD none
011 R  n.s.:v.4:no.2 (1990:June)                      MD 06/20/90  AD none
012 R  n.s.:v.4:no.3 (1990:Sept.)                     MD 09/11/90  AD none
```

EXAMPLE 1. (continued)

```
LTUL DONE                                                        ADD9169
                                                    OASIS ACQUISITIONS     TKJO
UL SERL LC    84643999 sc839219 sn833172 sn831995  ISSN 0745-5194
S/STAT c FREQ q S/T p
Medical anthropology quarterly. Vol. 14, no. 2 (Feb. 1983)-v. 17, no. 5 (Nov.
 1986); new ser., v. 1, no. 1 (Mar. 1987)-    . -- Washington, D.C. : Society
 for Medical Anthropology, c1983- Circulation Dept., Society for Medical
 Anthropology, 1703 New Hampshire Ave., N.W., Washington, DC 20009
PO#: 001ADD9169  11/03/88 ORDUNIT: SA RECUNIT: SA SCOPE: 2
VENDOR: FAXON/S    ACTINT: 0150 POP: x L1: us   L2:
VA:

NV: ORD 02/19/87
NO:
SOURCE: T.H. Charlton.                          REF:
DIV 001 CCN 001 NOTE: ==1222==;**207581**;
                                                              MED:     PCS:
001 BN v.18 (1987)-                E$        0.00 E# 00  AD none     MD 11/03/88
    FC MED       90/91 CUR usd AMT          40.00 C# 01 XPM a L3/4      ps
012 R  n.s.:v.4:no.3 (1990:Sept.)                      MD 09/11/90  AD none
013 R  n.s.:v.4:no.4 (1990:Dec.)                       MD 12/20/90  AD none
014 R  n.s.:v.5:no.1 (1991:Mar.)                       MD 03/07/91  AD none
015 R  n.s.:v.5:no.2 (1991:June)                       MD 06/11/91  AD 11/08/91
```

publicly displaying note. Examples of other types of publicly displaying coded notes are:

ask:	Ask at information desk
ci:	Only current issues retained
l:res	Latest on Reserve
lv3:ref	Latest 3 in Reference
rum:	Retained until microform received
sc:	Subscription cancelled
si:sm	Some issues/volumes in MAIN Serials Maintenance

Holdings for bound volumes are displayed in the opac following the print constant "Library has:." The holdings information displayed here comes from the NOTIS Volume Holdings Record. Holdings for current issues are displayed in the opac following the print constant "CURRENT ISSUES/VOLUMES:"; this information comes from receipt lines in the NOTIS Order/Pay/Receipt Record. This receipt information only displays if fixed field S/T (Type of serial) in the bibliographic record contains the value "p" or "n."

With implementation of the acquisitions module of OASIS, order information became available to the public via the opac. Messages, tailored to reflect the status of in-process materials, are displayed to the public. In Example 3 the opac message "ON ORDER, NOT YET RECEIVED." displays for the title "Poetry USA," which has, indeed, been ordered, but not yet received. When issues of this title are received, the appropriate codes in the OASIS record will be altered and the message displaying in the opac will change to "In process. To request cataloging for your use, ask at information desk."

Availability of on-order and in-process information in the opac provides us with invaluable patron input on priorities as library users are able to locate and request processing of items they need. On the other hand, availability of this information in the opac raises many authority control issues. While it is impractical to maintain strict authority control over all headings in acquisitions records, we do attempt to verify headings in acquisitions records in an effort to maintain the integrity of the opac. One incorrect heading in the opac can mislead a patron, who thinks that the single, incorrect result represents all that is available.

In addition to fully cataloged serial records and acquisitions records, OASIS contains "informational" serial records. The OASIS record for "Education times" (see Example 4) illustrates such a record; it was created to alert staff to the fact that this particular title is discarded. This

EXAMPLE 2. OASIS opac display for "Medical anthropology quarterly."

```
  OASIS search request:  T=MEDICAL ANTHROPOLOGY QUARTERLY
BIBLIOGRAPHIC RECORD -- NO. 1 OF 1 ENTRIES FOUND

Medical anthropology quarterly. -- Vol. 14, no. 2 (Feb. 1983)-v. 17, no. 5 (Nov.
  1986); new ser., v. 1, no. 1 (Mar. 1987)-    . -- Washington, D.C. : Society
  for Medical Anthropology, c1983-
  v. ; 28 cm.
  Quarterly
  Continues: Medical anthropology newsletter ISSN 0543-2499
  Title from cover.
 SUBJECT HEADINGS (Library of Congress; use s= ):
     Medical anthropology--Periodicals.
 SUBJECT HEADINGS (Medical; use sm= ):
     Anthropology--Periodicals.


             CONTINUED ON NEXT SCREEN:  press Return key
```

```
Type e to start over.      Type h for help.
Type command and press Return==>

  OASIS search request:  T=MEDICAL ANTHROPOLOGY QUARTERLY
BIBLIOGRAPHIC RECORD -- NO. 1 OF 1 ENTRIES FOUND  (CONTINUED)

Medical anthropology quarterly ...  c1983-   (CONTINUED)

Location: HEALTH SCIENCES
Call number:  No call number.
Library has a current subscription/order
Library has:
  n.s.:v.1 (1987)-n.s.:v.3 (1989)
  CURRENT ISSUES/VOLUMES:
    n.s.:v.4:no.1 (1990:Mar.)
    n.s.:v.4:no.2 (1990:June)
    n.s.:v.4:no.3 (1990:Sept.)
    n.s.:v.4:no.4 (1990:Dec.)
    n.s.:v.5:no.1 (1991:Mar.)
    n.s.:v.5:no.2 (1991:June)


                    Press Return key to see beginning of this record.


Type e to start over.      Type h for help.
Type command and press Return==>
```

EXAMPLE 3. OASIS opac display for a title on order, not yet received.

```
   OASIS search request:  T=POETRY USA
BIBLIOGRAPHIC RECORD -- NO. 1 OF 1 ENTRIES FOUND

Poetry USA.  Vol. 4, no. 16 (fall 1989)-  San Francisco : National Poetry Assn.

Copy for: MAIN
Temporary control number: ADZ6686
Library has a current subscription/order
     ON ORDER, NOT YET RECEIVED.  Ask staff for assistance.





Type e to start over.      Type h for help.
Type command and press Return==>
```

record displays in the opac with the message "THIS RECORD FOR STAFF USE.". With the next release of the NOTIS software (release 5.0), it will be possible to suppress records from opac display based on the value in fixed field D/S in the bibliographic record. If the value "D" is supplied in this field, the record will display in the opac; the value "S" will suppress the record from opac display. Informational serial records, such as the one shown in Example 4 will be suppressed from opac display in the future.

SERIAL INDEXING

Searching for serials in the opac can present some interesting challenges for the uninitiated. In our opac, for example, we have chosen to index subfield b of field 245. This subfield b information can be very useful when it is used to differentiate between monographs with generic titles,

EXAMPLE 4. OASIS opac display for an informational serial record.

```
  OASIS search request:   T=EDUCATION TIMES
BIBLIOGRAPHIC RECORD -- NO. 1 OF 1 ENTRIES FOUND

Education Times.

THIS RECORD IS FOR STAFF USE.
If another copy is not listed, ask staff for assistance.

Type e to start over.       Type h for help.
Type command and press Return==>
```

but it can cause considerable confusion when the user is not aware of its existence, which is often the case with serials.

A user searching for the serial "Archivum" (see Example 5) will expect to find this title indexed as a one-word title. The title search "fin t archivum" yields a result of 63 entries in our opac (see Example 6). The index entry produced by the 245 field in the bibliographic record occurs at line 61 because both subfield a and b are included in the index. The user would never think to look for this title alphabetized as "Archivum revista de la Facultad de Filosofia y Letras . . ." in the index result and would have come away empty handed if we had not anticipated this indexing quirk and added a NOTIS-defined "provisional" title field (field 924) for the one-word form of the title. It is this locally supplied 924 field that has created the index entry at line 2; through the use of this "trick," we are able to maintain fully standard cataloging while supplying a locally tagged field to circumvent this particular indexing idiosyncrasy.

Index entries for serials end with the first four characters of the place of publication, while index entries for nonserials end with the date of publication, making it relatively easy to skim through an index result and quickly differentiate between serial and nonserial entries. In Example 6, the entries at lines 1-2, 11-16 and 61 all represent serials. The index entries at lines 9 and 62, which lack date or place descriptive information, represent brief informational records for series whose volumes are classified separately. A single code in the STATUS field of the OASIS Copy Holdings Record for each of these two titles creates the following note in the opac: "ITEMS IN THIS SERIES ARE CATALOGED UNDER THEIR RESPECTIVE AUTHORS/TITLES. If desired item cannot be located, ask a staff member for assistance."

When a serial index entry is created from field 245, the place of publication is taken from subfield a of field 260. Unfortunately, when a serial index entry is created from provisional title field 924, the place of publication must also come from a provisional field rather than a "firm" field; the existence of place of publication in field 260 is ignored and if the corresponding provisional field for imprint information (field 926) is not supplied, the place of publication displays in the opac as "<—>." In our opac, therefore, in order to create a meaningful serial index entry from field 924, we also supply a 926 provisional field which duplicates the place of publication found in the 260 field.

With release 5.0 of the NOTIS software, up to ten characters of the place of publication will be provided in serial index entries and the designator "serial" will be added to each serial index entry.

EXAMPLE 5. MARC record for "Archivum."

```
LTUL DONE                                                    ADF8606
                                               NOTIS CATALOGING        TKJO
UL# ADF8606 FMT S RT a BL s DT 08/08/88 R/DT 03/26/91 STAT nn E/L 1 DCF   D/S D
SRC d PLACE sp  LANG spa MOD   OA   REPRO   S/STAT c DT/1 1951 DT/2 9999
CONT       S/T p FREQ b REG r MED   GOVT   TPA u IA u CIA u ISDS   CONF 0 SLE 0

022/1:  : .a 0570-7218
040:  : .a IaU .c IaU
245:00: .a Archivum; .b revista de la Facultad de Filosofia y Letras de la
Universidad de Oviedo.
260:11: .a Oviedo, Spain.
300/1:  : .a v. .c 24 cm.
362/1:0 : .a nueva ser., t. 1-   1951-
500/1:  : .a Vols. for   : "Revista de la Facultad de Filologia."
650/1: 0: .a Spanish literature .x Periodicals.
710/1:20: .a Universidad de Oviedo. .b Facultad de Filosofia y Letras.
710/2:20: .a Universidad de Oviedo. .b Facultad de Filologia.
924:00: .a Archivum.
926:00: .a Oviedo, Spain
973/1:00: .a Archivum; revista de la facultad de Filologia
```

EXAMPLE 6. Index display resulting from a search for the title "Archivum."

```
LTUL MORE
                                                   NOTIS INDEX SEARCH        TKJO
 AUTHOR/TITLE INDEX -- 63 ENTRIES FOUND, 1 - 21 DISPLAYED
  1 UL:ARCHIVUM <MUNC
  2 UL:ARCHIVUM <OVIE
  3 LL:ARCHIVUM +ARCHIVAL LEGISLATION 1970 1980 <1982
  4 UL:ARCHIVUM +ARCHIVAL LEGISLATION 1970 1980 <1982
  5 UL:ARCHIVUM +INTERNATIONAL DIRECTORY OF ARCHIVES ANNUAIRE INTERNATION <1988
  6 UL:ARCHIVUM +PROCEEDINGS OF THE 11TH INTERNATIONAL CONGRESS ON ARCHIV <1989
  7 UL:ARCHIVUM +PROCEEDINGS OF THE 9TH INTERNATIONAL CONGRESS ON ARCHIVE <1982
  8 UL:ARCHIVUM +PROFESSIONAL TRAINING OF ARCHIVISTS FORMATION PROFESSION <1988
  9 UL:ARCHIVUM CALDERONIANUM
 10 UL:ARCHIVUM CALDERONIANUM +TYRANNICIDE AND DRAMA <1987
 11 UL:ARCHIVUM EURASIAE MEDII AEVI <LISS
 12 UL:ARCHIVUM HISTOLOGICUM JAPONICUM NIPPON SOSHIKIGAKU KIROKU <NIIG
 13 UL:ARCHIVUM HISTORIAE PONTIFICIAE <ROMA
 14 UL:ARCHIVUM HISTORICUM SOCIETATIS IESU <ROMA
 15 UL:ARCHIVUM LATINATATIS MEDII AEVI +BULLETIN DU CANGE ARCHIVUM LATINA <BRUX
 16 UL:ARCHIVUM MATHEMATICUM SPISY PRIRODOVEDECKE FAKULTY UNIVERSITY J <BRNO
 17 UL:ARCHIVUM MUSICUM +TOCCATE E PARTITE DINTAVOLATURA LIBRO 20 <1980
 18 UL:ARCHIVUM MUSICUM ART DE LA FLUTE TRAVERSIERE +CONCERTOS NO 1 12 <1984
 19 UL:ARCHIVUM MUSICUM ART DE LA FLUTE TRAVERSIERE +CONCERTOS OP 37 <1986
 20 UL:ARCHIVUM MUSICUM ART DE LA FLUTE TRAVERSIERE +CONCERTS <1980
 21 UL:ARCHIVUM MUSICUM ART DE LA FLUTE TRAVERSIERE +LIVRE DE PIECES 1ER <1980
```

```
LTUL
                                               NOTIS INDEX SEARCH       TKJO
AUTHOR/TITLE INDEX -- 63 ENTRIES FOUND, 43 - 63 DISPLAYED
43 UL:ARCHIVUM MUSICUM CANTATA BAROCCA +CANTATAS <1980
44 UL:ARCHIVUM MUSICUM CANTATA BAROCCA +CANTATAS BOOK 3 <1983
45 UL:ARCHIVUM MUSICUM CANTATA BAROCCA +CONCERTI ECCLESIASTICI A 1 2 3 4 <1986
46 UL:ARCHIVUM MUSICUM COLLANA DI TESTI RARI +CANZONI FANTASIE ET CORREN <1980
47 UL:ARCHIVUM MUSICUM COLLANA DI TESTI RARI +CAPRICCI IN MUSICA A TRE V <1979
48 UL:ARCHIVUM MUSICUM COLLANA DI TESTI RARI +DIVERSI GENERI DI SONATE L <1979
49 UL:ARCHIVUM MUSICUM COLLANA DI TESTI RARI +DOLCIMELO <1979
50 UL:ARCHIVUM MUSICUM COLLANA DI TESTI RARI +INTAVOLATURA DE LEUTO <1979
51 UL:ARCHIVUM MUSICUM COLLANA DI TESTI RARI +INTAVOLATURA DI LIUTO ATTI <1979
52 UL:ARCHIVUM MUSICUM COLLANA DI TESTI RARI +TOCCATE DINTAVOLATURA DORG <1981
53 UL:ARCHIVUM MUSICUM COLLANA DI TESTI RARI +VILLANELLE LIBRO 1 4 <1982
54 UL:ARCHIVUM MUSICUM COLLANA DI TESTI RARI +WORKS <1981
55 UL:ARCHIVUM MUSICUM COLLANA DI TESTI RARI CANTATA BAROCCA <1980
56 UL:ARCHIVUM MUSICUM COLLANA DI TESTI RARI LART DE LA FLUTE TRAVERSI <1980
57 UL:ARCHIVUM MUSICUM COLLANA DI TESTI RARI STRUMENTALISMO ITALIANO N <1980
58 UL:ARCHIVUM MUSICUM LART DE LA FLUTE TRAVERSIERE +ARCHIVUM MUSICUM CO <1980
59 UL:ARCHIVUM MUSICUM STRUMENTALISMO ITALIANO NEL RI +ARCHIVUM MUSICUM <1980
60 UL:ARCHIVUM PHILOSOPHICUM ALOISIANUM +SANCTI THOMAE AQUINATIS HYMNORU <1951
61 UL:ARCHIVUM REVISTA DE LA FACULTAD DE FILOSOFIA Y LETRAS DE LA UNIV <OVIE
62 UL:ARCHIVUM SPECIAL VOLUME
63 UL:ARCHIVUM SPECIAL VOLUME +ACTES DE LA SECONDE CONFERENCE DES ARCHIV <1980
```

SERIAL PROBLEMS

One of the biggest concerns regarding the display of serial records in the OASIS opac stems from the fact that serial records are frequently long and complex. It is not unusual for bibliographic records to contain long histories of title changes, frequency variations, numbering peculiarities, spine titles, variations in issuing body, etc. Such complex bibliographic descriptions may extend onto many screens, forcing the holdings information that follows to be almost embarrassingly far removed from the first screen of the record.

In an attempt to minimize the long record problem, the decision was made at Iowa to suppress display of field 510 (Citation/References note) from the opac. In Example 7 the cataloging for "Journal of macromolecular science. Reviews in macromolecular chemistry and physics." contains nine 510 fields but, because these nine notes are suppressed from display in the opac, the entire record can be displayed on one opac screen (see Example 8).

In the current version of NOTIS software (release 4.6) an additional complication interacts with the long record problem to further frustrate the impatient opac user who wants to quickly get to current holdings information or circulation information; that is the display of current holdings and circulation information following the display of all other holdings information. With release 5.0 of the software, this display order will be flipped and current holdings and circulation information will display preceding the display of all other holdings information.

The opac display of holdings information for our first copy of "Life" illustrates this point (see Example 9). The bibliographic description displays on the first screen of the opac record, followed by a screen displaying location, call number, miscellaneous notes to the public and partial holdings of bound volumes. The third opac screen continues the display of bound volumes and their supplements. Finally, at the bottom of the third screen, the user encounters the first information relevant to current issues. This information spills over onto the fourth screen and is followed by a list of items charged out or not in their permanent location.

THE OPAC AND SERIALS PUBLIC SERVICE

Serials-specific public service is provided at a serials information window, located at one end of the serials area and manned by Library Assistants during the day and by students evenings and week-ends. At

EXAMPLE 7. MARC record for "Journal of macromolecular science. Reviews in macromolecular chemistry and physics."

```
LTUL MORE                                                    ADC4294
                                              NOTIS CATALOGING          TKJO
UL# ADC4294 FMT S RT a BL s DT 06/23/88 R/DT 02/18/91 STAT mc E/L   DCF a D/S D
SRC d PLACE nyu LANG eng MOD    OA    REPRO    S/STAT c DT/1 1982 DT/2 9999
CONT        S/T p FREQ t REG r MED    GOVT    TPA u IA u CIA u ISDS    CONF 0 SLE 0

010:   : .a sn 83000257
022/1:0 : .a 0736-6574
030/1:   : .a JMSPDH
035/1:   : .a (CStRLIN)IAUG835715
035/2:   : .a (CaOTULAS)159383223
040:   : .a NSDP .d IaU
042:   : .a nsdp
210/1:0 : .a J. macromol. sci., Rev. macromol. chem. phys.
222/1:00: .a Journal of macromolecular science. Reviews in macromolecular
chemistry and physics
245:00: .a Journal of macromolecular science. .p Reviews in macromolecular
chemistry and physics.
246/1:00: .a Reviews in macromolecular chemistry and physics
260:00: .a New York : .b M. Dekker, .c <1982-
300/1:   : .a v. : .b ill. ; .c 23 cm.
362/1:0 : .a Vol. C22, no. 1 (1982/83)-
```

EXAMPLE 7. (continued)

```
LTUL DONE                                                ADC4294
                                          NOTIS CATALOGING        TKJO

 510/1:0 : .a Chemical abstracts .x 0009-2258
 510/2:0 : .a Current contents/physical and chemical sciences
 510/3:0 : .a Engineering index
 510/4:0 : .a Index to scientific reviews
 510/5:0 : .a International bibliography of book reviews.
 510/6:0 : .a International bibliography of periodical literature
 510/7:0 : .a Journal of abstracts of the All-Union Institute of Scientific and
Technical Information of the USSR
 510/8:0 : .a Physikalische Berichte
 510/9:0 : .a Science citation index
 650/1: 0: .a Polymers .x Periodicals.
 780/1:00: .t Journal of macromolecular science.  Reviews in macromolecular
chemistry, .x 0022-2356
 998:  : .a 07/08/83 .t c .s 9110 .n IaU .w NJPG8354754 .d 07/08/83 .c CL  .b
TRE .i 830708 .l IAUG
```

EXAMPLE 8. OASIS opac display for "Journal of macromolecular science. Reviews in macromolecular chemistry and physics."

```
  OASIS search request:  T=JOURNAL OF MACROMOLECULAR SCIENCE
BIBLIOGRAPHIC RECORD -- NO. 5 OF 5 ENTRIES FOUND

Journal of macromolecular science. Reviews in macromolecular chemistry and
  physics. -- Vol. C22, no. 1 (1982/83)-    . -- New York : M. Dekker, <1982-
  v. : ill. ; 23 cm.
  Three times a year.
  Continues: Journal of macromolecular science.  Reviews in macromolecular
chemistry, ISSN 0022-2356
 SUBJECT HEADINGS (Library of Congress; use s= ):
     Polymers--Periodicals.

Location: CHEMISTRY
Call number:  No call number.
Library has a current subscription/order
Library has:
  v.C22 (1982/1983)-v.C27 (1986/1987)
  v.C28 (1988)-v.C29 (1989)


Type i to return to index.
Type e to start over.      Type h for help.
Type command and press Return==>
```

EXAMPLE 9. OASIS opac display for "Life."

```
  OASIS search request:   T=LIFE
BIBLIOGRAPHIC RECORD -- NO. 1 OF 3337 ENTRIES FOUND

Life. -- v. 1-73, Nov. 23, 1936-Dec. 29, 1972; <new ser.> v. 1-   Oct. 1978- --
  Chicago, Ill., Time Inc.
  v. ill. (part col.) ports. 33-36 cm.
  Monthly, 1978-
  Weekly, 1936-1972
  Title from cover.
  Some errors in numbering.
  Indexes: Vols. 7-32 (July 1939-June 1952).  1 v.



          CONTINUED ON NEXT SCREEN:  press Return key
```

```
Type n for next record.   Type i to return to index. Type g to return to guide.
Type e to start over.      Type h for help.
Type command and press Return==>

  OASIS search request:  T=LIFE
BIBLIOGRAPHIC RECORD -- NO. 1 OF 3337 ENTRIES FOUND  (CONTINUED)

Life ...   (CONTINUED)

Location: MAIN
Call number:  No call number.
Latest issue in Browsing Room
Current issues in Periodicals Reading Room
Library has a current subscription/order
Library has:
  v.2-3 (1937),v.4 (1938) inc.,v.5 (1938),
  v.6 (1939) inc.,v.7 (1939)-v.22 (1947),
  v.23 (1947) inc.,v.24 (1948)-v.37 (1954),
  v.38 (1955) inc.,v.39 (1955)-v.51 (1961),
  v.54 (1963),v.55 (1963) inc.,v.56 (1964)-
  v.67 (1969) inc.,v.68 (1970),v.69 (1970) inc.,
  v.70 (1971)-v.73 (1972)
  n.s.:v.1 (1978)-n.s. v.3 (1980) inc.,
                     CONTINUED ON NEXT SCREEN:  press Return key
```

EXAMPLE 9. (continued)

```
Type n for next record.    Type i to return to index. Type g to return to guide.
Type e to start over.       Type h for help.
Type command and press Return==>

  OASIS search request:   T=LIFE
BIBLIOGRAPHIC RECORD -- NO. 1 OF 3337 ENTRIES FOUND  (CONTINUED)

Life ...   (CONTINUED)

Location: MAIN
Call number:  No call number.
Library has:    (CONTINUED)
  n.s.:v.4 (1981)-n.s.:v.12 (1989)
  n.s.:v.13 (1990)

      SUPPLEMENTS:
  n.s.:v.7:spec. issue (1984)
  n.s.:v.8:spec. issue (1985)
  n.s.:v.9:anniv. issue (1986)
  CURRENT ISSUES/VOLUMES:
    v.14:no.1 (1991:Jan.)
    v.14:no.2 (1991:Feb.)
    v.14:no.3 (1991:Mar.)
                    CONTINUED ON NEXT SCREEN:  press Return key
```

```
Type n for next record.   Type i to return to index. Type g to return to guide.
Type e to start over.      Type h for help.
Type command and press Return==>

  OASIS search request:  T=LIFE
BIBLIOGRAPHIC RECORD -- NO. 1 OF 3337 ENTRIES FOUND  (CONTINUED)

Life ...   (CONTINUED)

Location: MAIN
Call number:  No call number.
ITEMS CHARGED OUT OR NOT IN ABOVE LOCATION:
   Item:  v.5 July-Dec. 1982 (incomplete)
      temporary location: MAIN Bind Hold
```

one time, public access to serial holdings was only available via the serials information window because the serials catalog and kardex, where all serial holdings were recorded on paper check-in cards, were housed in a non-public area. Although users still rely on serials information staff to supply holdings for serials which have not yet undergone retrospective conversion, the great majority of serial holdings information is now in machine-readable form and readily available to users of the OASIS database.

In addition to supplying manual holdings information to users, staff at the serials information window help patrons interpret serial cataloging records. The presence of both latest title cataloging and successive title cataloging in the opac, for example, can confuse patrons. Patrons may be confused by the filing of acronyms; in the opac they are treated as words, yet the shelving rules applied to our unclassified periodicals treat them as initialisms and we have neither the staff nor the space to correct this inconsistency.

Another conflict between entries as presented in the opac and actual shelving in our alphabetically arranged unclassified periodicals collection arises from the Utlas authority processing we had done. As I indicated, during authority processing headings in bibliographic records that matched old forms of headings in authority records were "flipped" to current forms. When these headings occurred as main entries in cataloging records for unclassified serials the result was that the heading in the opac no longer matched the entry under which the serial was shelved. Relabeling and reshelving the pieces under the new entry simply wasn't practical in most cases, so we have temporarily solved the problem by adding "Shelved as: . . ." notes to the appropriate holdings records.

SERIALS MAINTENANCE

One of the first lessons a serials cataloger learns is that the only constant associated with serials is change! It is not easy to keep serial entries current in the face of title changes, and numbering quirks and recataloging are an ongoing fact of life with serials. Because the full recataloging process associated with major changes can be slow, personnel in serials often make "interim" changes to the OASIS record as soon as the need to recatalog is identified; such changes provide pertinent information in the opac until full recataloging can be done.

In the case of a title change, for example, an "interim" 785 field might be added to the existing serial record to direct the user to cataloging for the new title. The fact that this field was not added by a cataloger would be noted in a NOTIS-defined field (field 940) to remind the cataloger to review this work at the time of full recataloging. Cataloging for the new title would be located on RLIN and passed into OASIS using GTO, or a provisional OASIS record would be created from scratch; this record would display in the opac as "In process" until the cataloger was able to finish the recataloging process.

WILSON INDEXES AND SERIAL HOLDINGS

In addition to the Online Public Access Catalog, we also make several H. W. Wilson indexes available to the public using NOTIS's Multiple Database Access System (MDAS). In the latest release of MDAS software, installed at Iowa in March 1991, the ISSN is used to create a link between citations to serials in the Wilson indexes and our holdings for these serials. In anticipation of availability of this new feature, Wilson provided us with lists of journals included in the pertinent Wilson indexes and their ISSNs. Using this information, we added ISSNs when they were lacking in our serial records and cleaned up any other ISSN problems identified by review of the lists. This "hook to holdings" has made it possible for users to view our local serial holdings while working in the Wilson database, thus avoiding the awkward process of exiting from WILS, accessing the opac and keying in an opac search for the desired serial title.

CONCLUSION

Due to their ongoing nature and their complexity, serials present unique problems in the online public access catalog. However, by combining the ability to customize the NOTIS software with a little "creativity," we have been able to find solutions to many of these problems and provide enhanced access to serials in the opac.

Sex, Lies, and Newspapers: *The Newspaper Cataloging and Union Listing Manual*

Todd Butler

SUMMARY. Three characteristics describe the bibliographic activities of the United States Newspaper Program (USNP). Participants catalog and inventory all newspapers published and held in the United States and its territories. The Program is primarily a retrospective cataloging and union list project. Newspaper files are incomplete and are scattered across the country. Defined by these characteristics, the Program has limited funds and a limited time in which to catalog and inventory the nation's newspapers. The *Newspaper Cataloging and Union Listing Manual*, the third such manual published for the United States Newspaper Program, attempts to facilitate the work of state newspaper projects characterized by the challenges of conducting a comprehensive inventory, the opportunity afforded by retrospective cataloging and union listing, and the mysteries of cataloging less-than-full runs. This article contains no information about sex. Judgement on truth is the prerogative of the reader.

Three characteristics describe the bibliographic activities of the United States Newspaper Program (USNP). The first characteristic is its comprehensiveness. Catalogers will seek out and examine any and all newspa-

---

Todd Butler formerly worked at the Library of Congress, Serial Record Division, as CONSER/USNP Specialist, where he prepared the *Newspaper Cataloging and Union Listing Manual*. Mr. Butler would like to acknowledge all participants of the United States Newspaper Program, who after five years, finally taught him how to catalog and union list newspapers, and to thank all the citizens of the United States of America and its territories, who paid his salary and allowed him to have a lot of fun and work with a lot of great folks.

Mr. Butler currently resides at 3688 Settlers Road, Dublin, OH, 43017.

pers as long as that newspaper is published and stored in the United States. The USNP motto is: "Have workforms, will travel."[1] It matters not whether the newspaper is currently published or ceased three centuries ago; whether its pages are still the buff color and soft texture of cotton or linen rag of the eighteenth century or the yellowed, broken leaves of the last decade; whether the issues are stored in a cool, dry vault or in a warm, damp bathroom; or, whether it is reproduced using the best techniques of preservation microfilming or by the hobbyist who gladly displays his own 35mm camera negatives.

The USNP is also a retrospective cataloging and union listing project. It is not a retrospective conversion project. Catalogers do not simply convert other peoples' records, whether they are AACR, ALA, latest or successive entry. Nor do they simply accept other peoples' inventories. They examine the actual issues, regardless of their condition, their storage, or their format. Only after dirtying their hands or straining their eyes do they then catalog the titles and inventory the issues.

Rarely does one find in the field a complete run of a newspaper. Much of the work includes collecting scattered issues in order to recreate the whole. After the cataloger collects and assembles the issues, he or she often finds that more is missing than collected. The all important first issue did not survive. Gaps in the run are common, during which time the paper changed its title. Non-extant titles are common. The less frequently published triweekly editions, mailed to the more rural areas, now exist only in bits and pieces, if at all.

These three characteristics–comprehensive inventory, retrospective cataloging, and the ubiquitous missing issues–stretch the limits of any cataloging code or union listing standard. Cataloging codes and union list standards do not provide the instruction necessary to inventory and describe the scattered remains from three hundred years of newspaper printing and publishing.

To establish bibliographic standards and procedures for a national program, the Council on Library Resources initiated a planning and documentation process that resulted in the publication of the *Newspaper Cataloging Manual*[2] in 1981. Prepared by Elaine W. Woods and patterned after CONSER's *MARC Serial Editing Guide*,[3] the *Manual* provided guidelines for tagging and inputting MARC records into the CONSER database via the facilities of OCLC, Inc. Although the *Manual* provides some cataloging instructions specifically for newspapers, it was primarily an editing guide.

In August 1982, the National Endowment for the Humanities awarded grants to six national newspaper repositories whose mission was to build a core database of approximately 35,000 titles describing newspapers from all fifty states. The collective experience of these projects resulted in a revision of Elaine Woods' *Manual.* Prepared by Robert Harriman and published by the Library of Congress in 1985, the CONSER/USNP edition of the *Newspaper Cataloging Manual*[4] combined an editing guide with a cataloging manual that used the *Anglo-American Cataloguing Rules,*[5] second edition, as a model. The new *Manual* provided specific instructions for cataloging newspapers and incorporated the suggestions of the initial repository projects. In anticipation of the next phase of the Program, which would include projects in all states and territories, the *Manual* predicted the need for further refinement of the rules and procedures.

The *Newspaper Cataloging and Union Listing Manual* represents that further refinement. It incorporates the changes and additions suggested by thirty-one state and territorial projects. The *Manual* provides an editing guide patterned after the *CONSER Editing Guide.*[6] It incorporates the union list guidelines, developed in 1983 by the six initial repositories, the Library of Congress, and OCLC, for recording the holdings of newspaper repositories in OCLC's Union List Subsystem. It also provides guidelines for union list maintenance. The cataloging portion of the manual consists of two sections, each with fully tagged examples: description and access and record set and access. The former describes individual titles and provides access to those titles. The latter pieces those titles together into a set of successive records and records for varying frequency editions.

The *Newspaper Cataloging and Union List Manual* attempts to facilitate the work of state newspaper projects characterized by the challenges of conducting a comprehensive inventory, the opportunity afforded by retrospective cataloging and union listing, and the mysteries of cataloging less-than-full runs. The *Manual*'s success or failure as a cataloging and union list guide depends upon its ability to accurately reflect and to successfully facilitate the work of state newspaper projects.

For participants of the USNP, much of the initial work includes searching out the parts that make up the newspaper and piecing together those parts. Newspapers change title, frequency, and publishers. They merge, split and procreate various editions. Repositories store them in various and sundry places within any one building and in various and sundry buildings sometimes located miles apart. One finds them loose, bound, in portfolios, filmed on reels, and reduced to fiche. The cataloger searches out the issues: whatever they are called, wherever they are stored, however they are stored, and regardless of who owns them. The cataloger then puts together the issues and recreates the whole.

The whole is called a bibliographic record set. The set may contain a newspaper with many titles that have changed over the centuries. The set may also contain several different frequency editions–a daily, a triweekly, and a weekly–all with different titles. On the other hand, the set may also consist of one: one title, possible with only one surviving issue.

Having recreated the whole, the cataloger again returns to the parts, the individual titles, to describe them and to provide access. This is bibliographic description: transcribe the titles, the numeric and chronological designations, and the imprints; provide the frequencies, a brief physical description, and any necessary bibliographic notes. Having described the parts, one then provides access to them. Points of access include title and places of publication, and if necessary, subject access and uniform title headings.

The cataloger now focuses on the individual issues. It is not uncommon to have only one extant issue. One reports it according to the ANSI Standard Z39.42, *Serial Holdings Statements at the Summary Level*,[7] as modified by USNP guidelines. If the newspaper published dutifully a daily for over one hundred years, along with a weekly and a tri- or semiweekly, one reports those issues, all 52,000 of them, according to ANSI Z39.42.

Having described the individual titles and provided access to the records describing those titles, and having inventoried one issue or thousands, the cataloger links the records together according to the practice of successive entry. The cataloger supplies the horizontal links (i.e., other editions available), as well as vertical links (i.e., preceding and succeeding entries). Sets pieced together in this manner have exceeded thirty bibliographic records based on thousands of issues.

This process may take years to complete. The cataloger assembles bits and pieces and inputs the catalog and union list records into OCLC. Over time, the cataloger finds more bits and pieces, modifies the description, enhances the OCLC catalog record, and edits the union list record. Acquiring additional issues, the cataloger establishes or changes the linking entry fields among titles, again enhances the OCLC catalog record, and again updates the union list record. This is a piecemeal process, one which reaches completion only when the cataloger finds all extant issues, or when the grant funds run out.

This limit in grant funding also characterizes the United States Newspaper Program. Grant funds do not last forever. Catalogers do not have the luxury of time to describe, inventory, and provide access to the nation's newspapers. This limit has directed and shaped newspaper cataloging. Because of the size and complexity of the Program, and because of the limit in resources, the Program has made its bibliographic choices. The instruction in the *Manual* reflect those choices.

One choice is to simplify bibliographic description. Newspaper catalogers provide only the information needed to identify a newspaper and to distinguish one newspaper from another. The descriptive model most closely resembles the first level of AACR2 description and fills only a few of the many slots offered by the *USMARC Format for Bibliographic Description.*[8]

To describe bibliographically a newspaper, one begins at the beginning, which begins at the top of the first page. There one finds the masthead, and within that chief source of information, one finds the title. There also one finds the first challenge of description.

The masthead is a marketing device, not a bibliographic one. The masthead is not analogous to the title page of a book, which has the purpose of identifying the book. Newspapers use mastheads to sell newspapers. The masthead is analogous to the dust jacket or book cover. With an emphasis on eye-appeal, those mastheads include fancy layouts and logos, trademarks, or other graphic devices with a few words scattered about. Those few, scattered words are the title, and they cause descriptive problems.

When the publisher of Russellville, Arkansas newspaper places the word "Weekly" above a finely crafted graphic device, and places the works "National" and "Tribune" on either side of the device, how does the cataloger "Transcribe the title exactly as to wording, order, and spelling . . ."?[9] Is the paper called *Weekly National Tribune, National Weekly Tribune,* or simply *National Tribune,* with the word "Weekly" a statement of frequency? The staff of the Arkansas Newspaper Project cannot call the publisher. He has been dead for a hundred years.

Those of us who once lay awake at night worrying about such significant topics quickly learned the value of descriptive simplification. Not only did we learn the value, we made it an asset. The *Manual* presents a simple rule for transcribing the title: "Transcribe the title of the newspaper." None of this exactly-as-to-wording order-or-spelling stuff. If it gets real difficult, as with the *Weekly National Tribune* (or, is it the *National Weekly Tribune*?), then don't worry. Be happy! Look to other areas in the issue, such as the publisher's statement or the running title, to suggest wording or order. Then write something in field 245 and the alternatives in one or more 246 fields. If necessary, provide an explanation of the title transcription in field 500: "The word 'weekly' appears above the masthead ornament."

The *Manual* encourages an equally simple treatment of other descriptive elements. Catalogers will note that the dates of publication, which usually includes the years of publication, are optional information for the imprint area of the description. Newspapers are issued frequently. By definition, they appear usually at least once a week, if not more frequently. Transcribing the years of publication does not describe a frequently issued publication.

A more descriptive area, the numerical and chronological designation, provides a better place for the dates of publication. The cataloger can include the month and day as well as the year. Within the area of the designation, in field 362, one may give the known dates, even if the issues themselves are not held. If the dates of publication are uncertain, the cataloger can even supply conjecture.

The guidelines for recording numerical and chronological designation represents a compromise between simplification and perceived need. Few patrons ask to see issue number 28,399 of *The Washington Post.* Most take a more sensible approach and request the issue for March 18, 1954. However, the USNP follows not the approach of the common man (or woman) but adheres to the national standards and records the numeric designation even though experience instructs that historically typesetters are sometimes a hard drinking lot who cannot count. On the other hand, the numeric designation fulfills an important need. Newspapers change titles frequently, and the issues of change often do not survive. The only way to identify and to describe successive titles with missing issues is to transcribe the numbering in each record. By counting and recording the numbering, the cataloger and user can follow the chain of successive records.

The *Manual* provides instructions about how to record designation if one holds the issues, which are the first and last issue of that particular title, from which the designation is transcribed. The *Manual* also explains how to record designation if one does not hold the requisite issues, which is often the case. Illustrations distinguish between formatted fields and unformatted fields, explain the use of conjecture, and the use of blank spaces. The *Manual* also instructs one not to record the designation if one has absolutely no idea of when the newspaper began or ceased, which is also often the case.

Simplification is applied towards alternative numbering. Assuming one holds a complete run, one need only record the alternative numbering if it appears for the entire run and if it appears as prominently as the first designation. For example, when two newspapers merge to form one, the new title may carry both designations. Fortunately, someone at the newspaper soon tires of this exercise, or more likely loses count, and drops one designation. The remaining is dutifully recorded in the bibliographic description as the sole designation.

Newspapers also change their numeric designations. Catalogers record all changes, even the ludicrous. (My favorite example is a Maryland newspaper that changed its numbering from volume 111 to volume III, which is transcribed as "-v. 111; v. 3-"). With some newspapers, the issues that provide the change in numeric designation did not survive. Because of these gaps, the record has gaps in the area of numeric description. The *Manual* provides instructions for leaping these gaps.

Catalogers will also note that most elements of the physical description are optional. The *Manual* requires the "v." because most local systems require USMARC field 300 in a serial record. The *Manual* fulfills that requirement. All other elements of the 300 field are optional. Catalogers need not count volumes, whether physical or bibliographic. Catalogers may omit any mention of illustrations. The notation "ill." or "ill. (chiefly advertisement)" provides no meaningful bibliographic information. Nor is size required. If one finds scattered issues of hardcopy in one repository and records the size, then later finds a few holdings of a different size elsewhere, one must then modify the bibliographic record. If another project later finds a few issues of a different size, then they modify the record. Continue *ad infinitum*. Afterward, collect all the issues, film them, and trash the hardcopy. (This author will take to his grave the memory of an outraged state librarian who exclaimed that "Those people are downstairs measuring those newspapers! Why?")

The *Manual* does not, however, instruct one to toss the baby with the bath. It goes to what at times appears to be great lengths to record significant descriptive information. Place of publication is significant. If it changes during the life of the newspaper, catalogers record subsequent places of publication. Fortunately, most newspapers are published locally for a local audience, and they rarely move from that locality–unless their publishers are pursued by invading armies. In retreat from the Grand Army of the Republic during the Civil War, a few southern publishers loaded their presses on railroad flatcars and published in a different town each week.

Frequency is important, and unfortunately, frequency changes more often. After place of publication, frequency is perhaps the second most descriptive element. ("Excuse me, sir, but is that the daily, triweekly, or weekly *Sandusky Register*?" asks the librarian of the patron.) The *Manual* advises catalogers to record all known frequencies and the dates of those frequencies. This is no mean feat if the newspaper has published 10,000 issues.

Bibliographic notes are kept to a minimum. Notes are added only if they explain an item of the description which cannot be explained, because of limitation of the code or the format, in the designated areas. Notes accompany statements of title and edition. They provide information about additional places of publication. They may explain complexities in designation. Language notes are added for all non-English language newspapers, including multilingual papers whether or not English is one of the languages. Catalogers also provide language codes for online and offline access.

Newspaper access represents a tug of war between traditional methods of newspaper access, which rely upon place of publication and key words from the title, and the title driven necessities of AACR2. Although the USNP goes to great lengths to record title as a part of our bibliographic description, title access historically is of little importance. Newspapers are not stored by title. Newspapers guides do not arrange by title. One rarely requests a newspaper by its title. Many patrons do not know the title of the newspaper they want.

Place of publication, however, is important. Steve Gutgesell arranged his *Guide to Ohio Newspapers, 1793-1973*[10] by place of publication. Next door, John Miller arranged his *Indiana Newspaper Bibliography*[11] by place of publication. At the Library of Congress, the first line on the request slip queries the patron for place of publication. The newspaper stacks in the Library's Newspaper and Periodical Reading Room are arranged by place of publication. When you are researching your rather famous or infamous family history, you want the birth announcements, marriage announcements, and obituaries of your grandparents' hometown newspaper. What are the titles of those hometown newspapers? (Unlike today's hometown, yesterday's hometown probably had several newspapers, which means the plural "titles.") You don't know, do you? You do know, however, where your folks lived, which is the place of publication.

The USNP uses MARC field 752 to provide access to place of publication. Originally defined for newspapers to contain a hierarchical form of geographic access for place of publication, the field is now valid for all formats, except computer files, ". . . to give access to a bibliographic record through a hierarchical form of a place name related to a particular attribute."[12] For newspapers, this simply allows the cataloger to use the field to provide access to the community served if it differs from the place of publication.

The goal of geographic access is to list together all newspapers published in and for a geographic community. For many communities, the surviving newspaper represents the most accessible, if not the only surviving, written record for that community. Some communities, such as western mining towns, did not survive, yet their events are chronicled in the newspapers that did.

Newspapers use the following hierarchy of geographic names: Country, state, county, and city. The *Manual* provides instructions for a host of complications that arise from a seemingly simple form of access. For example, the term "United States" is used even if the newspaper was published in an area outside of the United States and that area was subsequently included within the current boundaries, including territories. Consequently, newspapers published in Christiansted, Danish West Indies prior to 1917 are grouped together under the heading "United States–Virgin Islands–Saint Croix–Christiansted."

The USNP also provides subject access because not all newspapers are general interest newspapers published for a particular city, county, or state. *The Armenian Mirror-Spectator*, for example, publishes for all Armenians living in all the Americas. The primary audience is ethnic, not geographic. Subject access brings together in one list, either by arrangement or index, all newspapers published for or by a particular ethnic or national group. For some ethnic communities, their newspapers represent the most accessible, if not the only surviving, written record. Other ethnic communities have been totally assimilated or dispersed, and their newspapers provided a history of that community.

To provide ethnic access, the Subject Cataloging Division of the Library of Congress adopted the recommendations of the USNP for form of access. Because the Library did not classify its newspaper collection, the Library did not use the term "Newspaper" as a free-floating subdivision. The term previously used, "Periodicals," is a superordinate term and provides a less precise subdivision.

Using "Newspaper" as a free-floating subdivision, the Library adopted the following model of subject access: "Ethnic or national group–Geographic subdivision–Newspapers"; for example, "Armenians–United States–Newspapers." This form indicates that the heading describes a newspaper. Works about a newspaper use the form "Ethnic newspaper–Geographic Subdivision"; for example, "Armenian newspapers–United States." This heading identifies a book about Armenian newspapers published in the United States. For the same reason, and for the additional reason that it provides no meaningful access to a file which already numbers 100,000 bibliographic records, the USNP does not use the heading "American newspapers."

The *Manual* takes its list of headings for ethnic and national groups from the *Library of Congress Subject Headings.*[13] In order to compile this list, USNP staff at LC used *The Harvard Encyclopedia of American Ethnic Groups*[14] and a 1985 OCLC offline product consisting of 55,000 records to identify those groups who had or were likely to have published at least one newspaper in the United States.

This list does vary from Library policy in one category. With few exceptions, and those are Afro-Americans, French-Canadians, and Russian Germans, the Program does not use hyphenated or compound names to label a group. For the *Deutsche Zeitung* published in Charleston, South Carolina, the heading used is "Germans," not "German-Americans."

Having described the newspaper and having provided access to the records describing those titles, the cataloger now returns to the whole. To describe the whole, the *Manual* introduces the bibliographic record set, which is a group of related bibliographic records. The set may consist of records for successive titles and/or concurrently published frequency editions.

Newspapers, like periodicals and other serials, change their titles. AACR2, like its predecessor, uses the concept of successive entry to describe these changes. If the title of a newspaper changes, the cataloger enters a separate bibliographic record describing the new title. The cataloger then links the records of the older and newer titles with the appropriate linking entry fields.

The *Sandusky Register* illustrates the use of successive entry in newspaper cataloging. The currently published daily newspaper began in 1848 with the title *The Daily Sanduskian.* In 1851, only three years later, the newspaper changed its title to the *Daily Commercial Register*. Because a narrative quickly bores even a newspaper cataloger, these changes are better described with an outline:

The daily Sanduskian,	1848-1851
Daily commercial register,	1851-1867
Sandusky daily register,	1867-1894
Sandusky register,	1894-1897
Sandusky daily register,	1897-1910
The Sandusky register,	1910-1941
The Sandusky register star-news,	1941-1957
Sandusky register,	1957-

The *Register* also published a weekly and a triweekly edition. The weekly changed titles five times; the triweekly, three:

Sandusky weekly register
1851-18uu
Weekly Sandusky register
18uu-1876
Sandusky weekly register
1867-1894
Sandusky register
1894-1897
Sandusky weekly register
1897-1914

Sandusky triweekly register
1861-186u
Tri-weekly commercial register
186u-18uu
Sandusky tri-weekly register
18uu-1907

Successive entry cataloging does not provide this overview of the newspaper. It requires eight separate records for the daily, five separate records for the weekly, and three separate records for the triweekly. To correctly describe the *Register*, one must catalog and input sixteen records. If a goal of our profession is to bring similar items together in the catalog, then successive entry hampers that goal.

At best, the practice of successive entry cataloging provides the user with directions to the next record. The linking entry fields provide those directions. The linking entry field is the glue that holds the record set together, if not physically, then at least conceptually. The directions given include the title or the uniform title heading. The directions point to the next preceding record, the next succeeding record, and concurrently published editions. Those directions take one only to the next record. Once there, another linking entry field takes one to the next record.

It matters not whether the catalog is online, card, or book, each user bears the burden of piecing together the whole. If the user begins with the most current edition of the *Sandusky Register* and works backward, he must retrieve eight bibliographic records before obtaining the complete description of the daily edition of this newspaper. Somewhere in this journey, he will discover the two concurrently published frequency editions. He must retrieve eight more bibliographic records. Having retrieved sixteen records, the user now has the record set. With successive entry cataloging, each new user must piece together anew the record set.

Unfortunately, uniform title headings offer no assistance to the user. According to AACR2, "A uniform title provides the means for bringing together all catalogue entries for a work when various manifestations of it have appeared under various titles."[15] If this were the case, then one could assign one uniform title to all sixteen records of the *Register* and bring the record together under one heading.

As with serials, the uniform title heading does not bring together but instead separates. It is a unique title entry. The guidelines for uniform title headings for serials are from the *Library of Congress Rule Interpretations*[16] rule 25.5B. Headings are created when the title of a newspaper is identical to the title of another serial. Consequently, the uniform title heading is a unique title entry, designed to separate records, not to bring them together.

The use of successive entry cataloging has other practical limitations. The cataloging of newspaper indexes offers one illustration. How does one provide access to a separately published index of the *Register*? The title of the item indexed provides one form of access. However, the *Register* has sixteen titles. To provide title access, the catalog record for the index must contain sixteen title added entry fields. Because many of those titles are the same, then the added entry field must contain the uniform title headings taken from the bibliographic records for the newspaper. Each uniform title heading, in turn, requires a uniform title heading authority record.

The piecing together of a record set assumes, of course, that enough of the issues have survived for the cataloger to describe the set. One of the advantages of a retrospective cataloging project is that most of the titles have ceased. If enough issues survived, the cataloger can piece together the set.

One of the disadvantages of newspaper cataloging is that for many newspapers not enough issues survived to describe the set. For example, only thirty issues among the three triweekly editions have survived. We do not know when any of these titles began or ceased. We do not know with certainty whether they are correctly linked or whether intervening titles exist. One option is not to link and leave gaps in the set. However, if gaps exist in the set, then the cataloger cannot provide directions to the next record in the set, and the patron cannot piece the set together. The other option is to link without any measure of certainty. Because catalogers rarely find a complete run of a newspaper, the question of whether to link or not to link occurs frequently. Definitive cataloging is simply not possible.

Having described the newspaper and having provided access to it, one now must inventory the newspaper by recording the issues held and noting the repository holding those issues. This is union listing. It too is characterized by the challenge of comprehensiveness, the advantages of retrospective inventory, the frustration of missing and scattered issues, and the awareness that the grant clock is ticking. Like newspaper cataloging, which stretches the limits of the cataloging code, newspaper union listing stretches the limits of the union list standards.

One of the most difficult decisions any union list must make is whether to catalog microfilm reproductions as prescribed by AACR2 or to attach all holdings, regardless of format, to the bibliographic description of the hardcopy. The issue does not lend itself to compromise. One either does it one way or the other. In its *Union List: User Manual*,[17] OCLC recommends separate bibliographic records for each format. OCLC's *Manual*, however, permits users to attach holdings of both the original and reprints to the bibliographic record describing the original, paper item. The USNP adopted this latter approach.

The USNP uses what has become known as the master record convention to describe the various physical formats in which newspapers are held. With this simple, pre-multiple version of multiple versions, the bibliographic record identifies and describes the newspaper as it was originally published. Physical formats are described in the holdings records. Those formats include hardcopy, microform, and any eye-readable reprints. The holdings record also identifies the type of microform and the microform generation.

The USNP favor this technique because it cuts cataloging costs and is generally perceived to be more user friendly in both online and offline lists. Project participants input only one catalog record regardless of the number of reproductions held. The patron does not have to wade through a sea of similar-looking bibliographic records to get to the holdings. With the master record convention, the patron can easily identify the format and the microfilm generation.

This master record convention is not without cost, however. Although it works well for union lists, the master record convention performs poorly as a register for microform masters. The holdings record does not allow for a detailed description of the microform because it does not accommodate field 007 or field 533. Neither does it accommodate microform stock numbers (field 037) or source of acquisition (field 265). The OCLC three-character symbol identifies the holder of the printing master if one has a means to interpret that symbol. The best sources for symbol identification include the OCLC online Name-Address Directory, its published *OCLC Participating Institution List Arranged by OCLC Symbol*,[18] or its serial offline products.

Not only is descriptive information lost, but access is also sacrificed. The holdings record has no series added entry fields and does not easily accommodate information describing microform sets or series. Some projects have given this information in a free-text note subfield of the holdings record, but OCLC cannot index this subfield in its Online Union Catalog.

The OCLC holdings records are not as widely distributed as are the bibliographic records. OCLC makes the records available through its Online Union Catalog and its offline products. The Library of Congress, however, does not distribute USNP holdings records through its MARC Distribution Services (MDS). The Library does distribute the bibliographic records, but without the holdings records, and consequently, without format and preservation information. Similarly, OCLC's EPIC Service currently makes available only the bibliographic record and the OCLC three-character institution symbol. The EPIC Service does not contain the holdings records with its format and preservation information.

The holdings record used by the USNP is the OCLC local data record, most commonly called the LDR. The LDR identifies the repository holding the title, identifies a sublocation within that repository, describes the generation and type of microform reproduction, and lists the issues held. The holdings statement is a modification of the standard established by the *American National Standard for Serials Holdings Statements at the Summary Level*, ANSI Z39.42-1980.[19]

Newspaper holdings statements differ from Z39.42 in both style and substance. Z39.42 requires numerical designation when present, but the USNP does not report numerical designation. Program participants only report chronology. Because newspapers contain news on current events, the chronological designation better identifies the issue. Few patrons request newspaper by volume and issue number. Most require newspapers by date or range of dates.

Z39.42 reports holdings only at the highest, most inclusive level of chronological data. For newspapers, as for most serials, the year of publication is the highest, most inclusive level. Unfortunately, the year of publication does not offer the requisite detail for a daily newspaper. The Program reports holdings at a level that includes the year, month, and day. Participants use a numerical form, not a vernacular form. An issue for December 20, 1951 is reported as 1951:12:20.

Nor are holdings reported at a copy-specific level. OCLC's copy-specific field, known as the SCHD field, is used instead as a format-specific field. All copies of the original newsprint held at a specific sublocation are reported in a single, format-specific field. All copies of a microfilm held at a specific sublocation are reported in another format-specific field. Microfiche, if also held, is given in another, and all copies of an eye-readable reprint are given in a fourth format-specific field. Each field contains a free-text local note subfield that provides additional information about completeness, physical condition, retention, location, or restriction on use. If no clarification is needed, no note is input.

Perhaps the most disconcerting aspect of newspaper holdings are the angle brackets, "< >." The angle brackets were adopted in 1983 when NEH, LC, OCLC, and the initial repository projects met to devise a method of reporting widely scattered newspaper holdings. The brackets have evolved into a stylistic device. They group holdings together or separate holdings to improve readability. In most cases, as shown by the example below for a weekly newspaper, the angle brackets, as do the commas, indicate a gap in holdings. However, no gap exists between the first and second set of angle brackets. They simply bring together all issues for 1845 in one set and all issues for 1846 in another.

Cumberland Alleganian (Cumberland, Md. : 1844)

Cumberland Alleganian.

ISSN: CODEN: OCLC no: 12125967 Frequn: w Regulr: r

Hld Lib: TRNP COPY: FM

1 SCHD $d 8809 $g 0 $e 0 $y <1845:8:16-11:8,29, 12:13,27> <1846:1:3, 1:16-7:10> <1847:4:17-1848:6:10> 1848:6:24-1849: 3:10> <1849:3:24-6:30, 7:21, 8:11, 8:25-12:29> <1851:7:5-12:30>

The *Manual* provides no firm guidelines for the consistent application of angle brackets. As a stylistic device, they defy consistent application. Although required, their application varies from project to project and often among staff of the same project. If four different projects own the same service copies of a filmed newspaper, they will group holdings within angle brackets in four different ways. Consequently, a standardized style of reporting is not achieved. The best that can be said of angle brackets is that most project staff, except the terminal operator, gets used to them.

In addition to a format-specific field, the holdings statement provides a composite statement, the SIHD field, of all holdings in all formats. At this level, holdings are reported at the highest, most inclusive level, which is year. Angle brackets and notes are not used. The composite holdings statement actually functions as a combined composite/compressed statement that is manually entered at the terminal.

It is interesting to speculate what impact the widespread implementation of the *USMARC Format for Holdings Data*[20] and the widespread adoption of the *American National Standard for Information Sciences–*

Serials Holdings Statements,[21] ANSI Z39.44- 1986, will have on newspaper holdings statements. Because the holdings statements vary so much from the new standard, one doubts if they lend themselves to machine manipulation. The style of input does not lend itself to either compression or expansion. On the other hand, the statements should present no problems for communication across different systems because the information is carefully and correctly tagged and subfielded.

The implications for the *Newspaper Cataloging and Union Listing Manual* are obvious. The widespread implementation of the new format and the new standard will help render the *Manual* obsolete. A fourth edition will be needed. OCLC's reimplementation of its cataloging subsystem onto the PRISM Service has already dated the screen displays, searching techniques, and suggestions for title added entries. OCLC's reimplementation of its Union List Subsystem onto PRISM, if successful, will prompt further changes.

Other changes await. The specter of multiple versions already haunts the *Manual*, which describes the USNP's earlier, less sophisticated version of multiple versions. The Association of Research Libraries' *Guidelines for Bibliographic Records for Preservation Microform Masters*,[22] contrary to USNP practice, mandates the inclusion of preservation data in the bibliographic record. Such a practice, although necessary for preservation, makes union lists longer and more cumbersome to use.

Like most selections from the genre known as manual or guidelines, the current *Manual* suffers because it, like the ARL *Guideline*, had to aim at a moving target. At least the *Manual* is in excellent company. Only when the last newspaper is cataloged by the last project, when the library profession finds no more challenges and becomes static, and when the last newspaper is published in this country, will we know how newspapers should have been inventoried and cataloged. Let us anticipate with alacrity the first event and do everything possible to prevent the last two.

In conclusion, the *Newspaper Cataloging and Union Listing Manual* attempts to facilitate the work of state newspaper projects characterized by the challenges of conducting a comprehensive inventory, the opportunity afforded by retrospective cataloging and union listing, and the mysteries of cataloging less-than-full runs. Despite these often difficult characteristics, the United States Newspaper Program continues to succeed in its mission to find, inventory, and catalog the nation's newspapers. This success is due to the many people who apply the guidelines given in this and the previous manuals. The author hopes those folks find this manual worthy.

ENDNOTES

1. For a description of life on the road, see Beverley Geer-Butler's article "The Cataloging and Inventory Phase of the Maryland Newspaper Project" elsewhere in this volume.
2. Elaine W. Woods, *Newspaper Cataloging Manual* (Washington, D.C.: Library of Congress, 1981).
3. *MARC Serials Editing Guide*, CONSER edition (Washington, D.C.: Library of Congress, 1975).
4. Robert Harriman, *Newspaper Cataloging Manual* (Washington, D.C.: Serial Record Division, Library of Congress, 1984).
5. *Anglo-American Cataloguing Rules*, 2nd edition (Chicago, Ill.: American Library Association, 1976).
6. *CONSER Editing Guide* (Washington, D.C.: Serial Record Division, Library of Congress, 1985).
7. American National Standards Institute, *American National Standard for Serial Holdings Statements at the Summary Level*, ANSI Z39.42-1980 (New York, N.Y.: American National Standards Institute, 1980).
8. *USMARC Format for Bibliographic Description* (Washington, D.C.: Cataloging Distribution Service, Library of Congress, 1988).
9. *Anglo-American Cataloging Rules*, 2nd edition, 1988 revision (Chicago, Ill.: American Library Association, 1988), p. 18.
10. Stephen Gutgesell, ed., *Guide to Ohio Newspapers, 1793-1973* (Columbus, Ohio: Ohio Historical Society, 1974).
11. John W. Miller, *Indiana Newspaper Bibliography* (Indianapolis, Ind.: Indiana Historical Society, 1982).
12. *Library of Congress Rule Interpretations*, 2nd edition (Washington, D.C.: Cataloging Distribution Service, Library of Congress, 1989).
13. *Library of Congress Subject Headings*, 12th edition (Washington, D.C.: Cataloging Distribution Service, Library of Congress, 1989).
14. *Harvard Encyclopedia of American Ethnic Groups* (Cambridge, Mass.: Belknap Press of Harvard University, 1980).
15. *Anglo-American Cataloguing Rules*, 2nd edition, 1988 revision, p. 484.
16. *Library of Congress Rule Interpretations*, 2nd edition (Washington, D.C.: Cataloging Distribution Service, Library of Congress, 1989), p. 25.5B(1).
17. *Union List: User Manual* (Dublin, Ohio: OCLC Online Library Computer Center, 1989), p. 5:37.
18. *OCLC Participating Institutions Arranged by OCLC Symbol* (Dublin, Ohio: OCLC Online Computer Library Center, 1989).

19. *Op. cit.*

20. *USMARC Format for Holdings Data* (Washington, D.C.: Cataloging Distribution Service, Library of Congress, 1989).

21. American National Standards Committee on Library and Information Sciences and Related Publishing Practices, Z39, *American National Standard for Information Sciences–Serial Holdings Statements* (New York, N.Y.: American National Standards Institute, 1986).

22. *Guidelines for Bibliographic Records for Preservation Microform Masters* (Washington, D.C.: Association of Research Libraries, 1990).

The Cataloging and Inventory Phase of the Maryland Newspaper Project

Beverley Geer-Butler

SUMMARY. The cataloging and inventory phase of the Maryland Newspaper Project began in April, 1988 and was completed in November, 1990. The purpose of this paper is to describe a particular experience in conducting a newspaper cataloging project, to convey ideas for managing field work, and to describe the method the Maryland Newspaper Project used to determine when the cataloging and inventory phase was finished.

INTRODUCTION

In April, 1988 the Maryland Newspaper Project cataloging team attended the newspaper cataloging and union listing workshop conducted by Library of Congress personnel at OCLC. In May work began in earnest as stated in the monthly report submitted to the Project Director:

> We spend hours trying to find runs of papers. We are spending most of our time collating. We have found [OCLC] records which take up to 2 hours to figure out and we figured out that they are incorrect. We did not have a terminal this month and had to travel to College Park to search [OCLC] records. The entire project seemed cumbersome.[1]

Beverley Geer-Butler is Head, Copy Cataloging Section, The Ohio State University Libraries, 1858 Neil Ave. Mall, Columbus, OH 43210. The author held the position of Asst. Director/Cataloger for the Maryland Newspaper Project from August, 1989 through November, 1990.

The author would like to thank Christine Sandy, Debra Padgette Bixler, Peter Curtis and Todd Butler for their energy and good humor in bringing the cataloging and inventory phase to a successful conclusion.

The sentiment expressed here applies to any major cataloging project, but for newspaper projects, it aptly sums up the problems and frustrations inherent in conducting the cataloging and inventory phase. It is not the author's intention to instruct the reader in newspaper cataloging and union listing.[2] It is the author's intention to describe a particular experience in conducting a newspaper cataloging project, to convey ideas for managing field work, and to describe the method the Maryland Newspaper Project used to determine when the cataloging and inventory phase was finished.

BACKGROUND

The planning phase of the Maryland Newspaper Project (MNP), which was conducted by the Maryland State Archives (Archives) in 1984, concluded that approximately 1,800 newspaper titles had been published in Maryland since 1727. A preliminary list of titles and locations was prepared, and this list was used to plan for the second phase: cataloging and inventory. A grant proposal to accomplish the second phase was submitted to the National Endowment for the Humanities (NEH), and funding was granted in January, 1988, with work beginning in April of that year. The grant proposal included a plan and a schedule for visiting the 23 counties and a description of the institutions to be involved and their responsibilities.

The grant proposal also outlined how the cataloging and union listing would be done. All United States Newspaper Program (USNP) projects use the following to accomplish their work: OCLC's cataloging and union listing subsystems, *Newspaper Cataloging and Union Listing Manual*, *Anglo-American Cataloguing Rules (2nd ed., 1988 rev.)*, *Library of Congress Rules Interpretations*, and the *CONSER Editing Guide*. Newspaper cataloging utilizes the master record convention, meaning that the cataloging record is created for the original hard-copy version. The individual holdings records (local data records) indicate whether the library holds microfilm, microfiche, etc. The holdings records are detailed and are accessible through the union listing subsystem.

Many of the projects had devised cataloging and inventory forms. The Maryland Newspaper Project cataloging team asked several projects for samples of their cataloging and inventory forms and derived forms that we felt would be easy to read and interpret. Because the team would have no OCLC terminal in the field, the forms played an important part in our ability to record information accurately.

Armed with the Archives' survey and the plan that NEH approved, the Project moved forward.

THE CATALOGING AND INVENTORY PLAN

The plan was as follows: catalog and take inventory of the large collections at the Enoch Pratt Free Library (Pratt) and the Maryland Historical Society (MHS) in Baltimore and at the Maryland State Archives (Archives) in Annapolis. It was believed that after finishing these 3 sites, MNP Staff would have a large database of newspaper titles and holdings records to work with when processing the collections in the nearly 85 sites in the 23 counties. This premise proved to be true. In February, 1990, when the Project finished work at the Pratt, MHS and Archives and began work in the counties, close to 1,600 titles had been cataloged. This figure represents 62% of the total of 2,637 newspaper titles cataloged when the Project ended in November, 1990. The increase of 800 titles over the original estimate of 1,800 titles is the result of inclusion of non-Maryland titles in the inventory. The Project extended its purview to include non-Maryland titles with United States imprints when the cataloging team encountered a large collection of Afro-American titles on microfilm at a Baltimore university. The cataloging team continued to discover non-Maryland titles at many of the sites and believed that the users of a union list of newspaper titles would appreciate inclusion of newspaper titles from other states and territories. The number of non-Maryland titles cataloged is approximately 800, which verifies the original estimate of 1,800 Maryland titles.

THE ART OF ITINERANT CATALOGING

Abraham Lincoln spent part of his law career as a circuit judge, riding from city to city to hear cases and dispense law. The MNP cataloging team did not aspire to the presidency (we were as close to the roar and rumble of the District of Columbia and the White House as we cared to be), but we felt that we were doing something that would yield a useful product.

The mournful tone of the May, 1988 monthly report soon changed to enthusiasm as the workflow became stable and the cataloging and union listing statistics increased. Gaining control over the mass of materials was difficult because of the sheer size and weight of newspapers and because of the conditions in which they are stored. In 1986 Robert Harriman wrote a single sentence that effectively describes a newspaper project: "The work is different."[3] "He describes the cramped, dark and strange working conditions, but he also gives fine advice on making it work.[4] As stated above, the cataloging team (1 full-time cataloger, 1 full-time assistant and sporadic student help) began work at the Enoch Pratt Free Library, and it was there that procedures for cataloging and inventory were developed and refined. The newspaper collection at the Pratt is large and heavily used. The newspapers were scattered among many floors and locations, were in disarray, and were dangerously fragile. Today the collection is still large and is shelved in what space is available, but as a result of the MNP's work, the newspapers are in better order and many of the very fragile titles have been preserved on microfilm for public use.

The cataloging team began its task with collation of the hard copy of a title in the stacks and then moving into the microform area (located far from the stacks) to determine if any issues of the same title were held in microform. It is suggested that all physical formats of a title be collated simultaneously rather than cataloging the hard copy of *all* titles held at a site and then moving on to the microform collection. This method insures that a complete picture of that site's holdings of a particular title will be captured while the title is still fresh in your mind. It is also suggested that the whole family of titles (preceding, succeeding and related frequency editions) be cataloged as a group so that all the bibliographic links will be correct and fall into line. Information about a title and all of its kin was garnered from the issues themselves (masthead changes, publisher's block information, and articles about mergers and cessations) and from using other sources such as Brigham,[5] Gregory,[6] and Preston.[7] Harriman gives the following warning about the use of secondary sources for newspaper cataloging:

> . . . the key to the success of a project is the quality and comprehensiveness of the inventory in seeking out and working with the newspapers themselves, rather than relying on previous work. When the vast majority of newspapers published in the United States are local in character and coverage, it should come as no surprise to us to discover that the most complete holdings will be found closest to home. . . . Thus the need for reliance on secondary source materials to "fill out" the descriptive record should be minimal. Rather, these sources are used appropriately in providing preliminary inventory information and in providing extra "clues" to the cataloger attempting to solve bibliographic problems.[8]

With that advice in mind, the cataloging team attempted to edit existing bibliographic records and create new records based on concrete information gleaned from a site's holdings. It was hoped that questions about a title's bibliographic history would be answered when we began work in the other sites. As questions arose, they were filed in the county folder that represented the home county of the city of publication.

Many of the Pratt's newspapers were too fragile to handle and were sent to the Archives to be filmed before they were cataloged. Problems can arise from filming before cataloging in that the filmer may not spot changes of title or related titles that may have been interfiled. Cataloging before filming insures that distinct bibliographic units will be collated for the filmer. However, if the effort to collate and catalog endangers the life of the newspaper, the issues must be filmed before cataloging. A list of titles that were being filmed was retained, and they were cataloged as they returned. Many of the titles were not filmed until after the cataloging team had left the Pratt. The Pratt notified the cataloging team when the filmed titles returned and subsequent visits to catalog and take inventory of the filmed titles were made at a later date.

The cataloging team left the Pratt in December, 1989, having cataloged and collated every title found in its exploration and scrutiny of the stacks and microform area. The same procedures were used at the Maryland Historical Society and the Archives. Each of those locations presented its own problems and rewards, but the team soon found that life had been ordinary and routine compared to what awaited them in the counties.

FRIENDLY PERSUASION

None of the institutions surveyed in 1984 was obligated to participate in the Project. Therefore, it was the cataloging team's task to ask permission to visit the site and catalog and take inventory of its holdings. Because six years had passed since the survey was completed, it was assumed that the Project had been forgotten and that some public relations works had to be done. The team realized that in their concentration on their work at the Pratt, MHS and Archives, they had neglected to prepare the sites in the counties for their arrival.

In January, 1990 the cataloging team got together with a graphic artist working on the University of Maryland campus and designed an information brochure based on the handsome and informative brochure created by the Washington Newspaper Project. In March copies of the brochure were sent to persons and institutions on three mailing lists: Maryland state senators, newspaper offices in each county, and libraries and historical societies. The senators were approached to get attention and engender good will (it is uncertain whether this was effective since no responses were received from them). The newspaper offices, libraries and historical societies were sites that were canvassed in the 1984 survey or came to our attention through perusal of directories and telephone books. The cataloging team felt that the personnel at those sites would also direct us to other sources and collectors.

As stated above, the Project finished work at the three main sites (Pratt, MHS, and Archives) in February, 1990. During the time between January and April, when the brochure was being prepared and mailed and responses awaited, the cataloging team contacted the next county's sites by telephone and letter, asking them to participate in the Project. The process of requesting their participation included identifying and describing the Project to the director/administrator of the site, explaining our intentions, and describing our procedures. This took some time and was not effective because telephone conversations are not as official and consistent as letters and because the person to whom the request needed to be directed was not always available. Because the team had not allowed enough time for mail to be delivered and responded to, letter writing was not an efficient method of communication. Therefore, the team had to use the telephone for scheduling for a short period of time until the brochures were ready and a scheduling method was devised.

As soon as the brochures were ready, the cataloging team drew up a schedule for each county based on the tentative schedule presented in the grant proposal. Generally, the Archives' survey reported holdings for the public library, the county historical society and for at least one newspaper office in each county. Private collectors were also listed. The sites in each county were usually situated around the county seat and/or the major city in the county. Based on the number of titles listed for a site in the Archives' survey, the team made an estimate of how much time would be needed to process the collection. The schedule was also influenced by the distance to the site and by the season of the year. For example, the mountainous western part of the state was scheduled for the summer months when the roads would be passable; the eastern shore was scheduled for the fall when there would be less traffic to the beaches. If a site was more than two hours from home base in College Park, then hotel arrangements had to be made. One month in advance a letter was sent to the director/administrator of the site. The letter described the Maryland Newspaper Project and its purpose, asked permission to visit the site and gave a tentative date for our arrival. The recipient was asked to call and confirm the date or offer an alternative date. Along with the letter went a copy of the brochure and a brief description of MNP procedures that served to inform the site that the team would not disrupt their workflow or make any demands on their time. If a response was not received within two weeks of our visit, the site was called. This routine for contacting the sites proved to be an effective way to schedule the work and to get the counties interested in and excited about our arrival. For example, one of the remote sites was in Frostburg in western Maryland. One site director in Frostburg expressed her pleasure that the Project was interested in her site's collections. She said that "no one ever comes to see us!!" That site proved to be one of the most productive and enjoyable visits the team made.

The cataloging team also felt that good exposure would be gained from participation in the Maryland Library Association annual conference held in May. Because of our proximity to Washington, DC we were fortunate to have the assistance of Jeffrey Field, Assistant to the Director of NEH's Office of Preservation. Mr. Field along with three other panelists representing a public library, an academic library and an archives delivered an excellent discussion on preservation/conservation issues and possibilities. The purpose of the discussion was to get Maryland librarians interested in preservation/conservation and to let them know that any institution, no matter how big or small, can take advantage of grants and employ preservation/conservation techniques and knowledge. The discussion ended with a description of the Maryland Newspaper Project as a current and successful use of grant money and preservation microfilming. By the end of May, 1990 the Project was known, almost a household word. Letters and telephone calls were received with encouraging regularity.

COUNTRY ROADS

Recently Joanne E. Passet wrote an article on the itinerant librarians who worked in this country during the years 1887-1915.[9] The author gives details of the catalogers' lives and working conditions. Reading the article, this author was struck by the similarities between the conditions and attitudes those women faced and those that the cataloging team encountered.

> Itinerant librarians dealt with a wide range of people in the communities in which they worked: citizens, local women's clubs, library

> boards, and local library employees. Each body had different expectations, and these determined, in part, how much the organizer could accomplish.[10]

Public libraries ranged from small collections of fiction and popular magazines to large county systems with history rooms full of genealogical sources. Many of them had collections of both current and ceased newspapers. Robert Holley states in his article on the Utah Newspaper Project that "one unexpected problem was the difficulty in convincing small public libraries that we were interested in listing their limited newspaper subscriptions."[11] Bobby Weaver wrote in 1987 that the Texas Newspaper Project found that libraries and newspaper offices "either did not know the value of their local papers, did not have funding to work with their papers, or for a variety of reasons had neglected their local collection of papers."[12] The cataloging team quickly realized that the concern about the archival and historical value of newspaper collections that had prevailed at the Pratt, MHS and the Archives did not always exist out in the field. Many sites considered their newspapers to be ephemera that represented a terrible storage problem. More than once the team was told by a librarian, historical society curator or newspaper publisher that the newspapers were old, dirty and in bad shape and that we probably did not want to see them. It was our task to convince them that those were exactly the newspapers that concerned us.

A large number of the public libraries had limited retention policies for newspapers. This meant that the library could not be listed as a holdings location in the union list because they really had no collection at all. The union list was meant to report holdings that the user could count on finding at the site or, in the case of microfilm holdings, borrowing through interlibrary loan.

There also were many sites that were painfully aware of the value of their newspapers, but that were hard pressed to care for them properly. A constantly recurring problem was that of the free newspaper. In the past 20 years many cities have seen the beginning and end of local newspapers that were offered free on the newsstand or came unsolicited to homes. These newspapers funded themselves through advertising. The cataloging team discovered many sites that had broken runs of these newspapers. They were collected through any variety of means, including having a staff member collect the newspaper from the free newsstand. Because the site could not count on receiving the newspaper regularly through a subscription, efforts to collect the title met with little success. Many of these newspapers presented far more than local advertising.

There were articles, photographs, and editorials that reflected the times and constituted a snap shot of that city's history. These newspaper titles presented the most frustration. The publishing office was long gone or the newspaper had been bought and killed by the buyer. More often than not, the back issues had been thrown away. The cataloging team spent a great deal of time emphasizing the importance of keeping the newspapers. If a collection of newspapers (no matter how small) was in danger of being lost, the cataloging team alerted the Archives about its existence immediately. The Archives actively solicited collections of newspapers apart from their participation in the Maryland Newspaper Project. On many occasions the Archives was able to collect the newspapers from the site and store them for microfilming at a later date. This meant that the Archives could be listed as the holdings site for that title.

For the most part the sites were making fine efforts to maintain and preserve their newspapers. When the cataloging team arrived at a site, we would acquaint ourselves with the staff and then begin work. We encountered some skepticism, a small amount of fear of letting us handle the newspapers, and some confusion about what we were doing. More than once we were asked if we were indexing the newspapers, and one person asked us where our camera was because it was thought that we were going to film the newspapers on site. Our arrival at one site prompted the question, "Are you the cleaning lady?" Mostly we encountered people who were proud of their collections and who encouraged us to succeed with our Project. Many people asked us questions about what they could do to prolong the life of their collections. We were able to make recommendations about the purchase of acid-free boxes and about keeping the newspapers in a flat position and away from light.

Procedures did not change much from what had been devised while working at the Pratt. The site was usually much smaller than the Pratt or Archives so we were able to process the collection in good time. However, the working conditions varied drastically. Newspapers were found in well-lit libraries, drafty barns, busy bathrooms, bank vaults, and mansions on the hill. The team prepared for each site by compiling a list of titles that we hoped to find. That list was based on the Archives' survey and on clues and hints gleaned from working with the collections in other sites. Many librarians and curators had compiled their own lists and were very anxious to save us any trouble by letting us use the list rather than climbing up into the attic. Like the catalogers for the Pennsylvania Newspaper Project, we had learned "to assume nothing and to check everything."[13] Once again we worked with a title in all of its formats (hard copy and microfilm), and we worked with the whole family of titles (succeeding, preceding, and related frequency editions). Probably the single most valuable cataloging and union listing tool used was a printed union list that was ordered from OCLC every six months during the cataloging and inventory phase. The list contained all the titles cataloged and all the holdings listed for Maryland sites up to the point when the list was printed. Each entry in the list had the OCLC bibliographic record and the holdings records (local data records) attached to that bibliographic record. As we surveyed a site's holdings, the list was used to determine if the title had already been cataloged and if that site's holdings filled any gaps.

Very often it was discovered that a site held exactly the same run of microfilm or many of the same issues held at other sites. The team would list that site's holdings even though they were redundant. If the title was held in microfilm, it was listed because user's of the union list would benefit from knowing all the locations for the microfilm. If the newspaper was in hard copy, it was listed because the team felt that when the microfilming began, it would be better to have several sites listed so that the filmer could solicit the best copies for microfilming.

In many cases it was found that several sites had hard copy runs of newspapers that had been filmed. Those holdings were listed because a need could arise to refilm that title and the location of the hard copy would be useful. The cataloging team also discovered redundant holdings of historical issues. For example, many sites had a copy of the July 3, 1863 issue of *The Sun (Baltimore, Md.)* because there was a map of the Gettysburg battlefield. Such issues were not counted unless they represented something unique or endangered.

Private collectors presented an unique problem for the Project. Because their holdings were not publicly accessible, the collector could not be listed as a location. When a private collector was located, the team discussed the Project with him and attempted to make arrangements for the collector to donate the collection to the Archives or lend it for filming. There was a mixture of success and failure in persuading collectors to cooperate. If the collector would not allow access to the newspapers, then the newspaper collection was considered not found. In one instance a collector had issues of a newspaper the Project had never seen and which was not held anywhere else in Maryland or in the country. The team was not allowed to see them, and the collector would not allow the Archives to film them. The Archives maintains a list of the collectors and makes occasional efforts to persuade them to allow the newspapers to be filmed.

All decisions made about listing a site's holdings were made with the purpose of the Project in mind: to create a union list of holdings that would lead historians, researchers, and other interested persons to the information they needed and that would provide a list of unpreserved newspapers to the persons involved in the microfilming phase of the Maryland Newspaper Project.

When the team finished work in a county, letters of appreciation were sent to those who participated. If there were any titles that were not found, the director/administrators of the sites were asked to write articles for the local newspaper or the historical society newsletters, asking the citizenry to come forward with their newspapers. The team decided early on that rather than asking for newspapers before they visited a county, they would see what turned up in the sites and then try to locate unfound titles or more issues of titles that were found. It was felt that asking for help before we knew what we needed would result in a flood of newspapers that were not unique or did not fit into our purview. That decision may have been a mistake in that we may have missed out on discoveries, but when the cataloging and inventory phase ended in November, 1990, no new titles were found as a result of the articles written by the sites.

GOING HOME

The cataloging team was able to finish work in a county in an average of a week. Maryland is not a large state, and unlike other newspaper projects, no surprises were found.[14] We did not encounter any huge runs of newspapers that presented difficulties in cataloging or union listing nor did we discover any newspapers that had to be filmed before they could be cataloged. A few sites had to be visited a second time because new titles were acquired or titles that were not found during the first visit had turned up. The question before us was: are we finished? After the last county was visited, the team went through the cataloging records and holdings records, comparing them with the Archives' survey and the lists of titles we were unable to find. The cataloging team felt that it had made its best effort and that not too many opportunities had been missed. We had visited all the sites listed in the Archives' survey and several more that had been discovered along the way. Statistics showed that 2,637 Maryland and non-Maryland titles had been cataloged, and that approximately 5,000 holdings records had been created for 85 sites. The Archives' survey had estimated 1,800 Maryland titles, and the figures showed that the Project had cataloged approximately that many. We realized from the beginning that we would not find everything, but we were certain that our efforts had been productive and useful. The team had done a good day's work.

CONCLUSION

The author has attempted to describe the cataloging and inventory phase of a successful newspaper project and to offer suggestions for making the field work fruitful. Those suggestions are as follows:

1. To contact the participating sites well ahead of the visit so the schedule can work for both of you.
2. To take advantage of any and every opportunity for publicity.
3. To go to the site with a list of titles that you hope to find. The list can be derived from the initial survey done during the planning phase, from various bibliographies and from information you have gleaned in cataloging titles at other sites.
4. To ask the assistance of the site in locating titles. The curators and administrators of local collections are invaluable sources of information and are most likely to be the persons to whom the citizenry will respond favorably when they are asked to donate their newspapers.
5. To catalog the whole family of titles (preceding, succeeding, and related frequency editions) simultaneously.
6. To catalog a title in all of its forms (hard copy and microform) simultaneously.
7. To always keep in mind the purpose of the project: to create a union list of newspapers holdings that will lead historians, researchers and others to the information they need and that will provide persons involved in the microfilming phase with a list of unpreserved papers.

The author believes that the most important consideration is the maintenance of the information once the cataloging and inventory phase is finished. The cataloging data and the union list are not static so a mechanism for reporting changes is greatly needed. The maintenance of the cataloging and holdings information will require the cooperation and vigilance of all the sites or 50 years from now another newspaper project will have to be carried out. In the final report to the Project Director, the cataloging team made suggestions for maintaining the cataloging and union listing data.[15] For example, establish a clearing house for reporting title and holdings changes and reissue the printed union list at least annually.

The author also feels that the cooperation and devotion of newspaper publishers are needed if the unique form of history that they produce is to be preserved. Many states have depository arrangements whereby a copy of each issue published is sent to an archives or records center for storage. In some cases, the newspapers are filmed as part of an ongoing system. It will take vision and a love of history to carry on what the United States Newspaper Program has started.

Any serials cataloger will tell you that the work is never done, but the author feels that there is much to be learned from the effort. A great deal of money, time, effort and devotion goes into any cataloging project, but the gratification and benefits are not momentary.

> . . . cataloging is both an end in itself–the provision of access–and a means to an end–the assurance of access for future generations of researchers who will find newspapers one of the most valued resources for the study of American life and culture.[16]

NOTES

1. Monthly Report to the Project Director, Maryland Newspaper Project, May, 1988 (unpublished).

2. For rules and procedures concerning newspaper cataloging and union listing using OCLC see: Todd Butler, *Newspaper Cataloging and Union Listing Manual* (Washington, D.C.: Library of Congress, Serials Record Division, 1990).

3. Robert B. Harriman, Jr. "Coordination of Cataloging Practices in the United States Newspaper Program," *Cataloging & Classification Quarterly* 6, no. 4 (Summer 1986): 19.

4. *Ibid.*, p. 23-26.

5. Clarence S. Brigham, *History and Bibliography of American Newspapers, 1690-1820* (Westport, Conn.: Greenwood Press, 1976, c1975).

6. Winifred Gregory, ed., *American Newspapers, 1821-1936: a Union List of Files Available in the United States and Canada* (New York: H. W. Wilson, 1937).

7. Dickson Preston, *Newspapers of Maryland's Eastern Shore* (Centreville, MD: Tidewater Publishers, 1986).

8. Harriman, p. 25.

9. Joanne E. Passet, "Order is Heaven's First Law: Itinerant Librarians and Bibliographic Control, 1887-1915," *Library Quarterly* 60, no. 1 (Jan. 1990): 23-43.

10. *Ibid.*, p. 33.

11. Robert P. Holley, "The Utah Newspaper Project," *Library Resources & Technical Services* 31, no. 2 (Apr./June 1987): 187.

12. Bobby Weaver, "The Texas Newspaper Project: an Update," *Texas Libraries* 48 (Spring 1987): 16-17.

13. Rebecca A. Wilson and Lydia Suzanne Kellerman, "Challenges of On-Site Cataloging," *Cataloging & Classification Quarterly* 6, no. 4 (Summer 1986): 31.

14. Harriman, p. 19.

15. Final Report: Phase II: Cataloging and Inventory, Maryland Newspaper Project, 2 November 1990 (unpublished).

16. Jeffrey Field, "Foreword," *Cataloging & Classification Quarterly* 6, no. 4 (Summer 1986): 3

The Cataloguing of Serial Microform Reproductions at the National Library of Canada

John Clark
Wayne Jones

SUMMARY. The authors describe the cataloguing of serial microform reproductions at the National Library of Canada in the context of the current debate over the bibliographic control of multiple versions. NLC practice in each area of the bibliographic description is presented in detail with reference to *AACR2R* and MARC fields. The conclusion is that NLC practice satisfies current practical and theoretical demands, but that change is inevitable and necessary.

INTRODUCTION AND BACKGROUND

Take a look at a recent photograph of yourself. Depending on the accuracy of the likeness (or the generosity of the photographic process) you may say to a friend "This is me," or the friend may say "This doesn't look like you at all." Your eyes may be shut tight in reaction to the flash, you may be smiling unnaturally or there may be details about your features which are blatantly revealed. On the other hand, the photographic reproduction may be wonderful, and there will be no doubt that the person represented is indeed "you."

Now take a look at a microform reproduction of a local newspaper. The basic text of the newspaper is there, though there may be some deletions and rearrangements. There may even be additions made by the micropublishing agency, a title frame perhaps, or a target frame containing information about the microform as a physical object. In short, there

---

John Clark is a Cataloguer in the Serials Section of the National Library of Canada, 395 Wellington St., Ottawa, Ont., K1A 0N4. Wayne Jones is Head of the section.

will be characteristics about this microform that remind you it is a newspaper, and characteristics that remind you it is a reproduction. It is an object which contains a representation of another object. It is both itself and something else.

This fact explains in part the many problems associated with the cataloguing of microform reproductions. As Crystal Graham writes:

> the question of whether the bibliographic record should emphasize content or physical description is central to the discussion of multiple versions.[1]

A related problem is even more central to the debate over multiple versions.[2] Should there be separate bibliographic records for each version? Or, more specifically in the context of microform cataloguing, should the cataloguer create records for print and microform versions of serials? Should there be separate records for each kind of microform (typically microfilm and microfiche)? for each emulsion (diazo, vesicular, silver halide)? for each polarity (positive or negative)? for each generation (preservation master, service master, service copy)? and for versions from each micropublisher?

These are difficult and important questions of principle, but they cannot be answered without considering practicality and usefulness: how practical would it be to rigorously create so many records, and how useful would they be to searchers of the catalogue?

BASIC PRACTICE AT THE NATIONAL LIBRARY OF CANADA

The cataloguing of serial microform reproductions at the National Library of Canada is carried out with the working principle that there should be a separate record for each distinct physical version of a work. One of the results of this practice is that there may exist two, three or even more separate full records for the various versions of any one work. For example, on the DOBIS database on which the NLC catalogues there are currently four separate records for *The Toronto Star*, representing the newspaper in its original printed form as well as in the microfilm reproductions which have been done by several micropublishers.

The NLC is not absolutely rigorous, however, in its application of the principle of creating a record for each version. Separate records are indeed created for each specific kind of microform from each micropublisher, but some physical differences are interpreted to be not significant enough to necessitate separate records. Differences in polarity and in the emulsion of the film are the main ones here. The polarity of a microform (whether it is negative rather than positive) may be mentioned in the physical description area of the record, but a separate record is not created for versions with a different polarity but identical otherwise. Similarly for the emulsion of the microform (whether it is diazo, vesicular or silver halide): no separate record is created to account for differences in emulsion, and such information may be recorded only in the coded data in the MARC record distributed by NLC.

This separate-record approach, though consistent with generally accepted cataloguing principles, differs from the approach recommended by the Multiple Versions Forum held December 1989 at Airlie House in Virginia. That approach, called the two-tier hierarchical model, calls for the creation of an independent bibliographic record (level 1) for one version of a work, linked to dependent holdings records (level 2) for other versions.[3] The difference between NLC practice and the two-tier model consists chiefly in the amount of detail recorded in the level 2 records, and in the resulting inability of these records to be intelligible without reference to the level 1 record.

Another important aspect of the NLC's cataloguing of serial microform reproductions is the adherence to the *AACR2R* principle of describing an item according to its physical form:

> the starting point for description is the physical form of the item in hand, not the original or any previous form in which the work has been published.[4]

The result is that all areas of the bibliographic description except area 3 (numeric, etc., designation, MARC tag 362) and a single note in area 7 (MARC tag 534) contain information derived from the reproduction, *not* the original.

This is the most substantial difference between NLC practice and that of the Library of Congress. LC also creates separate records for microform reproductions, but its policy stipulates that all areas of the description should contain information derived from the original, except for a single note in area 7 (MARC tag 533).[5]

DETAILS OF NLC PRACTICE

Following is a rule-by-rule account of NLC's cataloguing practice for serial microform reproductions. Rules which do not apply, and rules for which NLC microform practice is the same as its practice for other types of material, are omitted.

Description

11.0B1 Sources of Information

For microform reproductions the chief source of information is the title frame (as specified in *AACR2R*) unless there is no title frame or unless "the information on the title frame is insufficient or is presented in such a way so as to cause doubt as to its reliability or accuracy."[6]

For microfilm the chief source of information is then the rest of the item, including the reproduced title page or reproduced title page substitute of the original.

For microfiche the chief source of information is then the header, or the accompanying eye-readable materials or container. If this information is insufficient, unreliable or inaccurate, then the rest of the item, including the reproduced title page or reproduced title page substitute of the original, is the chief source of information.

11.1D Parallel titles (MARC tag 246 1)

Inaccurate parallel titles appearing on the title frame or container are not transcribed in order to maintain consistency with any related print description.

11.3 Numeric and/or alphabetic, chronological, or other designation (MARC tag 362 0)

Rule 12.3B1 states that for a facsimile or other reprint, the designation should be that of the original publication. NLC considers a microform publication to fall into this category so the designation for the microform description is copied from the print description for the original in cases where the microform does not reproduce the first issue of the original.

In the above situation, the microform description will also include a "Description based on:" note citing the designation of the first issue reproduced.

e.g., the first issue reproduced for the newspaper *Leader (Toronto, Ont. : Morning)* is v. 17, no. 5140 (Jan. 1, 1870)

From another microform record, the cataloguer ascertains that the first issue designation is v. 3, no. 728 (Nov. 7, 1855).

The designations on the microform description would be:

362 0 Vol. 3, no. 728 (Nov. 7, 1855)-

500 Description based on: Vol. 17, no. 5140 (Jan. 1, 1870).

NLC would also take the ending designation from the original print record and include it in the microform description in cases where the last issue of the serial has not been microfilmed.

NLC does not cite designations in the note relating to the original, as displayed in the third example in rule 11.7B22.

NLC has written the following rule interpretation to clarify this practice:

> For serials reproduced in microform, give the numeric and/or alphabetic designation of the first issue of the original. This designation may or may not represent the designation of the first available issue of the microreproduction.[7]

11.4 Publication, distribution, etc., area (MARC tag 260)

For most microforms, identifying and recording the place, publisher, and date is straightforward; however, difficult or vague cases can be encountered. Several of these cases are illustrated below:

1. Imprint information on a microform title frame differs from imprint information on the container.

   e.g., title frame gives the place and publisher as:

   Scarborough, Ont. :$bStandard Microfilming,

   container gives the place and publisher as:

   Toronto :$bPreston Microfilming Services.

In this situation, Standard Microfilming has gone out of business and its film masters have been acquired by Preston. The title frame has not been updated or changed. For this microfilm, NLC treats Standard Microfilming as the original publisher while Preston is mentioned in the source of acquisition/subscription address field (MARC tag 265).

NLC does not consider the publisher to have changed as Preston has never published this microfilm, but only acquired the marketing rights.

2. A micropublisher has distribution rights to a microform published by a second micropublisher.

   e.g., Société canadienne du microfilm has distribution rights in Canada for a title published by the New York Public Library. NLC exercises the option cited in 11.4D1 resulting in the following 260:

   $aNew York :$bNew York Public Library; $aMontréal :$bSociété canadienne du microfilm [distributor], $c1964-

   Société canadienne du microfilm is cited in the 265.

3. A microfilming company is simply the manufacturer.

Where title frame or acquisition information clearly indicates a filming company is the manufacturer as opposed to the publisher, the name of this printer is not recorded in field 260 unless it is part of a phrase which includes the name of the publisher (see rule 1.4D3).

4. The same microform is marketed by two or more micropublishers.

   e.g., NLC has encountered situations where the same title is received once from a provincial archives and again from a commercial micropublisher. For both copies, the title frame reveals that the provincial archives is the publisher. In these cases, NLC treats the second title received as copy 2 and does not create separate records even though each copy is packaged in a different container.

5. There is no imprint information.

It is common to encounter film or fiche titles that have no imprint information. Either no title frame exists (a very common occurrence) or no imprint information appears on the title frame or container. In these cases, NLC records in square brackets any imprint information obtained from other sources. If there are no other sources of information, the imprint can be quite vague:

e.g., $a[Canada? :$bs.n.,$c19–]-

11.5 Physical description area (MARC tag 300)

It is rare for a micropublisher to begin a new reel or fiche at the issue where a serial title has changed. In most instances encountered at NLC, a title change occurs in mid fiche or reel. Where the exact number of reels or fiche is known for a dead serial and a title change has occurred, NLC uses the technique suggested in rule 11.5B3.

e.g., title 1 300$aon 11 of 16 reels

title 2 300$aon 6 of 16 reels

The same technique would apply to microfiche.

Where a film or fiche is negative polarity, light letters on a dark background, this information is included in the collation as per rule 11.5C1.

Where NLC receives two or more copies of a microform from the same micropublisher and the polarities differ, negative polarity is not recorded in the collation.

e.g., NLC receives two film copies of the *Canadian library journal* from Micromedia Ltd. One copy is negative, the other is positive. The collation does not include "negative" in 300$b.

12.7B7 Relationships with other serials (MARC tags 760-787)

Details about simple relationships such as "Continues" and "Continued by" are recorded outside the note relating to the original (MARC tag 534) because such title changes occur for the reproduction just as they occur for the original.

There are two situations where NLC would provide relationship information in field 534 instead of via separate 7XX linking entry fields.

The first occurs when microform reproductions do not exist for all related titles but accurate title transcriptions can be found on print descriptions. In these cases, the relationship is cited in a 534$n and is referred to as a blind link.

The second situation where relationship information is recorded in field 534 is when complex relationships such as mergers or splits occur. These relationships are considered to concern the originals, and so are recorded in the 534 as discussed below.

Some descriptions carry "incomplete" 7XX linking entry fields.

> e.g., the newspapers *Saskatoon daily star* and *Saskatoon phoenix* merge to become *Saskatoon star-phoenix.*
>
> Commonwealth Microfilming Products has filmed only the *Saskatoon phoenix* and the *Saskatoon star-phoenix.*
>
> The relationship information on the microform description for *Saskatoon phoenix* would appear as:
>
> 534$pReproduction of:$cSaskatoon.$nMerged with: *Saskatoon daily star*, to become: *Saskatoon star-phoenix.*
>
> 785 17 *Saskatoon star-phoenix*
>
> No 785 17 would appear on this description for the *Saskatoon daily star.*

NLC does not normally make another edition link (MARC field 775) between records for the reproductions of newspapers which have been issued in editions of different frequency. The reason is that the title changes may not coincide for the different editions. The daily edition may change title several times while the weekly's title remains constant. The result would be excessively complicated and cumbersome relationships, and so NLC practice now is to simply state the existence of the other frequency edition in a field 534$n.

> e.g., Issued also in a daily ed.

12.7B8 Numbering and chronological designation (MARC tag 362 1)

When beginning and/or ending designations are taken from a reference or some other source, they are cited in 362 1.

Where applicable, the source is also cited.

e.g., Began with Apr. 17, 1911 issue.$zCf. Hist. dir. Sask. newsp., 1878-1983.

When a source indicates only the beginning and/or ending year of publication, this information is cited in field 534$c. A 362 1 is not used in these cases.

Occasionally, a cataloguer will find conflicting designation information in different reference sources. When this occurs, more than one 362 1 may be used on the microform description.

e.g., Began with July 1, 1867 issue.$zCf. ULCNHCL. Began publication in June 1867.$zCf. Hist. dir. Sask. newsp., 1878-1983.

11.7B10 Physical description (MARC tag 500)

NLC does not give details on the nature (or emulsion) of the film in this note. These details are basically treated as local information (as discussed above). They are included only in the coded information of the MARC records which are distributed by NLC.

11.7B16 Other formats (MARC tag 530)

When records exist for the original print version of a reproduction, field 530 is supplied on these records to indicate the existence of a microform version. In conjunction with this note, a non-printing additional physical form available relationship (MARC tag 776) is constructed between the print and microform records.

e.g., Print record

530 $aIssued also on microfilm by: Toronto : Preston Microfilming Services.

776 1 link to microform record

Microform record

534 $pReproduction of:$cBelleville,

Ont.$mWeekly.$nIssued also in a daily ed.

776 1 link to print record

When a serial has been microfilmed by numerous micropublishers, or if the serial has been reproduced in more than one microformat, a generic 530 field is used.

e.g., Issued also on microfilm.

or

Issued also on microform.

11.7B21 "With" notes (MARC tag 500)

It sometimes happens that a micropublisher issues bibliographically unrelated titles together, with or without a collective title. NLC has received some with almost a hundred titles on a single microfilm reel.

A separate record is created for each of these titles. A general note explains the fact in general terms. A note beginning "Filmed with"and citing the title of the serial reproduced first is added to all records (except the first).

11.7B22 Note relating to the original (MARC tag 534)

This field is included in all *Canadiana* microform records and the examples given in rule 11.7B22 of *AACR2R* are fairly reflective of NLC practice. Except for designations and some relationships, all appropriate information pertaining to the original serial is cited in various subfields in field 534. This includes language and edition information.

12.7B23 Item described (MARC tag 500)

The NLC rule interpretation states in part:

> For serials reproduced in microform, if the numeric and/or alphabetic designation of the first issue of the original does not represent the designation of the first available issue of the microreproduction, give the item described.[8]

e.g., Description based on: Vol. 6, no. 1 (Jan. 1970).

Access Points

Name main and name added entries (MARC tags 1XX and 7XX)

On microform descriptions, NLC copies the choice of entry for names appearing on the original print record, where one exists.

> Exception: NLC would not follow the choice of entry from a print *AACR1* description where *AACR2R* practice differed.

The issue of differentiating identical titles proper is not addressed by *AACR2R*. NLC has prepared a lengthy rule interpretation listing the qualifier elements needed to create uniform title headings (MARC tag 130).

Where the original print description includes a uniform title heading, this heading is copied on the microform description.

Newspaper reproductions can present interesting problems in differentiating identical titles proper.

For long established newspaper titles, it is common to find cases in the 1800's and early 1900's where a newspaper was issued at the same time in a daily and weekly edition with both editions bearing the same title.

Where this situation is encountered, edition or frequency qualifiers are required to differentiate the identical titles proper.

> e.g., the *Globe* was issued for several years in both a daily and weekly edition. Only the weekly edition bears an edition statement. The uniform title headings would appear as follows:
>
> *Globe (Toronto, Ont. : Daily)*
>
> –frequency is used here as the qualifier
>
> *Globe (Toronto, Ont. : Weekly edition)*
>
> –the edition statement is used here as the qualifier

Other

Source of acquisition/subscription address (MARC tag 265)

Most NLC records appear in the national bibliography *Canadiana*. As this bibliography is widely used as an acquisitions tool, NLC routinely provides micropublisher addresses where applicable on its bibliographic descriptions.

Addresses are not provided for government micropublishers such as federal or provincial archives or for commercial and noncommercial micropublishers listed in the *Canadian ISBN Publishers' Directory.*

DESCRIPTIVE ELEMENTS (ORIGINAL VS. MICROFORM)

The following list of codes and fields illustrates the somewhat hybrid nature of a microform reproduction description:

245 choice of chief source depends upon the accuracy with which it transcribes the original title

250 records the microform edition statement

260 records the microform imprint

300 records the microform collation

362 records the numeric and/or chronological or other designation of the original

534 records any relevant information pertaining to the original serial

760-787 records titles of related microform descriptions

007 records the physical characteristics of the microform

008	c.p.6	publication status code	original
	c.p. 7-10	beginning date of pub.	original
	c.p. 11-14	ending date of pub.	original
	c.p. 15-17	country of pub. code	microform
	c.p. 18	frequency	microform
	c.p. 19	regularity	microform
	c.p. 21	type of serial designator	microform
	c.p. 22	form of original item	original
	c.p. 23	form of item	microform
	c.p. 28	gov't pub. indicator	microform
	c.p. 29	conference pub. indicator	original

c.p. 35-37	language code	original
c.p. 38	modified record code	original

NLC BIBLIOGRAPHIC PRODUCTS AND SERVICES

Records created by NLC for serial microform reproductions are available in a variety of ways. They are:

- in printed form in the publication *Canadiana*, which is published monthly with an annual cumulation
- on microfiche in *Canadiana*, again monthly with an annual cumulation; also in five-year cumulations beginning 1981
- on microfiche in *CONSER Microfiche*, which is published in annual supplements with annual cumulated indexes
- on magnetic tape in several options from the MARC Records Distribution Service, including those listing all NLC records or all CONSER records
- online on the NLC's DOBIS database
- online on OCLC's CONSER database

There are also NLC products which list subsets of all the serial records available:

- on microfiche in the *Union List of Serials in the Social Sciences and Humanities*, published annually
- on microfiche in the *Union List of Canadian Newspapers*, second edition to be published in 1991
- on CD-ROM in a union list of serials in the humanities, social sciences, and sciences (co-published by the Canada Institute for Scientific and Technical Information); first edition to be published late 1991
- on CD-ROM in *BiblioDisc* (co-published by the Canadian Telebook Agency), updated quarterly and consisting of the entire file of the agency plus the latest two years of *Canadiana*

CONCLUSION

NLC practice (like LC practice) lies somewhere between the two poles of strict cataloguing theory and practical necessity. Absolute adherence to theory would result in separate bibliographic descriptions not only for each obviously distinct microform version, but also for microform versions which differed in less obvious (but nonetheless substantial) ways. It is starting to become evident, however, that national cataloguing agencies must move closer to the pole of practicality. There are fewer and fewer resources (human and financial) for cataloguing, and databases are being filled with records which are virtually identical. There is also a more positive reason to consider creating fewer full records: the resulting file may be much more understandable and easier to get around in.

This movement towards practicality does not imply a rejection of the fundamentals of cataloguing, nor an expedient lowering of standards. As John C. Attig says, the decision to create fewer separate records is simply a decision to treat some bibliographic details as merely local information:

> In the past, the only way to achieve control over both works and the physical characteristics of their various manifestations was to describe each manifestation in a separate bibliographic record. This was because both the cataloging rules and the MARC formats had allowed little opportunity for recording local data in any kind of organized way . . . The existence of a holdings format provides the opportunity to think conceptually about which aspects of a bi[b]liographic entity should be described in a bibliographic record and which should be treated as local variations.[9]

It is instructive to note that when NLC was drafting its first microform cataloguing policies in 1986 there was never any question about the requirement for separate records for different versions. The main issue then was chief source of information: is it the title frame or container of the microform, or is it the reproduced title page or caption? A lot has changed in five years. Much more microform is being produced and acquired. The concern over the deterioration of publications of all sorts caused by brittle paper has led to an international effort to preserve the content of these publications through microfilming. Libraries are also attempting to deal with the problem of limited shelf space by acquiring microform copies of publications such as periodicals and local newspapers. In Canada, published microforms of all sorts became subject to legal deposit in 1988. NLC has also made an effort to purchase those microforms which were produced before then.

The result is much more microform to catalogue. For now, NLC policy will continue to call for separate records for different versions. Change is inevitable and necessary, though, as national cataloguing agencies, bibliographic utilities and users move to a better way.

REFERENCES

1. Crystal Graham, "Definition and Scope of Multiple Versions," *Cataloging & Classification Quarterly*, v. 11, no. 2 (1990), p. 13.

2. "Multiple versions" is the prevailing term used to describe the various physical manifestations in which a work may be issued. See Graham, pp. 11-15. The cataloguing of microform reproductions, which is the focus of this paper, is a subset of the broader issue of bibliographic control of multiple versions.

3. For a full discussion of the two-tier model see the *Multiple Versions Forum Report* (Washington: Network Development and MARC Standards Office, Library of Congress, 1990), pp. 7-21.

4. *Anglo-American Cataloguing Rules*, 2nd ed., 1988 rev. (Ottawa: Canadian Library Association, 1988), rule 0.24, p. 8.

5. See *Cataloging Service Bulletin*, no. 14 (fall 1981), pp. 56-58.

6. *Descriptive Cataloguing Manual* (Ottawa: National Library of Canada, Acquisitions and Bibliographic Services Branch, 1989-), rule 11.0B1.

7. *Descriptive Cataloguing Manual*, rule 11.3C.

8. *Descriptive Cataloguing Manual*, rule 12.7B23.

9. John C. Attig, "Descriptive Cataloging Rules and Machine-Readable Record Structures: Some Directions for Parallel Development," *The Conceptual Foundations of Descriptive Cataloging*, ed. Elaine Svenonius (San Diego: Academic Press, 1989), pp. 144-145.

Microform Reproductions and Multiple Versions: U.S. Cataloging Policy and Proposed Changes

Crystal Graham

SUMMARY. For over a decade, national standards for cataloging reproductions have caused cataloging bottlenecks, gobbled up preservation monies, and required maintenance of numerous duplicate records. Most importantly, the standards have made it difficult for people to find what they are looking for in the catalog! The United States Newspaper Program and the Association of Research Libraries have adopted alternative (but conflicting) approaches, while the Library of Congress and CONSER have formed task forces to study the problem. At the suggestion of the CONSER Policy Committee, a national summit conference was held to identify a technique for bibliographic control of these items. The Multiple Versions Forum, as it was called, recommended the use of a hierarchical structure to collocate "version" records. The ALA Committee on Cataloging: Description and Access is working to define the specific universe of materials for which this technique should be used and the ALA MARBI Committee is charged with revising the USMARC Format to accommodate the data needed for implementation of this much-needed solution.

Cataloging policy for microform reproductions is one of the hottest topics in cataloging circles. We endlessly debate questions such as:

Crystal Graham is Latin American Studies Cataloger, University of California, San Diego, 9500 Gilman Drive, Mail Code 0175K, La Jolla, CA 92093-0175. In 1989-90, she served as Association of Research Libraries Visting Program Officer charged with preparing guidelines for cataloging microfilm masters. Presently she is ALA Reproduction of Library Materials Section Liaison to the Committee on Cataloging: Description and Access.

Which publication should form the basis of the description? How much recataloging should be done? Are separate bibliographic records necessary? How can we communicate data about different versions? Should microforms be treated differently from other reproductions? The problems are so entangled that the answer to one question often depends upon resolution of another.

THE AACR2 CONTROVERSY

The issue of whether the original publication or the reproduction should be emphasized in the catalog record was first described in 1962 by Wesley Simonton in a study on bibliographic control of microforms for the Association of Research Libraries (ARL).[1] He identified two theories of microform cataloging, the "facsimile theory" and the "edition theory." The "facsimile theory" is primarily concerned with the intellectual content of the work, so the original work is described first, followed by the pertinent details of the microform. The "edition theory," on the other hand, is more concerned with the physical object. In describing the microform, prominence is given to the details of the microform over those of the original publication. The Simonton report recommended that the "facsimile theory" be adopted. The first edition of the *Anglo-American Cataloging Rules* (AACR1), published shortly thereafter, embodied this theory, prescribing description of the original with information about the microform reproduction given in a note.[2]

The second edition of the *Anglo-American Cataloguing Rules* (AACR2) completely reversed course, in effect embracing Simonton's "edition theory" by emphasizing the physical object instead of the original publication. The cardinal principle underlying AACR2 is given in Rule 0.24, a lengthy rule which says in sum: "The starting point for description is the physical form of the item in hand, not the original or any previous form in which the work has been published."[3] Chapter 11 of AACR2 prescribes that the body of the entry describe the microreproduction, with details of the original relegated to a note.

This new principle caused quite a furor in the library community. The idea that the physical object should take precedence over its content was assailed as "an obsession with principle to the exclusion of common sense."[4] Would users be able to find the item sought when the bibliographic description contained the place, publisher, and date of the reproduction rather than the original? Figure 1 shows an example of a brief

```
TITLE            Uno mas uno [microform]
PUBLISHED        La Jolla : University of California, San Diego,
                 1985-
DESCRIPTION      reels : ill. ; 35 mm.
```

Figure 1. Microform cataloged according to AACR2, Chapter 11

display in an online catalog for a microform reproduction cataloged according to Chapter 11 of AACR2.[5] The patron seeking the Mexican newspaper *Uno mas uno* may not recognize this as the desired publication, since the place and publisher of the microfilm are given rather than those of the original publication.[6]

The American Library Association Committee on Cataloging: Description and Access (CC:DA) considered three different proposals for revisions to the rules for cataloging microform reproductions at the 1980 ALA Annual Conference, but none of these were approved by a majority of the voting members. One of the chief reasons for rejecting a special rule for microform reproductions was the objection to treating microforms differently from other reproductions, a sentiment which has greatly influenced the multiple versions controversy described below.[7]

The Library of Congress studied the issue from both processing and public services perspectives, and concluded that when a microform is a reproduction of a previously-published item, it should be described primarily in terms of the original publication and secondarily in terms of the microform. In November 1980 the Library of Congress, the National Agricultural Library and the National Library of Medicine adopted an interim policy to describe microform reproductions as they did under AACR1.[8] Figure 2 illustrates the brief display of the reproduction of *Uno mas uno* cataloged according to that policy.

CC:DA sponsored an open hearing on the microform cataloging question at the 1981 ALA Midwinter Meeting, at which all but one speaker expressed concern about the impact of AACR2 on libraries and library users. In June 1981, CC:DA reversed its prior stand and voted in favor of the Library of Congress' interim policy.[9] When the Joint Steering Committee for the Revision of AACR2 (JSC) considered the issue, however, they decided not to revise the rules at that time, particularly since the issue had not been as thoroughly discussed in the other represented countries as in the United States. Following the JSC meeting, LC issued a rule interpretation of Chapter 11 which declared the interim policy "a final Library of Congress policy." The rule interpretation was adopted as network policy by RLIN and OCLC and thus became the de facto American national standard.[10]

```
TITLE           Uno mas uno [microform]
PUBLISHED       Mexico, D.F. : Editorial Uno S.A. de C.U., 1978-
DESCRIPTION     v. : ill. ; 46 cm.
```

Figure 2. Microform cataloged according to LC rule interpretation

LIBRARY OF CONGRESS PRACTICE

After many years of cataloging of microform serials in the same workflow with other serials, the Library of Congress Serial Record Division (SRD) in 1985 relegated all cataloging of reproduction microform serials to the newly-created CONSER Minimal Level Cataloging Section (CMLC). Contrary to what the name implies, microform reproductions of serials often receive cataloging which is more complete than minimal level. The only time a serial microform reproduction receives original minimal level cataloging is when no full level cataloging copy is available for the publication.[11]

When a full record for the microform already exists in the OCLC database, as is usually the case with commercially issued microforms, it is used by the CMLC Section. When a record for the hard copy or a different microform edition exists in OCLC, it is "cloned" as the basis for the new microform record. All appropriate descriptive information and access points are retained. Name and series headings are given in AACR2 form. When an AACR2 form of name heading does not exist in the Library of Congress name authority file (LCNAF), it is established by the CMLC Section, but no authority record is created. Series are traced only when a series authority record exists in the LCNAF. Subject headings and call numbers are accepted as found on the OCLC source record.

When no record is available online for items held by the Library in hard copy, the LC printed card for the hard copy is transcribed as the basis for the microform record. These records may be latest entry records, which are input in accord with the CONSER guidelines. Oddly, the call number and subject headings found on LC printed cards are not included in the microform record. It is unfortunate that the somewhat arbitrary distinction between microform records based on OCLC source records and those based on LC printed cards results in the loss of subject analysis for the latter category.

One of the biggest problems for the Serial Record Division (SRD) in the past was unreliable notification regarding the acquisition of microform reproductions. Now, incoming microform serials are routed through SRD before going to the Microform Reading Room, and serials selected for filming are cataloged by CMLC staff at the time the filming decision is made. In addition, the SRD has undertaken a project to catalog retrospectively the serial titles filmed by the Preservation Microfilming Office during the decades preceding the current system of notification.[12]

Microform reproductions of monographs have not received the same level of bibliographic control as serials. For many years, monographs filmed at the Library were merely noted in the LC shelflist as added copies.[13] Nowadays, existing monographic microforms are cataloged at minimal level in the Special Materials Cataloging Division, while monographs selected for filming are cataloged by the Preservation Microfilming Office. Despite having the full bibliographic record for the book in hand, the record for the microform is always minimal level. The choice of entry and call number from the original are recorded, but subject headings are never transcribed and some other access points and descriptive elements are omitted in accordance with LC's minimal level cataloging guidelines.[14]

ARL GUIDELINES

When AACR2 was first published, both OCLC and RLIN required that records input to their databases conform to AACR2 (as interpreted by LC) in terms of description, choice and form of access points. Catalogers had to create records for the microforms according to the new code, even when records for the original publications were available. This policy proved especially onerous in the case of serials, because AACR2 requires description based on the first available issue in contrast to AACR1 which specifies the most recent issue. The cataloger must literally "start from scratch." (Compare the records shown in Figures 3 and 4. The choice of entry, as well as most of the body of cataloging entry

```
AUTHOR          Seminar on the Acquisition of Latin American
                Library Materials.
TITLE           SALALM newsletter.
PUBLISHED       Austin, Tex., etc., SALALM Secretariat, University
                of Texas.
DESCRIPTION     v. 28 cm.
DESCRIPTION     1-    1973-
SUBJECT         Acquisition of Latin American publications--
                Periodicals.
SUBJECT         Seminar on the Acquisition of Latin American
                Library Materials--Periodicals.
OTHER TITLE     Seminar on the Acquisition of Latin American
                Library Materials. Newsletter.
```

Figure 3. AACR1 record for the original publication

TITLE	SALALM newsletter [microform]
PUBLISHED	Amherst, Mass. : SALALM Secretariat, University of Massachusetts Library,
DESCRIPTION	v. ; 28 cm.
DESCRIPTION	Began with: Vol. 1 (1973).
DESCRIPTION	Description based on: Vol. 3, no. 1 (May 1975).
NOTE	Microfilm. Vol. 3, no. 1 (May 1975)-v. 15, no. 2 (Dec. 1987). Los Angeles : Filmed for the University of California, San Diego by UCLA Photographic Services, 1990. 3 reels ; 35 mm.
SUBJECT	Acquisition of Latin American publications--Periodicals.
SUBJECT	Seminar on the Acquisition of Latin American Library Materials--Periodicals.
AUTHOR	Seminar on the Acquisition of Latin American Library Materials.
OTHER TITLE	Newsletter.

Figure 4. Microform cataloged according to LCRI of AACR2

differs, simply because the records were created under different editions of AACR.)

To avoid the expense of full-level original cataloging, some libraries have elected to create new records at minimal level. The result is that the catalog record for the master microform, which is essentially the official record for the nation's permanent copy, lacks subject headings, added entries and many notes.

The successful challenge to this requirement to create new records according to AACR2 came not from frustrated user services staff, angry catalogers, or frugal library administrators; the impetus for change arose from the preservation community. A heightened awareness of the need to preserve brittle books and serials, coupled with generous funding from National Endowment for the Humanities (NEH), has resulted in large-scale programs to microfilm library materials. In order to share resources and to prevent duplicative filming, bibliographic records for preservation masters must be readily available.[15]

Imagine the outrage of preservationists when they discovered that a large percentage amount of their preservation filming funding was going to pay for *recataloging*, instead of being used to film as many publications as possible.

In response to this concern, the Research Libraries Group modified the requirements of its bibliographic utility, RLIN. The new RLIN standard allowed catalogers to copy records for original publications without upgrading to AACR2.[16]

The Association of Research Libraries decided that a national standard was needed for the bibliographic records for preservation microform masters. Input was solicited from the library community, with several meetings of the ALCTS Task Force on Bibliographic Control of Microform Masters and the Committee to Study Serials Cataloging devoted to development of guidelines.[17] In September 1990, ARL issued *Guidelines for Bibliographic Records for Preservation Microform Masters.*[18]

The ARL *Guidelines* call for the application of "retrospective conversion standards" to the creation of records for microform masters. Whenever a record exists for the original publication, that record can be "cloned" to form the basis of the microform record. In other words, a record is created for the microform either by inputting the data as they appear on catalog cards for the original or by using a "copy" command ("cre*" in RLIN and "new" in OCLC) to create a new record just like the record for the original with the addition of a microform note, preservation information, and a general material designation (GMD). A basic set of data elements must be included, but the description is not changed to conform to AACR2. The choice of access points is not changed, but the headings are checked against the Library of Congress name authority file. If a heading has been established in AACR2 form, that new heading is used in the microform record.[19] The *Guidelines* describe how to deal with latest and successive entry records and provide guidance for creating new minimal level records, if no record is available for cloning. (Figure 5 illustrates a record created according to the ARL *Guidelines.*)

The National Endowment for the Humanities, the major funding agency for preservation microfilming, now requires libraries to adhere to the ARL *Guidelines* as part of their funding criteria. OCLC has agreed to endorse and distribute the ARL *Guidelines* rather than require libraries to create new records according to AACR2 as interpreted by LC. The

```
AUTHOR          Seminar on the Acquisition of Latin American
                Library Materials.
TITLE           SALALM newsletter [microform]
PUBLISHED       Austin, Tex., etc., SALALM Secretariat, University
                of Texas.
DESCRIPTION     v. 28 cm.
DESCRIPTION     1-   1973-
NOTE            Microfilm.  Vol. 3, no. 1 (May 1975)-v. 15, no. 2
                (Dec. 1987).  Los Angeles : Filmed for the
                University of California, San Diego by UCLA
                Photographic Services, 1990.  3 reels ; 35 mm.
SUBJECT         Acquisition of Latin American publications--
                Periodicals.
SUBJECT         Seminar on the Acquisition of Latin American
                Library Materials--Periodicals.
OTHER TITLE     Seminar on the Acquisition of Latin American
                Library Materials.  Newsletter.
```

Figure 5. Microform cataloged according to ARL Guidelines

ALCTS Task Force on Bibliographic Control of Microform Masters, originally formed to develop its own guidelines, has elected to endorse the ARL *Guidelines* as well.

During the development of the ARL *Guidelines*, two defects of the *USMARC Format for Bibliographic Data* (UFBD) were identified, both of which have subsequently been remedied. First, UFBD lacked a mechanism for identifying the numeric/chronological designation of the issues on the microform. The 362 field of the bibliographic record gave the designation of the issues originally published, yet often only some of those issues had been microfilmed. In early 1990 MARBI added "subfield m" to the 533 field for recording the designations of issues filmed. (In Figure 4, the second element in the note field illustrates the use of this data element.)

Second, the UFBD directed catalogers to code the 008 fixed field for the reproduction rather than for the original publication. For example, a microform reproduction produced by University Microfilms International of a serial published in Brazil, was assigned the country code for "Michigan" rather than "Brazil."[20] In winter 1990, MARBI approved a change to the UFBD directing the cataloger to code the 008 fixed field for the original, except for byte 23 (form of item). A "subfield 7" was defined for the 533 field where the data for the reproduction could be recorded.[21]

INTERNATIONAL COOPERATION

In May 1989, the International Federation of Library Association and Institutions (IFLA) sponsored the IFLA Symposium on Managing the Preservation of Serial Literature, held at the Library of Congress. The major theme was the importance of international cooperation in serials preservation.

While the degree of overlap is not known, most libraries collect literature of many countries. The preservation dollar, pound, or peso will stretch much further if a serial is microfilmed only once, with copies available to users around the world. Achieving this goal will require an international database of compatible bibliographic records of preserved items.[22]

The Commission on Preservation and Access (CPA) International Project is taking the lead to foster cooperation among U.S. libraries and institutions abroad. The Project's objectives are to determine the extent of existing preservation records, to identify the difficulties in converting these records to machine-readable format and entering them into a common database, to agree on the level of bibliographic detail needed to exchange records easily, and to determine the best method for creation of a shared database.[23] The Commission on Preservation and Access sponsored a meeting in Zurich, Switzerland on May 13-16, 1990 to begin work on an international register of microform masters. The Commission of European Communities has already done extensive planning for a *European Register of Microform Masters*, which will be based at the Bibliothèque nationale in Paris.[24] The intent of the CPA meeting was to "find the common ground" among American, Canadian, and European practices and to assure that records will be compatible, both bibliographically and technically.[25]

The biggest problem for bibliographic compatibility is the "AACR2" issue discussed earlier: should the record emphasize the microform or the original? The Canadians, who use AACR2 as written, have graciously agreed to develop conversion programs so that their records will conform to the American and European practice of emphasizing the original publication. The Canadians hope that universal adoption of the "multiple versions" solution (described below) will eliminate such incompatibility.[26] The most troublesome dilemma identified to date is that serial linking entries are recorded so differently in the UNIMARC format and the USMARC format that it may not be possible to convert this information from one system to the other.

THE MULTIPLE VERSIONS PROBLEM

The "retrospective conversion standard" described in the ARL *Guidelines* was hailed as a way to communicate records for microform masters without causing enormous cataloging backlogs. It did nothing, however, to alleviate the confusion and expense caused by separate bibliographic records for each version of a publication.

In the days before machine-readable cataloging, a library owning a publication in both paper and microform could describe both on a single record. AACR1 included special provisions for the treatment of such multiple versions, which it called "issues," saying that "if variations between issues are so great that the publications cannot be treated as copies but the title and text of the works are the same, they are cataloged as different issues."[27] These issues were noted on catalog cards by means of a dash entry. Since AACR2 prescribes description of the physical piece in hand, it contains no provisions for the use of dash entries to record issues. Likewise, the *USMARC Format for Bibliographic Data* requires a separate record for each version.

Let's look at a simple example of the confusion caused by creating essentially duplicate records for every version. You are looking for an article published in 1987 in *Information Technology and Libraries*. You search the OPAC and retrieve three citations. (See Figure 6.) You select the first item listed and discover that it lists current issues only. (See Figure 7.) If you happen to remember that there were other selections, you go back to the summary screen. (Look again at Figure 6.) The second selection says microform, but upon calling up the record, you see the holdings are for 1982-1984 only. (See Figure 8.) Once again you go back to the menu screen. (Look again at Figure 6.) Indeed, there is another microform listing, and when you look at it, you find what you are looking for. (See Figure 9.) If you are curious as to why there were three postings, you can call up the full records, (See Figures 10, 11, 12), and you will see that the library has partial runs in microfilm, microfiche, and paper. When the cataloging records are prepared under different catalog codes, the displays are even more difficult to comprehend.[28]

Widespread dissatisfaction with microform cataloging standards has caused librarians to explore other alternatives to AACR2 as interpreted by the Library of Congress. Many libraries simply ignore national standards and append their holdings of microforms to records for the original publication. In fact, many union lists require participants to do just that in order to accommodate version and holdings data in an intelligible fashion. An informal survey taken at a 1985 RTSD Serials Section Research Libraries Discussion Group meeting revealed that about 50% of the participants worked in libraries which deviated from national standards for cataloging microform reproductions of serials.[29] At the 1986 ACRL Conference, librarians from Ohio State described their practice of using a single bibliographic record and appending holdings information for different versions in item records in their local system.[30]

```
You searched for title: Information technology and libraries

3 titles found; Titles 1-3 are:

1) Information technology and libraries
2) Information technology and libraries [microform]
3) Information technology and libraries [microform]
```

Figure 6. Browse screen for multiple versions

```
TITLE           Information technology and libraries.
PUBLISHED       Chicago, IL : Library and Information Technology
                Association, c1982-
DESCRIPTION     v. : ill. ; 24 cm.
```

```
LOCATION: Current Periodicals Room
CALL NO.: Z678.9.A1I53
HOLDINGS: Current issues
```

Figure 7.

```
TITLE           Information technology and libraries [microform]
PUBLISHED       Chicago, IL : Library and Information Technology
                Association, c1982-
DESCRIPTION     v. : ill. ; 24 cm.
```

```
LOCATION: Microform Reading Room
CALL NO.: Film 555
HOLDINGS: 1 (1982)-3 (1984)
```

Figure 8.

```
TITLE           Information technology and libraries [microform]
PUBLISHED       Chicago, IL : Library and Information Technology
                Association, c1982-
DESCRIPTION     v. : ill. ; 24 cm.
```

```
LOC: Microform Reading Room
CALL: X8065
HOLD: 4 (1985)-
```

Figure 9.

UNITED STATES NEWSPAPER PROGRAM

The United States Newspaper Program (USNP) is a major national program funded largely by the National Endowment for the Humanities, to identify, preserve, and catalog all newspapers ever published in the United States. Catalogers are responsible for determining the publication history of each paper–a formidable assignment given the generic titles and frequent title changes of many papers–and also for recording the specific issues held by each institution. Consider that many newspapers

TITLE	Information technology and libraries.
PUBLISHED	Chicago, IL : Library and Information Technology Association, c1982-
DESCRIPTION	v. : ill. ; 24 cm.
NOTE	Vol. 1, no. 1 (Mar. 1982)-
NOTE	Title from cover.
NOTE	Official publication of the Library and Information Technology Association.
NOTE	Continues: Journal of library automation.
SUBJECT	Information science--Periodicals.
SUBJECT	Libraries--Automation--Periodicals.
SUBJECT	Information storage and retrieval systems--Periodicals.
AUTHOR	Library and Information Technology Association (U.S.)

Figure 10.

TITLE	Information technology and libraries [microform]
PUBLISHED	Chicago, IL : Library and Information Technology Association, c1982-
DESCRIPTION	v. : ill. ; 24 cm.
NOTE	Vol. 1, no. 1 (Mar. 1982)-
NOTE	Title from cover.
NOTE	Official publication of the Library and Information Technology Association.
NOTE	Continues: Journal of library automation.
NOTE	Microfilm. Ann Arbor, Mich. : University Microfilms. reels ; 35 mm.
SUBJECT	Information science--Periodicals.
SUBJECT	Libraries--Automation--Periodicals.
SUBJECT	Information storage and retrieval systems--Periodicals.
AUTHOR	Library and Information Technology Association (U.S.)

Figure 11.

have been microfilmed by various agencies over the years, and you can begin to picture how complex a job it is to create intelligible records for these newspaper runs.

USNP coordinators opted to take a "master record" approach, utilizing the capabilities of OCLC's union list subsystem. A single bibliographic record for the original publication is created, with local data records attached giving locations, holdings, and physical format.[31] This single record approach overcomes many problems. It's much easier for users to consult a single record than to flip back and forth amongst a host of records; it's cheaper than creating, storing, and maintaining duplicate records; and it's a lot less work for catalogers. At first glance, it seems perfect, but the major flaw with USNP is its lack of full preservation information. Although the local data records indicate the format of the

TITLE	Information technology and libraries [microform]
PUBLISHED	Chicago, IL : Library and Information Technology Association, c1982-
DESCRIPTION	v. : ill. ; 24 cm.
NOTE	Vol. 1, no. 1 (Mar. 1982)-
NOTE	Title from cover.
NOTE	Official publication of the Library and Information Technology Association.
NOTE	Continues: Journal of library automation.
NOTE	Microfiche. Ann Arbor, Mich. : University Microfilms. microfiche ; 11 x 15 cm.
SUBJECT	Information science--Periodicals.
SUBJECT	Libraries--Automation--Periodicals.
SUBJECT	Information storage and retrieval systems--Periodicals.
AUTHOR	Library and Information Technology Association (U.S.)

Figure 12.

holdings, no information is given about the availability or physical characteristics of the microforms.

At the time USNP adopted this approach, Lucia Rather, then Director of Cataloging at the Library of Congress, said that it should not be considered a precedent. Yet the success of the USNP approach was a major impetus for further investigation into the feasibility of adopting a ''master record concept'' for multiple versions.[32]

MULTIPLE VERSIONS STUDIES

The Library of Congress recognized the growing incompatibility of bibliographic records for microforms. Within the CONSER database alone, Canadian records follow AACR2 as published, most American records conform to the Library of Congress rule interpretation, and the USNP records use a ''master record'' convention. In 1984, LC decided that a comprehensive study should be undertaken of the problem, with a scope much wider than microform cataloging. The term ''multiple versions'' or ''mulver'' was coined to encompass all publications that are identical in content but different in physical format, such as sound recordings on cassette and disk, motion pictures in dubbed and subtitled versions, and videocassettes in Beta and VHS format. Helen Schmierer was hired by LC as a consultant to make recommendations on the bibliographic treatment of multiple versions. She concluded that separate records should be made for different versions, except that ''for some categories of reproductions, the separate record may in some well-defined instances be a holdings record identifying the changed physical format.''[33]

LC then appointed an in-house committee to investigate the multiple versions issue. Their fundamental conclusion was that the essence of the problem is not caused by the standards for cataloging and communicating the records, but rather by the display conventions of individual systems and bibliographic networks. The Committee recommended the continued use of separate bibliographic records for related versions, but with explicit links among the version records.[34] The idea was that these links would clarify the relationships of the version records and that programs could be developed to display the records as a cluster in local catalogs and bibliographic utilities.

This scheme was not well received by some members of the library community, as the fundamental question of the utility and expense of creating largely duplicate catalog records had not been addressed. The linking technique was criticized for increasing cataloging workloads, since the catalogers would need to identify all the version records and create and maintain links among them. Local systems were expected to eliminate the redundancy in display formats, but the Committee considered it beyond its purview to suggest how that could be done.

The LC Committee gave serious consideration to the use of the *USMARC Format for Holdings Data* for describing multiple versions, observing that it ''could represent a promising strategy.''[35] Their reasons for rejecting the strategy were two-fold. First of all, they found that approach was not satisfactory for all types of versions. Their conviction that a single solution must be applied to all version types forestalled consideration of using the *Holdings Format* for any of them. Secondly, the Committee recognized that this technique would require all libraries to use the *Holdings Format*. How curious that use of a recognized national standard was seen as a defect, especially in a report emanating from the Library of Congress, the very creators of the USMARC Format!

In the meantime, the CONSER Program formed a task force to study the multiple versions problem. This group never did reach a consensus, as some me/mbers favored the status quo while others adamantly supported use of the *USMARC Format for Holdings Data*.[36] Given the lack of progress in resolving the multiple versions problem, the CONSER Policy Committee approached LC with the idea of bringing together a group of interested parties to reach a consensus.

MULTIPLE VERSIONS FORUM

In December 1989 an invitational meeting was held at Airlie House in Virginia. This meeting was funded by the Council on Library Resources and organized by the Library of Congress. Participants represented a variety of affected parties: national libraries, bibliographic utilities, local systems, cataloging theoreticians, programmers, CONSER, ALA's Committees on Cataloging: Description and Access (CC:DA) and Machine-Readable Bibliographic Information (MARBI), and some hands-on catalogers.[37]

The goal of the Multiple Versions Forum was to identify a technique for communicating bibliographic data about versions, that is, items with equivalent artistic and intellectual content but differences in physical format. While the Forum considered many types of versions, it was apparent that microreproductions were the most crucial category. All options were considered with an emphasis on their potential for resolution of microform cataloging problems. The pros and cons of separate records, composite records, and two- and three-tiered hierarchical records were debated.

The composite record approach was quickly discarded due to the impossibility of adding and replacing version information in a single record in a multi-network environment. The difficulty of relating multiple fields relating to different versions, linking holdings information to such a record, and generating bibliographic products also precluded its acceptance. The linked but separate record model was rejected, since it would be as unwieldy as the current situation and "the prospect of having system-specific links among records would lead to great confusion and ambiguity in inter-system record transfer."[38] The three-tier hierarchical approach was found to be the most theoretically attractive alternative, but the costs of implementing this option seemed entirely out of proportion to its potential benefits, since a three-tier hierarchy would require a new structure which would be incompatible with existing databases.[39]

The Multiple Versions Forum recommended using a "two-tier hierarchical technique;" in other words, using the *USMARC Format for Holdings Data*. In this scenario, holdings records containing version information are linked to a master bibliographic record. In the case of microreproductions, the full bibliographic record describes the original publication and each holdings record describes a reproduction.

This technique was attractive to the Forum participants because it "eliminate[s] the confusion brought about by having multiple instances of 'near-match-but-somehow-different' records. Version data can be displayed in a clear and unambiguous manner because the salient data about each version is concentrated in each of the attached USMARC holdings records.''[40] The method is perceived as cost-effective, because it eliminates the requirement to create separate bibliographic records for each version, liberating catalogers from the onerous workload described above, and it utilizes a machine-readable format which library automation vendors and utilities are already committed to implement.[41]

This solution is similar to the USNP approach: a description of the original publication with holdings information appended. It is better than USNP, however, because it utilizes a standardized format, the *USMARC Format for Holdings Data*, rather than OCLC's union list system. In addition, the *USMARC Format for Holdings Data* provides for bibliographic description of the microform (e.g., publisher and physical description) and for preservation data (which appears in coded form in the 007 field).

CC:DA MULTIPLE VERSIONS TASK FORCE

The Multiple Versions Forum identified the conceptual model for communicating bibliographic data about multiple versions; that is, use of a hierarchical technique. The responsibility for defining the scope of materials to which the technique should be applied was assumed by the ALA Committee on Cataloging: Description and Access (CC:DA), which formed a Multiple Versions Task Force. As of this writing, the Task Force report has not yet been presented to the full Committee, so all recommendations described below must be regarded as preliminary.

Identifying precisely what materials belong under the ''multiple versions'' rubric bogged down many discussions.[42] The members of the LC Committee, the CONSER Task Force, the Multiple Versions Forum, and the CC:DA Task Force all agreed that the materials under consideration should have ''equivalent'' content[43] and that variant editions (e.g., revisions, translations, adaptations) and ''side-car'' publications (e.g., supplements, cumulations, indexes) should be excluded. Reproductions of both print and non-print materials were specifically identified by the Multiple Versions Forum as materials which could be effectively represented using the hierarchical technique. The question of simultaneously issued publications was referred to specialists in each non-print area.[44]

The CC:DA Task Force established subcommittees to consider the application of the technique to different categories of materials. Interest groups such as the Music Library Association and OnLine Audiovisual Catalogers were contacted. The Task Force concluded that the hierarchical technique was suitable for data about all types of reproductions, such as microformats, sound records and video materials that contain copies of previously existing works. This decision extends the benefits of the technique beyond the print community, and also satisfies the objections mentioned earlier about treating microforms differently from other reproductions.

The CC:DA Task Force recommended against the application of the hierarchical approach to simultaneously issued versions, such as cassettes and disks, Beta and VHS videocassettes, or foreign editions, for two reasons. First, few savings were realized when only the data elements common to both versions were contained in a rather barren bibliographic record, while the data elements unique to each version were contained in detailed holdings records. Secondly, the task of determining whether versions are indeed equivalent in content would place a new and difficult burden on catalogers.

Reprints proved to be one of the most controversial types of versions. Monographic catalogers tend to think of reprints as variant editions, while serials librarians view them as substitutes for the original publication. One of the most pressing reasons to adopt the "multiple versions solution" is the need to collocate all the holdings of a serial run held by a library. Exclusion of reprints would result in catalog displays giving a library's holdings of the hard copy, photocopied issues, microfilm and microfiche issues in one record, while listing the issues held in reprint in a separate, unrelated record. The Multiple Versions Forum report specifically excluded monographic reprints from consideration,[45] but the CC:DA Task Force reconsidered that recommendation in the hope that one set of guidelines could be applied to both serials and monographs.

And what of the cataloging rules themselves? The cardinal principle of AACR2 to describe the physical piece was, to a large extent, what stirred up all this trouble in the first place. The Multiple Versions Forum report contended that no change to the rules was needed, rationalizing that since the bibliographic data in the separate holdings record for the version will describe only the physical item in the cataloger's hands, not the original or any other version, it could be considered to be in accord with the emphasis of AACR2 on the description of the physical item.[46] This twisted logic failed to acknowledge that the cataloger may need to create the bibliographic record for the original publication, using the reproduction in hand as the basis of the description.

The CC:DA Task Force has proposed a rule revision which would resolve the conflict. The cardinal principle is reworded to maintain the concept of describing the item in hand according to the chapter appropriate to the type of material, but eliminating the directive to use the piece in hand as the starting point for description. An optional rule would be added to sanction the use of a multilevel description for reproductions.[47]

MARBI AND MULTIPLE VERSIONS

While CC:DA is responsible for identifying the scope of the "multiple versions" application, decisions about the USMARC format fall to ALA's Committee on Machine-Readable Bibliographic Information (MARBI). In addition, bibliographic utilities and local system vendors must decide how to display the data to users.

The *USMARC Format for Holdings Data* was originally designed to accommodate a limited amount of bibliographic data about reproductions. The format includes an 843 field for reproduction notes (similar to the 533 in the bibliographic format) and an 007 field for coded physical description of microforms. The limitations of the current structure pose a number of problems for implementation of the "multiple versions technique." Additional data elements beyond those allowed in the 843 will no doubt be needed, such as edition statements, other titles, and notes which relate to the reproduction only. In fact, the CC:DA Task Force identified the need in the subordinate record for virtually every field in the bibliographic format.

One of the most technically difficult areas is the need to provide access points, and therefore, to index portions of the holdings record. While the current format provides for inclusion of a series statement, no series tracing is allowed. Likewise, variant titles, editors of reprints, and other entries may be required.

In order to facilitate the addition of data elements and the indexing of access points, the Library of Congress has proposed a new structure for the *Holdings Format*. In the new model, each data element would be contained in a separate field rather than residing in subfields of a single field. Other commentators have observed that the large amount of bibliographic data that will be given in the holdings record, resulting in considerable redundancy of that description in union databases, points toward reconsideration of the three-tiered model previously rejected. Part of the dilemma is due to the desire to accomplish two different objectives with a single solution: (1) The desire to collocate records by version in bibliographic utilities and (2) The desire to display serial holdings in chronological order.

Without knowing the details of the communications format, the bibliographic utilities and local systems cannot design the displays for their systems. Yet it is difficult to make recommendations for revisions to the *Holdings Format* without some notion of the impact such decisions will have on the end product. A further consideration is the impact these decisions will have on cataloging products, such as cards, tapes, and the profile-matching programs used to supply analytics of microform sets.

Other topics which MARBI will need to address include the provision of non-roman data in the Holdings Format, delineation of the linking mechanism between holdings and bibliographic records, and the need for coded data about the reproduction.

CONCLUSION

Dissatisfaction with the requirements of AACR2 for cataloging microform reproductions has generated a panoply of alternative approaches, rule interpretations, and national studies. The American decision to emphasize the original publication in bibliographic description has provided the opportunity to streamline cataloging without impairing access. The provision for "cloning" existing records set forth in the ARL *Guidelines* and endorsed by the bibliographic utilities has expedited processing of preservation microforms. The USNP "master record" approach has demonstrated the feasibility of using a single bibliographic record to collocate all versions of a library's holdings. The technique identified by the Multiple Versions Forum has the potential for enhancing access, facilitating cataloging, and rationalizing the treatment of materials in different formats. Systems designers face a monumental challenge in the development of a communications format and creation of intelligible online displays. The key to the success of the "multiple versions technique" will be its implementation by the bibliographic utilities and local systems. The realization of uniform and intelligible access to bibliographic records for microform reproductions depends upon their success.

REFERENCES

1. Wesley Simonton, "The Bibliographic Control of Microforms," *Library Resources & Technical Services* 6, no. 1 (winter 1962): 29-40.

2. *Anglo-American Cataloging Rules. North American Text.* (Chicago: American Library Association, 1967), 253-254. (Rule 191)

3. *Anglo-American Cataloguing Rules*, 2nd Ed., 1988 Revision. (Ottawa and

Chicago: Canadian Library Association, American Library Association, 1988), 8. (Rule 0.24)

4. Louis Charles Willard, "Microforms and AACR2, Chapter 11: Is the Cardinal Principle a Peter Principle?" *Microform Review* 10, no. 2 (spring 1981): 76.

5. While the publications cited in the examples in this article are real, the reproduction data and online catalog displays have been created for illustration purposes.

6. For other examples of the problems this policy would have caused for serials, see: Diane Stine, "The Cataloging of Serials in Microform under AACRII Rules," *The Serials Librarian* 5, no. 3 (spring 1981): 19-23.

7. Janet Swan Hill, "Descriptions of Reproductions of Previously Existing Works: Another View," *Microform Review* 11, no. 1 (winter 1982): 14-21.

8. "Decision on Microforms," *Library of Congress Information Bulletin* 39, no. 47 (Nov. 21, 1980): 448.

9. Richard W. Boss, *Cataloging Titles in Microform Sets: Report of a Study Conducted in 1980 for the Association of Research Libraries by Information Systems Consultants, Inc.* (Washington, D.C.: Association of Research Libraries, 1983), 58-59.

10. "Library of Congress Policy for Cataloging of Microreproductions," *Cataloging Service Bulletin* 14 (fall 1981): 56-58.

11. Jean Hirons, Head of the CONSER Minimal Level Cataloging Section, Library of Congress, letter to the author, Nov. 11, 1990.

12. Jean Hirons, "Report on Serial Microform Cataloging Activities," *Library of Congress Information Bulletin* 49, no. 7 (March 26, 1990): 124-125.

13. Boss, *Cataloging Titles in Microform Sets,* 58-59.

14. Jeffrey Heynen, Special Materials Cataloging Division, Library of Congress, electronic mail message, Feb. 28, 1991.

15. For an excellent overview of the importance of bibliographic control for preservation microfilms, as well as instructions for cataloging microfilms, see: Nancy E. Gwinn, ed. "Preservation Microfilming and Bibliographic Control," *Preservation Microfilming: A Guide for Librarians and Archivists.* (Chicago: American Library Association, 1987), 132-147.

16. *RLG Preservation Manual.* 2nd ed. (Palo Alto: Research Libraries Group, 1986): 72.

17. Crystal Graham, "Guidelines for Cataloging Microform Masters (Serials)," *RTSD Newsletter* 14, no. 6: 53-54.

18. *Guidelines for Bibliographic Records for Preservation Microform Masters.* (Washington, D.C.: Association of Research Libraries, 1990). The 1990 guidelines cover both books and serials, superseding the guidelines for books issued in 1989.

19. The only significant difference between the ARL *Guidelines* and the practices of LC's CONSER Minimal Cataloging Section is that the *Guidelines* allow libraries to use pre-AACR2 forms of headings when the AACR2 form is not available in the LCNAF, while the CMLC Section formulates the AACR2 form of a name heading if it has not already been established.

20. Another example of the fixed field problem was the date coding for monographs. The initial date position (which is usually the one displayed and indexed) was the date of the reproduction rather than the original, unlike the coding for serials which gave the dates of the original.

21. MARBI Proposal no. 90-8. Approved Nov. 21, 1990.

22. Patricia Battin, "Information Collection and Preservation and Sharing in the Global Context," in *Managing the Preservation of Serial Literature*. Ed. Merrily Smith. (Munich: K.G. Saur, forthcoming. IFLA publication #57).

23. Commission on Preservation and Access, *Annual Report* (July 1, 1989-June 30, 1990): 22-23.

24. G. Vitiello, "EROMM: A European Bibliographic Tool." June 1990.

25. Hans Rütimann, Program Officer, Commission on Preservation and Access, telephone conversation with the author, Mar. 7, 1991.

26. Margaret Stewart, National Library of Canada, telephone conversation with the author, Nov. 30, 1990.

27. *Anglo-American Cataloging Rules. North American Text. Chapter 6.* (Chicago: American Library Association, 1974), 100-101. (Rule 152B)

28. Additional examples of the problems caused by the creation of independent records can be found in: Crystal Graham, "Rethinking National Policy for Cataloging Microform Reproductions," *Cataloging & Classification Quarterly* 6, no. 4 (summer 1986): 69-83.

29. "Cataloging for Print and Microform Serials: One Record or Two?" Meeting of the American Library Association, Resources and Technical Services Division, Serials Section, Research Libraries Discussion Group, Washington, D.C., Jan. 1985. Coordinated by Crystal Graham. Reported in *The Serials Librarian* 10, no. 4 (summer 1986): 163, and *Library of Congress Information Bulletin* 44, no. 28 (July 15, 1985): 181-182.

30. Marjorie E. Adams and Daphne C. Hsueh. "Handling of Serials in Micro-Reproduction: Single Bibliographic Record–An Ohio State University Experience," in *Energies for Transition: Proceedings of the Fourth National Conference of the Association of College and Research Libraries, Baltimore, Maryland, April 9-12, 1986*. Ed. Danuta A. Nitecki. (Chicago: American Library Association, 1986), 23-26.

31. Robert B. Harriman, "Coordination of Cataloging Practices in the United States Newspaper Program," *Cataloging & Classification Quarterly* 6, no. 4 (summer 1986): 69-83.

32. Ruth C. Carter, "Editorial," *Cataloging & Classification Quarterly* 8, no. 2 (1987/88): 2-3.

33. Helen F. Schmierer, "Multiple Versions: A Consideration," October 1985 draft.

34. Library of Congress Multiple Versions Committee, *"Communication of Records for Multiple Versions."* April 27, 1988. (Distributed as MARBI Discussion Paper no. 21.)

35. *Ibid.*, 8.

36. CONSER Multiple Versions Task Force. "Final Report." June 1989.

37. The serials community was represented by Linda Bartley (Library of Congress, CONSER Operations Coordinator), Linda West (member of the CONSER Policy Committee), Betsy Humphries (chair of the CONSER Multiple Versions Task Force) and Crystal Graham (cataloger).

38. *Multiple Versions Forum report* (Washington, D.C.: Network Development and MARC Standards Office, Library of Congress, 1990), 29.

39. *Ibid.*, 28.

40. *Ibid.*, 11.

41. *Ibid.*, 12.

42. For an exhaustive discussion on the topic, see Crystal Graham, "Scope and Definition of Multiple Versions," *Cataloging & Classification Quarterly* 11, no. 2 (1990): 5-32.

43. The term "equivalence" was first applied to bibliographic relationships by Barbara Tillett in her *Bibliographic Relationships: Toward a Conceptual Structure of Bibliographic Information Used in Cataloging*. (Thesis (Ph. D.)–UCLA, 1987). Photocopy. Ann Arbor, Mich.: University Microfilms International, 1989. (Catalog no. 8721068), 24-25.

44. *Multiple Versions Forum Report*, 10.

45. *Ibid.*, 10.

46. *Ibid.*, 17.

47. "Multilevel Description Applied to Reproductions," a memorandum from John Attig to Verna Urbanski, Oct. 13, 1990

Serials Cataloging Time and Costs: Results of an Ongoing Study at Iowa State University

Lori L. Osmus
Dilys E. Morris

SUMMARY. All Technical Services staff at Iowa State University (ISU) Library are involved in an ongoing time and cost study which began in April 1987. Since the initiation of this research project, nineteen one-week samples have been taken. In this article we will analyze the data for the Serials Cataloging Section, present times and costs associated with serials cataloging at ISU, compare them with monographic cataloging times and costs, and explain the use and importance of the information.

TIME AND COST STUDY METHODOLOGY

All Technical Services staff at Iowa State University participate in an ongoing time and cost study. They maintain records of the total time worked during the course of a sample week. For two years samples were gathered every other month, but during the third year the collection periods were reduced to four times a year. All work is divided into seven Centers and each Center into tasks. An eighth Center, Leave, tracks sick leave, vacation, and holiday time. The Centers are defined as follows:

ORDERING/RECEIVING/CLAIMING: Includes all the order, receiving and claiming functions as well as the maintenance of associated files but not the selection of materials.

Lori L. Osmus is Head of the Serials Cataloging Section and Dilys E. Morris is Assistant Director for Technical Services at Iowa State University.

CATALOGING: Includes copy and original cataloging, searching for copy, authority work, recataloging, and internal file maintenance associated with cataloging.

VOLUME PREPARATION: Includes all functions associated with marking materials, binding, Tattle Taping, and minor in-house binding.

CATALOG MAINTENANCE: Includes the activities involved in maintaining online databases (OPAC, union lists, OCLC, etc.), card catalogs and shelf lists, making holdings and location changes, and entering into OCLC cataloging completed off-line.

AUTOMATION: Tracks the impact of the introduction of personal computers, the maintenance of the Library's computer files for a former PC-based online catalog, troubleshooting and general automation maintenance of the PC-based online catalog.

CONVERSION: Covers a long-term retrospective monographic bibliographic conversion project.

MISCELLANEOUS: Includes all administration time, meeting attendance, non-divisional library and university work, professional service and research, and any other work time not associated with one Center.

LEAVE: Vacation, sick leave, and holidays occurring during the sample week.

Each Center includes all the time associated with that activity except meetings. Nearly every Center contains the activities of Training, Procedure and Policy Documentation, Consulting and Referring, Solving Problems, Sorting /Shelving/Distributing/Receiving, Revising, and Other. There is a total of 139 tasks divided among the Centers as shown in Table 1. The task definitions are based on logical differentiations between work activities, identification of activities anticipated to change with automation, and uniformity of task definitions across Centers to facilitate analysis on a wider basis.

Time is recorded in increments of a quarter hour and is rounded to the nearest quarter of an hour. (Example: Copy Cataloging for 1 hour and 10

TABLE 1

TECHNICAL SERVICES CENTERS AND TASKS

Centers	Number of Tasks
Ordering/Receiving/Claiming	27
Cataloging	15
Volume Preparation	19
Catalog Maintenance	24
Automation	12
Conversion	15
Miscellaneous	24
Leave	3

minutes would be recorded as 1.25 on a time sheet.) Break time is not recorded; instead employees spread break time over the tasks worked.

The time studies are conducted anonymously. Staff identify themselves by a position number which reflects their position in the organizational hierarchy. Using these position numbers, data were extracted for the Serials Cataloging Section. Employees submit time sheets to the Assistant Director's secretary who checks each for mathematical accuracy and any obvious errors. Periodically, supervisors review time sheets to be certain no problems have arisen, but these reviews are announced prior to the study period. Later, supervisory meetings are held to review the continuing accuracy of task definitions and to identify needed changes.

Technical Services faculty frequently work more than 40 hours a week but are not reimbursed for this time. The time portion of the reports thus reflects this greater than 40 hour week. Because the study software computes hourly salaries and multiplies task hours by hourly salaries, the costs reflect dollars which the University did not pay. To adjust for these unreimbursed hours, records are kept of the faculty time worked over 40 hours during a sample week, but there is no way of knowing in what activities the time was spent. Thus, the over-40 inflated costs are removed across the board from all Centers. This amounts to four percent of the Serials Cataloging Section costs.

Costs are based on actual salaries plus benefits and are updated for each study period. The Miscellaneous and Leave Center times are apportioned across all the other six Centers as overhead.

SERIALS CATALOGING SECTION STAFFING

A description of the staffing and responsibilities of the Serials Cataloging Section may be helpful to place the time and cost study data in context. The Section consists of the Section Head and two other faculty catalogers, three Library Assistant (LA) IIIs, one of whom is half-time, two LA IIs, one of whom is three-quarters-time, and ten to fifteen hours per week of student assistance. The Section Head and faculty catalogers are expected to engage in professional activities, undertake research and scholarship, and also have supervisory responsibilities. One faculty cataloger supervises the LA IIIs, who perform copy cataloging. The other faculty cataloger supervises the LA IIs, one of whom is primarily responsible for pre-cataloging searching, while the other supervises the clerical processing of material before and after it is handled by the catalogers, including work done by the student assistants. The LA IIs also engage in some of the less time-consuming recataloging, and are part of a central staff who update records in the online catalog for the Cataloging Department as a whole.

AVERAGE WEEKLY HOURS

Of the 3,106 average weekly hours worked in Technical Services during the time and cost study, the Serials Cataloging Section accounts for 311, or about 10% of the Division's time. Although the Section's 7.25 F.T.E. staff working 40 hours a week would work 290 hours, the 21-hour difference comes from the time faculty work over 40 hours (averages 9.26 weekly) without additional compensation, and the hours worked by student assistants.

The Section's largest cost center, not surprisingly, is Cataloging (see Table 2), and the 152 hours the Section spends in that cost center is 29.12% of the 522 hours spent weekly in the Technical Services Cataloging Center.

What is surprising is that only 48.87% of the Section's time is spent in the Cataloging Center. The next largest category is Miscellaneous, 24.76%, which includes administration, writing reports, reading memos, personal professional time and all meeting attendance. Leave (vacation

TABLE 2

WEEKLY AVERAGES

Cost Centers	Technical Services Hours	Serials Cataloging Section Hours	Serials Percentages Total Section Time	Serials Percentages Total Division Time	Monographic Cataloging Section Hours	Monographic Percentages Total Section Time	Monographic Percentages Total Division Time
Ordering	796	0	0.00%	0.00%	43	8.40%	1.38%
Cataloging	522	152	48.87%	4.89%	290	56.64%	9.34%
Catalog Maintenance	378	34	10.93%	1.09%	5	0.98%	0.16%
Volume Preparation	291	3	0.96%	0.10%	0	0.00%	0.00%
Conversion	145	1	0.32%	0.03%	41	8.01%	1.32%
Automation	35	1	0.32%	0.03%	1	0.20%	0.03%
Miscellaneous	619	77	24.76%	2.48%	74	14.45%	2.38%
Leave	320	43	13.83%	1.38%	58	11.33%	1.87%
Total	3106	311	100.00%	10.01%	512	100.00%	16.48%
F.T.E.	77.65	7.78			12.8		

and sick leave) is the next largest use of time, an average of 43 hours a week out of the 311, or 13.83%. The Section was responsible for a number of Catalog Maintenance tasks during the course of the cost study, such as shelf list card filing and revision, sequencing records for a local serials data base, cleaning up serial records in the online catalog, and sorting OCLC serial card receipts. Some of these activities over the course of the study have been discontinued or are no longer performed in the Section, and some, such as inputting records in the OPAC, were added. They account for an average of 10.93% of the Section's work. Activities in the remaining Centers account for 1% or less of the Section's work.

Out of all the Centers, the Serials Cataloging Section's top ten tasks in both time and cost are, in order starting with the highest: recataloging, administration, copy cataloging, vacation, sick leave, meetings, personal professional work, copy searching, authority work, and sorting. The average weekly times and costs of these tasks, as well as percentages of the Section's total time and cost, are shown in Table 3. These tasks account for 73.19% of the Section's time and 75.2% of its costs.

Since there is not space in this article to analyze every task performed in the Serials Cataloging Section, it seems most useful to concentrate on the Section's largest cost center, Cataloging. The five Cataloging tasks in the Section's overall top ten tasks account for 83.25% of the time and 81.24% of the cost in the Section's Cataloging Center. Original cataloging falls immediately after the top five Cataloging tasks and accounts for 4.23% of the time but 4.87% of the cost because it is performed exclusively by faculty catalogers. The order of the other Cataloging tasks can be seen in Table 4, along with their average weekly times and costs and percentages of the Cataloging Center. Descriptions of the Cataloging Center tasks are in Appendix A at the end of this article.

For some tasks, the average time and cost per week can be deceiving. By taking the ratio of the standard deviation to the average of each task to obtain the coefficient of variation, one can see which tasks are per-

TABLE 3

TEN LARGEST TASKS

Centers	Tasks	Time (of Section Time)	Cost
Cataloging	Recataloging	22.89%	22.78%
Miscellaneous	Administration	9.12%	10.10%
Cataloging	Copy Cataloging	8.74%	8.96%
Leave	Vacation	7.18%	7.78%
Leave	Sick Leave	5.72%	5.47%
Miscellaneous	Meetings	5.55%	6.17%
Miscellaneous	Personal Professional	4.81%	6.14%
Cataloging	Copy Searching	3.21%	2.73%
Cataloging	Authority Work	3.00%	2.58%
Cataloging	Sorting and Shelving	2.97%	2.49%
	Totals	73.19%	75.20%

TABLE 4

WEEKLY AVERAGES FOR CATALOGING TASKS

Definitions	Percent Time (of Center Time)	Percent Cost	Hours	Hourly Salary	Cost (+Over40)
Recataloging	46.53%	46.46%	71.37	$13.89	$991
Copy Cataloging	17.77%	18.20%	27.24	$14.32	$390
Authority Work	6.39%	5.77%	9.34	$12.01	$112
Searching Copy	6.56%	5.72%	10.01	$11.84	$119
Sorting & Shelving	6.00%	5.09%	9.25	$11.70	$108
Original Cataloging	4.23%	4.87%	6.80	$15.89	$108
Consulting	2.92%	3.55%	4.54	$16.87	$77
Revision	3.01%	3.42%	4.79	$16.08	$77
Solving Problems	1.75%	2.24%	2.58	$17.22	$44
Procedure & Policy	1.48%	1.66%	2.33	$15.47	$36
File Maintenance	1.65%	1.02%	2.55	$8.82	$23
Training	0.58%	0.77%	0.91	$19.83	$18
Training (Trainee)	0.27%	0.23%	0.43	$13.98	$6
Other	0.00%	0.00%	0.00	$0.00	$0
Totals	100.00%	100.00%	153.49	$14.70	$2,133

formed less steadily or with greater variation from week to week, and thus where the average presents a less accurate picture of normal weekly activities. In the Cataloging Center, three tasks have a coefficient of variation above 1.00: training performed by the trainer; training received by the trainee, in which no work was accomplished; and procedures and policy documentation. These tend to be sporadic rather than regular tasks. Training is especially so because of unusually low staff turnover in the Section, only one position in the last five years.

The necessity for both training and revised procedures results from changes which are not regular and predictable. The work of the Serials Cataloging Section underwent considerable change since the time and cost study began on April 5, 1987. These changes included implementation of a CARLYLE Systems online catalog in July 1987 and switching to a NOTIS online catalog in September 1990. All kinds of cataloging in the Section included filling out cards and forms to have information added not only to OCLC and the online catalog, but also to a local serials data base, which since 1973 has used an older version of the MARC format to produce a book-format *Serials Catalog* and supplements. This aspect of serials cataloging has undergone the most recent change, by being discontinued in April 1991, and through the time and cost study it may be possible to find out how this change impacted productivity. Overall, the Section has been moving towards greater efficiency in the use of automation and less direct involvement in catalog maintenance functions.

Other cataloging tasks show little variance from week to week, and these have relatively low coefficients of variation, all below 0.50. The most stable activities, in order, are: recataloging, copy cataloging, sorting, searching copy, and consulting. The averages for these tasks are probably an accurate indicator of the actual time or cost in any given week.

CATALOGING COSTS

The cost study should be an ideal opportunity to find out from one sample week to another the time and costs of cataloging a title. Unfortunately, statistics on the number of titles cataloged per cost study week were not kept until recently. Instead the number of titles per week was extrapolated from the monthly cataloging figures, giving some strange results for the weeks in which zero hours were spent on original cataloging. However, over the entire nineteen samples, it is expected that the averages present an accurate picture. In fact, the recent studies when actual cataloging figures were kept correlate almost exactly with the overall averages.

Cost can be figured three different ways (see Table 5): the cost of the specific tasks for copy, original, or recataloging; the average cost of all three of these cataloging tasks; or the average cost of these three cataloging tasks plus Technical Services overhead (Miscellaneous and Leave Centers). The cost per title with overhead averages $41.83 while without overhead it is $24.32 per title. Per-title costs of specific kinds of cataloging without overhead are $19.35 for copy cataloging, $31.31 for original cataloging, and $16.53 for recataloging. Time per title is a simple average, not involving overhead, and comes to 1.35 hours to catalog a serial with copy, 1.97 hours to catalog a serial originally, and 1.19 hours to recatalog a serial.

Recataloging

Recataloging includes title changes, cessations, closing holdings due to subscription cancellation, adding notes, changing or adding corporate body headings, and adding copies or volumes to holdings. Unless other recataloging is involved, it does not include transfers, noting lacking issues, retention changes, and withdrawals, which are counted in the Catalog Maintenance Center. Of all the tasks performed in the Serials

TABLE 5

CATALOGING TIME & COSTS

	Copy Cataloging	Original Cataloging	Recataloging	All Cataloging
Time Per Title in Hours				
Serials	1.35	1.97	1.19	1.82
Monographs	0.32	1.32	0.31	0.49
Costs Per Title: Without Overhead				
Serials	$19.35	$31.31	$16.53	$24.32
Monographs	$4.41	$19.06	$3.62	$9.45
Cost Per Title: With Overhead				
Serials				$41.83
Monographs				$11.53

Cataloging Section, recataloging takes the largest proportion of time, 22.89% or 71.37 hours per week, more than twice as much as any other task. A cost and time analysis does not reveal that some recataloging is very easy, such as making a simple note, while other recataloging, such as sorting through numerous title and corporate body name changes, takes hours or days. The cost of $991 per week for recataloging serials may seem large, but the cost per hour is a moderate $13.89 due to the level of staff who do most of the work. Statistics indicate that the Section recatalogs an average of 253 titles per month, compared to only about 100 new titles cataloged, both copy and original. The cost per title is lower than for new title cataloging because it is performed mostly by Library Assistants. These data put to rest any notion that recataloging is a trivial part of the work of serials catalogers. It is their primary activity, at least at Iowa State University.

Copy Cataloging

Copy cataloging costs $14.32 per hour, slightly more than recataloging because it is performed by LA IIIs and faculty catalogers. Faculty catalogers normally work only with copy which has no Library of Congress classification number or requires special language expertise. Most of the copy cataloging is performed by LA IIIs. The serials catalogers catalog new titles with copy by writing on OCLC printouts. Editing of the data online is handled by other staff in the Cataloging Department. Copy cataloging is the third highest task in the Serials Cataloging Section, coming after recataloging and administration, and accounts for 8.74% of the time, or an average of 27.24 hours weekly. An average of 86 new serials are cataloged with copy per month.

Original Cataloging

Original cataloging occurs less steadily as demonstrated by its coefficient of variation of .92 in time. While averaging 6.80 hours per week, it actually ranged from 0 hours during two weeks to 18.75 hours during the most recent week of the time and cost study. Original cataloging is performed by faculty catalogers filling out worksheets when no OCLC copy is available and costs $15.89 per hour. The two faculty serials catalogers create an average of 14 original records per month.

COMPARISONS WITH MONOGRAPHIC CATALOGING

The percent of time devoted to monographic cataloging tasks is very different from serials cataloging and reflects the differences in the nature of the publication types, the completeness and currency of the OCLC records, and the resulting cataloging requirements. A review of these differences is very revealing.

The Monographs Cataloging Section at Iowa State has more staff than the Serials Cataloging Section, and their time therefore accounts for 16.48% of the average hours per week worked in Technical Services, compared to 10.01% for Serials Cataloging (see Table 2). Besides monographic cataloging the Section is also responsible for pre-order searching. There is an even greater difference in the quantity of cataloging produced per average month: 2051 monographs cataloged with copy, 135 cataloged originally, and 275 recataloged. The Monographs Cataloging Section actually recatalogs more titles than the Serials Cataloging Section, but the recataloging task accounts for only 3.61% of their time.

Copy cataloging is the major task in the Monographs Cataloging Section, consuming 30.87% of their time, or an average 158 hours per week. The other top ten tasks in descending order are: original cataloging, vacation, order searching, retrospective conversion, recataloging, administration, cataloging consulting, meetings, and sick leave. Order searching and converting manual records are not part of Serials Cataloging tasks because for serials, order searching is done in the Serials Acquisitions Section, and all serials cataloging is already in machine-readable form.

The cost of cataloging a monograph is considerably lower than the cost of cataloging a serial (see Table 5). With Technical Services overhead, the cost of cataloging a monograph is $11.53, compared to $41.83 for a serial. Without overhead, cataloging a monograph with copy costs $4.41 as opposed to $19.35 for a serial; cataloging originally, $19.06, compared to $31.31 for serials; and recataloging monographs costs $3.62 while recataloging a serial is $16.53 per title. Time spent on cataloging a monograph averaged .32 hours for copy cataloging, 1.32 hours for original cataloging, and .31 hours for recataloging.

These statistics reveal that original cataloging time is about a third greater for serials than for monographs, but monographic original cataloging does include minimal level original cataloging for the first 17 sample weeks. Copy and recataloging times, however, are much greater for serials than for monographs (+76% for copy, +74% for recataloging). Monographic copy catalogers do examine every OCLC record and make enhancements as necessary, but for the great bulk the changes are limited. This is not the case for serial copy cataloging and recataloging. Most records need to be upgraded, because they are incomplete by the time Iowa State handles them. Furthermore, once the records enter the local database Public Services staff request even additional enhancements to provide greater access. Iowa State University has a world renowned scientific serials collection, and it is heavily used for research and undergraduate education. A queueing study completed in 1979 showed that the printed *Serials Catalog* was used 60% of the time by patrons, while the card catalog, which contains no serial records, was used only 40% of the time.[1] Usage of this nature requires current serials cataloging and explains the Public Service need for continual enhancements to records.

The significantly higher cataloging times and costs for serials copy cataloging and recataloging demonstrate a serious problem with copy cataloging using OCLC records. Since only a limited number of CONSER libraries are allowed to enhance serial records and because serials are constantly changing, the records tend to be incomplete. Libraries can elect, as Iowa State does at enormously high costs, to enhance records, thus providing greater access and links between related titles in order to support the research needs of clientele. It is assumed that other research libraries are making similar changes to their records at probably similar costs; however, research is required to determine the nature and extent of editing of OCLC serial records by member libraries.

With monographic records OCLC Enhance libraries are authorized to change any non-national level library record within the format or formats they have agreed to enhance. If for serial records OCLC libraries could be authorized to enhance non-CONSER authenticated records, serials cataloging and recataloging costs would drop. However, it is doubtful that these costs could ever be as low as monographic ones since ongoing changes in serials as well as discrepancies between existing local records and an enhanced OCLC serials record would probably continue to require greater editing of serial records. OCLC's evolving Contribution Pricing would encourage libraries to update the national data base if it were possible to do so.

USE OF THE TIME AND COST STUDY DATA AT ISU

The time and cost study data are useful in tracking the effects of changes, as well as in developing an overall picture of which activities are emphasized because they absorb the most time and money. Some were obvious, but others were surprising because subjective interpretations in the past had de-emphasized the time spent in some areas, such as serials recataloging. There is finally objective information on how the work of various units differs in terms of time spent on various tasks, and the portion of work for which the unit is responsible. When tasks are being considered for transfer from one unit to another, a good estimate of the time involved is readily available. The financial impact of using different levels of staff to perform certain tasks also becomes concretely apparent, rather than theoretical. However, one must use caution in interpreting averages, and realize the data represent the activities of specific weeks.

A Section Head can find a wealth of information in the time and cost study data other than the general information reported in this article. Trends in the Section's activities can be tracked, and highs and lows in times or costs for various tasks can be examined and interpreted in light of the forces at work during those specific weeks. Comparisons are possible between the time and costs of various activities which provides new opportunities and data to evaluate the appropriateness or the desirability of change. The time and cost study is thus a useful tool for providing factual information to encourage change as well as a useful tool for analyzing change.

NOTE

1. Charles Sage et al., "A Queueing Study of Public Catalog Use," *College and Research Libraries* 42, no. 4, p. 323.

APPENDIX A
CATALOGING CENTER TASKS AND DEFINITIONS

CA01. Training (trainer only).
Used only by individuals training others.

CA02. Procedures and policy documentation.

CA03. Consulting and referring/responding to inquiries associated with cost center.
Includes CDC work, giving demonstrations/presentations, filling out questionnaires, requests for review of cataloging, in-process requests.

CA04. Solving problems.
Resolving (or working on) problems which fall out of normal procedures and cannot be handled following the usual guidelines. Often work falling into this category is referred because an individual did not know how to proceed. Problem solving does not refer to complex investigation/verification, etc. which is part of an assigned task.

CA05. Sorting, shelving, distributing, and retrieving.
Handling of any material prior to or immediately after cataloging; also includes sequencing of volumes for Holding cage. Sorting Cat As.

CA06. Searching for cataloging copy. (Use only if performed as separate task, otherwise count as type of cataloging).
Includes printing.

CA07. Maintaining Unit/Holding Files.
Includes pre-cataloging filing and recording of accession numbers in the on-order file.

CA08. Cataloging with copy.
Includes assigning classification numbers.

CA09. Full level original cataloging.

CA10. Recataloging
Cessations, title changes, library has closings, notes, reclassifications, entry changes, added copies/volumes, retention changes; as well as withdrawals and transfers only when other recataloging is involved.

CA11. Authority work. (Use only if performed as separate task, otherwise count as type of cataloging).
Includes searching, verifying, resolving, printing.

CA12. Revision.
Includes all reviewing of others work, but does not include training staff in new tasks.

APPENDIX A (continued)

CA13. Other

CA14. Training (trainee only).

Used by the individual being trained only if no work is accomplished during training; such as programmed learning tutorials, reading manuals.

CA15. Minimal level original cataloging: (ISU theses, SCHOLAR only records, ISU Lecture Series)

ISBD(S) Revised Edition and AACR2 1988 Revision: A Comparison

Patrick F. Callahan

SUMMARY. In 1988, a revision of AACR2 and a revised edition of ISBD(S) were published. The first part of this paper briefly discusses the origins of these two standards and their relationship. The remainder of the paper is a detailed, though not exhaustive, comparison of AACR2 (Rev.) and ISBD(S) (Rev.). It concentrates on inconsistencies between the two texts and evaluates their compatibility. It concludes that there is a high degree of compatibility on major points but that relatively little progress has been made since the original editions in reducing the substantial number of minor differences.

INTRODUCTION

In 1988 revisions of both the *Anglo-American Cataloguing Rules, 2nd edition* (hereafter AACR2 (Rev.)) and *ISBD(S): International Standard Bibliographic Description for Serials* were published.[1] While the practical impact on serials catalogers is considerably less dramatic than that occa-

Patrick F. Callahan is Assistant Dean for Library Technical Services at Ball State University.

sioned by the publication of the original AACR2 and ISBD(S), it was nonetheless a significant juxtaposition of events for the serials cataloging community both in the United States and worldwide. Despite their acknowledged importance, there remains considerable confusion among librarians as to the relationship between ISBD(S) and AACR2 and the extent to which their rules coincide with or deviate from one another. This paper examines this relationship and compares the specific provisions of AACR2 (Rev.) with ISBD(S) (Rev.).

BACKGROUND OF ISBD(S)

The International Standard Bibliographic Descriptions are often mistakenly thought of as cataloging codes and are, in fact, used in this manner by some countries that lack national cataloging codes. However, the ISBDs only deal with bibliographic description. They lack rules concerning choice and form of entry that true cataloging codes must contain. Actually they were designed by the Committee on Cataloguing of the International Federation of Library Associations and Institutions (IFLA) to serve as "an internationally accepted framework for the representation of descriptive information in bibliographic records" in order to assure mutual intelligibility of bibliographic information produced in different countries and to facilitate the exchange of bibliographic records.[2] ISBD has been remarkably successful in reaching its goals, becoming as Michael Gorman says "a kind of bibliographic lingua franca, its punctuation and other conventions recognizable throughout the world."[3]

As Gorman has also observed, ISBD has accomplished all of this while developing in a counter-logical manner. ISBDs for specific formats were developed before a generalized ISBD was in place.[4] The effect of this is evident in the history of ISBD(S). Without a unifying standard, the framers of the preliminary edition of ISBD(S), published in 1974, were faced with the dilemma of striving for compatibility with a monographic standard, ISBD(M), while keeping faith with the more format appropriate guidelines of the International Serials Data System (ISDS).[5]

Recognition of the problems this created led to the publication in 1977 of a generalized framework, ISBD(G), and the first standard edition of ISBD(S).[6] This first standard edition was heavily influenced by the development of ISBD(G) and conformed to its structure. Also, in 1977, IFLA decided that all ISBDs should have a five year life span. Consequently, the ISBD Review Committee was formed and started work in 1981 on a revision of the four existing specific ISBDs, including ISBD(S). After a laborious cycle of drafting, soliciting comment, and redrafting, the revised edition of ISBD(S) was published in 1988.

RELATIONSHIP OF ISBD(S) (REV.) AND AACR2 (REV.)

The history of AACR2 and its 1988 revision is well known to most catalogers but a few points need to be emphasized to clarify its relationship to ISBD(S). There was early consensus that ISBD(S) should serve as the basis for the revision of Chapter 7 of AACR1. Also, the creation of ISBD(G) was stimulated by a Joint Steering Committee for Revision of AACR (JSC) proposal to IFLA that was designed to foster the compatibility of the ISBDs and AACR2. JSC subsequently adopted ISBD(G) as the framework for the AACR2 rules of description.

Thus it is apparent that IFLA and JSC have tried to coordinate their activities in an effort to make AACR2 and the ISBDs compatible. The following comparison will explore how successful they were in the case of ISBD(S) (Rev.) and the rules for describing serials in AACR2 (Rev.).

COMPARING ISBD(S) (REV.) AND AACR2 (REV.)

This comparison of ISBD(S) (Rev.) and AACR2 (Rev.) is based on the texts as published. It does not reflect Library of Congress (LC) interpretations of AACR2 (Rev.) except when specifically cited. The reason for this is that other national libraries can and frequently do differ from LC in their interpretation of the code. It should also be kept in mind that this is exclusively a comparison of rules of description, not rules involving choice of entry and forms of headings.

It is necessary to refer to the rules on serials in Chapter 12 of AACR2 (Rev.) and the general rules in Chapter 1 since the two chapters are interdependent. There is no parallel relationship between ISBD(S) and ISBD(G). ISBD(S) adheres to the framework of ISBD(G) but does not refer the cataloger back to the general rules in ISBD(G).

General Rules

There are a number of stylistic differences, mostly involving punctuation, between ISBD(S) (Rev.) and AACR2 (Rev.). For instance, ISBD(S) .10 authorizes the use of [!] as well as [sic] for identifying misprints while AACR2 (Rev.) 1.0F only allows the use of [sic]. ISBD(S) is also somewhat more consistent in its use of brackets, usually reserving them for "information found outside the prescribed sources of information" (0.4.8) /while putting information from outside the piece in a note. AACR2 (Rev.) is more ambiguous since brackets can signal information supplied by a cataloger or data from outside the prescribed sources.

These stylistic differences run throughout the various areas of the description. For example, a qualifier to the place of publication, that appears in the prescribed source, is enclosed in parentheses according to ISBD(S) (Rev.) 4.1.9 (e.g., Cambridge (Mass.)) but follows a comma in AACR2 (Rev.) 1.4C3 (e.g., Carbondale, Ill.). Occasionally different abbreviations are used such as for copyright. It is abbreviated as "cop." in ISBD(S) (Rev.) 4.4.4 and as "c" in AACR2 (Rev.) 1.4F5.

A more substantive difference involves the prescribed sources of information in ISBD(S) (Rev.) 0.5 and AACR2 (Rev.) 12.0B1. This rule illustrates a conscious effort, though only partially successful, to bring AACR2 (Rev.) into agreement with ISBD(S) (Rev.). AACR2 (Rev.) has adopted the ISBD terminology and definition of "Title page" as opposed to the original AACR2 phrase, "Chief source of information." However, the prescribed sources still differ for Areas 2, 3, 4, 5, and 6 (See Figures 1-2). The effect of these differences is that ISBD(S) is more restrictive for Areas 2 and 6 while AACR2 (Rev.) is more restrictive for Areas 3 and 4. The difference in Area 5, physical description, is one of semantics.

U.S. serial catalogers recognized some difficulties with the AACR2

Figure 1. Prescribed sources of information as found in AACR2 (Rev.) 12.0B1.

AREA	PRESCRIBED SOURCES OF INFORMATION
Title and statement of responsibility	Title page
Edition	Title page, other preliminaries, colophon
Numeric and/or alphabetic, chronological, or other designation	Title page, other preliminaries, colophon
Publication, distribution, etc.	Title page, other preliminaries, colophon
Physical description	The whole publication
Series	The whole publication
Note	Any source
Standard number and terms of availability	Any source

Figure 2. Prescribed sources of information as found in ISBD(S) (Rev.) 0.5.2.1.

AREA NO.	AREA NAME	PRESCRIBED SOURCES OF INFORMATION
1.	Title and statement of responsibility	Title page
2.	Edition	Title page
3.	Numbering	Title page, cover, caption, masthead, editorial pages, colophon and other preliminaries
4.	Publication, distribution, etc.	Title page, cover, caption, masthead, editorial pages, colophon and other preliminaries
5.	Physical description	The issue itself
6.	Series	Title page, cover, caption, masthead, editorial pages, colophon and other preliminaries
7.	Note	Any source
8.	Standard number (or alternative) and terms of availability	Any source

(Rev.) list of prescribed sources and LC and the American Library Association have both endorsed a proposal to JSC which would reduce the amount of bracketing required by strict adherence to the rules. The effect of this change, however, would be to increase the disparity between ISBD(S) and AACR2 (Rev.) by making the latter less restrictive in areas 2-6. There is also a slight difference in the definition of "preliminaries" since ISBD(S) specifies the spine as a preliminary while AACR2 (Rev.) lists the cover instead. The cover is, however, usually implicitly included via the phrase "pages preceding the title page."

ISBD(S) and AACR2 (Rev.) also differ in the presentation of the prescribed sources in that ISBD(S) provides a second list for ceased titles and limited runs (See Figure 3) while AACR2 (Rev.) employs a single list. This allows ISBD(S) to be more precise. For example, it specifies "the first and last issue" for Area 3 which is obviously necessary, while AACR2 (Rev.) 12.0B1 only refers to the first issue.

A final difference worth noting is that AACR2 (Rev.) 1.OD specifical-

Figure 3. **Basis for the description and prescribed sources of information for serials that have ceased publication or for limited runs of issues, as found in ISBD(S) (Rev.) 0.5.2.2.**

AREA NO.	BASIS FOR THE DESCRIPTION (Note: The parenthetical text applies to the case where a limited run of issues is being described)	PRESCRIBED SOURCES OF INFORMATION
1.	The first (or first available) issue	Title page
2.	The first (or first available) issue	Title page
3.	The first and last issue (or the first and last available issue)	Title page, cover, caption, masthead, editorial pages, colophon and other preliminaries
4.	The first (or the first available issue) Note: In case of the date of publication and/or printing the first and the last issue (or the first and last available issue)	Title page, cover caption, masthead, colophon and other preliminaries
5.	The whole publication (or the limited run)	The issues themselves
6.	The whole publication (or the limited run)	Title page, cover, caption, masthead, colophon and other preliminaries
7.	The whole publication (or the limited run)	Any source
8.	The whole publication (or the limited run)	Any source

ly authorizes three levels of description, each varying in the degree of comprehensiveness of elements included. ISBD(S) does not employ such tiering.

Area 1–Title and Statement of Responsibility Area

ISBD(S) and AACR2 (Rev.) are similar in regard to choice of the title proper. However, ISBD(S) 1.1.3.2 and AACR2 (Rev.) 1.0H differ slightly in how to handle serials with multiple title pages in multiple languages. Both instruct to select the title page in the language and/or script of the main content of the issue as the chief source. When this standard cannot be applied, ISBD(S) states that the right hand of two facing title pages is preferred. AACR2 (Rev.) leaves this detail to a rule interpretation.

The two also differ on the choice of title proper when a set of initials or an acronym plus its spelled out form appear on the title page. ISBD(S) 1.1.2.3 and 1.4.3 say to use the initialism or acronym as the title proper as long as it is "prominently displayed." The expanded form is given as other title information. If the expanded form appears in the issue, but not on the title page, it is still recorded as other title information but enclosed in square brackets.

The first edition of AACR2 agreed with ISBD(S) that the initialism or acronym could be, and in practice usually was, selected as the title proper. However, AACR2 (Rev.) 12.1B2 instructs to "choose the full form as the title proper unless the acronym or initialism is the only form of title presented in other locations in the serial." The purpose of the exception is, presumably, to provide a mechanism for discerning the publisher's intentions as to what the serial should be called. *JAMA : journal of the American Medical Association* is an example of the application of this rule. Both the initialism and the spelled out form appear on the title page but the initialism is chosen as the title proper because it is consistently used elsewhere in the serial. The initialism or acronym, when not chosen as the title proper, is recorded as other title information (12.1E1). Unlike ISBD(S), however, this is only done when the initialism or acronym appears on the title page. If it appears elsewhere in the piece, it is recorded as a note.

As with choice of title, the rules for transcribing the title are similar but there are some differences. Both ISBD(S) 1.1.4.1 and AACR2 (Rev.) 1.1B4 allow the abridgement of lengthy titles proper if this can be done without the loss of "essential information." AACR2 (Rev.) 1.1B4 is more restrictive, however, in that it prohibits omission of any of the first five words of the title. The same distinction applies to other title information (ISBD(S) 1.4.5.2 and AACR2 (Rev.) 1.1E3).

The meaning of ISBD(S) 1.1.4.2 dealing with dependent titles (called section or supplement titles in AACR2) is essentially the same as AACR2 (Rev.) 12.1B4 and 12.1B5 though the instructions in AACR2 (Rev.) are clearer. It is necessary to refer to the examples in ISBD(S) to be sure what to do. ISBD(S) again permits the recording of a dependent title, in brackets, that appears in the issue but not on the title page. AACR2 (Rev.) 12.1B4 explicitly states that both the common and section titles must appear on the chief source. (This difference persists throughout the texts, for example see AACR2 (Rev.) 1.1D4 and ISBD(S) (Rev.) 1.3.3.3 on transcribing parallel titles.) 12.1B6 instructs that when the title of the "section or supplement is presented in the chief source of information without the title that is common to all sections, give the title of the section or supplement as the title proper." ISBD(S) includes a similar provision in 1.1.5.3.1 though it treats it as part of the rules on title changes. It is somewhat unclear as to how 1.1.5.3.1 is reconciled with the ability to transcribe a dependent title appearing outside the title page which is granted by 1.1.4.2.

ISBD(S) 1.1.5.1 provides another example of fuzzy wording in ISBD(S). It states that "variations of the title *proper* occurring in the issue being described are given in Area 7 (see 7.1.1.3)." Given the definition of "title proper," it is not clear until one looks at 7.1.1.3 that this is meant to include cover titles, caption titles, etc. AACR2 (Rev.) 12.7B4 instruction to "make notes on titles borne by the serial other than the title proper" is less ambiguous.

A major change between AACR2 and AACR2 (Rev.) is in the treatment of title changes. AACR2 21.2A defined a title change as occurring when there was any change in the first five words, or any "important words" were added, deleted, or changed, or there was a change in word order. This was more restrictive than ISBD(S). Eliminating this discrepancy was one motivation for the rule changes that were incorporated into AACR2 (Rev.). The revised 21.2A added a number of exceptions to the basic title change definition. Changes in representation of a word (e.g., abbreviation vs. spelled out form), changes after the first five words that do not change the meaning of the title, addition or deletion of the name of the issuing body, and changes in punctuation are not to be considered title changes. AACR2 (Rev.) is still not in complete harmony with ISBD(S) 1.1.5.2 and 7.1.1.6 since ISBD(S) does include the exception for additions, deletions, and changes beyond the first five words of the title. ISBD(S) 7.1.1.6 also does not consider transitory changes in the order of parallel titles to be title changes. AACR2 (Rev.) does not have such a provision although the Library of Congress Rule Interpretation follows ISBD(S).

There are some minor differences concerning General Material Designations (GMD) though both codes consider them to be optional. ISBD(S) 1.2.2 allows the use of "Printed text" while AACR2 (Rev.) 1.1C1 uses "Text." As applied by the Library of Congress, a GMD is not used for printed serials.

ISBD(S) 1.3.3.2 says to record only three parallel titles with others listed in a note. However, it permits deviations from this standard when "national considerations" prevail. In AACR2 (Rev.) 1.1D2 the transcription of parallel titles depends on the level of description being used, a concept not present in ISBD(S). In a second level description, the first parallel title and a subsequent one, if it is in English, are recorded. For a level three description, all parallel titles are transcribed.

ISBD(S) 1.5.4.3 states that "when the names of several persons or corporate bodies are represented in a single statement of responsibility . . . the number of names transcribed is at the discretion of the bibliographic agency." AACR2 (Rev.) 1.1F5 reduces this discretionary latitude by instructing to omit all but the first if there are three or more individuals or bodies performing the same function. A somewhat curious provision of ISBD(S) is rule 1.5.4.11 which says that when there are multiple statements of responsibility, one for a person and one naming a corporate body, and the person's name precedes that of the corporate body, the name of the corporate body should be transcribed first. AACR2 (Rev.) transcribes them in the order presented.

AACR2 (Rev.) 12.1F3 specifies, in strange prose, that "statements of responsibility statements relating to persons that are editors of serials" are only recorded if thought to be important by the cataloger and then only in a note. ISBD(S) does not discriminate against editors in this fashion.

Area 2–Edition

The only significant difference in Area 2 concerns supplements or inserts. ISBD(S) 2.1.4.6 allows such statements to be recorded in the edition area (e.g., – with supplements in four languages.) whereas AACR2 (Rev.) records these statements in the Note Area (12.7B7j).

Area 3–Numbering

In general, ISBD(S) is superior to AACR2 (Rev.) in providing detailed sensible instructions for handling numeric and chronological designations, though in some cases AACR2 (Rev.) deficiencies have been remedied by LCRIs. ISBD(S) clarifies several common sources of confusion. For example, it warns catalogers that the chronological designation may be different than the dates of publication and that the designation of the serial should not be confused with a library's local holdings. In addition, it explicitly states that Area 3 is only omitted when both the first and last issues of the serial are unavailable. AACR2 (Rev.) provides no guidance on what to do when the last issue of serial is available but the first is not.

AACR2 (Rev.) 12.3B1 and 12.3C1 state that the designations are given as they appear on the piece. Strict adherence to this rule leads to chronological designations such as 1970-1971-1980-1981 when the first and last issues of the serial span more than one calendar year. ISBD(S)

3.1.3 sensibly allows the substitution of a diagonal slash for the hyphen in such circumstances. Thus the above example is transformed into the less confusing 1970/1971-1980/1981.

Another AACR2 (Rev.) shortcoming is 12.3C4 which mandates that the numeric designation always precede the chronological designation. This is not helpful when the number is a division of the date with the issue numbers repeated each year. In order to eliminate the ambiguity in a designation such as No. 1 (1971)-no. 12 (1975) it is necessary to add a note stating that "Numbering begins each year with no. 1." ISBD(S) 3.3 provides a simpler solution by allowing the number to be transcribed after the date when it represents a division of the date (e.g., 1971, no. 1-1975, no. 12).

Of more debatable value is ISBD(S) 3.5 which provides the option of recording parallel designations (e.g., Vol. = T. = Bd. 20-). AACR2 (Rev.) eliminates that option and prefers the designation in the language of the title proper.

Area 4–Publication, Distribution, etc.

Most of the differences between ISBD(S) and AACR2 (Rev.) in Area 4 have to do with multiple places of publication and/or publishers. In such cases, ISBD(S) 4.1.3 and 4.2.1 say to record the place or publisher given prominence by typography and if this does not apply, then give the one named first. AACR2 (Rev.) 1.4C5 and 1.4D5 virtually reverses the hierarchy by preferring the first named place or publisher. Subsequent places or publishers given prominence by typography are also recorded. ISBD(S) 4.1.4 and 4.2.2 leave it up to the cataloging agency to decide if subsequent places or publishers are important enough to be recorded. AACR2 (Rev.) 1.4C5 and 1.4D5 go into detail as to when subsequent places and publishers are to be transcribed, in effect defining what is important. Another difference is that ISBD(S) 4.1.5 and 4.2.3 allow the cataloger to supply "etc." when subsequent places or publishers are omitted (e.g., Lausanne [etc.] : Payot [etc.]). AACR2 (Rev.) merely omits those not considered important without using "etc."

Area 5–Physical Description

The one minor discrepancy in Area 5 concerns changes in the dimensions of the serial. ISBD(S) 5.3.4 says to record variations in the dimensions of issues in a note while AACR2 (Rev.) 12.5D1 allows the range of dimensions to be recorded in Area 5 (e.g., v. : ill. ; 27-32 cm.).

Area 6–Series

The differences in Area 6 are more in the realm of nuance rather than outright contradictions. ISBD(S) 6.4.1 mandates the transcription of the first statement of responsibility when the series title is a generic term. AACR2 (Rev.) 1.6E1 does not require this though the cataloger is told to record statements of responsibility "necessary for identification of the series." The practical application of the two rules should produce the same results in almost all instances.

There is also a subtle distinction between ISBD(S) 6.5 which says to record the ISSN when it is known and AACR2 (Rev.) 1.6F1 which says to do so when the ISSN appears in the item.

Area 7–Notes

Both ISBD(S) and AACR2 (Rev.) grant the cataloger more latitude in the note area than in the other areas of the description. Therefore it is not surprising that there are a number of differences between the two sets of rules. Many of these are fairly inconsequential such as a differing prescribed order for the notes.

The most important difference is in the form of the notes used to cite serial titles which are linked to the description of another serial (e.g., Continued by:). ISBD(S) prefers the use of the key title and the ISSN as in "Continued by: Annual report of the General Manager–Transport Department, Glasgow Corporation = ISSN 0308-4140." AACR2 (Rev.) 12.7A2 prefers the use of the "title or name/title under which that serial is entered in the catalogue." Thus the above example would be cited as "Glasgow Corporation. Transport Dept. Annual report of the General Manager." When the serial is not in the catalogue it can be cited as: title proper/statement of responsibility, but the key title is not even an option. ISBD(S) only allows use of the catalogue form when the key title is unknown.

In general, ISBD(S) is more prescriptive and provides more detailed instructions on the note area than does AACR2 (Rev.) (This is demonstrated by comparing the notes on statements of responsibility, ISBD(S) 7.1.5 and AACR2 (Rev.) 12.7B6). ISBD(S) also lists a number of notes that AACR2 (Rev.) does not include. For example, ISBD(S) 7.1.1.4 authorizes use of an "Expanded form of title proper" note for spelled out forms of initialisms, acronyms, and numerals. AACR2 (Rev.) does not have such a note. ISBD(S) 7.2.8 uses another non-AACR2 (Rev.) note: "Published under the same title during . . ." for serials that have reverted to a previous title. AACR2 (Rev.) only calls for citations to the immediately preceding and succeeding titles. ISBD(S) 7.2.11, 7.6.1, and 7.6.2 all allow the use of notes listing series and subseries even when these are repeated in Area 6. AACR2 (Rev.) has no such provision.

There are, however, some examples of AACR2 (Rev.) notes which are not addressed by ISBD(S). For instance, AACR2 (Rev.) 12.7B8 specifically says to make notes concerning the report year or dates of coverage for annuals on less frequent serials when it is other than the calendar year. ISBD(S) ignores this. There is also no equivalent in ISBD(S) for AACR2 (Rev.) 12.7B14, dealing with intended audience, and 12.7B16, which lists other formats in which the serial has been issued.

In some cases ISBD(S) remedies deficiencies in AACR2 (Rev.). The most glaring of these is AACR2 (Rev.)'s failure to provide a single example of the commonly needed notes "Began with" and "Ceased with." ISBD(S) spells these out clearly in 7.3.2.

ISBD(S) also tends to make finer distinctions among serial relationships. For example, 7.2.10 distinguishes between "Supplement to" and "Inset in" while AACR2 (Rev.) does not have a comparable rule. ISBD(S) 7.2.4 also retains the distinction between "Continues" and "Supersedes" which was dropped in the migration from AACR1 to AACR2. It is debatable whether this is important since the numbering in Area 3 should provide sufficient clues as to whether the serial maintains the numbering system of its predecessor. ISBD(S) is remiss in not defining the difference between "Continues" and "Supersedes."

Area 8–Standard Number and Terms of Availability

The rules in AACR2 (Rev.) and ISBD(S) are virtually identical for this area.

CONCLUSION

In 1982, Jim Cole compared the first editions of AACR2 and ISBD(S). At that time he concluded that "while both documents are based on ISBD(G), there is a wide divergence rather than a close correspondence between the two." It could logically be assumed that the revised editions of AACR2 and ISBD(S) would address the disparities between the two that Cole had identified. This is true, however, of only a small number of rules and many of the discrepancies noted by Cole remain in the revised editions.

While the number of minor discrepancies is large, it is debatable whether these now add up to a "wide divergence." Though this is in part, an exercise in semantics, it is an important point in regard to the international exchange and intelligibility of bibliographic records created in accord with the two standards. AACR2 (Rev.) and ISBD(S) (Rev.) correspond closely enough so that, in the vast majority of cases, the descriptions of a serial that they engender are very similar, if not identical.

However, the fact that the differences between the two are, with a few exceptions, mostly minor raises the question of why these discrepancies need to exist at all. In a few cases, particularly Area 3, ISBD(S) (Rev.) offers clear advantages to AACR2 (Rev.). However, many of these provisions in ISBD(S) (Rev.) have been incorporated into Library of Congress rule interpretations thus making the practical applications identical. On the other hand, ISBD(S) occasionally goes into too much detail for an international standard and would be better off leaving these particulars to national cataloging codes. This problem results from its attempt to serve two purposes, its stated objective of being an international standard for the exchange of bibliographic information and its unstated role as a de facto cataloging code for those countries who lack a national standard.

The international library community would be better served if the relationship between ISBD(S) (Rev.) and AACR2 (Rev.) were more explicitly defined. It is also necessary to ask whether the advantages gained from maintaining national autonomy on matters of bibliographic description are that significant. The first edition of AACR2 was a major stride toward compatibility with ISBD(S). It would be fairly simple to bring ISBD(S) (Rev.) and AACR2 (Rev.) into complete correspondence. The question is whether there is a consensus among librarians that this is a worthwhile goal.

REFERENCES

1. *Anglo-American Cataloguing Rules*, 2nd ed., 1988 rev. (Chicago: American Library Association, 1988); *ISBD(S): International Standard Bibliographic Description for Serials*, Rev. ed. (London: IFLA Universal Bibliographic Control and International MARC Programme, 1988).

2. *ISBD(M): International Standard Bibliographic Descriptions for Monographic Publications*, 1st standard ed. (London: IFLA Committee on Cataloging, 1974), p. vii.

3. Michael Gorman, "Bibliographic Description, Past, Present, and Future," *International Cataloging* 16 (Oct. 1987): 43.

4. Ibid.

5. Eva Verona, "A Decade of IFLA'S Work on the Standardization of Bibliographic Description," *IFLA Journal* 6 (1980): 220.

6. *ISBD(G): General International Standard Bibliographic Description* (London: IFLA International Office for UBC, 1977); *ISBD(S): International Standard Bibliographic Description for Serials*, 1st standard ed. (London: IFLA International Office for UBC, 1977).

7. Jim E. Cole, "AACR2 and ISBD(S): Correspondence or Divergence?" *Serials Review* 8 (Fall 1982): 69.

ISDS, ISBD(S) and AACR2: Divergence and Convergence

Albert A. Mullis

SUMMARY. The origins of the International Serials Data System (ISDS) are described. The early moves towards compatibility between the *Guidelines for ISDS* and the 1974 draft of *ISBD(S)* were undone in the latter's first standard edition in 1977. Concern by some national bibliographic agencies over creation of records to two different conventions and consequent dual processing were addressed by the ISDS Governing Board. The wholesale revision of the *Guidelines* and their transformation into the *ISDS Manual* are detailed. Many of the original conflicts and discrepancies between ISDS and *ISBD(S)* have been resolved. Although perfect and absolute compatibility has not been achieved there is now a workable harmonization. The possibility of further improvements in accessibility of ISDS records is noted. Current usage of ISDS records in catalogues in several European countries is then briefly described.

The International Serials Data System (ISDS) is a worldwide system for the identification and registration of serial publications. Its most visible function and, indeed, its primary function is the assignment of a standard number, the International Standard Serial Number (ISSN), to each serial publication so that it may be uniquely identified and unequivocally distinguished from any other serial publication.

ISDS originates in proposals from a feasibility study on the establishment of a world science information system (UNISIST) which had been

---

Albert A. Mullis is Serials Officer, The British Library Humanities and Social Sciences, Great Russell Street, London WCIB 3DG, United Kingdom. Mullis was formerly Head of Serials Office, British Library Bibliographic Services Division (1981-84), Head of Processing, English Language Collections (1984-87). He served on the ISDS Governing Board (1981-88) and was consecutively Rapporteur, Chairman and Past Chairman. He edited the *ISDS Manual.*

jointly set up by Unesco and the International Council of Scientific Unions (ICSU). The UNISIST/ICSU-Abstracting Board Working Group on Bibliographic Descriptions recommended the creation of an international network for periodical titles. The network, it was recommended, should establish a world list of journal titles and a register of title word abbreviations, and it should issue supplementary lists of changes and additions to the world list and issue cumulated revised editions of the list.

INSPEC, at the Institution of Electrical Engineers in London, was commissioned to carry out a feasibility study on these proposals. That study[1] recommended the establishment of ISDS and described a proposed design of the system and its supporting network. The authors of the study, Martin and Barnes, particularly stressed:[2]

> The *difficulty* of maintaining an accurate serials data base. All experience shows that the population of serial titles is complex, inhomogeneous, and subject to frequent change. Many publications which are undoubtedly serials do not follow any regular pattern; many publishers of serials operate on a somewhat casual basis. Any attempt to develop an ISDS is doomed to failure, or at least only a very partial success, if it does not begin with an awareness that the system will have to handle some extremely complex and difficult problems, and will require a high level of bibliographic expertise in its day-to-day operations.

In July 1972 Unesco and the Government of the French Republic signed a provisional agreement establishing the International Centre for the Registration of Serial Publications in Paris. A final agreement was signed in November 1974 and the International Centre, whose first Director, the late Marie Rosenbaum, had already been appointed in 1971, came formally into existence in January 1976 after ratification of its Statutes by the French Parliament in December 1975.

The aim of the Centre was to introduce and operate an automated system for the registration of serials, covering the whole range of recorded knowledge and all kinds of serials irrespective of physical format. Thus the original proposals, which concentrated on periodical or journal literature in science and technology, were broadened out.

While these various political moves to establish the Centre were going on, Technical Committee 46 of the International Organization for Standardization (ISO/TC 46) had developed a proposal for the ISSN as ISO 3297,[3] firmly based on ANSI Z39.9-1971: *Identification Numbers for Serial Publications*. ISO 3297-1975, as it was originally, has been subjected to the normal ISO review procedure and in its present form is ISO 3297-1986. That later date, however, indicates review and not revision. The definition of a serial given in this international standard is used also in the *International Standard Bibliographic Description for Serials (ISBD(S))*:[4]

> A publication, in printed form or not, issued in successive parts usually having numerical or chronological designations and intended to be continued indefinitely. Serials include periodicals, newspapers, annuals (reports, yearbooks, directories, etc.), the journals, memoirs, proceedings, transactions, etc. of societies, and monographic series. The definition does not include works produced in parts for a period predetermined as finite.

The AACR2 definition, while in most respects similar, says "bearing numeric or chronological designations," that is not admitting undesignated serials, the idea of which is, perhaps, a contradiction in terms, although an unnumbered preliminary issue or issues of a serial is not unknown. It also excludes the reference to part works (perhaps on the grounds that such exclusion is implicit in the definition).

In November 1972 the Director General of Unesco had circulated a letter to Member States announcing the establishment of the International Centre and inviting them to establish their own national centres. Attached to that letter was a copy of 'Provisional guidelines for ISDS' explaining in more detail the scope, structure and functions of the system. These provisional guidelines were revised by the then ISDS Technical Advisory Committee and finalized by the Director of the International Centre as *Guidelines for ISDS*[5] in 1973.

ISO 3297 gives four brief rules on the construction of a key title, that is the unique name assigned to a serial by the ISDS and inseparably linked with its ISSN. The *Guidelines* expanded these rules on key title to seventeen liberally spaced pages.

What must be clearly understood about ISDS is that serials are entered in ISDS files by title, without exception. The key title was designed as a uniform construction for entry to allow for the differences which occur or might occur between the different cataloguing codes used otherwise by the parent bodies of ISDS centres. Not all these parent bodies use AACR2, even though more than half of the 530,000 records in the international file as of 31 December 1990 were created by centres whose parent bodies use that code. There were and, in some instances, there remain differences in practice between ISDS, *ISBD(S)* and AACR2 which will be addressed later when looking at the former's rules as now given in the *ISDS Manual*. ISDS is not, primarily, a cataloguing service, although it can be said to be the most notable attempt at international serials control to date. ISDS is primarily concerned with the unique identification of serials and therefore need not subordinate its requirements to the omnipotent monograph.

The *Guidelines for ISDS* were published in 1973 and were followed in 1974 by the final draft of the recommendations of the Joint Working Group on the International Standard Bibliographic Description for Serials. The draft attempted some compatibility with ISDS rules. While it incorporated the basic structure and concepts of the ISBD for Monographs it also reflected some of the principles of ISDS in the title and statement of responsibility areas.[6] It included the concept of 'distinctive' title, which was a reflection of the key title concept of ISDS, rather than the title proper of ISBD(M). The 'distinctive' title was the key title without qualifiers (where they existed as part of the key title) on the basis that information which otherwise would be qualifying data in a key title could clearly be found in the descriptive ISBD(S) entry.

Such limited compatibility was to be short lived. The expansion of IFLA's ISBD programme and the progress on revision of AACR brought to light incompatibilities and inconsistencies in the ISBD texts. A general framework for the description of all library materials was developed as the *International Standard Bibliographic Description (General)* to serve as a model for all other ISBDs. In the ensuing revision of the draft 1974 *ISBD(S)* discussion of the rival merits of *ISBD(G)* and the *Guidelines for ISDS* led to the adoption of the concept of title proper. The identifying 'distinctive' title was no longer tenable within the guidelines laid down by *ISBD(G)*. The abandonment of the concept of 'distinctive' title led to a change in emphasis in which description is based largely on a single issue. Only in these terms can a title proper be regarded as a valid concept in serials cataloguing. In the first standard edition of *ISBD(S)*[7] the key title is relegated to Area 8 (ISSN and Terms of Availability Area).

ISDS national centres are, without exception, within either the national library or a national documentation centre. While much of the intellectual effort of creating an ISDS record and a national cataloguing record is the same there is, nevertheless, information unique to each kind of record which must be separately established or recorded and the data may need to be separately processed. This dual input is wasteful. More could be done by national bibliographic agencies to use the ISDS record as a basis for the national cataloguing record and more could be done to make processing, both manual and automated, more efficient to reduce and even eliminate most of the apparent effects of dual input. The useful, detailed, but now dated, study by Françoise Bouffez and Annette Grousseaud is relevant here.[8]

Reflecting the concerns of many national bibliographic agencies the ISDS Governing Board passed a resolution in 1981 urging improved compatibility between *ISBD(S)* and the ISDS bibliographic conventions. The uniform application of the *Guidelines for ISDS* had only been achieved by continuing cooperative maintenance within the ISDS network. The extension of that network to countries using a wide variation of languages and scripts and with differing publishing traditions created the need to extend and amend basic rules. Additionally, the centres found themselves faced with problems in day to day operations which were not covered in the existing *Guidelines*. A draft revision of the *Guidelines* was circulated to ISDS centres for comment during 1981. That draft, together with the comments which had been received from various centres, was discussed extensively at a meeting of directors of ISDS centres in October 1981. It was agreed at that meeting that a final English text should be prepared and an editor was appointed. In the earliest stages of editing it became apparent that what was needed was not simply an extensively revised edition of the *Guidelines* but an entire replacement. The new text which evolved and which was published in 1983 was the *ISDS Manual*[9] and replaced the *Guidelines for ISDS*. The modest 74 liberally laid out pages of the *Guidelines* had developed into the much more closely packed 257 pages of the *Manual*. There have been three sets of amendments issued, all relatively minor or reflecting changes in procedures rather than principles. A revised edition of the *Manual* is promised for the foreseeable future and will presumably be published in a more convenient looseleaf format.

During the revision and editing process care was taken to ensure compatibility with the practices of other international systems and with international bibliographic standards, in particular *ISBD(S)*, then under review. The ISBD(S) Working Group met with the editor of the *ISDS Manual* immediately prior to the meeting of directors of ISDS centres in October 1982, and the editor and the chairman of the Working Group, Judith Szilvássy, exchanged views by correspondence, which sometimes reflected their differing philosophies and attitudes, with the Director of the International Centre, Marie Rosenbaum, acting as honest broker between them.

The eventual outcome was that many of the original conflicts and discrepancies between ISDS and *ISBD(S)* have been satisfactorily resolved. The more important compromises and resolutions of differences and difficulties are:

- Some early efforts had been made to get the ISDS key title completely identical to *ISBD(S)* title information, but it was soon accepted that they served different functions. It was finally agreed that the title proper, where it differed from the key title, should be added to ISDS records thus enabling *ISBD(S)* records to be built from ISDS data and vice versa.
- In the *Guidelines for ISDS*, edition statements were an integral part of the key title and were not delimited. In order to improve mapping of data elements between ISDS and *ISBD(S)*, edition statements in ISDS records are now delimited as qualifying information in key titles.
- The *Guidelines for ISDS* had conventions on title changes which had caused difficulties for some national bibliographic agencies; but *ISBD(S)* had no guidelines on title changes, simply referring to national cataloguing practices. The ISDS specifications were considerably modified and have been incorporated in *ISBD(S)*.
- Greater consistency between the two systems has been made possible by modification of the *ISBD(S)* linking entry information specifications to allow key title and ISSN in linking entry notes.
- Some compatibility has been achieved in punctuation conventions.
- In order to accommodate *ISBD(S)* requirements more closely the *ISDS Manual* permits some flexibility in the imprint area.

Perfect and absolute compatibility between the *ISDS Manual* and *ISBD(S)* has not been achieved, and may never be achieved; but there is now a workable harmonization of the two systems. Dorothy Anderson[10] and Judith Szilvássy[11] have authoritatively and comprehensively described the compatibility issues.

Some basic facts need to be kept in mind in relation to ISDS records:

- There are a number of descriptive elements in the ISDS record which are the same as those which appear in bibliographic records following *ISBD(S)* practices. These include: title proper, issuing or corporate body, place of publication, name of publisher, date of publication, linking elements relating to the bibliographic history of the serial.
- The ISDS record does not: (a) describe a particular issue of a serial either in respect of content or physical format; (b) include number-

ing relating to volume or issue; (c) include physical description of a serial; (d) include the terms of availability relating to a serial.
- The ISDS record is independent of cataloguing rules relating to headings and is expected to stand by itself.

There are thirty data elements which may be present in an ISDS record. All but two of these are mandatory or mandatory if available or applicable. The two optional elements are notes on CODEN and other codes and notes on coverage by indexing and abstracting services. Nine of the elements are in the information codes (008) field and all those are mandatory except end date of publication which, of course, can only be mandatory when a particular title ceases to exist. The ISSN, UDC or DDC class number, abbreviated key title, and imprint are mandatory. Title proper, variant title, the name of the issuing body as established by national cataloguing practice, and nine data elements concerning related titles are mandatory if available or applicable. The title proper, in particular, is mandatory if it is different from subfield $a of the key title in content or subfielding which would be required in field 245.

As has been said, there are remaining differences between the ISDS rules and *ISBD(S)* and, for that matter, AACR2. Where do those differences lie? Information in the data element 'variant title,' such as cover title, parallel title, expanded forms of key title (where, for example, the key title is an acronym or initialism and it is spelled out here), titles with minor changes which do not attract a new key title, and so on, appears in the Note Area in *ISBD(S)* and in AACR2 12.7. Whereas notes in those rules will indicate that the title is a cover title or whatever, in ISDS the variant title will be shown printed out with the MARC tag, indicators and subfield codes so that the nature of the variant title is not immediately apparent unless the user is familiar with the ISDS MARC coding. That is not to say that such indications as 'cover title' or 'parallel title' could not be generated by program. The nature of the ISDS record is that it is primarily machine-held and is, as it were, a series of building blocks from which an appropriate catalogue record can be built. Similar treatment is given to the series of data elements which cover linked titles (other language editions, subseries, both when the key title of the record is part of a subseries or has a subseries itself, insets, supplements, former titles, successor titles, and related titles, that is any other serial which is related in a manner not otherwise specified). Both the key title and the ISSN of the linked title are given but its relationship has to be discerned from the MARC coding. The relationship, again, could be shown in natural language generated by program. These correspond to the prescriptions of *ISBD(S)* area 7.2, 'Notes on the edition area and the bibliographic history of the serial,' and to AACR2 12.7B7.

In the imprint ISDS records the name of each place of publication and each publisher given on the publication. *ISBD(S)*, in the Publication, Distribution, etc., Area, stipulates only the first or most prominently named place of publication and says that a second or subsequent place *may* be given. Similar treatment is accorded to publishers. While AACR2 goes a bit further there is, nonetheless, a strong similarity between its prescriptions and those of *ISBD(S)*, It has to be said, however, that some ISDS centres use discretion in applying these rules and tend to use *ISBD(S)*, AACR2 or other local practices.

The only date of publication which appears in the ISDS imprint area is the date of publication of a reprint, facsimile edition, etc., when it is different from the date given in the coded information. The date of publication is in the record, nevertheless, and is there to be manipulated.

The *ISDS Manual* gives a choice so far as the name of an issuing body is concerned. The rule states: "When the information on the title source includes a generic term such as bulletin, technical bulletin, journal, transactions, proceedings, newsletter, report, etc., or its equivalent in other languages, and that generic term is linguistically separate from and/or typographically distinguished from the name of the issuing body, the key title is the generic term followed by the name of the issuing body, unless the language prevents this. Transcribe the name of the issuing body in the sequence and form given on the title source. The generic term is separated from the name of the issuing body by a space hyphen space."[12] Thus we get:

> Transactions - North Carolina Medical Society = ISSN 0361-5537
> Bulletin - Bach Society = ISSN 0309-7021

But, contrary to that, we have, because of their natural language construction:

> Journal of the American Chemical Society = ISSN 0002-7863
> British Pteridological Society bulletin = ISSN 0301-9195

The prescription that the name of the issuing body should be entered "in the sequence and form given on the title source" does lead to variant and inconsistent versions of the name of the same issuing body appearing in the file.

Centres have the choice, however, of entering the name of an issuing body in the form established by national cataloguing practice "when the name of the issuing body is not otherwise present in the record . . ."[13] There is a rider to this ISDS rule which states: "Centres subject to the bibliographic agreements of the CONSER . . . Project may transcribe the name of the issuing body in the form established by national cataloguing practice for use in headings and other access points."[14] Strictly that rider applies only to the United States and Canada but in recent years the British Library has adopted it even though the Library is not "subject to the bibliographic agreements of the CONSER . . . Project."

AACR2 makes no provision for distinguishing what would otherwise be identical titles, although the ABACUS libraries have devised a formula for uniform titles (or, as they are called in the United Kingdom in relation to serials, unique titles). The UK formulation prescribes qualification of a title proper to make it unique when it is identical with one or more titles within the same file (or if such conflict is thought to be likely in the future). The *ISDS Manual* states:[15] "When a proposed key title is identical with an existing key title in the ISDS database . . . or when it is otherwise known that there is another serial with an identical title, the proposed key title must be made unique by the addition of qualifying information . . ."

The UK formulation of the ABACUS practice prescribes qualifiers to be used in the order: place of publication, name of issuing or publishing corporate body (in the form used as an access point), any other term or combination of terms such as date, other title information, edition statement, language, format, etc. The latter may be added to place of publication or name of corporate body if further specificity is necessary. The *ISDS Manual* prescribes the order: place of publication, place and date of first publication, date alone (if an earlier title is resumed after a change of title), other information such as frequency, type of publication, etc., issuing body, and publisher (when nothing else will serve). This different ordering of qualifiers may lead occasionally to a key title and a unique title differing.

ISBD(S) has adopted the ISDS rules for minor changes of title, that is those instances where a change does not warrant a new entry or a new key title, as the case may be, and these rules have been adopted by AACR2 21.2A.

There are other differences between ISDS, *ISBD(S)* and AACR2 of a minor nature an account of which might stretch this paper to unacceptable limits. *ISBD(S)* gives an outline comparison of ISDS and *ISBS(S)*[16] and goes on to say:

> . . . the present ISBD(S) text results from a major effort to harmonize differences between [ISBD(S) and ISDS]. It should be noted in this connection that the ISBD(S) treatment of common/section titles, of main series/sub-series titles and of main publication/supplement or inset titles adheres closely to the ISDS treatment now, including the details of terminology and, moreover, the concepts behind the terms that can be seen in the ISDS Manual . . .

Elsewhere[17] it says: "It is suggested that for many libraries and for some library functions a short and authoritative record for a serial can be obtained from the data files of the International Serials Data System (ISDS)."

Günter Franzmeier, in a closely argued paper,[18] puts quite the opposite view:

> ISDS records as they are now, cannot and should not replace ISBD(S) records, much less can they replace full bibliographic records as offered by the national bibliographies . . . This will remain true in spite of the compatibility between ISDS and ISBD(S) achieved recently . . . It is true not so much because an ISDS record may still not contain information needed by the user of the national bibliography . . . but mainly for the reasons described in this paper, that is to say the different approach to the question of "entry," the absence in ISDS of satisfactory access and retrieval facilities. The latter point seems particularly regrettable since ISDS is often contrasted with the more "descriptive" task of cataloguing as being mainly, or even exclusively devoted to "identification." If "identification" means more than just distinguishing one title from another and one serial from another, then it should include satisfactory facilities for really identifying, i.e., finding a certain title amongst many other, sometimes very similar titles. This, unfortunately is not the case now . . .[19]

He goes on to propose a study "to assess in more detail the lack of, and the necessity for, refined retrieval facilities for ISDS."[20] It must be admitted that the ISDS Register on microfiche is not especially user friendly and much could be done to improve it. In 1991 the ISDS Governing Board is commissioning a professional market survey and some, if not all, of the improvements Günter Franzmeier wishes to see may be some of the outcomes of the follow-up to that survey.

The machine-readable file is there, however, to be manipulated. There are several current applications of ISDS data being used to create catalogue records. The oldest is NOSP (the *Nordisk Samkatalog over Periodika*) which is a union catalogue of foreign serials in the five Scandinavian countries established in 1977.[21] Record content is: key title, ISSN, parallel titles, publisher, place of publication, dates of first and last issue published, holdings according to country. References are made to former and successor titles and from issuing bodies. Within the Nordic countries Denmark's union catalogue of serials is based on ISDS records. In this context it is worth noting that the Danish manual on serials[22] is an amalgamation of AACR2 chapters 1 and 12 with some rules taken from *ISBD(S)* and the *ISDS Manual*. In Sweden, when the Swedish version of AACR2 was being prepared, it was decided, after consultation with the library community, that the key title would be the main entry for serials: ". . . we felt that the key title . . . is the most commonly used identifier of a serial, and you should see to it that that form of the title is really used as an entry in all catalogues . . . You reach that goal only by making the title the main entry."[23]

The relationship between the French national union catalogue of serials, *Catalogue collectif national informatisé des publications en série* (CCN), is very close. CCN policy is to base bibliographic description entirely on the ISDS file which constitutes an authority file. The principal complaints which have been levelled at ISDS by CCN are on inadequate access to issuing bodies and classification data.[24]

At the international level the Advisory Committee for the Coordination of Information Systems (ACCIS) of the United Nations is working closely with the ISDS International Centre to facilitate the registration process and the regular updating of data. The International Centre establishes bibliographic records for all serial titles of United Nations organizations (except for the World Bank, the records of which are processed by NSDP). A database of United Nations serial titles, derived from ISDS data, is maintained by the ACCIS Secretariat. The second edition of the *Register of United Nations Serial Publications*, derived from that database, was published in 1988 and contained about 3600 titles of 38 organizations within the UN.

In 1979 the British Library proposed to a national forum it had convened on the implementation of AACR2 and DDC19 that the Library should generate serials records only to ISDS standards. At that time the UK National Serials Data Centre, responsible for assignment of ISSN and registration of ISDS records for UK serial publications and for editing the *British Union-Catalogue of Periodicals. New Periodical Titles* (BUCOP.NPT), had the prospect of taking over responsibility for cataloguing UK serials for the UKMARC database and with the replacement of *BUCOP.NPT* by *Serials in the British Library*. The new office was thus faced with cataloguing UK serials to two standards, AACR2 and ISDS. The forum, at the time, considered the proposal to be worth further consideration. Within six months the Library had come back to the forum withdrawing its proposal on the grounds that the Library would be out of step with the other ABACUS libraries, the British Library Reference Division found it unacceptable and that additional data and structured access points would have to be created. Clearly other counsels had prevailed; the time was obviously not right for such a bold step. It is a pity that, at least, the nettle was not grasped of entering all serials by title thus lightening the burden and reducing bewilderment for us and our libraries' users. If one national library had taken that bold step perhaps others would have been encouraged to follow.

REFERENCES

1. Martin, M. D. and Barnes, C. I. *Report on the Feasibility of an International Serials Data System, and Preliminary Systems Design*; prepared for UNISIST/ ICSU-AB Working Group on Bibliographic Descriptions. (London: INSPEC, 1970.)

2. *Ibid.* section 2.1.

3. International Organization for Standardization. *ISO 3297-1986: Documentation-International Standard Serial Numbering (ISSN)*. (Geneva: ISO, 1986.)

4. International Federation of Library Associations and Institutions. *ISBD(S): International Standard Bibliographic Description for Serials*. Revised ed. (London: IFLA Universal Bibliographic Control and International MARC Programme, 1988.)

5. International Centre for the Registration of Serial Publications. *Guidelines for ISDS*. (Paris: Unesco, 1973.) (SC/WS/538).

6. Price, Mary S. "National and International Serial Standards," *The Serials Librarian* 12, no. 1/2 (1987): 3-7.

7. International Federation of Library Associations and Institutions. *ISBD(S): International Standard Bibliographic Description for Serials*. lst standard ed. (London: IFLA International Office for UBC, 1977.)

8. Bouffez, Françoise and Grousseaud, Annette. *Comparative Study on the Handling of Serials by ISDS Centres and National Bibliographic Agencies*. (Paris: Unesco, 1980.) (PGI/80/WS/13).

9. ISDS International Centre. *ISDS Manual*; edited by A. A. Mullis. (Paris: ISDS International Centre, 1983.)

10. Anderson, Dorothy. "Compatibility of ISDS and ISBD(S) Records in

International Exchange: the Background," *International Cataloguing* 12, no. 2 (April/June 1983): 14-17.

11. Szilvássy, Judith. "ISDS and ISBD(S) Records in International Exchange: Compatibility Issues." *International Cataloguing* 12, no. 4 (October/December 1983): 38-41.

12. *ISDS Manual.* Part 2, 3.2.2.3.

13. *Ibid.* Part 1, 8.3.1

14. *Ibid.* Part 2, 3.2.2.3

15. *Ibid.* Part 2, 3.2.8.

16. *ISBD(S)*, 0.3.3, 0.3.3.1.

17. *Ibid.* 0.1.3.1.

18. Franzmeier, Günter. "Can ISDS Replace ISBD(S)?" *International Cataloguing* 12, no. 4 (October/December 1983): 41-44.

19. *Ibid.* p. 44.

20. *Ibid.* p. 44.

21. Salomonsen, Annika. "NOSP: *NO*rdisk *S*amkatalog over *P*eriodika,"*International Cataloguing* 12, no. 4 (October/December 1983): 44-46.

22. Spangen, Inger Cathrine. "Implementation of AACR2 in the Nordic Countries," *Catalogue & Index* no. 81 (Summer 1986):2.

23. Hedberg, Sten. "Serials Cataloguing in Sweden," *The Serials Librarian* 12, no. 1/2 (1987): 12.

24. Lupovici, Christian and Bourgain, Jacques. "The French National Union Catalogue for Serial Publications (C.C.N)," *News from ISDS* no. 8 (1985): 1-6.

AACR2 and Serials Cataloguing in the United Kingdom

Albert A. Mullis

SUMMARY. The British Library implemented AACR2 in January 1981. The diverse origins of the Library and the differences in practice that still exist and which stem from those origins are described. The organization of cataloguing in the Library is explained. Continuing economic problems and increasing numbers of legal deposit items have forced the Library to make economies in cataloguing. The conclusion of a survey of user reaction to serials records in existing catalogues is noted. There is little evidence of concern or particular interest in serials cataloguing among British librarians. Listings which adequately identify titles and designate holdings are seen as much more important than 'authoritative' records created according to AACR2.

The British Library's implementation of AACR2 in the United Kingdom was not without controversy. A forum of interested parties (the bibliographic utilities, the MARC Users' Group, the Cataloguing and Indexing Group of the [British] Library Association, and others) was established by the Library before implementation to air concerns and to smooth progress. The Library was committed, along with the Library of Congress and the National Library of Canada, to implementation on 1 January 1981. The United Kingdom Serials Group was not represented on the forum and the direct impact on the cataloguing of serials was not a concern. Indeed, the principal and overwhelming concern was economic and what actions the Library proposed to take to ease the burden of implementation.

Albert A. Mullis ALA, is Serials Officer in the British Library Humanities and Social Sciences, Great Russell Street, London WC1B 3DG, United Kingdom (formerly Head of Serials Office, Bibliographic Services Division, 1981-1984, and Head of Processing, English Language Collections, Humanities and Social Sciences, 1984-1987).

The move towards revision of AACR67 was driven in the UK more by political and economic reasons on the part of the British Library and the Library Association than by an upsurge of grassroots dissatisfaction. The 'political' reasons were the part the Library, as the national library, and the Library Association, as the principal professional body, considered they must play in the revision of AACR and the need to avoid any possible, but unthinkable, move by the Americans to go down the revision path without us. The British needed to be seen to be giving unequivocal support if they were to have an equal voice in the revision process and if they were to derive maximum benefit. Peter Lewis explains in an article in 1978[1] the differences of approach between the United States and the United Kingdom.

> Almost simultaneously with the British Library's declaration of interest in this field, the American Library Association put forward a formal proposal for a revised edition of AACR. With the hindsight of observation of the very energetic and comprehensive scrutiny and review of the 1967 text that the Americans were later able to pack into the two very short years they had to carry it out, I should say that the dynamic of the ALA's initiative sprang from a very much greater dissatisfaction with the 1967 text at the grassroots level than was ever expressed to us here in this country, rather more than from the broadly political and economic reasons, if you like, for which the British Library and the Library Association endorsed the proposal.

The British Library was criticized at the time for implementing AACR2 too precipitately when developments in technology over the coming five years would, so it was said, considerably ease conversion and reduce costs. The drama is well described by one of the principal players at the time, David Buckle[2] (although recounting it from a very partial point of view). Some of the developments which it was predicted would happen have yet still to happen. With hindsight it was wise, perhaps, for the Library to have gone ahead as it did. Seemingly it was adopting Macbeth's attitude of: "If it were done when 'tis done, then 'twere well it were done quickly. . . . "

It is useful to have some understanding of the origins of the British Library as background to the different approaches taken within the Library and the attitudes of other libraries in the UK to it and its practices. The Library, as a corporate entity, is still relatively young, having been established by the British Library Act, 1972. Its original components were the British Museum Library (now the Humanities and Social Sciences division), the National Reference Library for Science and Invention (itself an offshoot of the British Museum Library and the Patent Office Library and now the Science Reference and Information Service), the National Lending Library for Science and Technology (now the Document Supply Centre), the British National Bibliography (now an integral part of the Acquisitions Processing and Cataloguing directorate and the National Bibliographic Service), the National Central Library (most of which was merged into the former Lending Division, and the remainder, the *British Union-Catalogue of Periodicals* (BUCOP), was merged into the then Bibliographic Services Division), and the Office of Scientific and Technical Information (then part of the Department of Education and Science and now the Library's Research and Development Department). Later, in the early 1980s, these were joined by the India Office Library and Records (now, with Oriental Collections, part of H&SS division's Special Collections directorate) and the British Institute of Recorded Sound (now the National Sound Archive).

These various components ranged in age from the eighteenth century origins of the British Museum Library (1753), through the nineteenth century origins of the Patent Office Library (1885) to the then more recently established National Lending Library for Science and Technology (1962) and the British National Bibliography (1949). Inevitably there were, and there remain, several disparate traditions and practices, not least in cataloguing. Each addressed, and in their present manifestations, still address, different audiences for different purposes.

The *British National Bibliography* (BNB) when it came into the Library used AACR67, with some local practices, and as the cataloguing arm of the then Bibliographic Services Division was in the forefront, not only in the Library but also in the country, in the adoption of AACR2. BUCOP had its origins in the British Museum and as *BUCOP. New Periodical Titles* (BUCOP.NPT) was the responsibility of the National Central Library. Its approach to serials cataloguing was a set of fairly basic inhouse rules, entering all serials by title and using the principle of successive entry, unlike its progenitor which had used earliest entry and, equally important, entered titles under corporate authors and places and authors, as appropriate. BUCOP.NPT was succeeded in 1981 by *Serials in British Library* (SBL) which, of course, uses AACR2.

It was intended that *Serials in the British Library* should include titles newly acquired not only by the various departments of the Library but also a number of other libraries with significant collections of serials in the United Kingdom and Ireland. They included the other five copyright deposit libraries (National Library of Scotland, National Library of Wales, the Bodleian Library at the University of Oxford, Cambridge University Library, and the library of Trinity College, Dublin). Other libraries were selected on the basis of either geographical location or because of strengths in particular subject areas. While it was intended that British Library contributions should be at AACR2 levels 3 or 2, other libraries were intended to submit their contributions at least to AACR2 level 1, and these would be enhanced where possible. There were difficulties, however, in getting all input to the required standard, not only from libraries outside the British Library but also from departments within the Library. The two principal stumbling blocks from within the Library were the then Lending Division (now the Document Supply Centre(DSC)) and the Science Reference Library (now the Science Reference and Information Service(SRIS)).

DSC used, and uses, its own cataloguing conventions. When its precursor, the National Lending Library for Science and Technology (NLLST), was established some of the UK library community was "shocked" by the decision to organize its holdings on shelves, where appropriate, by title. Its cataloguing rules are quite simple and wholly adequate for its purposes. Serials are, without exception, entered by title. Its general practices are not dissimilar to those of the International Serials Data System (ISDS), although that organization was not established until 1971 and NLLST had been set up in 1962. This writer finds difficulty in understanding why some UK librarians were "shocked" by the NLLST cataloguing and shelf arrangement practices when they seem to him to be eminently sensible and wholly pragmatic. Twenty eight years of existence has not proved that decision to be wrong or ill-judged.

The DSC's practices created some difficulties for the SBL editorial team. Because of the divergences in their practices from AACR2 it was not possible simply to work from records. Instead photocopies of covers and/or title pages and any other pages containing pertinent bibliographic data, together with shelf mark and start date of holdings were used as surrogates. Another problem area was SRIS because it continued to use AACR67 and without the actual serial or an acceptable surrogate it was not always possible to 'translate' records created according to the prescriptions of AACR67 into AACR2-style records. SRIS practice is a hybrid of AACR2, AACR67 and local rules. AACR67 is applied to determine the main entry, although headings are constructed in accordance with AACR2. Description is according to AACR2 with some local variations. Again, within the context of this particular library, these practices are seen by its staff to work. SRIS was also concerned not to create a split catalogue, as were other libraries; the move by AACR2 to entry of a far greater number of serials under title was not met with complete equanimity.

There were also problems with some records received from outside the Library in that they were patently not created according to correct AACR2 practice. Equally there were problems with some records received from the Library's Reference Division (now largely the Humanities and Social Sciences division). Each language area in that division created its own records, and standards varied in spite of some attempt at centralized editorial control.

Difficulties multiplied and the downward pressures on resources (staff numbers and money) eventually led to SBL being restricted, as it is now, to including only titles newly acquired by the London-based parts of the Library. Where titles which are unique to a particular department are not catalogued according to the prescriptions of AACR2 they are, nevertheless, entered in SBL.

It would be helpful here to say something about the organization of cataloguing in the Library now and in recent past. There is no central processing department and there has not been one during the Library's relatively short history. On its foundation there were not only different standards applied by its components but also different practices stemming from diverse traditions. The BNB was incorporated into what was then the Bibliographic Services Division (BSD) and from the point of view of cataloguing this is the face of the Library most other libraries see. It is responsible for cataloguing the UK legal deposit intake and as such is the largest single centre for cataloguing in the Library. BSD was also the 'guardian' of the UKMARC format and bibliographic standards (those roles have now been taken by the National Bibliographic Service). BSD has now been disbanded and restructured as three separate directorates: Acquisitions Processing & Cataloguing, Computing & Telecommunications, and National Bibliographic Service.

The former Reference Division (now Humanities and Social Sciences division and SRIS, but soon to be brought together again as 'London Services') had within it its own diversity. The organization of its services (not just information services but also selection and acquisitions processing and record creation) is broadly based on language or kind of material (for example the British Library Information Science Service (BLISS)). Each area, at present, is responsible for its own cataloguing. The Reference Division (with the exception of what is now SRIS) was early to adopt AACR2, although maintaining some divergent practices as the division, in its latest manifestation as Humanities and Social Sciences, still does. The division gradually moved towards closure of the *General Catalogue of Printed Books* (GK), now renamed the *British Library Catalogue of Printed Books to 1975* (BLC), with its own rules and structure firmly rooted in the nineteenth century and Panizzi's original rules, and which now make it something of a bibliographic curiosity.

The original intention had been that BSD would be responsible for cataloguing not only the copyright intake but also modern books and serials in English published outside the UK and Ireland. Eventually the dual problems of increasing publishing output and diminishing staff numbers caused the return of the non-UK and Ireland cataloguing responsibility to the Reference Division in 1982. The wheel is now in process of turning full circle as in 1992 the newly created Acquisitions Processing & Cataloguing (AP&C) directorate will take responsibility for modern overseas English material (as it is known) when AP&C relocates from London to Boston Spa in Yorkshire. Presumably any divergences that may still exist will be eliminated by this merger, at least so far as modern English language material is concerned.

There are no definitely stated plans to include the cataloguing of foreign language material in AP&C, although it may be that the mainstream West European languages (French, German, Spanish and Italian) will be included. It seems that any move in that direction may well be strongly resisted. It is highly unlikely that there will ever be one all-embracing cataloguing department in the Library. The cataloguing of foreign language material, special materials, such as maps, printed music, sound recordings, manuscripts, graphic materials, and newspapers, and older materials are likely to remain outside AP&C's orbit. While it is planned that the mainstream English language materials at SRIS will be catalogued by AP&C as from 1991 it seems probable that DSC will successfully resist incorporation of its cataloguing procedures into that directorate. There comes a point at which the perceived advantages of uniformity become counterproductive.

The standards applied in AP&C should be viewed as those the Library should use in an ideal situation; other practices, whatever good reasons there may be for their continued use, must be regarded as non-standard. The British Library, by the very nature of its diverse origins, is, by and large, a federal institution; its road to a true corporate identity being evolutionary rather than revolutionary.

Standards and their application, even in AP&C, do not stand still. Absolute concurrence with the practical application of AACR2 between the ABACUS libraries (that is, the British Library, the National Library of Australia, the National Library of Canada, and the Library of Congress) does not exist and never has existed. While AACR67 had, unfortunately, separate British and North American texts, AACR2 does not leave us without the opportunity to diverge from one another by its use of optional additions, options and alternative rules. The British Library's final position on options and so forth is set out in the newsletter of the former Bibliographic Services Division.[3] The Library has issued *Cataloguing Practice Notes for UKMARC Records*[4] but in number and bulk they are insignificant compared with the rule interpretations of the Library of Congress. The British Library's attitude has long been one of permitting discretion to its cataloguers (once properly trained) rather than give them voluminous written instructions. Humanities and Social Sciences has its own cataloguing practice manual, which is somewhat more substantial. This pragmatic approach does, however, have disadvantages in that not all cataloguers will arrive at the same answer and there is likely to be some disregard for standards and a growth of incoherence in the catalogue. AP&C, at least, does tend to adhere fairly rigidly to the principles of AACR2.

H&SS, because of the growth of its cataloguing backlogs to an unacceptable level, has freely used derived cataloguing, notably from the LCMARC files and the OCLC database; but because of remaining differences between the British Library and the Library of Congress (or for that matter between the UK and the United States) over practice and interpretation of AACR2, cataloguers do need to check headings to ensure that they are in conformity with our practices.

The continuing downward trend in the amount of money the Library receives from the Treasury and the continuing upward trend in the number of new titles published led the then Bibliographic Services to issue a consultative paper, *Currency with Coverage: the Future Development of the British National Bibliographic Database*,[5] in July 1987. This proposed a selective application of AACR2 level 1 to the legal deposit intake and certain reductions in subject coverage. The objectives are to produce records in a more timely fashion and to eliminate backlogs of processing in a reasonably short time but without reduction of coverage or quality. The outcry at the time from some parts of the UK library community was more against the timing and manner of the proposals than the proposals themselves; although there was some unhappiness about the loss of some data, such as other title information and subject data and the impact that would have for subject retrieval from OPACs. Some modifications were made later as a result of representations from the library community.[6] The MARC Users' Group commissioned a survey from the Centre for Bibliographic Management at the University of

Bath[7] from which no firm conclusions could be drawn on the deleterious impact of the Library's proposals.

Humanities and Social Sciences adopted the proposals, although with some local differences. Insofar as serial titles are concerned it may be useful to indicate what differences there are between AP&C and H&SS. AP&C makes some effort to establish and supply data for the UKMARC 255 field, designation area, whereas it is left blank by H&SS if the information is not readily to hand, especially if holdings are other than from the first issue. Whereas AP&C strictly observes AACR2 level 1 by the omission of place of publication, H&SS includes first place of publication. In AP&C added entries are made at 710, 711, 740 and 745 as appropriate but H&SS no longer makes added entries for related titles. There are also some other minor differences.

The differences of practice already noted above do not end there and one other significant difference should be noted. The Newspaper Library (which is part of H&SS) uses inhouse rules and applies the principle of earliest entry in contrast to AACR2's prescription of successive entry. Not all titles held at the Newspaper Library are by any known definition 'newspapers.' As a general rule publications appearing more frequently than monthly are also held at the Newspaper Library and these non-newspaper serials are recorded in the same way as the rest of the stock. There is the contradiction that new legal deposit titles destined for the Newspaper Library are catalogued according to the prescriptions of AACR2 for BNB and *Serials in the British Library* but are catalogued separately and differently by that library.

At the beginning of this article a generalised statement was made that the direct impact on the cataloguing of serials was not a concern of the forum on AACR2. That is not wholly true. The British Library did put forward a proposal that serials records should be generated only to the standards of the International Serials Data System (ISDS). There was concern in Bibliographic Services Division at the time that serials would be catalogued by two standards, AACR2 for the UKMARC database and other internal purposes and ISDS. While there was double input the intellectual effort to produce two different records was not doubled. When the proposal was mooted it was not dismissed out of hand but "considered worthy of further investigation" by the forum. But six months later the British Library withdrew the proposal on the grounds that: (i) the Library would be out of step with the other ABACUS libraries, (ii) the Reference Division found the proposal unacceptable for its needs (the legal deposit intake which is recorded for the UKMARC file is held within what is now H&SS and SRIS), and (iii) additional data such as structured access points would have to be created. The Library made one other, rather curious, point: "The ISDS key-title is unique, but does not necessarily mean anything to the user." The Library's change of heart was accepted by the forum.[8]

Ross Bourne in a paper given to a seminar on AACR2[9] in 1979, among other things drew attention to the need for unique titles to distinguish otherwise identical titles one from another. This was a lacuna in AACR2 and this 'oversight' was put right by the ABACUS libraries. While not a rule amendment the device of unique title (as it is known in the UK) is, nevertheless, within the spirit of the code. As presented to the UK library community the decision reads:[10]

> If the title proper of a serial, or a title which is used as an added entry, is identical with one or more titles within the same file (or if such conflict is thought to be likely in the future) establish a unique title by adding to the title a qualifier based upon which ever of the following criteria best serves to identify the work meaningfully in this order:
>
> a. first named place of publication, distribution, etc.
> b. name of corporate body by which it was issued or published (in the form in which used as an access point)
> c. any other term or combination of terms such as date, other title information, edition statement, language, format, etc.
> These may be added to a. and b.

Günter Franzmeier makes the point[11] that in *Serials in the British Library* (and, for that matter, in *New Serial Titles*) an entry may have as many as four different titles, the unique, or uniform title, the title proper, the ISDS key title, and the ISDS abbreviated key title. Some are remarkably similar, differing only in terms of punctuation and capitalization of initial letters. He wonders whether this is the result of ten years effort to standardize, rationalize and internationalize serials cataloguing. Some of the blame he lays at the door of AACR2 for largely dropping entry under corporate author for so many serials.

One particular aspect of AACR2 which has bemused some is its adoption of the punctuation and other prescriptions of the international standard bibliographic descriptions (ISBD). Philip Bryant, Director of the Centre for Bibliographic Management at the University of Bath, was commissioned by the British Library in 1986:[12] "To discover the needs of users in respect of bibliographic access (i.e., the amount of bibliographic description required) to the British Library's serials collections and to determine the most effective way in which those needs might be met.'' Limited time and resources restricted the study to the main Reading Room and the Official Publications and Social Sciences Service reading room in the British Museum building. In effect only the Humanities and Social Sciences division was being looked at (and even then the Oriental Collections, the India Office Library and the Newspaper Library were excluded because of their location in other buildings).

There were and, indeed, still are two particular problems when attempting to trace details of serials held in the Library. Users (and that includes members of staff) often do not appear to understand the content, arrangement and presentation of data in existing catalogues and staff are unable to search for items held in other parts of the Library except by looking through a range of catalogues compiled in a diversity of ways.

While some of Bryant's findings are relevant just to the British Library, nevertheless some have relevance to the wider library community. The conclusions are worth noting in full:

- i. Accurate holdings data are considered far more important by users than bibliographic details.
- ii. Ideally users would like to have correlation of volume numbers with dates in the holdings statement but many users recognized this was an almost impossible task because of the sheer magnitude of the problem.
- iii. Very few users want a journal as an artefact. Most would be well satisfied with a surrogate such as a photocopy or microfilm if this could be supplied immediately and with good enough quality.
- iv. There was little evidence that users of long experience are necessarily more knowledgeable about data in the catalogue entries than new users.
- v. Clarity of presentation and layout of the entries is far more important to users than additional data. Particular problems are caused by:
  - a. Over abbreviation, e.g., *v.* instead of *vol.*, *ill.* instead of *illus.*
  - b. Ambiguous use of punctuation, especially the ISBD convention of using dashes which get confused with hyphens used in dates.
  - c. The use of jargon terms in entries such as 'holdings,' 'imprint,' 'cover title,' etc.
  - d. Lack of labelling of certain data elements (e.g., 'Publ. by').
  - e. Lack of clarity of terms used, such as 'continued as' instead of 'split into,' or the omission of words such as 'by' or 'at' in relation to publishers or places of publication.
  - f. The considerable lack of understanding of the difference be-

tween the 'bibliographic' date and the 'holdings' date. It would appear that, in general, use of just the latter would be much less confusing to the user.

g. Lack of 'paragraphing' of data, e.g., if a title changes, give each change a fresh line and, if possible, the appropriate dates.

Regrettably it has not yet been possible to put into effect any of Philip Bryant's findings: that must wait until the day when an integrated database is economically feasible.

Elsewhere[13] he has made some play with the ISBD punctuation conventions. He quotes a few of the users' comments made during the course of his study for the Library:

> "I find things in spite of, not because of, library cataloguing."
> "Why do I need to know this?"
> "*Not* very helpful!"
> "This entry is rubbish . . . designed to confuse!"
> "What is that hyphen doing, anyway?"

Much earlier, Jane Wainwright,[14] in reviewing the *International Standard Bibliographic Description for Serials: ISBD(S)* (first standard edition, 1977) cites an example from the ISBD(S) prefacing it by: "Try . . . explaining this to a reader . . ."

British librarians, on the whole, seem to be unconcerned with, if not positively uninterested in, serials cataloguing. Practitioners coming together at the workplace may argue long and fiercely over certain cataloguing minutiae and matters of rule interpretation but whatever they feel does not often see its way into print. We could not, in the United Kingdom, emulate the RTSD Serials Section bibliography of articles and monographs on serials, the fifth of which appeared in *Serials Review* 12, no. 2 (Summer 1987). Among its twenty four entries under cataloguing (covering only three years) not one item is British or by a Briton. *Serials: the Journal of the United Kingdom Serials Group* and its predecessor the *United Kingdom Serials Group Newsletter* in their combined twelve years of existence can muster only two articles specifically on serials cataloguing, although there are references here and there within other articles. In its fourteen annual conferences, including the upcoming 1991 conference, the UKSG has had only one paper specifically on serials cataloguing. The Cataloguing and Indexing Group of the Library Association at its conferences and in its journal *Catalogue & Index* does little better.

Serials, by and large, are not treated with any special reverence in cataloguing, although their differences and problems are fully recognized. The separate serials cataloguing section is a rarity in British libraries. Throughout the British Library only the Document Supply Centre has a separate section dealing exclusively with serials cataloguing, if you exclude the UK National Serials Data Centre (the UK ISDS centre) in AP&C. The latter's predecessor body, Bibliographic Services, had a Serials Office from late 1980 until 1985 when it was merged into the mainstream cataloguing function.

Well known (at least in the UK) and heavily used listings such as the DSC's *Current Serials Recived, Keyword Index to Serial Titles* (KIST), and the Cambridge University Library listing all have entries stripped down to the bare essentials and lack the elaboration to be found in *Serials in the British Library* and BNB. In spite of that, they work; and that, when all is said and done, is what really matters. For those requiring authoritative records compiled in conformity with the prescriptions of AACR2, BNB and the UKMARC database will provide them, at least so long as they are legal deposit items. The current catalogues and the databases deriving from them of Humanities and Social Sciences and the Science Reference and Information Service (such as SBL) will provide 'authoritative' records, after their own fashion, of non-UK items in their collections.

The apparent elaboration required by AACR2 and ISBD(S) seems not to be to British taste but, on the whole, there is a general observance of the broad principles of AACR2. This is inevitable given the number of libraries which use UKMARC records through one source or another. The unconcern about cataloguing came across in a workshop on serials held at the MARC Users' Group conference in 1988.[15] There the concern was not with the standard or authority of records but rather with the need for a 'national' database which gave information on which libraries hold what for the purposes of interlibrary lending, consultation and collection development. There was little or no concern that such a database should hold records which could be derived or used for copying.

Perhaps Michael Gorman sums it all up. Unlike David Buckle[16] I do not look upon Michael Gorman as a personal guru, but he does occasionally write and say something which illuminates by its forthrightness or iconoclasm and which has much appeal, as he does in an article on the ISBDs:[17]

> There is not, nor has there ever been, any conclusively proven demand for this type of full bibliographic description . . . The overwhelming majority of records listing serials are working tools con-

> cerned primarily with the identification and location of specific titles and with the recording and registering of the library's holdings . . . The niceties and fine distinctions . . . are not relevant to the needs of most serials librarians.

The foregoing, concentrating as it has so heavily on the British Library, would seem to give the lie to its title. That an account of the application of AACR2 in the UK should give so much attention to the British Library is inevitable given the Library's position at the apex of the UK library community pyramid and its roles as the guardian of cataloguing standards and the producer of authoritative UKMARC records for British legal deposit material. Whenever the British Library makes any significant changes in practice controversy and concern seem to follow from a number of libraries in the UK. It is not the case, and never has been one, of what is good for the British Library is good for the rest of the UK library community. The Library is sometimes torn between its international and national obligations and between the needs of other libraries and its own needs. This situation will remain, unfortunately, so long as we are in a situation where expenditure on the public sector remains on the very tight rein it has done over the last ten years or so.

REFERENCES

1. Lewis, Peter. "Introducing the Second Edition of AACR," *Catalogue & Index* no. 51 (Winter 1978): 3.

2. Buckle, David. "AACR2 Implementation Five Years on," *Catalogue & Index* no. 80 (Spring 1986): 1, 3-5.

3. "AACR2 Optional Additions, Options and Alternative Rules: the British Library's Position," *British Library Bibliographic Services Division Newsletter* no. 16-17 (May 1980): 3-6.

4. *Cataloguing Practice Notes for UKMARC Records.* No. 1- . (London: British Library Automated Information Service, 1981- .)

5. British Library. Bibliographic Services. *Currency with Coverage: the Future Development of the British National Bibliographic Database.* (London: British ibrary Bibliographic Services, 1987.)

6. *British Library Bibliographic Services Newsletter* no. 44 (October 1987): 1-3.

7. MARC Users' Group. *Currency with Coverage–a Survey: Report; Prepared by the Centre for Bibliographic Management* (London: MARC Users' Group, 1989).

8. *British Library Bibliographic Services Division Newsletter* no. 14 (August 1979):5.

9. Bourne, Ross. ''AACR2: Cataloguing of Serials'' in *Seminar on AACR2: Proceedings of a Seminar. . . 20-22 April 1979*, ed. Graham Roe: (London: Library Association, 1980): 50-59.

10. *British Library Bibliographic Services Division Newsletter* no. 20 (February 1981): 2.

11. Franzmeier, Günter. ''The Miraculous Multiplication of Serial Titles,'' *International Cataloguing* 11, no. 1 (January/March 1982): 9.

12. Bryant, Philip. ''Bibliographic Access to Serials: a Study for the British Library'' *Serials* 1, no. 3 (November 1988): 41-46.

13. Bryant, Philip. ''What Is That Hyphen Doing Anyway? Cataloguing and Classification of Serials and the New Technologies,'' *International Cataloguing and Bibliographic Control* 18, no. 2 (April/June 1989): 27-29.

14. *Catalogue & Index* no. 47 (Winter 1977): 6.

15. MARC Users' Group. *The Future of the National Bibliographic Database: Proceedings of the 14th Annual Seminar. . . of the MARC Users' Group. . . 13-15 September 1988*. (London: MARC Users' Group, 1990): 51-53.

16. Op. cit., p. 4.

17. Gorman, Michael. ''International Standard Bibliographic Description and the New ISBDs'' *Journal of Librarianship* 10, no. 2 (April 1978): 132.

National Bibliographic Control of Serials in Australia, 1980-1990

Jasmine Cameron

SUMMARY. There is a long history of effective co-operation and national initiatives in controlling and sharing serial data in Australia. Prior to the 1980's this largely took the form of manually produced national union catalogues such as *Scientific Serials in Australian Libraries*; *Serials in Australian Libraries, Social Sciences and the Humanities*; and *Newspapers in Australian Libraries*. The commencement of the Australian Bibliographic Network (ABN) in 1980 provided the mechanism for both a national shared cataloguing venture and a truly national on-line union catalogue. *The National Union Catalogue of Serials* produced from ABN was dependent on the addition of holdings by ABN participating libraries. Several factors contributed to the growth of serials data on the national bibliographic database–notably the steady increase in the number of ABN participants undertaking serials cataloguing on ABN, serial conversion work on titles in the National Library card catalogues, and major serial conversion work undertaken by other Australian libraries. Although much has been achieved in the 1980's there remains much to be done to enhance the coverage of bibliographic and holdings data for serials on ABN.

The increasing focus of library thinking in Australia in the 1980's on the concept of the National Bibliographic Database (NBD) has created opportunities for sound initiatives in the national bibliographic control of serials in Australia. The all too familiar tightening of library budgets, and the trend towards automated serials systems have also turned the attention of Australian libraries towards the co-operative collection and control of serials on a national basis.

Jasmine Cameron is Chief Serials Librarian, National Library of Australia, Canberra, ACT 2601 Australia.

There is a long history of effective co-operation and national initiatives in controlling and sharing serial data in Australia. The National Library of Australia and the Commonwealth Scientific and Industrial Research Organization (CSIRO) were for many years responsible for the production of two major complementary national union catalogues of serial holdings–*Scientific Serials in Australian Libraries (SSAL)*, produced by the CSIRO and first issued in 1930 and *Serials in Australian Libraries, Social Sciences and the Humanities (SALSSAH)*, produced by the National Library and first issued in 1952. The National Library also commenced the production of a national union catalogue of newspapers held in Australian libraries–*Newspapers in Australian Libraries (NAL)*–in 1960. Each of these national union catalogues was updated by means of contributed cards received from a large number of Australian libraries. Their main function was to facilitate inter-library lending and resource sharing between Australian libraries.

The production of these union catalogues was by nature very labour intensive and delays in updating entries were common. This problem was partially overcome with the introduction of microfiche formats but it was not until the implementation of the Australian Bibliographic Network (ABN) in 1980, with its shared cataloguing facility, that *national* bibliographic control of serials based on up-to-date cataloguing and holdings information became a reality.

Since the early 1970's the concept of a single national database has been widely accepted by the Australian library community. In 1981 ABN (based on the Washington Library Network software) commenced operation as a shared cataloguing facility following a successful pilot project. The introduction of ABN provided the mechanism for the development of an online national union catalogue of serials to replace the earlier printed and microfiche catalogues.

Although the early success or failure of ABN was seen largely in terms of its success or failure as a shared cataloguing venture, it had always been envisaged that ABN would play a wider role, and particularly for serials in relation to the union cataloguing function. Harrison Bryan, Director General of the National Library at the time of ABN implementation, praised the shared cataloguing aspect of ABN but said during a memorial lecture in 1982, "Even more significant, perhaps, will be the growing value of the system for co-operative use of cataloguing resources. Every Australian location included on it helps to sound the death knell of the present cumbersome, inefficient and inevitably obsolete tools for interlibrary loan: *NUCOM*, *SSAL* and *SALSSAH* . . . A single integrated on-line union list of serials has suddenly become a reality."[1]

Work on the feasibility of producing *SALSSAH* and *SSAL* from ABN progressed rapidly and the National Library began the transfer of data from the union catalogues to ABN. In addition to online access, the National Library produced the first issue of the *National Union Catalogue of Serials (NUCOS)* in 1984. *NUCOS* was issued as a microfiche product and included all serials on ABN to which a holdings statement was attached.

The national aspect of *NUCOS* was stressed from the beginning and it was seen as crucial that both serial bibliographic and holdings data should be contributed co-operatively by ABN participants and the national union cataloguing agencies. The rapid growth of *NUCOS* testified to the success of the National Bibliographic Database (NBD) as a mechanism for resource sharing. By the end of 1985 *NUCOS* included holdings data for 103,000 titles. At the end of 1987 the National Library responded to the decline in card reports to *NUCOS* and announced that card reports would no longer be accepted. From this stage onwards the growth of *NUCOS* was dependent on the addition of holdings to the NBD by ABN contributing libraries, with the National Library taking some responsibility for adding serial holdings data in cases where insufficient holdings had been identified on the NBD. By the end of 1989 over 210,000 serial records included at least one holdings statement on the NBD.

Several factors contributed to this continued growth–notably the increase in the number of ABN participants undertaking serials cataloguing on ABN, serial conversion work on titles in the National Library card catalogues, and major serial conversion work undertaken by other Australian libraries.

SERIALS CATALOGUING AND RETROSPECTIVE SERIALS CONVERSION AT THE NATIONAL LIBRARY OF AUSTRALIA

In 1980 the Australian Bibliographic Network pilot project commenced and the National Library began cataloguing its current intake of monographs onto ABN. Following the success of the pilot project the National Library closed its Serials Card Catalogue in April 1981 and became the first ABN participant to undertake serials cataloguing on ABN. This meant that all newly acquired titles and title changes were catalogued onto the network. Good progress was made with the addition of serial records to ABN and in June 1982 bibliographic records for serials included in the *Australian National Bibliography (ANB)* were added to ABN. This was made possible with the introduction of the Australian MARC Serials Format. The Serials Format was developed by staff at the National Library and was introduced to *ANB* in 1982. Although the cataloguing of current serial titles and title changes onto ABN produced a steady increase in the number of National Library serial holdings on ABN most of the National Library's collection of 190,000 overseas and Australian titles were not represented on the database. In an effort to expand coverage of the National Library's serial collection a series of retrospective conversion projects was launched.

In December 1985 staff from the Library's Serial Section commenced a three month project to add holdings and call number information to ABN for major journals. For the purposes of this project major journals were considered to be those titles most frequently requested via the National Library's Loan and Copy Service and which were indexed in major indexes such as *Social Sciences Citation Index* and *Medline*. The first phase of the project was completed in March 1986 with the addition of 6,700 holdings to existing ABN records and the creation of 360 original cataloguing records. The second phase of the project began in June 1986. By the end of April 1987 an additional 11,000 serial holdings had been added to ABN and 2,500 original serial records had been created. The results of this conversion project showed the Australian library community that serials cataloguing and retrospective conversion of mainstream serial titles on ABN not only yielded benefits in terms of better collection control but were a worthwhile venture in terms of productivity.

The project demonstrated that copy cataloguing of mainstream journal titles was an efficient cost-effective operation due to the high hit rate (85%) on ABN. Staff reached a processing rate of 20 titles per day during the project. At the time this project was undertaken the ABN database contained approximately 510,000 serial records gathered by the regular addition of MARC serial records from various bibliographic agencies including the Library of Congress, National Library of Canada, British Library and the National Library of New Zealand.

The benefits of this serial conversion project were such that plans were made for further conversion work by the National Library and other Australian libraries as well. The National Library's first conversion project had achieved several major objectives including the provision of the basis for the Library's Document Supply Service to operate a priority 'fast lane' loan and copy service for requests which quoted the National Library's call (shelf location) number. The provision of information concerning the Library's holdings and cancellations through ABN also assisted Australian libraries involved in collection rationalization.

A second conversion project was launched in January 1988 with the aim of converting the 65,000 titles which remained in the Library's Serials Card Catalogue (all titles received and fully catalogued between 1967 and 1980) onto ABN. At the commencement of the project it was acknowledged that the component of original cataloguing would be much higher due to the large number of Australian and non-mainstream overseas titles in the catalogue. However, the substantial contribution of original cataloguing was recognised as essential in terms of opening up access to the Library's rich collection of serial material, much of which (e.g., material from the United Nations and other inter-governmental agencies) is not widely held in Australia or is held uniquely within Australia by the National Library.

The retrospective serials conversion project is still underway at the National Library and has so far taken the form of a series of mini-projects in which different categories of material have been targeted. Much of the more recent conversion work has been driven by the need for the National Library to prepare a database for an integrated library management system. More positive moves towards co-operative collection and control of library material in Australia in the late 1980's have also placed a greater importance on the need to add the Library's serial holdings to ABN as quickly as possible so that the NBD is a viable vehicle for the co-operative collection and control of serials.

NEW DIRECTIONS AND ISSUES

In 1988 a consultative meeting of the peak library organisations in Australia, known as the Australian Libraries Summit, was held to discuss future directions for library and information services in Australia. The Australian Libraries Summit addressed the issue of the role of the NBD and formed a set of resolutions including:

- support for the concept of a central database operated through the National Library as the major component of a national database for the forseeable future
- encouragement of the National Library and other appropriate institutions to ensure that as high a proportion as possible of the bibliographic record of the national collection, including the holdings of non-ABN participants, is accessible online

In response to the need to address the bibliographic resolutions of the Australian Libraries Summit, the National Library established a Bibliographic Planning Group in 1989 to co-ordinate an effective approach to the delivery of bibliographic data to the nation via the NBD. Although ABN has a very wide coverage there are still significant gaps in regional coverage and some major institutions are not yet represented on the database. One objective of the Bibliographic Planning Group is to investigate methods to improve this coverage of holdings and bibliographic data on ABN. Attention has been given recently to the idea of loading MARC files onto the database from non-ABN participants such as the serials file of the University of Queensland which, when loaded, will fill a major gap in serial holdings on the NBD. Although there has been considerable progress in the 1980's there remains much to be done to enhance the coverage of bibliographic records and holdings data for serials on ABN.

REFERENCE

1. Harrison Bryan, "The Development of ABN," *Cataloguing Australia* 8, no. 1(March 1982): 2-18.

Serials Cataloging in Italy

Rossella Dini

SUMMARY. The article provides an outline from an historical standpoint of how Italian cataloging rules have dealt with serials and gives a general picture of the current situation and trends. The most recent of the three national codes issued up to the present time (1921, 1956, and 1979) recommends the creation of a separate catalog for this type of publication in conformity with a national standard (UNI norm 6392) conceived outside the framework of the functions of the general library catalog.

There exists, however, a substantially uniform cataloging tradition that allows access by title and deals with title changes in accordance with the principle of successive entry.

The only existing national periodical file was created by the Istituto di studi sulla ricerca e documentazione scientifica (ISRDS) of the Consiglio nazionale delle ricerche (CNR), set up in conformity with UNI norm 6392.

The existence of this file, whose records are to be adapted and converted, forms the basis of a government project to create a periodical file within the catalog of the National Library Service (SBN).

INTRODUCTION

The aim of this paper is to provide an outline from an historical standpoint of how cataloging rules in Italy have dealt with serials as well as to give a general picture of the current situation and trends.

Our examination will be conducted on the basis of the three cataloging codes issued up to the present time: the *Regole* of 1921[1] and 1956[2] and RICA of 1979,[3] with particular reference to the central questions regarding serials cataloging: (1) rules for entry and heading, (2) rules for description, (3) title change, and (4) title differentiation.

Rossella Dini, Via della Fornace di San Giorgio, n. 30, 51100 Pistoia, Italy, is Chief of the Publishing Office, Regione Toscana, Florence, Italy.

A preliminary consideration must, however, be made: Italian cataloging tradition does not take *serials* into account as a specific topic in the wider sense of the term, but only one of its segments, the periodicals.[4] All reference to the term *serial/serials* in this article is to be understood in this more limited sense. We would have the reader note, however, that the most recent standards which we shall comment further on–UNI 6392 and RICA–point out that the instructions for cataloging are to be extended to all serial publications.

THE FIRST CATALOGING RULES: THE HISTORICAL CONTEXT

The decree signed on June 11, 1921, by Benedetto Croce, Minister of Public Education at that time, gave Italian libraries their first set of cataloging rules for compiling alphabetical catalogs. The date is significant as it is just before the advent of Fascism, at the very end of the process of national unity that had been begun with the proclamation of the Kingdom of Italy in 1861.

The general picture of national life was characterized at that time, in the words of the Neapolitan historian Pasquale Villari, by "17 million illiterates and 3 million 'Arcadians.'"[5]

The absence of a reading public and the fundamentally conservative character of Italian culture were at the very origin of a concept of the library as a bibliographical museum, not a viable tool for cultural development. The preindustrial state of publishing, the unequal distribution of public libraries in relation to the national territory and the lack of means at their disposal, and the practically nonexistent professional know-how of librarians (for the most part humanists and philologists) complete the picture.[6]

Notwithstanding the organic insufficiency of their overall framework, Italian libraries had a "promising spring" in the last quarter of the century, thanks to the happy combination created by the appointment of the highly cultured and dynamic Ferdinando Martini as General Secretary of the Ministry of Public Education and the presence of a handful of "task-force" librarians like Desiderio Chilovi, Prefect of the National Library of Florence, Guido Biagi, librarian at the Marucellian Library of Florence, and Giuseppe Fumagalli, deputy librarian at the National Library of Rome.

Among other things, Chilovi has to his credit the launching of the *Bollettino delle pubblicazioni italiane (Bulletin of Italian Publications)*, which listed works received on legal deposit by the National Library of Florence and was the first true national bibliography of Italy, and the founding of *Indici e cataloghi*, a series of volumes aimed at publicizing printed and manuscript collections owned by Italian libraries, the first issue of which was dedicated significantly to periodicals and constituted their first union catalog having a national basis.[7]

Biagi's particular merit was in the production of tools that contributed to the modernization of Italian bibliographical scholarship, opening it to advances made in other countries. From 1887 to 1893 he edited the series *Biblioteca di bibliografia e paleografia*, published by Sansoni, where important translations appeared (e.g., the *Regole* of Karl Dziatko and those of Jewett, translated by Biagi himself). In 1888 he founded the *Rivista delle biblioteche*,[8] which he edited until his death in 1925.

A venture of particular relevance to our topic, proposed by Desiderio Chilovi and supported by Ferdinando Martini, was the announcement of a series of bibliographical awards, one of which was to be given to the author of "the most rational and practical rules for drafting catalogs alphabetically or by subject matter, and for compiling indexes for particular bibliographical materials." Giuseppe Fumagalli received the award for his essay *Cataloghi di biblioteche e indici bibliografici*, which was later published in 1887 by Sansoni in the series edited by Biagi.[9]

This was the first important proposal for a unified code of rules and the result of the author's personal experience first in Florence[10] and then in Rome,[11] as well as of his study of specialized literature and cataloging rules used in other countries.[12]

In particular, for his alphabetical catalog, Fumagalli borrowed from American experience, principally Jewett and Cutter. In rule LIV, dealing with periodicals, his appreciation of Cutter was quite evident: in the *scolio* to the rule the four features of a periodical as described by Cutter in rule 54[13] were practically translated. The general instruction was that newspapers and periodicals were always to be cataloged as anonymous works and thus under their title even if they had only one compiler. Although Fumagalli accepted the principle of cataloging publications issued by a corporate body under its name (rule XXXXIX),[14] he clearly excluded periodicals (rule L, scolio I).

Title changes were handled according to the single entry principle, under the earliest title; later titles were noted on the card and references were made from them. The principle of successive entry was introduced, however, for any title change that brought about "more substantial modifications" in the overall features of the periodical–if it had started its numbering over again or if "in some other way it [had] become a new periodical." In this case it was "convenient to enter each part under its own title with notes at the bottom of the card to this effect: *For continuation, see* etc., and: *For preceding volumes, see* etc." In other words, the mere formal criterion of change of title wasn't enough to establish a bibliographical identity: to define a periodical change, more intrinsic evaluations as to its nature were necessary.

As far as description was concerned, periodical publications were not substantially different from monographic ones. After the title (including possible statements of authors, collaborators, etc., and of edition) came, in the following order, the place of publication, name of the publisher, and year of publication, followed by printing data if different (rules LXXVI and LXXVII); the number of volumes, format, illustrations (rule LXXVI); the frequency and dates of the first and last issues (rule XC).

References were prescribed for archaic forms of nouns used as entry words, individual editors and editors-in-chief, and other titles and later titles (rule XCVIII).

In spite of the Ministerial award, Fumagalli's work was never translated into a code of rules. Undoubtedly "it was used as a text in Italian libraries, but . . . unfortunately it didn't set down fixed rules, and only outlined the various problems, listing the different solutions that could be given for each. For this reason it could be held responsible for the disorder that reigned on the subject"–such was the opinion of Fumagalli himself when remarking on "the actual anarchy that reigned in the cataloging system"[15] in Italian libraries at the end of the last century.

The result of his proposal to submit a set of cataloging rules drawn up by the Società bibliografica italiana to the Government was the publication in 1901 of a *Progetto di norme uniche per la compilazione dei cataloghi alfabetici*,[16] a rather scant set of instructions written in a very modest way and closely tied to the editorial features of a book. Periodical publications were mentioned in relation to only one, but quite relevant, aspect: titles changes, for which successive entry was basically prescribed:

> For magazines that change their title or are merged with others . . . the later titles are to be preceded by the note "*Continued* by . . ." and under each new title a full entry is to be compiled, giving the preceding title in the note "*Continues* . . ."[17]

These instructions, which no longer abided by Fumagalli's principle of single entry, prefigured what would become a constant in Italian cataloging codes from 1921 up to the present time.

Chilovi had already expressed his skepticism for operations like the *Progetto* of the Società bibliografica. When he was called upon by Biagi to respond to the proposal of Princeton University's librarian, E. C. Richardson, for participating in an international cooperative cataloging project based on uniform cataloging rules,[18] he answered:

> Though . . . there are examples of rules and attempts to apply them, I think that at the present moment it would be very difficult for Italy's libraries to reach an agreement among themselves . . . The *Istruzioni* published on May 10th, 1899, for the alphabetical catalogs in the libraries of Prussia, and for the Prussian general catalog, could be the basis of an international agreement.[19]

On the other hand, quite different advice was given by Biagi in subsequent years. In pronouncing himself against the decision of the first International Congress of Archivists and Librarians (Bruxelles, 1910) to set up an international cataloging code that took into account the various national norms, he stated:

> If we accept the Anglo-American rules as a basis, it will be easy to give the catalog an international form; it would be a matter of choosing *entry words* in international form, but the principles of cataloging will still be *Anglo-American.*[20]

The publication of the *Joint Code* of 1908 was for Biagi an essential point of reference whose importance he was often to emphasize. Although he recognized the "indisputable superiority" of the *Joint Code* to all preceding codes, including Fumagalli's work, he stated in the report written for the commission in charge of proposing a code of rules that he felt the commission "should nonetheless reach the conclusion that it would be necessary to make several modifications." These would not alter the essential part of the code, which continued "to represent a great advance in cataloging, in comparison with the empirical methods that all of us have used and are using."[21]

In the opening editorial of the new series of the *Rivista*, he was even more radical in recognizing that Croce's rules were nothing other than "the adaptation of those worked out by the English and American library associations."[22]

THE 1921 AND 1956 RULES

The code of 1921 and its successor that appeared in 1956 can be examined in close connection. The latter, in fact, though much more detailed, moves substantially from within the structure of the former without introducing any real modifications or advances.[23]

The 1921 code differed from the Italian empirical tradition in two significant ways: (a) corporate bodies, whose publications up to that time had been generally entered as anonymous works (that is, under title), were now considered as authors, in agreement with Fumagalli's principle; and (b) anonymous works, which up to then had been entered by choosing as entry word the first noun in the title–either the initial substantive or the most meaningful word–now took as their entry word the first word of the title that was not an article.

The influence of the *Joint Code* was visible in the formulation of distinct rules for the different types of periodical publications: Periodicals (95); and Political Newspapers, Almanacs, Annals, Guides (96). Here, however, any analogy must end. The Italian code maintained the tradition that had characterized both norms and practices in Italy since the second half of the nineteenth century: periodical publications were entered under title with an added entry for the editor when his name appeared on the title page (rule 95). Some of the rules regarding publications of corporate bodies that were to be entered under their name (rules 65, 69, 71, and 76) contained a rather ambiguous provision: the decision to enter either under the body or under the title was based on how well known the title was, a rather elusive criterion that was subject to interpretation. But the scale generally weighed decisively in favor of the title, if we take into consideration the very clear statement of rule 95: "A periodical published regularly by a society, an institute, or an office is entered under its own title (see articles 65, 69, 71)."

This statement was to be substantially maintained in the 1956 code: "A periodical published regularly by a body (society, institute, or office) is entered under its own title with an added entry for the body (cf. art. 65, 69, 71, 76)." But the articles to which this rule referred introduced an important clarification in respect to the analogous 1921 rules:

> The periodical publications of a society [of an institute, of ministries and offices] are entered under their title with an added entry for the society [institute, name of office], unless they are annuals, bulletins, etc., that prevalently provide reports on the activities of the body [of the office by which they are issued].

The ambiguous criterion of how well known the title was, which was found in the first code, was resolved in the second, where the choice of heading was linked to the contents of the publication. However, even in the second code of rules a difference exists between monographic publications (always entered under the name of the body) and periodical publications (entered under the name of the body *sub condicione*).

The treatment of series was analogous to that of periodicals: they were always entered under their titles (97, 1921; 98, 1956).

A significant divergence of the 1921 code from preceding Italian tradition as well as from the *Joint Code* concerned the treatment of title changes: "When a periodical changes its title, a new entry is to be made, and the various titles are linked by notes" says the next-to-last paragraph of rule 95 (which becomes almost to the letter rule 96 of the 1956 code).

The dilemma found in Anglo-American cataloging tradition regarding the bibliographic identity of serial publications that change their titles doesn't seem to have concerned Italian cataloging, which from Biagi's code up to the present time has maintained the principle of successive entry.

In the first two codes there was, however, absolute silence as to what variations constituted a title change. Consequently, the same silence persisted in regards to simple variations in title.

Particular provisions regarding description were totally lacking, except for the one inevitable statement common, for that much, to continuations and periodicals still in course of publication: to complete an open entry, one was to record in place of the date only "the first year of printing" (139, 1921) or "the year the publication first appeared" (138, 1956) and to leave the number of volumes blank.

UNI NORM 6392 AND RICA

The development of a national standard specific to periodical cataloging was to occur between the 1956 code and the most recent Italian cataloging code.

UNI norm 6392, developed by the Commissione documentazione of the UNI (Ente italiano di unificazione, an ISO member), aimed at meeting the needs of the scientific, technical, and business sectors. It was published as an experimental measure in 1968 and was revised during the period in which the new national cataloging code was being written, as proposed by the Gruppo razionalizzazione, meccanizzazione, automazione of the Associazione italiana biblioteche.[24]

The final version (now being revised) was published in 1976 as *Norma UNI 6392. Documentazione e riproduzione documentaria. Cataloghi alfabetici di periodici.*

As its title implies, it was intended to be used in the construction of a manual or computerized catalog of periodicals of a single library or a group of libraries. The standard's principle features are the following:

a. the title is without exception the main access to the periodical; names of bodies are relegated, as optional, to secondary access points;
b. the term *title* is intended as *distinctive title*, that is, the chief title sufficient in itself for the identification of the periodical (2.2.1); expressions consisting of a generic term plus the name of a body are to be considered together as constituting the title (2.2.3); statements relating to a section or a supplement are also part of the *distinctive title*, as are edition statements (2.2.4-2.2.6);
c. "enumeration and dates" (as data regarding the extent of publication of the periodical) are recorded after the place of publication and the name of the publisher; they are not to be confused with holdings data, which are to be recorded as the last information given;
d. notes give information about any element contained in the description; e.g., the periodical's bibliographic history (preceding titles, later titles, etc.), or any other feature (frequency, language, etc.);
e. for title changes, the principle of successive entry is to be adopted (2.2.7) with reference to the most recent form for current periodicals and the one of longest duration for periodicals that have ceased (2.2.7.2); points 2.2.7.1 and 2.2.7.2 set out, respectively, those variations that are to be considered title changes and those that are not to be considered as such;
f. the alphabetization of entries in the catalog is according to meaningful words, omitting articles, prepositions, conjunctions, etc.
g. the eventuality of identical titles is to be taken into consideration only for the purpose of filing (4.8):

> For the filing of periodicals having the same title, the place of publication is to be considered . . . If the place is the same, the first date of publication is to be considered.
> e.g., Il Piemonte. Torino, 1855-
> Il Piemonte. Torino, 1910-

The framework of RICA is quite different from preceding codes. It is subdivided into three parts according to logically comprehensible divisions that reflect (although they are not arranged in logical sequence) the three phases in the cataloging process: Part I, Choice of heading; Part II, Form of heading; Part III, Description. Five specific rules are given for periodical publications in Part I (41-45), ten in Part III (140-149).[25]

A somewhat peculiar preamble to the rules for the choice of heading points out that:

> The present rules are valid for entries that are part of an author catalog. It is recommended, however, that every library should set up a catalog for periodicals, in which particular rules can be adopted *(UNI 6392, Documentazione e riproduzione documentaria; Cataloghi alfabetici di periodici, 1976).*

Actually RICA seems to accept with resignation the fact that in the general catalog of the library there should be entries concerning its periodicals (Carlo Revelli had termed the provision of rules for periodicals in a general cataloging code a "total misfit").[26] It dictates rules for the libraries that choose to do so; but it is oriented decidedly in the direction of a separate catalog, compiled according to a standard substantially extraneous to the recognized functions of a library catalog.

For periodical cataloging, the influence of the UNI norm upon RICA is in reality quite considerable, as we shall see further on.

Rule 41, entitled "General Rules," states that "periodical publications, and more generally serial publications, are to be entered under their title" (41.1).

For names of bodies (41.1), the following apply:

a. added entries are mandatory, if the names are "linked to generic titles insufficient in themselves to identify a publication";
b. added entries are optional for bodies "in some way connected with the publication (publishers, sponsors, and similar entities)."

Periodicals "issued by a body" are to be entered under the name of the body only under two conditions, which must both be met (41.3):

a. if they have a prevalently administrative, legislative or documentary character with reference to the activity of the body itself
   and
b. if they have a generic title.[27]

What a generic title is, is not defined, nor is it made clear from the only example appended to this rule: the *Bollettino ufficiale del Ministero dell'interno*, to be entered under the body *(Italia. Ministero dell'interno)*, with an added entry under the title. This example seems to be a source of some perplexity, since the title, having a grammatical link between *Bollettino ufficiale* and the name of the body, is not at all *generic* but, if anything, *contains a generic term*, which is something quite different.

It is obvious that we have here a further limitation of the provisions of the Paris Principles. Paragraph 11.14 of the Principles, stating that works, including serials and periodicals known primarily or conventionally by title, are to be entered under title, has proved itself to be quite unsatisfactory[28] and is to be, in any case, coordinated[29] with paragraph 9.11, stating that when a work is by its nature necessarily an expression of the collective thought or activity of the body, it is to be entered under the body, as well as with paragraph 9.12, which states that when the wording of the title or title-page, taken in conjunction with the nature of the work, clearly implies that the corporate body is collectively responsible for the contents of the work, the main entry is to be under the name of the body. Thus RICA actually utilizes only paragraph 9.11, while limiting its application to generic titles.

This formal requisite of title "genericity" for entry of periodicals under a body's name has rather heavy consequences for the consistency of the catalog.

In the first place, it creates a clear distinction between monographs and serials. The "works with an administrative, legislative, or documentary character that by their very nature are necessarily expressions of its activity" (rule 23) and "works of an intellectual character that expressly and formally present themselves as manifestations of its collective thought or as a result of its activity" (rule 24) are to be entered under the body if they are *monographs*; but if they are *periodicals*, only the principle stated in rule 23 is valid. Moreover, since this principle is applicable only in the case of title "genericity," a further division is produced within the category of serials: between those having a specific title and those with a generic title. These prescripts invalidate the collocative functions of the catalog: the third function (to convey information about all the works of each author), since under the heading of the same body we will not be able to find all its works but only the monographs and periodicals with generic titles; as well as the second function (to convey information about the various manifestations of each work), since by relegating the name of the body to secondary access when the title is not generic, retrieval of the document is made possible but, by denying the body the main heading, identification of the work is not permitted. This is because "the main entry is the name we use to identify a work, and defining it generally requires the intersection of the name of an individual (or corporate body) and the name of a bibliographical unit created by that individual or body.''[30]

Of course the authors of RICA were quite aware of the illogical aspects of the rules. As Carlo Revelli wrote: ''On a logical ground, the rule we have suggested seems absurd . . . Nonetheless, I feel it is preferable to accept its incongruity rather than attempt to draft a norm based on contents, which would inevitably present limits too indistinct.''[31] He continues:

> the norm concerning periodicals is an obvious compromise aimed at drawing together standards for an eventual periodical catalog (calling for arrangement by title and only by title) with those applying to periodical entries in an author catalog, preferring the greater possibilities of retrieval it provides to the rigorous application of the concept of corporate authorship. The latter nonetheless can always be expressed, a somewhat brutal consolation, through an added entry.[32]

In reality the reason for this choice was substantially to avoid any conflicts with UNI norm 6392 as far as possible.

The influence of this norm on RICA is in fact quite evident in the concept of the title of periodicals that both codes have.

Although the authors of RICA have often stated[33] that the ISBD standards have constituted a point of reference for structuring that section of the rules dealing with description, this is only partially true.[34] The relative autonomy of the description from the various access points (as established by ISBD formats) is not really assimilated by RICA. Its rules for description and those for headings are often inextricably intertwined; this is the case with rule 41.2, which introduces a descriptive standard into the general rules for headings:

> If the name of the body precedes the generic title and is not connected to it grammatically, it can be placed after the title itself. The transposition may be indicated in the notes.

In addition, in the rules for the description it is clearly stated that the title is not the title proper of ISBD, but the *distinctive title*. Rule 140, regarding the transcription of the title in the ''Title and Authorship Statement Area,'' reads as follows:

1. The title is to be transcribed as it appears and in a form complete enough to identify the periodical (distinctive title) . . .

2. In the case of a generic title *(Annali, Atti, Bollettino, Notiziario,* etc.) accompanied by the name of a body, if the name of the body precedes the generic title and is not linked to it grammatically, it is to be transposed (see par. 41.2).
3. In the case of a generic title accompanied by the name of the body, if the body is adopted as the heading (see par. 41.3) and appears in the same form in the title as well, its name is not to be repeated.
   e.g., **Italia.** Ministero dell'interno
   Bollettino ufficiale <del Ministero dell'interno>

These are instructions altogether different from those given for the description of monographs, which incorporate the ISBD concept of title proper. Is this a residue from the 1974 edition of ISBD(S) or an approach towards the UNI norm? This is difficult to establish; what is certain is that the 1977 edition of ISBD(S), which freed Area 1 of the concept of distinctive title, so misleading for bibliographic description,[35] didn't influence the drafting of RICA.

This can be deduced from an examination of the other rules for the description of periodicals: (a) in RICA there is no edition area (as on the other hand exists for monographs), and any eventual statements of this kind are absorbed into the Area 1 and recorded as other title information (141, *Subtitle*, e.g., *Le scienze. Edizione italiana di Scientific American*); (b) the numerical and/or chronological designations (ISBD(S) Area 3) are not taken into consideration; (c) publication data are limited to the place and publisher (143); and (d) the holdings statement (145-147) is to be placed after the collation (144) and before the notes area (148).

RICA also adopts, as do the preceding codes, the principle of successive entry for title changes, according to rule 43:

> If the title of a periodical varies, a new entry is to be made for each title; the preceding title and the succeeding title are recorded in the notes. In the case of minor variations the most constant, or if there is any doubt, the most recent form, is to be selected; any variants can be indicated in the notes.

What "minor" variations are–that is to say, those that don't necessitate a new entry–is not established. The acceptance of the provisions contained in UNI norm 6392 is probably implicit. These were in fact conceived as related to an alphabetization (letter by letter, taking into consideration the meaningful words) quite different from RICA's (letter by letter, word by word).

As stated above, moreover, the form that is to be taken as the basis for the title entry is the most constant, or, in case of doubt, the most recent; the same can be said for the rest of the description: 141.1 for the subtitle; 143 for publication data; 144 for dimensions.

THEORY AND PRACTICE: LISTS AND DATABASES

There has always been a considerable gap between catalog codes and the real cataloging situation in Italy.

Notwithstanding the existence of a national code, the National Library of Florence and its *Bollettino* remained faithful even after 1921 to the tradition of cataloging as anonymous works those publications that could not be attributed to a personal author, in this way simply ignoring the provisions of the code relating to corporate bodies. The same treatment was maintained for periodicals, but with more reason, if the code's almost unimportant overture to the possibility of alternative entry (under the name of the body) is considered in its relationship to how well known the title was. This is what we are able to verify from the list *Periodici italiani 1886-1957*.[36]

The policies of the national library services changed, however, with the birth of the *Bibliografia nazionale italiana* (BNI).[37] From the beginning this publication has been compiled in conformity with cataloging rules–first with the 1956 code and then with the 1979 rules. We can see their application to periodicals in two lists that were produced as extracts of the information available in BNI.[38]

For the rest, however, things have gone quite differently.

In a survey on printed periodical catalogs in Italian libraries published in 1968, G. Nobile Stolp makes a bold assumption that Italian libraries were simply unaware of any codes: "quite often compilers do not even provide any justification for the nonobservance [of the rules], which allows us to suppose that they don't even know of their existence."[39]

From this survey and another one conducted at the same time but chronologically more limited,[40] we can get quite a good overall picture of the situation from the second half of the nineteenth century to the first half of the twentieth.

Almost all the catalogs utilized the title as the main access to the periodical, even in the case of titles consisting of a generic term. The bibliographic data recorded were quite varied: from descriptions extremely concise (title and place) to detailed descriptions (title, subtitle, editors, compilers, place, publisher, initial date, frequency, variations, holdings). The filing systems were also diversified, ranging from a strictly alphabetical system to alphabetical arrangement by meaningful words.

Often we are dealing with mere finding lists, with no references and no indexes. More complex structures and more elaborate reference facilities are to be found only in catalogs having a high degree of bibliographic value issued by institutes of national importance, such as the *Elenco delle pubblicazioni periodiche ricevute dalle biblioteche pubbliche governative d'Italia nel 1884*, or of regional importance like the *Catalogo dei periodici delle biblioteche lombarde* compiled by the Municipal Library of Milan (1964); or works more properly classified as bibliographies rather than catalogs, such as *La stampa periodica romana dell'Ottocento* by Olga Majolo Molinari (1963).

The high number of periodical catalogs published from the 1950s (seventy in the first decade alone from 1957 to 1967, while from 1859 to 1945, almost a century, only eighty six were produced, according to the survey by Nobile Stolp) is, however, a phenomenon "less comforting than it seems at first sight . . . since it reveals the lack of any central organization set up to coordinate these efforts and to produce union catalogs, both central and regional, such as are already realities in other countries."[41]

They are almost totally catalogs of single libraries or union catalogs from a fairly circumscribed territory. There are five having national scope, but with a limited coverage: (a) by libraries,[42] (b) by subject matter,[43] or (c) by libraries and subject matter.[44] Of the four regional catalogs in the survey, one that deals only with regional periodicals describes the holdings of nongovernmental libraries of Campania and Calabria.[45] The other three refer to Lombardy; two are subject-oriented (medical and chemical periodicals),[46] and one is general[47] and constitutes somewhat of a milestone: it is the first union periodical catalog of an entire regional territory, compiled without any subject limitations. Published in seven volumes from 1964 to 1979, it describes about 55,000 periodicals from 187 libraries. The catalog is quite structured and compiled according to the 1956 rules: main entry either by title, or by body when the periodical reports its activity; summary description: title, subtitle, place, indication of the first year of publication; former and later titles; holdings. The only exception to the rules regards the alphabetical arrangement, which ignores articles and prepositions. Identical titles are not distinguished; any distinctions are to be found in the rest of the description.

The first two surveys that we have cited (Nobile Stolp and Califano

Tentori) were continued in a survey compiled by the Istituto centrale per il catalogo unico (ICCU), covering the period 1966-1981,[48] in which 190 catalogs are identified and summarily described. The general trends registered in the first surveys are confirmed: access is mainly by title, and description formats are extremely variable. Some–very few–catalogs follow the national code (RICA); and at the same time there is a greater, though still limited, diffusion of UNI norm 6392.

In the period considered above a trend was registered that was to be continued later in the 1980s: in the absence of any national government projects, activity continues with regional projects, usually promoted and financed or in some way supported by the regional governments.

In 1981 the regional government of Lombardy launched an important cataloging project for current periodicals in the regional libraries. It was designed to integrate the excellent periodical catalog that had just been finished. After a sample volume limited to the letter ''A,''[49] the work was completed in 1989 with about 30,000 entries from over 600 libraries.[50] The indexes (by issuing body and Universal Decimal Classification) are in course of publication. Catalog data are available in printed form and can be consulted also online by those capable of accessing the database of the Lombardia Informatica.

An important aspect of this catalog, compiled in accordance with UNI norm 6392, was the fact that it was the result of a partnership with the Istituto di studi sulla ricerca e documentazione scientifica (ISRDS) of the Consiglio nazionale delle ricerche (CNR) for programming, technical assistance, and data processing, as well as for the use of its database in a relationship of mutual exchange.

In 1975 this institute became by government decision the Italian national ISDS center, charged with the national bibliographic control of periodical literature.[51]

Moreover, since 1972 the institute has worked on setting up the Archivio collettivo nazionale delle pubblicazioni periodiche (the Collective National File of Periodical Publications, ACNP), which currently contains over 72,000 entries of periodicals in the sciences and humanities from more than 1,800 libraries. The file, compiled in conformity with UNI norm 6392, can be consulted online, as an internal service, from the data processing center of the CNUCE of Pisa, from the Libera università degli studi sociali (LUISS) of Rome, and from the Coordinamento interfacoltà per le biblioteche (CIB) of Bologna. The file is to be issued in the near future on CD-ROM.[52]

During the 1980s there has been a constant increase in the production of printed periodical catalogs created in partnership with ISRDS/CNR similar to those described above. This experience has made the gap between cataloging rules and current cataloging practices even more evident. (However, the national code itself has favored this development, recommending the formation of separate catalogs compiled in accordance with UNI norm 6392).

PERIODICALS CATALOGING IN THE NATIONAL LIBRARY SERVICE

Also in the 1980s, a project called Servizio bibliotecario nazionale (the National Library Service, SBN) reached the experimental stage. The project was conceived at the central government level to create a network of computerized libraries for the purpose of cooperation in resource sharing among member institutions through the identification, location, and circulation of materials. The creation of a catalog is at the center of the various system functions. A guide to cataloging[53] was drawn up as a basis for compiling the catalog to be used by all the participating institutions. The guide deals with the cataloging of both monographic and serial publications and is based on the 1978 edition of ISBD(M) and the 1977 edition of ISBD(S) for description and on RICA for headings.

For the first time in the history of serials cataloging in Italy, the overlapping of the functions of description with those of access was surmounted (in RICA, as we have seen, this overlapping had remained, not for monographs but only for periodicals). Description and access are now clearly distinct. This made it possible to deal with the problem of the distinctive title as "another title," different from the title that appears in the bibliographic description (title proper).[54]

The distinctive title, however, is still connected to an ill-identified "generic title" (an expression and a concept that disappeared from Anglo-American cataloging some time ago):

> When a serial or a series has a generic title, a distinctive title is to be created. This title will be formed by the generic title followed by the statement of responsibility or by the edition statement.[55]

The problem of having to differentiate among periodicals with identical titles, which has been resolved in Anglo-American experience by applying the concept of the "unique serial title," continues to be ignored in Italian cataloging.

Within the framework of the catalog of the SBN, a periodicals project is being worked out to create a database using the ACNP of

ISRDS/CNR.[56] Data from the ACNP, currently in the CNR format, are to be dumped into the central index of the SBN catalog. The operational phases of this project, involving the computerized comparison and conversion of data from the CNR format into the SBN format and the installation of the periodical database into the central index of SBN, are being developed by various organizations (ITALSIEL, ISRDS/CNR, CSI/Piedmont, and the Piedmont regional government) under the coordination of the ICCU.[57]

The Piedmont regional government is at the center of the project, since it has produced a catalog of current periodicals in Piedmont's libraries and has tested the formula for the computerized comparison of data from the files of the National Library of Torino with data from the ACNP in the SBN perspective.[58] The result is a catalog still halfway between UNI norm 6392 and the SBN format (i.e., ISBD(S)).

In particular, entries are arranged by title; there are no headings for bodies or any title-headings; and the task of distinguishing between identical titles is left to the description. In fact, the alphabetization (in contrast to that of the SBN) is still that of the UNI norm–only by the meaningful words of the title proper, to which are added those of the statement of responsibility in cases where the title proper is generic.

CONCLUSIONS

The cataloging of periodicals in Italy has never been the object of particular attention (the same thing could be said of cataloging in general). The most recent of the three national codes issued up to the present moment (1921, 1956, and 1979) recommends the establishment of a separate catalog for this type of publication, in conformity with a national standard (UNI norm 6392) conceived outside the framework of the functions of the general library catalog.

There exists, however, a substantially uniform cataloging tradition that allows access by title and deals with title changes in accordance with the principle of successive entry.

The only existing national periodical file was created by the Istituto di studi sulla ricerca e documentazione scientifica (ISRDS) of the Consiglio nazionale delle ricerche (CNR), set up in conformity with UNI norm 6392.

The existence of this file, whose records are to be adapted and converted, forms the basis of a government project to create a periodical file within the catalog of the National Library Service (SBN).

NOTES

1. *Regole per la compilazione del catalogo alfabetico*. Roma: Nardecchia, 1922.

2. *Regole per la compilazione del catalogo alfabetico per autori nelle biblioteche italiane*. Roma: Palombi, 1956.

3. *Regole italiane di catalogazione per autori*. Roma: Istituto centrale per il catalogo unico delle biblioteche italiane e per le informazioni bibliografiche, 1979.

4. The very Italian term *seriale*, based on the English *serial*, is a neologism introduced by the author of this paper into the Italian edition (Roma: Associazione italiana biblioteche, 1987) of *ISBD(G)*. London: IFLA International Office for UBC, 1977.

5. Quoted from: Mollica, Carmela. *Le biblioteche popolari italiane nell'Ottocento*. Roma: Tip. Agostiniana, 1935, p. 63.

6. For a historical study in English of the situation of Italian libraries in this and successive periods, see: Dean, Elizabeth A. "The organization of Italian libraries from the Unification until 1940." *Library quarterly*. 53 (Oct. 1983), p. 399-419.

7. *Elenco delle pubblicazioni periodiche ricevute dalle biblioteche pubbliche governative d'Italia nel 1884*. Roma: Presso i principali librai, 1885. (Indici e cataloghi ; 1). The following year, another volume appeared (as its complement) listing the categories of periodicals not included in the first: *Indice dei giornali politici e d'altri che trattano di cose locali ricevuti dalla Biblioteca nazionale centrale di Firenze: 1o luglio 1885-30 giugno 1886*. Roma: Presso i principali librai, 1886. (Indici e cataloghi ; 6).

8. *Rivista delle biblioteche: periodico di biblioteconomia e di bibliografia* [since 1895 *Rivista delle biblioteche e degli archivi: periodico di biblioteconomia e di bibliografia di paleografia e di archivistica*]. Diretto dal Dr. Guido Biagi. A. 1, n. 1/2 (genn./febbr. 1888)-A. 36, n. 7/12 (luglio/dic. 1926). Firenze: Tip. Carnesecchi, 1888-1926.

9. For a detailed account of the awards and an exposition of Fumagalli's rules, see Galli, Giovanni. *Regole italiane di catalogazione per autori tra Ottocento e Novecento*. Milano: Bibliografica, c1989, p. 58-77.

10. The *Istruzioni per la compilazione e la copia del catalogo alfabetico*, Enclosure G of the *Regolamento per il servizio della Biblioteca nazionale di Firenze* (Firenze, agosto 1881) were almost entirely compiled by Fumagalli (cf. *Cataloghi di biblioteche e indici bibliografici*. Firenze: Sansoni, 1887, p. 3).

11. It is quite probable that Fumagalli was also the author of Biblioteca nazionale centrale di Roma. *Norme per la compilazione e l'ordinamento delle schede del catalogo alfabetico*, [1882?] (see Galli, Giovanni. *Regole italiane di catalogazione per autori tra Ottocento e Novecento*, cit., p. 53).

12. Fumagalli, Giuseppe. *Cataloghi di biblioteche e indici bibliografici*, cit., p. vii.

13. Cf. Cutter, Charles A. *Rules for a printed dictionary catalogue*. Washington: Government Printing Office, 1876.

14. This principle was incorporated into the *Istruzioni* of the National Library of Florence (rule 19), while the *Norme* of the National Library of Rome required it to be applied to official publications (rule 21).

15. *Rivista delle biblioteche e degli archivi.* 10, n. 11/12 (1889), p. 45. The *Bollettino della Società bibliografica italiana* has been published in the *Rivista* since 1897.

16. Società bibliografica italiana. *Progetto* . . . Pavia: Tip. Ponzio, 1901. The proposal, which several times appeared on the agenda of the Society's conventions, was never discussed and was finally abandoned because of skepticism on the part of some members (D. Chilovi) and an explicit opposition on the part of others (see *Rivista delle biblioteche e degli archivi.* 15, n. 8/10 (ott./ago. 1904), p. 161-162).

17. Cf. Società bibliografica italiana. *Progetto*. . . , p. 6.

18. Biagi, Guido. "Una proposta americana per un catalogo cooperativo." *Rivista delle biblioteche e degli archivi.* 13, n. 4 (apr. 1902), p. 50-53.

19. Chilovi, Desiderio. "A proposito di una proposta americana per un catalogo cooperativo." *Rivista delle biblioteche e degli archivi.* 13, n. 5 (magg./giu. 1902), p. 78-79.

20. *Rivista delle biblioteche e degli archivi.* 21, n. 8/10 (ago./ott. 1910), p. 145.

21. *Regole per la compilazione del catalogo alfabetico*, p. ix-xix, passim.

22. Biagi, Guido. "Dopo trenta e più anni." *Rivista delle biblioteche e degli archivi.* 33, n. 1/2 (genn./febbr. 1923), p. 3. As to the points where there is agreement between the Italian code and the *Joint Code*, see Hanson, J.C.M. *A comparative study of cataloging rules based on the Anglo-American Code of 1908*. Chicago: University of Chicago Press, 1939, passim.

23. The reasons are outlined in Barberi, Francesco. "Catalogue code revision in Italy." *UNESCO bulletin for libraries.* 12 (1958), p. 116-119.

24. Berruti, Maria Teresa [et al.] "Catalogazione di periodici: le tendenze attuali e la nuova norma UNI." *Accademie e biblioteche d'Italia.* N.s. 25, n. 6 (1974), p. 409-421.

25. For an examination of periodical description in RICA, see Merola, Giovanna. "Descrizione dei periodici (RICA, par. 140-149)." *Le regole italiane di catalogazione per autori e la loro applicazione.* Roma: ICCU, 1985, p. 53-58.

26. Revelli, Carlo. "Le nuove norme italiane di catalogazione per autori." Associazione italiana biblioteche. *Bollettino d'informazioni.* N.s. 13, n. 1 (genn./magg. 1973), p. 10.

27. In an important work preliminary to the revision of the code of rules, Diego Maltese suggested an almost exclusively formal norm: "A periodical published regularly by a body (society, institute, office) is to be entered under its own title with . . . an added entry under the body, unless its title is made up of a generic term . . . specified only by the name of the body, whose activity is in some way reported in the publication . . ." (Maltese, Diego. *Principi di catalogazione e regole italiane.* Firenze: Olschki, 1965, p. 117).

28. The obvious vacuity of paragraph 11.14 (subject to being applied in almost totally arbitrary terms) caused the Americans to eliminate it in the 1967 AACR (cf. Introduction, p. 3); while instead it was incorporated into RICA, rule

4 (see the critique on this point by Alberto Petrucciani: *Funzione e struttura del catalogo per autore*. Firenze: Giunta regionale toscana: La nuova Italia, 1984, p. 73-74; "Le Regole italiane di catalogazione per autori." Associazione italiana biblioteche. *Bollettino d'informazioni*. N.s., 27, n. 2 (1987), p. 156).

29. *Statement of principles adopted at the International Conference on Cataloguing Principles, Paris, October 1961*. Annotated ed. by Eva Verona. London: IFLA Committee on Cataloguing, 1971, p. 101.

30. Malinconico, S. Michael. "Technology and standards for bibliographic control." *Library quarterly*. 47, no. 3 (July 1977), p. 319.

31. Revelli, Carlo. "Gli enti collettivi nel catalogo per autori." *Annali della Scuola speciale per archivisti e bibliotecari*. 3 (1963), p. 151.

32. Revelli, Carlo. "Divagazioni sul concetto di autore." *Studi di biblioteconomia e di storia del libro in onore di Francesco Barberi*. Roma: AIB, 1976, p. 474.

33. Cf. Maltese, Diego. *Introduzione alle nuove regole di catalogazione per autore*. Brindisi: [Amministrazione provinciale], 1981, p. 21.

34. For observations of a general character on this relationship in RICA, see Dini, Rossella. "Come le tigri dai denti a sciabola?" *Biblioteche oggi*. 4, n. 4 (luglio/ago. 1986), p. 89-94.

35. Cf. Franzmeier, Günter. "Multiplication of serial titles forever?" *The Serials Librarian*. 12, 1/2 (1987), p. 64.

36. *Periodici italiani 1886-1957*. Roma: ICCU, 1980, is the printout of periodicals extracted from the CUBI tapes. CUBI is the *Catalogo cumulativo 1886-1957 del Bollettino delle pubblicazioni italiane ricevute per diritto di stampa dalla Biblioteca nazionale centrale di Firenze* (Nendeln, Liechtenstein: Kraus reprint, 1968-1969, in 41 printed volumes but also available on tape).

37. The BNI, produced by the National Library of Florence, has been issued since 1958 as a monthly bulletin and an annual cumulation. It continues the *Bollettino delle pubblicazioni italiane*. Since 1975 data contained therein have also been made available on tape and can be consulted online through the services of the Italian Supreme Court, the Chamber of Deputies, and the Library of Pedagogic Documentation.

38. *Bibliografia nazionale italiana. Periodici 1958-1967*. Roma: Centro nazionale per il catalogo unico delle biblioteche italiane e per le informazioni bibliografiche, 1972; and *Periodici italiani 1968-1981*. Roma: ICCU, 1983.

39. Nobile Stolp, Gertrude. *Cataloghi a stampa dei periodici delle biblioteche italiane (1859-1967)*. Firenze: Olschki, 1968, p. ix.

40. Califano Tentori, Maria. *Elenchi e cataloghi di periodici in Italia, 1946-1966*. Roma: Consiglio nazionale delle ricerche, 1967.

41. *Ibid.*, p. v.

42. *Elenco delle pubblicazioni periodiche ricevute dalle biblioteche pubbliche governative d'Italia nel 1884*, cit.

43. Pinto, Olga. *A union list of American periodicals in Italy*. Roma: Ministero della pubblica istruzione, 1958; Majolo Molinari, Olga. *La stampa periodica romana dell'Ottocento*. Roma: Istituto di studi romani, 1963.

44. Gulì, Giuseppe. *Elenco delle pubblicazioni periodiche straniere acquistate dalle biblioteche pubbliche governative del Regno d'Italia. Anno 1913.* Roma: Biblioteca nazionale Vittorio Emanuele II, 1915; Magrini, Giovanni. *Periodici stranieri che si trovano nelle biblioteche degli istituti scientifici italiani.* Roma: Consiglio nazionale delle ricerche, 1930.

45. Tamburrino, Maria and Rita. *Pubblicazioni periodiche a carattere regionale esistenti in biblioteche non governative della Campania e della Calabria.* Napoli: Sopraintendenza bibliografica per la Campania e la Calabria, 1957.

46. Società lombarda di medicina. *Catalogo dei periodici medici raccolti nelle biblioteche lombarde.* Milano: Pirola, 1936 (further editions: 1949, 1959); Cuboni, E. and Devalle, G. *Catalogo dei periodici chimici raccolti nelle biblioteche lombarde.* Milano: Istituto sieroterapico milanese "S. Belfanti," 1960.

47. *Catalogo dei periodici delle biblioteche lombarde redatto dalla Biblioteca comunale di Milano.* Milano: Comune, 1964-1979.

48. *Cataloghi italiani di periodici, 1966-1981.* Roma: ICCU, 1982. For an examination of the latest catalogs, see Maini, Roberto. "Cataloghi di periodici, soprattutto quotidiani." *La rivisteria.* 4, 11 (1987), p. 12-15.

49. *Catalogo di periodici correnti delle biblioteche lombarde.* A-*Archives e titoli collegati.* Milano: Regione Lombardia, 1981.

50. *Catalogo dei periodici correnti delle biblioteche lombarde.* Milano: Bibliografica, 1985-1989.

51. See Salimei, Matilde. "Dieci anni di vita del sistema ISDS, 1976-1985." CNR. ISRDS. *Quaderni.* 17-18 (1986), p. 189-197.

52. For a thorough description of the database, see Bianchi, Gianfranco and Petrucci, Antonio. "L'Archivio collettivo nazionale delle pubblicazioni periodiche." CNR. ISRDS. *Editoria elettronica: ricerca e applicazioni.* Roma: ISRDS, 1988, p. 115-142. In 1990 the printed catalog of the ISRDS was issued: CNR. ISRDS. *Catalogo collettivo nazionale delle pubblicazioni periodiche.* Roma: ISRDS, 1990 (70,709 periodicals are described from 1,730 libraries).

53. ICCU. *Guida alla catalogazione nell'ambito del Servizio bibliotecario nazionale.* Roma: ICCU, 1987. There is also a bulletin, SBN *notizie* (Roma: ICCU, 1989-), which reports any modifications applied to the *Guida.* Every issue provides a bibliography of contributions on SBN. For more detailed information on SBN, in English, see: Grignani, Elisa. "Bibliographic databases produced in Italy." *Cataloging & classification quarterly.* 8, 3/4 (1988), p. 225-238.

54. Among the preliminary documents to the *Guida*, see: Brunetti, T. "Confronto ISBD(S)-RICA-UNI." Ministero per i beni culturali e ambientali. ICCU. *Notizie.* 8 (mar. 1984), p. 25-27.

55. *Guida alla catalogazione nell'ambito del Servizio bibliotecario nazionale,* cit., vol. 1, p. 143.

56. *SBN notizie.* 1990, 1, p. 11.

57. These are, as we have stated above, formats based on different cataloging standards: the CNR format is based on UNI norm 6392, the SBN format on the 1977 edition of *ISBD(S).* At the moment it is being revised in relation to the 1988 ISBD(S) edition. This edition of the standard has been the object of much

critical observation: see Dini, Rossella. *ISBD(S): introduzione ed esercizi.* Milano: Bibliografica, 1989 and Petrucciani, Alberto and Scolari, Alberto. ''Presente e futuro della descrizione bibliografica.'' *Biblioteche oggi.* 7, 2 (mar./apr. 1989), p. 165-194.

58. *Catalogo dei periodici correnti della Biblioteca nazionale universitaria di Torino.* Torino: Regione Piemonte, Assessorato alla cultura, 1990

Serials in the Current National Bibliography

Kremena Zotova

SUMMARY. Serials registration in the current national bibliography is discussed along the following lines: serials as a subject of the current national bibliography; international recommendations regarding serials registration therein; sources of serials registration; the coverage of serials; their bibliographic description; the representation of their content; forms of their registration; and the importance of their registration.

The importance of serials in the modern world may best be illustrated by the words of the great English biologist T. H. Huxley:

> If all the books in the world perish, except "Philosophical Transactions," it may be said for certain that the bases of science will not be affected and that all colossal achievements of human thought during the last 200 years will be saved, laid on paper, although in an incomplete form.[1]

Therefore, the objective of this article is to prove, by considering the status of serials bibliographic control in the current national bibliography, the necessity of its constant improvement.

In our publications we have been trying continuously to clarify the nature and the methods of bibliography,[2] its future development,[3] and especially its functions. In the articles "Essay on Bibliographic Apology" and "La bibliographie dans la perspective de la bibliologie" (1989),[4] we have stated that the specific function of the bibliography is a modelling one, i.e., the creation of models both of the individual docu-

Kremena Zotova, Leonardo da Vinci 9, 1504 Sofia, Bulgaria, is the former Deputy Director of the Cyril and Methodius National Library in Sofia.

ment (bibliographic description) and of the file of documents (bibliographic list, directory, catalog, etc.).

The bibliographic models are used as a means of substitution for objectively existing documents that were or are circulating in the society. Thus, we feel that the bibliography creates–and should create–not only descriptive models of the extrinsic characteristics of the documents (physical characteristics included), but first and foremost models of the information contained therein. Consequently, the main object of bibliography is the creation of information models for the documents. Insofar as the documents represent communication channels, the bibliography may be perceived as a superchannel in the communication process or a channel transmitting information relating to the documents. In addition, we have demonstrated that bibliography, in the process of its historical development, broadens the spectrum of its objects, i.e., the world of documents, and that it depends more and more heavily on the document users' interests in information. In this respect, we consider that the modelling in bibliography has an alternative character, that the document model or documentary file model is defined not only by the characteristics of the documents themselves, but also by the interests of the users for whom the information contained therein is designed. Thus, the document's characteristics and the users' interests are simultaneously reflected in the model of the document or file of documents.

The different types of bibliography have a number of other functions in addition to the modelling one, depending on the specific interests of the users. Therefore, since the current national bibliography does not satisfy the specific interests of one group or another of users but of society as a whole, we may enumerate its functions as follows, as found in the monograph The *Optimum Model for the Current National Bibliography in Bulgaria* (1982):[5] the identifying and documenting functions, as well as the informational, statistical, cultural and historical, and evaluative ones.

We shall try, in the light of these general theoretical formulations, to consider the present and future status of serials registration in the current national bibliography along the following lines: serials as a subject of the current national bibliography; international recommendations regarding serials registration in the current national bibliography; sources of serials registration in the current national bibliography; the coverage of serials by the current national bibliography; the bibliographic description of serials in the current national bibliography; the representation of serials content in the current national bibliography; forms of serials registration in the current national bibliography; and the importance of serials registration in the current national bibliography.

SERIALS AS A SUBJECT OF THE CURRENT NATIONAL BIBLIOGRAPHY

Of all the documents submitted to the current national bibliography, serials have the most complex character.

The typological characteristics of serials have been studied in detail in our article "Bibliographic Control of Serials in Bulgaria" (1990).[6] Therefore, we shall dwell here only on the point that the concept of *serial* includes two different categories of documents: publications circulating under one and the same title, i.e., their different issues, published at definite or indefinite intervals of time, don't have their own titles and in principle represent collections of articles or other materials (newspapers are included here); and publications having their own title and author (or authors), and which are included in a "series" or "monographic series." The first category, customarily designated by the term *periodicals*, represents the core of serials. So, when we speak about serials registration in the current national bibliography, it is exactly this category that is meant, since publications included in monographic series are registered as books or other documents (scores, maps, sound recordings, etc.) on an equal footing with them. The registration of monographic series as a whole has, or may have, a supplementary character in the current national bibliography (most frequently in the form of indexes).

However, this does not exhaust the complex nature of serials. This results first of all from the fact that serials are documents published in parts and that their continuance in time is not determined in advance, which means that their character is exceptionally dynamic–they appear, they exist (with or without a modification of title), and the greatest part of them cease to appear. Moreover, their dynamic character is also demonstrated by changes in the institutions and persons publishing them, the subjects that they cover and the purpose of their publication, their typological characteristics (newspapers, journals, yearbooks, etc.), the frequency of their publication, and the designation of their individual parts (number, issue, volume, etc.).

All this shows that serials registration in the current national bibliography should not be an elementary one, but one that is of maximum completeness and authority. However, not all national bibliographic centers are in a position to meet such requirements. Nevertheless, if we study the information on serials found in *Les services bibliographiques dans le monde*[7] for the period 1960-1979, we see that bibliographic control is improving (Figure 1):

According to *An Annotated Guide to Current National Bibliographies* (1986) prepared by B. L. Bell,[8] the total number of current national bibliographies is 108, and serials are registered in about 100 of them. However, the character of such registration is quite diverse and generally unsatisfactory. In our opinion, the reasons for this situation are, on the one hand, the complex nature of serials themselves, as we have already emphasized; and, on the other, the international recommendations that were made concerning serials and the current national bibliography.

INTERNATIONAL RECOMMENDATIONS REGARDING SERIALS REGISTRATION IN THE CURRENT NATIONAL BIBLIOGRAPHY

As early as the International Bibliographic Congress in 1897, it was recommended that the national bibliographic agencies should record the currently published books, booklets, periodicals, private publications, and publications of public and governmental organizations.

For the first time the International Congress on Improvement of Bibliographic Services, organized by UNESCO in Paris in 1950, determined all categories of publications to be recorded in the current national bibliographies. The well-known "minimum model" for publications covered by the current national bibliography was incorporated into the decisions of the congress, which also included guidelines for published newspapers and journals.[9] These recommendations were also later included in K. Larsen's *Les services bibliographiques nationaux*, published by UNESCO in 1955.[10]

Period	Total number of current national bibliographies	Number of current national bibliographies covering serials
1960-1964	53	36
1965-1969	64	38
1970-1974	104	68
1975-1979	102	80

Figure 1. The number of national bibliographies and those that cover serials, 1960-1979.

Following the creation of the international program of Universal Bibliographic Control (UBC) by the International Federation of Library Associations in 1971, the problems related to the coverage of the current national bibliography have attained an exceptionally urgent significance. Thereafter, the 39th IFLA session (Grenoble, 1973) was entirely devoted to UBC. The first version of the *Synoptic Tables Concerning the Current National Bibliographies*, which were published in their final form in 1975, was submitted at this session.[11] The *Tables* included information on periodicals as well as on all categories of publications in the current national bibliography. M. Line's report,[12] in which he suggested that the current national bibliography should cover only new periodicals, including those that had undergone a change (title change, merger, separation, dincontinuance), had the strongest impact on the further development of serials registration in the current national bibliography. This formulation was entirely accepted in the main report delivered at the International Congress on National Bibliographies (Paris, 1977),[13] in its recommendations,[14] and in the *Guidelines for the National Bibliographic Agency and the National Bibliography*,[15] published by UNESCO in 1979.

Of course, this limited concept of serials coverage by the current national bibliography expressed at the 39th IFLA session has its opponents. The report by K. Zotova[16] emphasized that it was necessary to extend to the maximum the limits of the current national bibliography to include first of all the registration of audiovisual materials, periodicals, articles, and bibliographic publications. This report drew attention especially to the fact that the inclusion of just new periodicals in the current national bibliography was utterly inadequate and that the future improvement of the current national bibliography had to be oriented toward a complete annual registration of all periodicals (i.e., both new periodicals and those already being published, together with all their issues). In this respect, three types of modern current national bibliographies were differentiated in the report: *limited* ones that published information on just books and new periodicals; *extended* ones that also controlled other types of documents (scores, maps, dissertations, etc.) in addition to books and new periodicals; and *advanced* ones that established complete bibliographic control of all types of documents (traditional and nontraditional), including bibliographic publications and literature in the field of "exteriorica," with complete information on periodicals as a whole and analytically being particularly characteristic thereof. This formulation was expressed later in the report of R. Cybulski and K. Zotova[17] delivered at the 45th IFLA session (Copenhagen, 1979). Unfortunately, only new serials and serials with altered titles ("First issue of new or altered titles") were included again in the IFLA recommendations entitled "Coverage of Documents in Current National Bibliographies" (1982)[18] prepared by a working group consisting of K. Zotova (Bulgaria), W. Bergmann (GDR), R. Cybulski (Poland), and N. Gruzinskaya (USSR). This was necessary, since on the basis of inquiries made before publishing the recommendations it became clear that the greatest number of representatives of the national bibliographic centers considered that the complete registration of periodicals was related to the retrospective national bibliography and not to the current national bibliography.

This problem was thoroughly discussed at the 7th International Conference of Experts of the Socialist Countries on the Problems of the Current National Bibliography (Warsaw, 1984), which was especially devoted to serials registration in the current national bibliography. Reports were made by K. Zotova (Bulgaria), G. Rost (GDR), J. Kowalczyk and B. Karamaç (Poland), J. Creţeanu (Romania), G. Nadd and P. Zonnevend (Hungary) and A. Kucianova (Czechoslovakia).[19] The opinion that serials bibliography was part of the current national bibliography and that the complete registration of every issue (and not merely the first) was obligatory, was accepted.

SOURCES OF SERIALS REGISTRATION IN THE CURRENT NATIONAL BIBLIOGRAPHY

It is well known that the main source for the compilation of the current national bibliography is the mandatory legal deposit of documents in the national bibliographic agency. The necessity of depositing newspapers and journals is also indicated in K. Larsen's guide mentioned above. In 1977 UNESCO and IFLA entrusted the drafting of a model law on legal deposit to J. Lunn of the National Library of Canada. Its latest version was discussed at a joint meeting of the National Library Section and the Section on Bibliography during the 46th IFLA session (Manila, 1980).[20] As for serials, it was assumed in this model that at the discretion of the relevant national bibliographic agency some newspapers may not be deposited. Furthermore, general recommendations were made therein relating to the exclusion of some publications such as confidential documents, office orders, and ephemeral publications.

The "Model Law of Legal Deposit for the Socialist Countries,"[21] prepared by K. Zotova and accepted at the 8th International Conference of Experts of the Socialist Countries (Leipzig, 1987) provides for the deposit of all serials, regional publications of central newspapers, and serials published by diplomatic missions and other official institutions abroad (whether in the original or in translation).

L'étude sur le traitement des publications en série par les centres ISDS et les agences bibliographiques nationales,[22] prepared by F. Bouffez and A. Grousseaud on the basis of a survey in which 45 countries participated, offers information relating to the exclusion of the following categories of documents from the legal deposit requirements of a number of countries: official publications, house organs, local publications, commercial publications, confidential and ephemeral publications, newspapers, and publications having no scholarly value. Thus it is possible to say that J. Lunn's model law has had a considerable influence on the whole world. However, the exclusion of such documents from the law is very dangerous for the bibliographic control of serials. It enables institutions other than the national bibliographic agency to carry out the selection within the current national bibliography. In this respect, the above-mentioned model law of the former socialist countries permits the exclusion of only photostatic copies of documents and confidential and unpublished documents. In addition, it should be explained here that insofar as the inclusion of serials published abroad is provided for, such publications may also be obtained from sources other than legal deposit. This is especially valid for countries that collect and control all serials in the field of "exteriorica" (e.g., Hungary).

COVERAGE OF SERIALS BY THE CURRENT NATIONAL BIBLIOGRAPHY

As has already been emphasized, serials registration in the current national bibliography is extremely varied. Hence, there are four types of current national bibliographies:

- bibliographies that do not cover serials at all as an object of registration (e.g., Egypt, China);
- bibliographies covering new serials or serials that have undergone a change of title, i.e., bibliographies documenting only the initial publication of a serial (this is the prevailing number of bibliographies);
- bibliographies showing new serials and discontinued serials, i.e., showing the initial and final publication dates for serials (e.g., Belgium, Denmark, Mexico); and
- bibliographies in which the coverage of all types of serials, including all their issues, is complete (e.g., Bulgaria, Norway, Poland).

However, the above-mentioned study of F. Bouffez and A. Grousseaud, which does not differentiate between current and retrospective national bibliographies, indicates that complete or nearly complete bibliographic control is made only in the following countries: Australia, Austria, Bulgaria, Great Britain, the German Democratic Republic, Israel, Hungary, and Finland–thus demonstrating how small the number of countries is that meet the requirements of the modern functions of the current national bibliography.

BIBLIOGRAPHIC DESCRIPTION OF SERIALS IN THE CURRENT NATIONAL BIBLIOGRAPHY

The majority of current national bibliographies have already introduced ISBD(S), which leads to an ever increasing standardization of bibliographic data. However, it is possible to apply ISBD(S) successfully only in current national bibliographies, the only objective of which is to establish that a serial has appeared (i.e., to record information about a new publication on the basis of its first issue).

Current national bibliographies that maintain complete bibliographic information about serials usually make a bibliographic description on two levels, the general and the individual (i.e., the description identifies the serial both as a whole and as an incomplete or complete series of individual issues). However, the introduction of ISBD(S) by these bibliographies requires considerable additions related to the second level.

The differences in the bibliographic descriptions in the various current national bibliographies are also due to the possibility of each national bibliographic agency's accepting some or other decisions relating to the heading or the incorporation of optional elements. Two types of headings are generally used: the title proper of the serial and the key title. The use of the key title as a heading is not efficient, since the key title would then have to be included twice (in the heading and at the end of the description). Moreover, a large percentage of key titles repeat verbatim the title proper. Another important argument in favor of the use of the title proper as a heading is that every national bibliographic agency has the responsibility of maintaining authoritative information about the titles of the serials published in the country.

To identify the serials completely in the current national bibliography, it is also necessary to include in the description all elements and notes provided for by ISBD(S). Without such an application of ISBD(S), it will never be possible to bring out the entire nature of a serial and especially its dynamics, i.e., its appearance, the changes that have occurred in its subtitle and statement(s) of responsibility, the numbers and dates of issues, the imprint, its physical characteristics, bibliographic history, discontinuance, etc. However, this is not to imply that in connection with the relevant national agency's participation in the international exchange of bibliographic information it is impossible to communicate brief descriptions of serials.

REPRESENTATION OF SERIALS CONTENT IN THE CURRENT NATIONAL BIBLIOGRAPHY

As has already been pointed out, the main object of bibliography, in our opinion, is to create information models for documents, i.e., not to make a blind description of their extrinsic characteristics, but first and foremost to bring out their content in every aspect by means of different information retrieval languages (classification schemes, subject headings, descriptors, etc.). Of course, here we are discussing the content of serials as a whole, since their analytical description in detail is made only by the bibliographic registration of articles or other materials contained therein.

The recommendations of the Congress on National Bibliographies contain no special instructions on how to represent serials content in the current national bibliography. Serials are included in the general recommendation that current national bibliographies should use international classifications (Dewey, UDC). However, it should be emphasized here that such classifications are used mostly by current national bibliographies that record only new serials and serials that have changed title. The countries that continue to publish special annual or multiannual directories present their information in alphabetical order. In these cases, only the title and subtitle serve to reveal the content, but it is well known how little information these two sources contain. Admittedly, alphabetical order affords the greatest possibilities for rapid search and identification of serials by their title, but this does not free the national bibliographic agency of its obligation to submit information relating to the content of serials either by incorporating relevant classification numbers into the description or by compiling Dewey or UDC indexes or a subject index.

It is not by chance that the report by B. Kelm and W. Traiser made at the IFLA Conference in Brighton (1987)[23] says that the subject index should represent an integral part of the current national bibliography. The simultaneous use of hierarchic and subject information retrieval languages is necessitated in the current national bibliography not only by the requirement to bring out document content in every aspect (serials included), but also by the possibility of the automation of the current national bibliography, which is much more effective if better conditions are provided for searching and sorting according to a large number of different characteristics (formal, physical, semantic). In some countries where the bibliographic processes are not yet automated (e.g., Bulgaria, the USSR), a large number of indexes are included in serials directories. The permanent incorporation of ISSN indexes (e.g., the FRG) is a particularly important obligation of every modern current national bibliography.

FORMS OF SERIALS REGISTRATION IN THE CURRENT NATIONAL BIBLIOGRAPHY

The phrase "forms of serials registration in the current national bibliography" means the bibliographic publications themselves, whether traditional or nontraditional, through which the information is distributed. It also includes the identical data in machine-readable form in the automated systems of the current national bibliography.

The studies of different current national bibliographies show that serials information, when limited to new serials or serials that have changed title (including discontinued serials as well), is usually published together with information on books (e.g., Great Britain, Belgium). However, other countries submit such information in appendices or individual directories of varying periodicity: monthly (France), annual (Japan), quinquennial (Finland). Information regarding new serials, title changes, and discontinued serials is published together with information on books in the Federal Republic of Germany; the serials information is also issued in separate cumulations covering a varying number of years. Many current national bibliographies simultaneously publish information about new serials, information about serials that have changed title, and complete information about all serials for a certain period of time. The first type of information is published either together with that for books (e.g., Hungary) or in separate sections in publications dealing with books (e.g., Bulgaria)[24] or in individual directories (e.g., quarterly in Poland; annual in the USSR).

The complete registration of serials is always made in individual bibliographic directories. Here the differences between the individual current national bibliographies are shown by whether they contain information about monographic series and by the period they cover. Annual directories are the most common, but there are also biennial (e.g., Czechoslovakia) and quinquennial ones (e.g., Denmark).

There is no doubt that the simultaneous registration of new serials, serials that have changed title, and all currently published serials is to be adopted as the optimum one by any current national bibliography. It is desirable to publish the first type of registration in a differentiated way from that of the other categories of documents in the current national bibliography (irrespective of whether in independent sections or separate directories). The optimum complete registration is the annual one. It is also possible to choose longer periods which, however, should not be greater than five years.

An annual registration corresponds most accurately to the specific character of the majority of serials (newspapers, journals). In principle their numbering and dating change every year. Therefore, the bibliographic unit of such publications is not and cannot be the first issue, but all issues in a year. In connection with the intervals of publication of the complete information about serials, we should in addition like to emphasize that this type of information should not be considered retrospective. It represents, without exception, current cumulative information about serials similar to the current cumulative information pertaining to other types of documents (books, dissertations, scores, etc.). The registration of all issues of a serial during a certain period of time is exactly the same thing as the registration of all volumes of a multivolume monograph. Just as it is obligatory to record in the current national bibliography all volumes of a multivolume monograph irrespective of the frequency of its publication, so should the registration of all issues of serials also be obligatory.

Moreover, as all current cumulative directories in the current national bibliography are used to compile later retrospective bibliographies of national literature covering longer periods of time, so current cumulative directories of serials form the basis of their retrospective national bibliography. They are even the cornerstone of such bibliography, because it is absurd to compile a retrospective bibliography only on the basis of the registration of new serials and serials that have changed title. The restoration of the whole picture of the serials in a country for long periods of time on the basis of such partial information is like the restoration of skeletons of pre-historic animals with only one of their bones to serve as a basis.

However, all these problems lose their importance after automation of the bibliographic processes. The automation of the current national bibliography affords the opportunity for the constant mainenance of a serials file in a given country and its continuous updating through the modification of the existing records and the creation of additional records for new titles. On the other hand, the ability to process data rapidly permits the publication of both partial and complete records for serials on different data carriers (paper, magnetic tape, magnetic disk, etc.) for shorter or longer periods of time, with the serials being classified according to various characteristics (formal, physical, semantic). However, this can be done only when the relevant national bibliographic agency possesses the required electronic computing equipment and when all such options are carefully considered and programmed before the information is processed. The selection of an appropriate format for information exchange both on national and international levels is not the last point. Of course, such a complex problem is most frequently solved by conversion of the national format into an international format.

THE IMPORTANCE OF SERIALS REGISTRATION IN THE CURRENT NATIONAL BIBLIOGRAPHY

The significance of the current national bibliography today from national and international points of view was discussed in detail at the Congress on National Bibliographies (Paris, 1977) and the 53rd General IFLA Conference (Brighton, 1987), which prepared a special National Bibliographies Seminar[25] on the occasion of the tenth anniversary of the congress. It is without doubt that the importance of the current national bibliography also relates to the registration of serials, where the political, economic, scholarly, and cultural life of each country is reflected most rapidly. This is especially conspicuous now in the countries of Eastern Europe where democratic reforms have contributed first of all to freedom of speech and hence to the rapid increase in the number of newspapers and journals of varying content and purpose. In Bulgaria alone in 1990 about 400 new serials began publication. However, in these circumstances it is necessary to consider the question of registration by the current national bibliography in light of the existence and development of ISDS. The reason for the creation of ISDS in the early 1970s was the poor international bibliographic control of serials and especially of scientific publications. On the other hand, however, the existence of ISDS with its decentralized collection of information would be impossible without the participation of the national bibliographic agencies and their activities related to the implementation of legal deposit and the compilation of the current national bibliography (even in countries where there are national ISDS centres). In this way a closed circuit is formed. It can be broken only if the necessary efforts are made internationally for the strengthening and future development of complete serials registration in the current national bibliography, which plays–as it should–a primary role even for ISDS.

However, in this respect it is necessary on the international level to draw up special recommendations for serials registration in the current national bibliography. First and foremost, such recommendations must carefully explain the concept of a serial, since it does not cover even newspapers in a number of countries. Moreover, it is also necessary to explain the notion of partial and total registration and the distinction between current and retrospective national bibliographies. Special recommendations should be made regarding improving the coverage of registration, the bibliographic description, the representation of content, and the types of indexes; and particular efforts should be paid to the relative standardization of the forms of registration (both traditional and nontraditional) and the intervals of their publication. Only on the basis of such recommendations will it be possible to assume that serials registration in the current national bibliography will occupy the place it is entitled to and is worthy of, since serials are documents having an exceptional national and international importance as carriers of information.

NOTES

1. Translation quoted per: Focket, D., "O niekotoryh sociologičeskih aspektah formal'nyh sistem peredači znanij" [On some sociological aspects of the formal systems of education].–In: *Problemy informatiki : sbornik statej*.–Moscow, 1973, 60-61.

2. Zotova, K., "Săštnost i metodi na bibliografijata" [Essence and methods of bibliography].–In: *Bălgarska bibliografija* '85, 1986, 19-46.

3. Zotova, K., "Bădešteto na bibliotekite i bibliografijata" [The future of libraries and bibliography]. –In: *Bălgarska bibliografija* '84, 1985, 17-42.

4. Zotova, K., "Opit apologii bibliografii" [Essay on bibliographic apology].–*Sovetskaja bibliografija*, 1989, No. 3, 7-14.

5. Zotova, K., "La bibliographie dans la perspective de la bibliologie." –*Revue de bibliologie*, 1989, No. 31, 10-13.

6. Zotova, K., *Optimal'naja model' tekuščej nacional'noj bibliografii Bolgarii* [The optimum model for the current national bibliography in Bulgaria].–Sofia, 1982.–231 p.

7. Zotova, K., "Bibliographic Control of Serials in Bulgaria."–*The Serials Librarian*, 1990, 18, No. 1-2, 181-196.

8. Avicenne, P., *Les services bibliographiques dans le monde* 1960-1964 ; 1965-1969.–Paris: UNESCO, 1967 ; 1972.–233 p. ; 320 p.

9. Beaudiquez, M., *Les services bibliographiques dans le monde* 1970-1974; 1975-1979.–Paris : UNESCO, 1977 ; 1983.–391 p. ; 488 p.

10. Bell, B. L., *An Annotated Guide to Current National Bibliographies*–Alexandria, Va., 1986. – 407 p.

11. *Compte-rendu de la Conférence sur l'amélioration des services bibliographiques, Paris,* 7-10 nov. 1950.–Paris : UNESCO, 1978.–27 p.

12. Larsen, K., *Les services bibliographiques nationaux : création et fonctionnement.*–Paris : UNESCO, 1955.–171 p.

13. *Synoptic Tables Concerning the Current National Bibliographies* / compiled by G. Pomassl and a working group of the Deutsche Bücherei.–Berlin; Leipzig, 1975.–3 S., 25. gef. Bl.

14. Line, M. B., *Inclusion of Materials in Current National Bibliographies.* –11 p.–(IFLA. 39th session, Grenoble, 1973. Committee on Bibliography).

15. *The National Bibliography: Present Role and Future Developments* / prepared by the IFLA International Office for UBC.–Paris : UNESCO, 1977.–vii, 97 p.

16. *International Congress on National Bibliographies, Paris, 12-15 Sept. 1977 : Draft Recommendations.*–Paris : UNESCO, 1977.–4 p.

17. *Guidelines for the National Bibliographic Agency and the National Bibliography* / prepared by the IFLA International Office for UBC.–Paris : UNESCO, 1979.–50, 20 p.

18. Zotova, K., *Universal Bibliographic Control and the Problems of Current National Bibliography.* –23 p.–(IFLA. 39th session, Grenoble, 1973. Committee on Bibliography).

19. Cybulski, R. and K. Zotova, *The Dynamic Model of Coverage of the Current National Bibliography.*–28 p.–(IFLA. 45th session, Copenhagen 1979. Section on Bibliography).

20. "Coverage of Documents in Current National Bibliographies" / R. Cybulski, K. Zotova, W. Bergmann, N. Gruzinskaya.–International Cataloguing, 1982, January/March, 11, No. 1, 4-7.

21. *VII meždunarodnoe soveščanie ekspertov socialističeskih stran po voprosam tekuščej nacional' noj bibliografii* [7th International Conference of Experts of the Socialist Countries on the Problems of the Current National Bibliography], Warszawa, 9-12 Oct. 1984.–Warszawa, 1987.–171 p.

22. Lunn, J., *Study on a Model Law of Legal Deposit.*–Third draft.–Ottawa, 1980.–101 p.– (IFLA. 46th session, Manila, 1980. Section on Bibliography and National Library Section).

23. Zotova, K., Otnosno *"Modela na zakona na zadălžitelnija depozit na socialističeskite strani"* [On a model law of legal deposit for the socialist countries].–In: *90 godini zakonodatelstvo za zadălžitelnija depozit i tekuštata nacionalna bibliografija na Bălgarija.*–Sofia, 1988, 247-256.

24. Bouffez, F. and A. Grousseaud, *L'étude sur le traitement des publications en série par les centres ISDS et les agences bibliographiques nationales.*–Paris : UNESCO, 1980.–142 p.

25. Kelm, B. and W. Traiser, "Die Anwendung von Klassifikationssystemen in Nationalbibliographien."–In: *National Bibliographies Seminar.*–London, 1987, 13-15.–(53rd IFLA council and general conference, Brighton, 1987. Division of Bibliographic Control).

26. Catalog cards for new serials and serials that have changed title are also printed in Bulgaria.

27. *National Bibliographies Seminar.*–17 p.–(53rd IFLA council and general conference, Brighton, 1987. Division of Bibliographic Control).

OPTIONS FOR CHANGE

Latest Entry Cataloging Locally and Nationwide: Some Observations

Mary M. Case
Kevin M. Randall

SUMMARY. Northwestern University Library began experimenting with a return to the use of latest entry cataloging for selected title changes in spring 1985. An informal user survey conducted in 1989 suggests that patrons may be helped by latest entry records in finding needed information, but may be hindered by the separate records required by successive entry. While the Library of Congress Rule Interpretations and the recent AACR2 rule changes lean more toward earliest entry, 52% of the sixty-four ARL libraries responding to a 1990 survey indicated that they too were using latest entry cataloging in circumstances ranging from limited use in retrospective conversion to extensive use in current cataloging. Until there is more sophisticated manipulation of the MARC record for indexes and displays, the authors believe latest entry cataloging can help patrons and staff.

Latest entry cataloging, the use of a single entry under which to record the history of a serial's titles, was among the methods of processing title

Mary M. Case is Head, Serials and Acquisitions Services, and Kevin M. Randall is Head, Serials Cataloging Section, Northwestern University Library, Evanston, IL 60208-2300.

changes that was supported by various cataloging codes until the publication of the *Anglo-American Cataloging Rules* (AACR) in 1967. AACR dropped latest entry as an option and prescribed the exclusive use of successive entry cataloging, the creation of a new record for each change in a serial's title. The use of latest entry continued, however, until the Library of Congress finally adopted successive entry in 1971. Although intended to simplify the cataloging rules, the practice of successive entry led to the creation of numerous records for seemingly insignificant, minor, and unintended title variations. This effect was exacerbated in libraries with online integrated systems where title changes resulted in not only bibliographic data, but also order, payment, receipt, holdings, and circulation information dispersed among many records. Staff and patrons needing to consult a full serial run were often forced to search for, display, and interpret many records.

Seriously inconvenienced in dealing with multiple records in the processing of title changes, we at Northwestern University Library began an experiment in spring 1985 in a return to the use of latest entry cataloging.[1] With the support of public services, systems, and technical services staff, we decided to revive the use of latest entry on an experimental basis for selected title changes. After a few years of practice and refinement of procedures, we developed a set of "Latest Entry Cataloging Rules" to be used as a supplement to AACR2.[2] To date we have created over 800 latest entry records. Response from Library staff has generally been positive, with one departmental library preferring the use of latest entry whenever possible.

A USER SURVEY[3]

While staff supported latest entry, we believed that its use could only be justified as a permanent option if this method actually helped users. So, in the spring of 1989, we conducted an informal survey to gather information on user response to latest entry. With the help of the staff in the Reference Department, we constructed a brief questionnaire that asked for information about five serial publications. Four of these involved title changes, two of which had been cataloged using latest entry cataloging and two using successive entry. Surveys were handed out at two locations in the Library during ten, one-hour time periods. Patrons were asked to search the online catalog in order to complete the survey and to return the completed forms to a public services desk. We collected 112 usable surveys. Table 1 summarizes the results.

QUESTION	CORRECT ANSWER	INCORRECT OR NO ANSWER
Latest Entry 1	97 (87%)	15 (13%)
Latest Entry 2	111 (99.5%)	1 (0.5%)
No Title Change	107 (96%)	5 (4%)
Successive Entry 1	14 (13%)	98 (87%)
Successive Entry 2	29 (26%)	83 (74%)

Table 1. User Survey: Numbers of Respondents with Correct and Incorrect Answers by Type of Question (n=112)

For the two questions involving latest entry records, information about earlier titles was asked. In the first case, ninety-seven respondents (87%) gave the correct answer, the call number of the Main Library copy of the title. Fourteen respondents (12.5%) gave the call number of the Law Library's copy, which displayed first in the online catalog, and one user did not respond to this question. For the second latest entry question, virtually 100% of the respondents (111) were able to identify correctly the earliest issue of the first of three titles included in the record (one questionnaire had no response to this question). This "correct" response was even greater than that for a question which involved no title change, where the presence of a monograph with the same title misled five respondents.

The two successive entry questions asked about a current title in combination with information about earlier or later titles. A right answer would result from reading the linking notes of the first title and then performing another search to access the earlier or later title record. The first question asked if the Library owned volume 1 of *Journal of the Southwest* and what year that volume was published. The serial began as *Arizona and the West* in 1959 and then changed title with volume 29 in 1987. Only fourteen respondents (13%) answered that volume 1 was published in 1959 or gave some indication that they had noticed that the title had changed. The second question asked whether the Library held the February 1988 issue of *Dun's Business Month* and any later current issues. *Dun's* had changed title in early 1987 to *Business Month.* In this case, twenty-nine respondents (26%) indicated that the Library owned the February 1988 and later issues. Variables such as type of user (student, faculty, staff) or frequency of use of the online catalog had no discernable impact on the results of the survey.

The data collected, of course, do not explain why it appeared easier to answer the latest entry questions than the successive entry ones. We could suggest that the latest entry records do indeed provide all the necessary information within the bibliographic notes and that this information is easily read and understood by patrons. However, we are more inclined to believe, based on discussions with public services staff, that most patrons are not reading the bibliographic data at all. Upon finding the record, patrons appear to move immediately to the location and holdings information, without noticing that the title at the top of the display is not the one they used to access the record. If this behavior is typical, latest entry may have the advantage of leading patrons to the needed information transparently.

In the case of the successive entry questions, it is possible that the respondents might have interpreted the questions too literally. We do not, strictly speaking, own volume 1 of *Journal of the Southwest* or the February 1988 issue of *Dun's Business Month.* It was difficult to word questions which suggested further possibilities without explicitly instructing the patron to look at another record. Again, it is not clear whether all the respondents read the bibliographic data; if they had, would the linking notes have made it obvious to them that they needed to look further?

Although there is obviously a need for additional and more rigorous research on this topic, we believe that this survey has given us some indication that latest entry records, rather than confusing patrons, may actually assist them in finding earlier titles. At the same time, the survey results also point to the need for further exploration of the display and manipulation of successive entry records.

AN ARL SERIALS CATALOGING SURVEY

The Library of Congress has made it clear that it does not intend to return to latest entry; at the same time, LC's rule interpretations and the subsequent changes to AACR2 21.1 are moving national standards toward earliest entry. Although Northwestern has been a strong advocate of latest entry and the topic has been discussed heatedly at ALA and NASIG, we were not certain whether other libraries were employing latest or earliest entry options.

In the fall of 1990, we polled our colleagues in ARL libraries about how they handle serial title changes. We identified this group of libraries as the one most likely to have a large number of cataloged serial titles, as well as large manual files needing conversion. One hundred twenty-four questionnaires were sent out and we received sixty-four responses (52%). (Northwestern was not included in the survey.)

The responses fell into two main categories (see Table 2):

1. Libraries which use latest entry cataloging to some extent or accept its existence in the catalog. Practices range from using latest entry for retrospective conversion only, to using existing pre-AACR latest entry records on national databases for current serials, to creating latest entry records for title changes occurring after the advent of AACR2. Thirty-three libraries (about 52%) fell into this group.[4]
2. Libraries which use successive entry cataloging exclusively or have used latest entry cataloging in retrospective conversion, but are intending to redo these records as successive entry records (or are in the process of doing so). This group consists of thirty-one libraries (about 48%).

We found no instance of a strict use of earliest entry cataloging in the survey responses. Although a few libraries reported using earliest entry, other responses on the forms indicated that they meant successive entry. Two libraries did say, however, that they "cheat" with "title varies slightly" notes and that they use variant title access (MARC tag 246) for "frivolous, unconvincing, or inconsequential" title changes, a procedure which leans toward the earliest entry approach.

Libraries Using Latest Entry Cataloging

Of the thirty-three libraries using latest entry cataloging to some extent, twenty-two (67%, or 34% of the total sample) employ it only for

METHOD OF CATALOGING	NUMBER OF LIBRARIES	PERCENTAGE OF LIBRARIES
Successive Entry exclusively	31	48%
Latest Entry	33	52%
TOTAL	64	100%

Table 2. ARL Survey: Number of Respondents by Method of Cataloging Title Changes

retrospective conversion or the current processing of older materials for which latest entry copy is available (although even such limited use may be kept to a minimum). Expediency is the prime reason for using latest entry in these cases. Four of these libraries had discussed using latest entry more broadly. In one, discussion was undertaken without any serious thought of further expansion; another library rejected expansion; and the two others were, at the time of the survey, still undecided. Factors mentioned as initiating discussions on the use of latest entry included the belief that it would work well with the NOTIS acquisitions module, reduce the cataloging workload on RLIN, reduce computer disk space, and generally be more helpful in an OPAC environment.

The major reason given for not using latest entry cataloging for current materials was adherence to national standards. This point was cited by ten libraries in the following ways: CONSER membership (three); membership in cataloging utilities (three); facilitating the use of LC records/cards (two); multi-institution union catalog requirements (one); and, in the words of one respondent, "problems we have already encountered by not conforming to national standards & LC practice." Other reasons given were: the lack of advantage in recataloging existing successive entry records since latest entry would be a benefit only for future title changes; problems caused by past use of latest entry, including, for example, relabelling and shifting of unclassified periodicals; the existing Kardex system already based on successive entry cataloging; difficulties in matching holdings to records in the online catalog; and problems in union listing.

In eleven libraries (33% of the latest entry group, or 17% of the total sample), latest entry is (or has been) used in the processing of new materials. One library used latest entry experimentally on a small number of records and has put the practice "on hold," but has not yet abandoned it. In eight it is used to a limited extent or rarely, usually being reserved for certain classes of materials, various "problem" situations, or certain types of title changes (e.g., vacillating titles, changes in corporate body main entry only, title changes of brief duration or very minor changes). In two libraries it is used regularly (one of them stating that it is used "whenever possible"). Five of the libraries returned to the use of latest entry sometime between 1986 and 1989; one renewed it in 1981; and five have been using it to some extent since before AACR. The reasons most cited for using latest entry for current cataloging were: (1) ease of access to records for check-in purposes, for use of the public catalog, or for reference use (cited by seven libraries); and (2) ease of processing in either cataloging or recording holdings (cited by five libraries). Table 3

TYPE OF USE OF LATEST ENTRY	NUMBER OF LIBRARIES	PERCENTAGE OF LATEST ENTRY USERS (n=33)	PERCENTAGE OF TOTAL SAMPLE (n=64)
Retrospective Conversion or Old Materials Only	22	67%	34%
Current Materials	11	33%	17%

Table 3. ARL Survey: Users of Latest Entry by Type of Use

summarizes the type of use of latest entry by the thirty-three libraries which use this method.

When asked about any problems encountered in using latest entry, five libraries reported no problems. Two libraries mentioned lack of familiarity with the rules (especially for newer catalogers), and one also said that the inability to input original latest entry records into OCLC was a major problem. Two libraries stated that reporting holdings to union lists was difficult when the local records were latest entry and the lists' records were successive entry. One of the libraries which uses latest entry only for retrospective conversion or older materials believes that the major problems encountered were not related specifically to latest entry but were common to all methods of serials cataloging: challenges related to the choice and form of entry, numbering inconsistencies, and complicated relationships among families of serials.

We have data from twenty-one of the latest entry libraries on their use of cataloging utilities. Ten of these are libraries that use latest entry only for retrospective conversion or old materials, and all ten catalog directly on a utility and download the records to local systems. The other eleven are the libraries which use (or have used) latest entry more broadly; seven catalog primarily on a utility, and the other four download some records (three of these also upload) but edit records primarily on local systems. Two of the seven that catalog primarily on a utility said that they will create successive entry records on OCLC and edit them for local use as latest entry records; one other library said that they will modify existing records to make them latest entry, but will follow national standards if creating original records.

The library which has put latest entry "on hold" relies heavily on CONSER copy from RLIN and union list records from OCLC, and is thus "somewhat committed to the use of successive entry," finding it more convenient to use that copy rather than to create latest entry records. In union list reporting, holdings were split among corresponding successive entry records; this was not reported specifically as a problem, perhaps due to the rather small number of records involved.

The reported responses of staff and patrons to latest entry were on the whole more positive than negative. Nine libraries reported positive reactions from staff to the use of latest entry, and one library also noted positive reactions from users. Another respondent–the library which has suspended latest entry for current materials–said that favorable comments had been made upon explanation of the practice, but there had been no comments about any actual records. The most cited reason for favoring latest entry was the ability to find holdings more easily for title changes.

Four libraries (including three from the paragraph above) reported negative reactions to latest entry. In three, the negative reactions were from technical services staff (in two of these, some catalogers were unhappy with variance from national standards). In the fourth library, the respondent reported that "staff and patrons don't understand" latest entry and "cannot find the titles."

Other libraries had no comments from staff or patrons. One survey respondent, who had queried the heads of branch libraries on the topic, said "few had strong opinions or understanding of the differences between latest entry & successive. They stressed they were in favor of whatever 'increased access.'"

Libraries Using Successive Entry Cataloging Exclusively

Of the sixty-four respondents, thirty-one (48%) indicated that they use successive entry cataloging exclusively. Included within this group are a few institutions who have used latest entry cataloging in retrospective conversion but plan to recatalog these records if they have not already done so.

Eighteen libraries (58% of the successive entry group, or 28% of the total sample) have not discussed using latest or earliest entry cataloging. Twelve libraries (39%, or 19% of the total sample) have discussed the issue but indicated that the discussions were brief and informal, and that latest entry was not seriously considered. The discussion usually arose as a result of articles in the literature, investigations into saving cataloging time and easing the entering of holdings, dissatisfaction on the part of non-technical services staff with both the indexing of serial titles in the online catalog and the existence of multiple records for "one" serial. All of these libraries cited national standards as the primary reason for rejecting the use of latest or earliest entry cataloging. National standards cited included AACR2 cataloging rules, CONSER requirements, LC practice, and OCLC and RLIN input standards.

Other reasons for continuing the exclusive use of successive entry cataloging were regional union listing requirements; participation in a consortial database for which joint policy decisions are made; the possibility of long, complicated records resulting from latest or earliest entry cataloging; the linkage between OCLC successive entry records and the institution's records for interlibrary loan purposes; lack of staff to do original cataloging for latest or earliest entry; the easing of the rules defining title changes; and the difficulty in finding and verifying specific serial history details.

Twelve members of this group (39%) indicated that they had continued to use latest entry cataloging even after the Library of Congress discontinued this practice in 1971. All, however, had stopped using it by the implementation of AACR2 in 1981.

In comparing the libraries which use latest entry with those which use only successive entry, we discovered only one factor which seemed to differ substantially between the two groups. The latest entry group had more libraries in which the serials acquisitions records were linked to the serial bibliographic records in the respondents' online systems (see Table 4). Of the twenty-three libraries in this group having serials acquisitions functions automated, sixteen (70%) indicated that these records were integrated with or linked in some way to the bibliographic records. In the successive entry group, only nine libraries (45%) out of twenty with automated serials acquisitions functions reported that these records were linked to the bibliographic records. The ease of access and processing in an automated system was mentioned by at least twelve of the respondents as the primary factor leading to the decision to use latest entry to some extent. These data suggest that as libraries continue to automate and to link their acquisitions and cataloging records, there might be further discussions of possible alternatives to successive entry.

CONCLUSION

Title changes, significant and trivial, have been and will always be an integral part of serials cataloging. Three ways that catalogers have attempted to deal with these changes have been latest entry, earliest entry, and successive entry. All three have their detractors, and all three also

METHOD OF CATALOGING	NUMBER OF LIBRARIES WITH SERIALS ACQUISITIONS FUNCTIONS AUTOMATED	ACQUISITIONS RECORDS LINKED TO BIBLIOGRAPHIC RECORDS	ACQUISITIONS RECORDS NOT LINKED TO BIBLIOGRAPHIC RECORDS
Latest Entry	23	16 (70%)	7 (30%)
Successive Entry	20	9 (45%)	11 (55%)
TOTAL	43	25 (58%)	18 (42%)

Table 4. ARL Survey: Number of Respondents with Automated Acquisitions Functions (by Method of Cataloging)

have their champions. Though we heard from none in the earliest entry camp in our survey of ARL libraries, we did hear from several who are interested in latest entry. One librarian, whose institution uses latest entry for retrospective conversion only, favors a broader application locally; another, whose library uses latest entry for some current processing, said that her library was very interested in it; another expressed strong support; and four–including one from an institution which uses successive entry exclusively–stated a desire for a national return to latest entry.

Our belief at Northwestern is as strong as ever in the need for easier access to the holdings of the entire run of a serial publication. To that end, we continue to use latest entry, even though we realize that it is not the ideal solution. The matter of standards still concerns us, now even more so given recent developments.

At the time we began to use latest entry, we belonged to the Research Libraries Group. Given that each library has its own records in the RLIN database, our cataloging practices created no problems in sharing records. In 1989 we joined OCLC and have been adding our holdings to the Online Union Catalog through regular tapeloads. This change has had no impact on our style of cataloging. If, however, we were to begin inputting original cataloging directly into OCLC, latest entry could have an extremely significant impact on our cataloging workflow. Title changes which are not represented on OCLC would have to forego latest entry on NOTIS, or be cataloged twice (once on OCLC for successive entry, and again on NOTIS for latest entry), or otherwise remain unrepresented on OCLC.

Sharing of volume-specific holdings data is still under consideration. Manual intervention is always a theoretical possibility for reducing or eliminating record-matching problems that arise from the application of different cataloging methods. The magnitude of the files in a large research library, however, makes this a practical impossibility. Consequently, machine matching of records becomes critical. Current developments in defining and applying the USMARC Format for Holdings Data (MFHD) do not seem to be addressing this problem. Nor does adherence to successive entry eliminate the problem entirely, especially as the rules defining title changes keep evolving. Different interpretations of AACR2 sometimes result in different successive entry records, in effect adding the problem of matching successive entry records with *earliest entry* records.

If there is an ideal solution to the processing of serial title changes, we believe that it has to come from much more sophisticated manipulation of the MARC record in the online catalog. Staff and patrons must be able to readily interpret index and record displays and to move from title to title with a single keystroke. Careful screen design and complex programming will be needed. We spend countless time and energy entering serials data into our online systems. We must ensure that this fundamental information is as easily accessible and understandable to our patrons as possible. Until developments in OPAC design bring an answer to the problem of title changes, latest entry cataloging can help.

NOTES

1. Priscilla W. Andre et al., "Serials Control in an Online Integrated System: Can Latest Entry Cataloging Help?" *Cataloging & Classification Quarterly* 7, no. 1 (winter 1986): 39-53.

2. Mary M. Case et al., "Rules for Latest Entry Cataloging: Northwestern University Library Supplement to AACR2," *Cataloging & Classification Quarterly* 9, no. 2 (1988): 41-54.

3. Our thanks to Bradley D. Carrington, Head of Cataloging at the University of Kentucky Libraries, who, while Head of Serials Cataloging at Northwestern, helped to construct and analyze this survey. Carrington and Case discussed the results of this survey as part of a workshop on latest entry cataloging at the NASIG Annual Conference in June 1989.

4. One of these libraries is not actually using latest entry for current processing, and has not yet done retrospective conversion; however, they stated that the CONSER guidelines, which allow latest entry for retrospective conversion when no successive entry records exist for any of the titles involved, would be used whenever retrospective conversion is undertaken. Because of this intention, the library seemed to belong with this group.

The Linked Systems Project and Serials Cataloging: An Update

Mary Ann Sheble
Carolyn Havens

SUMMARY. In the previous study by Havens, "The Networks Merger and Serials Control," the implications of the Linked Systems Project (LSP) for serials control and particularly serials cataloging were explored.[1] Since the paper's publication, considerable progress has been made with the LSP, and substantial changes have occurred with the participants which could have a vast impact on the project's continued development. As a follow-up article to the previous paper, this article will explore the applications of the LSP which are currently operative (name authorities) and which are projected (widespread bibliographic record exchange and, for the more distant future, full-text document exchange) and their relationship to the cataloging of serials.

Mary Ann Sheble is a Serials Cataloger in the University of Alabama Libraries, Cataloging Department, Main Library, University of Alabama, P. O. Box 870266, Tuscaloosa, AL 35487-0266.

Carolyn Havens is a Serials Cataloger in the Auburn University Libraries, Serials Department, Ralph Draughon Library, Auburn University, AL 36849-5606.

Research support for this paper was provided by the Auburn University Libraries.

The assistance of Tammy Roundy of the University of Georgia Libraries is gratefully acknowledged.

INTRODUCTION AND BACKGROUND OF THE LINKED SYSTEMS PROJECT

Because of economic realities, libraries must share information resources to meet the needs of their users. The development of the MARC format in the middle 1960s made resource sharing possible via computer networking. Shortly after the Library of Congress (LC) developed the MARC format, the Online Computer Library Center (OCLC) implemented its system, manifesting some of the possibilities of an online system for library operations.[2] Although OCLC was originally designed as a cooperative endeavor within Ohio, its services quickly spread beyond state boundaries.

By the middle 1970s, two other bibliographic networks had been developed: the Bibliographic Automation of Large Library Operations (BALLOTS), which later evolved into the Research Libraries Group (RLG) and its network, the Research Libraries Information Network (RLIN), and the Washington (now Western) Library Network (WLN). This development resulted in what Richard McCoy has referred to as a bibliographic tower of Babel: three distinct bibliographic utilities, each with its own computer system, database and membership.[3] Although the member libraries of each utility share resources within their utility, each utility has been isolated from the others. This isolation has led to the costly duplication of cataloging and conversion activities within the United States.[4]

In its most basic sense, the Linked Systems Project (LSP) is an effort to circumvent this isolation through the development of a communications protocol enabling heterogeneous computer systems to exchange information. Although the impetus for coordinating the efforts of the major U. S. bibliographic utilities can be traced to the middle 1970s, the Linked Systems Project had its formal beginning in 1980, when the Council on Library Resources (CLR) made a decision to fund the project.[5] The initial participants in the project were the Library of Congress, the Washington Library Network (WLN) and the Research Libraries Group (RLG). OCLC joined the project in 1984.

Developments within the LSP can be divided into two components: (1) the communications facility, the Standard Network Interconnection (SNI), and (2) the applications software that allows the three utilities to share bibliographic and authority information. The SNI is based on the International Organization for Standardization's (ISO) Open Systems Interconnection (OSI) Reference Model. This model was developed by ISO as a generic protocol to overcome the complexity of exchanging information between systems with different hardware, software, and data representation.[6]

The OSI model is composed of seven layers. Each layer consists of procedures required for disparate systems to communicate. When a message is sent from system A to system B, the message is passed to the top (7th) layer of system A's protocol. This application layer arranges the information into a generic form that can be understood by the 7th layer of system B. This information in its new form is then passed to the 6th or "presentation" layer of system A. This layer is designed to perform encryption, character code conversion and similar functions. The 5th or "session layer" adds information about the requirements of the two computer systems and ensures that the messages received and sent between the systems do not become mixed with other dialogue. The message then passes to the lower four levels, which are primarily concerned with moving information accurately and efficiently across the chosen telecommunications network.[7] On the receiving system B, the message from system A is reassembled, routed and converted as it is moved up through the corresponding layers of the OSI protocol.

The major advantage of the OSI protocol for communications exchange between bibliographic utilities is that users employ the procedures and language of their local system for both inputting and searching records. Responses made to users at their terminals are displayed in the format of the local system, regardless of the system of origin of the information.

The LSP is not, then, as numerous information specialists have maintained, an effort to create a single unified nationwide network. It is, rather, a cooperative endeavor between the Library of Congress and the three major U. S. bibliographic utilities. Each utility will retain its autonomy with regard to membership, structure, and governing system. The primary role of the LSP will be to reduce the duplication of cataloging and authority work and to promote the efficient use and exchange of library materials on a national scale. Authority work is the aspect of the LSP in which the most progress has been made up to this point.

AUTHORITY RECORD EXCHANGE: IMPLICATIONS FOR SERIALS CATALOGERS

The importance of authority control in an online environment has been documented in papers by Malinconico,[8] Avram,[9] and others.[10,11] Yet, developing and maintaining an authority file is one of the most labor intensive and expensive aspects of cataloging. In recognition of these issues, the first application of the LSP has been directed toward authority file work.[12] This application of the LSP has been built on the National Coordinated Cataloging Operations Project (NACO), formerly the Name Authority Cooperative. This program began in the late 1970s as a joint project between the Library of Congress and the U. S. Government Printing Office.[13] Since 1977, the program has grown to include 41 contributing libraries.

As summarized by Clack, NACO is the mechanism by which the Library of Congress has been able to avoid a large backlog of authority work and increase the size of its authority file at a fairly constant rate.[14] NACO permits participating libraries to contribute records for name and series headings to the Library of Congress for inclusion in the LC authority file. Although Harvard University Library and the University of Chicago Library input authority records directly into the LC file, the majority of the NACO participants have their records screened by LC before the time that they are incorporated into the LC master authority file. These procedures have led to a high degree of consistency and integrity in the file. The file is later distributed via the MARC Distribution Service to all subscribers.

Prior to the implementation of the LSP, the majority of transactions between NACO participants and the Library of Congress were handled through the U. S. mail.[15] This method was slow and often resulted in duplicate efforts between NACO participants. Some of the NACO participants did not have immediate access to LC machine-readable files and thus would submit records for approval that had already been incorporated into the latest edition of the master authority file. Even for participating libraries with online access to LC files, mailing delays created situations in which LC and other NACO participants submitted duplicate records.

This duplication of effort was substantially reduced with the implementation of the LSP. Through their bibliographic utilities, NACO libraries contribute records to the LC master authority file. With the exception of libraries with direct input authorization, these records are placed in a holding queue. All records are reviewed within 24 hours of the time they are received.[16] If a record input from a NACO participant fails edits, the master file system produces a notification for the participant's utility, indicating the reasons for the error. The record is then deleted from the LC authority file queue. If a NACO participant wishes to correct and resubmit the record, it may retrieve the record from its bibliographic utility file. Records that pass all edits are added to the LC master authority file and are distributed to subscribers either online or on tape.[17]

In about 1988, LC was distributing an average of 2,500 authority records to RLIN and OCLC daily over the LSP link, giving access to all users of the two utilities a copy of the LC's authority file, current within 24 hours. This work includes early notice records (preliminary notices of work that is underway for records that have not previously been made available outside of the Library of Congress).[18] Although the current arrangement allows only for the exchange of data between LC and each utility, the system is designed to facilitate searching between utilities. Intersystem searching will permit members of one utility to search the authority files of other utilities for records not currently in the LC authority file.[19] WLN, for example, has maintained its own authority file for a number of years.[20] Many of the WLN authority records predate the NACO program. This resource is constantly augmented by WLN members who are non-NACO participants. RLIN also has a valuable authority resource: the authority file of the New York Public Library. With the implementation of the LSP, these records will at least in theory be available to members of all three utilities. This option would be especially attractive to OCLC member libraries, who currently have access to only the LC authority file.

Such improvements in the quantity and currency of authority records should make the cataloging of serials much easier. The vast majority of authority work for serials involves establishing corporate headings. Whereas personal authors may publish under variant names and occasionally change their names, corporate bodies are notorious for both frequent and complex name changes. International investment firms, for example, may have an extremely loose and complex corporate structure, with a confusing, complex set of headings. Local institutions, such as social, church, and charitable organizations may present a similar set of problems in establishing headings. This situation is particularly true when the cataloging agency is not within the locality of the institution or society for which an authorized heading needs to be established.

This latter difficulty has been made very apparent in a current project at the University of Alabama Library. The library is participating in a SOLINET project, sponsored by the National Endowment for the Humanities, to microfilm deteriorating materials. As its part in the project, the University of Alabama is submitting a number of records to OCLC for an early Louisiana pamphlet collection. Authority records for the majority of the corporate bodies are not available through the LC authority file. The majority of these materials were published in the 1700s and early 1800s; they frequently emanate from fairly obscure and short-lived corporate bodies, and no one locally is likely to be familiar with these bodies.

Hence, the lack of existing authority records has resulted in a great deal of work for the library. Since the library is not a NACO participant, the research required to establish headings for these entities will result only in local authority records. Other libraries with similar holdings will have to duplicate this research.

The lack of shared authority control has also created problems for the University of Alabama Library in searching OCLC for existing bibliographic records. Many of the serials have generic titles such as "annual report" and must be searched by corporate body. In the absence of established authorities for these bodies, it is possible that existing records will be overlooked, especially if the corporate body name has appeared in variant forms on different issues of the serial. This type of situation is especially problematic when inputting and searching libraries have limited runs of a serial and are working from different issues.

The LSP may make it practical for OCLC and RLIN to investigate creating utility-specific authority files similar to that maintained by WLN. The maintenance of such files could be beneficial for libraries in several ways. First, these files could serve as a resource for NACO participants. Member libraries which are not NACO participants could input records into these files, doing at least a minimal amount of the required research. NACO participants could draw on these records and add any other available information when these headings are encountered and submitted to the LC master authority file. This procedure would reduce at least some duplication of effort between libraries. These records could also serve as a resource among utility members to reduce duplicate research for establishing authority records for their local files. This resource would seem to be of special value in reducing efforts for retrospective conversion activities, in which a great deal of research is frequently required to establish headings. Some type of standards would, of course, need to be established and enforced by the utilities to make these authority records a viable resource.

In spite of its problems, the name authority aspect of the LSP is at least functioning, and progress continues to occur with it. But the next projected phase, that of massive intersystem bibliographic record exchange, is sorely needed today and will remain so until its implementation. In fact, bibliographic record exchange is possible now, and OCLC and RLIN have already exchanged almost 500,000 records as part of a cooperative agreement between the two networks regarding RLG's Preservation Program, which began in 1974. The exchanged records are for materials preserved on microfilm, and this cooperative agreement is an important step toward total internetwork cooperation, but widespread exchange of all bibliographic records in all three networks as well as the Library of Congress' database needs to be made possible and the sooner the better. The problems associated with the implementation of total bibliographic record exchange simply need to be systematically resolved for the greater good of the affected libraries and library users.

Conceivably, intersystem bibliographic record exchange could be implemented fairly quickly and easily if the databases of all three networks and that of the Library of Congress were all loaded or merged into one master database, with the three utilities remaining separate and autonomous, which would greatly decrease problems of governance. A record de-duping program could be implemented whereby duplicate records could be merged, with the unique elements as well as the shared elements of all merged records retained. Each network that had input a version of the merged records could still retain credit for having done so, and, if desired, each network could retain its own subfile within the combined database in one configuration or another. Subfile boundaries could be invisible, with users being able to search in only one master file rather than having to search through multiple subfiles.

Failing any possibility of a master database, at very least the need exists for libraries to be able to transfer bibliographic records directly between databases and stop the duplication of original cataloging. A member of any of the networks should also be able to load records from any of them into its own online system such as NOTIS and be charged for the use of the records. The library would not even necessarily have to do any editing of the records on OCLC or the other utilities. At the absolute very least, "search only" memberships in both RLIN and WLN need to be much more readily available to OCLC libraries than is the case at present.

POTENTIAL PROBLEMS AND SOLUTIONS INVOLVED IN BIBLIOGRAPHIC RECORD EXCHANGE

The lack of indexing continuity across the three systems has been identified by several individuals as a potential problem in intersystem searching.[21] This discontinuity especially affects title searches and, because the title is often the major access point for periodicals, this issue will be of concern to serialists. One utility may index only the title proper of a document, another utility may index both the title proper and subtitle and a third may index the title proper, subtitle, key title, and uniform title. As noted by McCallum,[22] users need to be educated about these differences before they attempt intersystem searching. It is especially important that individuals searching for serial records be aware of these indexing differences, as many serials are entered under uniform titles or have generic titles that contain information in the delimiter "p" (part) subfield. Unless the individual conducting the search is aware of indexing variations between systems, time and money can be wasted by inefficient search strategies.

Other concerns relate to the economics of day-to-day search queries for cataloging and interlibrary loan. Searching for serial titles in large bibliographic databases presents a unique conglomerate of problems for librarians. Serials can be extremely difficult and expensive to search even within a single bibliographic database. This problem is especially severe with generic titles, such as "annual reports" whose corporate author's heading contains one or more stopwords (i.e., words that cannot be searched) and whose beginning date of publication is unknown to the searching library. Although Boolean capabilities alleviate this problem to some extent, libraries may need to be able to monitor costs during intersystem searching to determine when original cataloging will be more economical than attempting to obtain a record from the database of an outside utility.

Since many serials are entered under corporate body, changes in the rules for construction of corporate body names have had far-reaching implications for serials. Older serials must frequently be searched under both older and current forms of heading. If a title has been input as part of a library's retrospective conversion project, it is likely that the serial can be accessed using the current form. If, however, the record predates AACRII, it is likely that the title will be accessed under the older forms and occasionally under unauthorized forms. Under these conditions, serial titles may be overlooked in one database and located on another. (Utility-specific name authority files might at least help alleviate this problem.) If an OCLC member library overlooks a record on the OCLC database and uses a record from RLIN, will OCLC penalize the library for overlooking the record on its "home utility" database? Will any tracking mechanisms exist to detect this use? This question brings up, again, the issue of migrating records from one utility to another. Will this practice be authorized and under what circumstances will it be authorized? Such issues will need to be resolved, but a number of sensible solutions should be possible.

An additional characteristic of serials that makes searching for them especially problematic on large bibliographic databases relates to the shift from latest entry to successive entry cataloging. Perhaps problems associated with latest entry records in general would multiply in a combined database, but perhaps such records could be permanently corrected and upgraded using the cut and paste feature of OCLC's new Passport software which makes it possible to do block editing which was not available in OCLC's first system.

Although differences in the search keys of the three bibliographic networks in fact also remain, OCLC has bridged and decreased some of the differences with its current implementation of its new Prism Service and accompanying Passport software. This second version of OCLC's online system, which has been in development for years, is being installed in OCLC member libraries nationwide on a daily basis and is operational in many others at the time of this writing. The Passport software provides enhanced searching capabilities which not only make searching in OCLC easier but also make it more similar to searching in RLIN, particularly through the introduction of the "fin" and "scan ti" commands and the new capacity to combine author and title search algorithms with the Boolean operator *and.* Although keyword and subject search capacity and more Boolean logic are unquestionably still needed in OCLC, searching for serial records is now greatly facilitated and should be correspondingly so in intersystem searching in the LSP's projected bibliographic record exchange phase. If/when this phase occurs (and may it come quickly), OCLC users will already be somewhat familiar with searching in RLIN, which should prove helpful.

Another concern relates to the use of a "better" record by non-member libraries when a duplicate of inferior quality is found in the database of the library's own utility. For example, will OCLC participants be able to use an RLIN or WLN serial record, when the only record available on OCLC is an unenhanced MULS record? If so, how will the pricing mechanism work? If a better record is located for a particular serial title, can the member library transfer this record to its bibliographic utility? Who will pay, the library or the bibliographic utility receiving the updated record? How will this affect the ability of a bibliographic utility to have its member libraries upgrade the quality of its database? Again, such issues will need to be resolved by thoughtful and responsible dialogue between the utilities and knowledgeable representatives of member libraries.

The issue of entering original cataloging for a record that may be in the database of another utility raises an additional set of concerns. At this time it is impossible to find information relating to the extent to which libraries will be obligated to view the LSP network as a national database. It may be, for example, that libraries will be free to simply use intersystem searching as an occasional option, as each individual library deems necessary. It may be that for specific cataloging activities, guidelines will be implemented. Several individuals at the Library of Congress have shown concern about the lack of a nationally coordinated effort for retrospective conversion.[23] It is possible that the Library of Congress and the three utilities will decide to cooperate as a national database and will mandate intersystem searching for retrospective conversion and other special projects, while allowing optional intersystem searching for normal day-to-day activities.

As a further note on the subject of retrospective conversion, if all records from all three utilities were loaded into one giant database, then a nationally coordinated recon project would essentially have begun. Such a merger would certainly go a long way in the right direction of the formation of such a project. Although many libraries have already converted their records, sufficient time still remains for the Linked Systems Project to help many others with conversion. Auburn University Library is still engaged in the conversion of serials. Many needed records not found in OCLC almost surely reside within the WLN and RLIN databases, and the Auburn serials catalogers want them to be available in some way to transfer into their NOTIS system, preferably through OCLC since it is the system to which Auburn subscribes.

Correspondingly, the LSP could also promote more efficient information sharing between libraries which are members of CONSER (formerly the Conversion of Serials Project, now the Cooperative Online Serials Program).[24] The CONSER records are distributed on MARC tapes. The most up-to-date information is always in OCLC, except for records created or updated by RLIN CONSER participants. Several members of CONSER are members of RLIN and lack the means to (1) search the OCLC database for existing records and (2) input records into the RLIN system to be transmitted to OCLC so that CONSER members of OCLC will not duplicate the efforts of non-OCLC CONSER members. Currently, tape transmission between utilities is being used but is far too slow to be effective.

Finally remains the unexplored issue of the impact of the LSP on cataloging as a profession and the workflow of cataloging departments. Original cataloging is time-consuming, but it is also interesting and challenging. Searching bibliographic databases can be time-consuming but in general is not particularly interesting. In many libraries, the majority of searching on OCLC is delegated to paraprofessional staff and student employees. For libraries whose participation in intersystem searching will be extensive, a shift in the responsibilities of the professional cataloger can be anticipated. Little doubt also exists that changes will occur in workflow patterns and the composition of cataloging and serials departments, but such changes take place each time a library enters a new phase of automation, and they are to be expected as a matter of course, as are the fiscal adjustments which accompany its implementation.

FISCAL CONCERNS REGARDING FULLER IMPLEMENTATION OF THE LSP

Gillham and Beckman suggest conditions that must be met for a library network to be successful: participation is voluntary; costs and benefits are viewed by all participants as distributed equitably; the central organization coordinates but does not control the activities of the participants; and standards are set, accepted, and maintained by all participants.[25] Barbara Markuson maintains that networking can be successful only when it is a grass-roots effort and that it cannot be successful when imposed from the top down.[26] Other authors have focused on the ability of networks to fill crucial needs of libraries in a era of heightened patron expectations.[27]

Although these authors have approached network viability from different perspectives, all seem to suggest that the success of library networks, current and future, depends on the ability of networks to provide financial relief for individual libraries and serve workflow functions more efficiently than would be possible if the libraries were operating as self-contained units. As stated by Susan Martin, "Networks will survive and perhaps flourish if it is perceived that the benefits they offer outweigh the costs."[28]

Although the LSP can extend accessibility to information resources, it also has the potential for increasing costs to member libraries. The majority of development efforts have been funded from outside resources. The initial plan had a budget of $6 million. Since 1980, the Council on Library Resources (CLR) has made approximately $2.5 million available in grants for LSP related efforts.[29] The bibliographic utilities have attempted to secure third-party funding to help defray the cost of in-house hardware and software development.[30] However, no doubt exists that the majority of the project's day-to-day costs once it is fully implemented will be passed on to member libraries. Librarians may agree in theory that the idea of a nationwide network is a valid pursuit but whether they will agree to provide initial and continued support will depend on project costs and the benefits for their individual libraries. In brief, how much does the LSP help the patron waiting in line for an uncataloged serial at a branch library in Birmingham, Alabama?

The issue of whether enough libraries will benefit sufficiently from the LSP to justify the expense of the project has been raised by Malinconico.[31] Malinconico has argued that the LSP is a "patrician pursuit," that the primary beneficiaries of the LSP will be large research libraries. The argument constructed by Malinconico rests on two characteristics of the OCLC database: (1) the composition of the database, and (2) the hit rate (i.e., successful record retrieval). Of records contributed by member libraries, 46% were used only by the contributing library. Since contributed records constitute approximately 70% of the OCLC database, approximately one-third of the records are of benefit to only the inputting library. Given the high hit rates achieved by most OCLC member libraries, the primary function of the LSP will be to provide access to a wide range of little used, idiosyncratic records. Malinconico argues that the users of these materials will be a "small highly exclusive elite."[32] The question of equity is raised by Malinconico. Is it fair to distribute costs to all utility members for enhancements that do not benefit the general library community?

Since a breakdown does not exist between serial and non-serial formats in the OCLC database for contributed records, it is difficult to judge the applicability of Maliconico's argument for serial records. A significant number of serial publications are issued by specific universities, colleges and other corporate bodies. The majority of these publications will fall into Malinconico's idiosyncratic contribution and use category.

Despite the lack of concrete information, our experience as serials catalogers leads us to believe that most serial publications are going to be held by more than one library and, in fact, by a fairly wide range of libraries. If information is perceived as important enough to be issued on a regular, continuous basis, in most cases it is probably going to be important enough to be distributed and retained by a significant number of libraries. If this reasoning is correct, it raises two issues. First, if the majority of serial publications have a moderate to wide range of distribution, it is highly probable that most of these records can be retrieved from a library's "home utility." This likelihood would make intersystem searching unnecessary for the majority of serial publications. In this regard, our argument follows Malinconico's and questions the utility of the LSP's projected manifestation. However, again, if the databases of all three utilities were combined, records for serial titles would not need to be input three times over in three separate home utilities.

The second issue relates to materials with limited distribution and/or limited retention. Again, based on experience, one can estimate that the majority of the materials in this category are of several types: (1) older materials that have not been converted to MARC format, (2) materials that are highly specialized in terms of subject content, and (3) materials with a limited geographic distribution. Records for highly specialized materials would be of limited use in the general library community. It seems probable, however, that the other two types of materials would be used by a fairly broad range of libraries and library patrons. Records for these materials would be used for both interlibrary loan and cataloging purposes. Intersystem search capabilities could be useful for locating these records. It is difficult, however, to construct a definitive argument for or against the LSP on this basis, since the argument is based on conjecture rather than statistics.

Ronald Segal has argued for the cost formula for LSP services to be based on use.[33] He suggests that libraries be allowed to determine their level of participation on an individual basis: "Each member should be allowed to choose which services it will buy, which services it will provide to others, and to whom it will provide them. Those who provide service must be free to determine its quality, price, level of support and availability. . .The long-term success of an integrated nationwide network requires that on-going operations be paid for by those who are receiving the benefits."[34]

Few would disagree with Segal's observations. It seems only fair that costs be assumed by those who accumulate them. For direct operational costs, Segal's argument may be workable. However, questions about the distribution of indirect costs remain. Indirect costs can include everything from the development of new software to accommodate LSP hardware[35] to the revision of accounting systems so that utilities are able to track both transactions in their database from non-member utilities and transactions of member libraries in other utility databases. It seems very likely that such costs would be distributed to all utility members, regardless of their level of participation in the LSP. The resolution of this situation would be that individual member libraries' participation in the LSP could be optional. If the three networks remain administratively and fiscally separate entities, member libraries could elect to belong to only their home networks and thus avoid any additional costs incurred by membership in the LSP. If an effort is truly cooperative, various options of this nature should be possible.

Other fiscal matters could surely be worked out fairly simply if, as suggested by former OCLC president Rowland C. W. Brown in 1986, the membership structure of the utilities could simply be changed. The three networks could share each other's records and simply charge each other's members for using them just as they presently charge their own members for using records. This level of internetwork cooperation within the United States could lead to increased international cooperation which could eventually and ideally include the exchange of full-text documents.

INTERNATIONAL COOPERATION AND SERIALS APPLICATIONS

The groundwork for the international exchange of bibliographic information in machine-readable form was established in 1975, when the International MARC Network Committee was formed. The Committee was composed of representatives from national libraries with MARC programs. The original concept of the committee involved the exchange of MARC data among national libraries, which would then be responsible for distributing these records to agencies within their respective countries. As noted by Avram, the current activities of international MARC are accompanied by a host of problems. The majority of these problems have their roots in two developments: (1) MARC records have become a commodity, and (2) the altruistic climate that once encouraged the exchange of data on both the national and international levels is eroding.[36]

Use of the Linked Systems protocol on an international scale would do nothing to circumvent these problems and, because of an unprecedented set of possibilities for information exchange, would add an entirely new set of problems. Although data exchange via magnetic tape can be monitored to some extent because it requires intermediaries on both the sending and receiving ends, the LSP protocol makes possible the direct exchange of information between libraries and individual library patrons. As noted by Buckland and Lynch, the international use of the Linked Systems protocol would enable ". . . a cataloger in Manchester to search a catalog in Munich and a scholar in Singapore to search files in Seattle."[37]

Libraries have historically shown interest in developing international standards to extend efficient communication worldwide in the information community.[38] As early as 1985, Canada was working with the United States on application layer protocol standards to ensure that the standards would support both interactive applications (i.e., LSP) and remote operation application, such as those developed in Canada. Norway has done extensive testing in this area for the European information community. As a result of these activities, the ISO Technical Committee 46 organized a Working Group, composed of representatives from the United States, Canada, Great Britain, Norway, Denmark and other nations to develop international standards for information exchange between heterogeneous computer systems.

As with many other projects, technology is not the limiting factor. The major problems in developing an international information exchange are organizational, cultural, economic and political.[39] Because the United States is such a large and diverse country, Americans tend to underestimate cultural factors as barriers to cross-national information exchange and to take a fairly liberal attitude toward information dissemination. Although all governments, including our own, restrict the cross-national flow of scientific and technological information (STI) identified as important for national security, the U. S. has a long history of viewing information as a public domain commodity. The idea of sharing information from U.S. libraries in exchange for the right to view the information of foreign libraries does not seem inappropriate from a U.S. perspective.

This perspective is not necessarily shared by other countries, however. In Japan, for example, responsibility for the selection of materials for university libraries is placed in the hands of teaching faculty. An earlier study by Humphreys[40] found that only 1.9% of all materials purchased for Japanese universities had been selected by library staffs. Faculty members tend to be possessive about the resources they have selected. "The idea that such books could be considered as part of a national resource would be anathema to many professors."[41] Under such conditions, providing incentives for sharing this information on an international scale could be difficult.

Political and legal factors present an equally formidable set of barriers to international cooperation in information exchange. This set of factors is especially strong regarding the transmission of full-text documents. However, full-text document delivery would be the ultimate goal of information exchange on the international level. Knowing that a library in Tokyo holds the desired issue of a journal does little to help the patron waiting in line for an article in Eugene, Oregon. The complexities of multiple copyright laws and regulations can be expected to create an enormous set of problems, as utilities extend their capabilities beyond the transmission of records to full text transmission.[42] Copyright issues related to the databases themselves may also prove problematic, as shown by OCLC's attempt to copyright the OCLC database.

Another area of concern relates to variations in assumptions and procedures that have guided cataloging practices in different countries.[43,44] These differences, combined with multiple languages and character sets have created a complex set of problems and issues. As stated by Buckland and Lynch, ". . . problems that have been largely solved at the national level would have to be resolved again for international bibliographic searching."[45] A discussion of issues which illustrate these problems follows.

LACK OF INTERNATIONAL CATALOGING STANDARDS FOR SERIALS

Although the International Standard Bibliographic Description (ISBD) has helped to standardize the descriptive aspect of cataloging, significant variations continue to exist in regard to standardization of choice and form of heading.[46] Even the current edition of the *Anglo-American Cataloguing Rules* (AACRII) allows for significant differences in the construction of access points.

For serials, a great deal of disparity exists between countries in the way title changes have been handled. Prior to AACRI, the U. S. used latest entry cataloging, collating all titles of a serial on the same record. This practice was followed through 1966 in U. S. libraries. AACRI shifted to successive entry cataloging (separate entries for each title change). However, the Library of Congress continued to use latest entry cataloging for some time, even after AACRI had been implemented. In contrast, U. K. collated their serials by earliest entry; all titles were entered on one record under the first title of the serial. Although successive entry is currently practiced in both countries, older records that were constructed under previous rules would limit the utility of these records for cross-national exchange. Again, latest entry cataloging of serials is a bibliographic problem which needs to be addressed at least in the United States, preferably by correcting all latest entry records in all databases or in the preferred merged database.

The lack of cataloging standardization for serials presents an additional problem for libraries in regard to full-text transmission. For monographs, it is sufficient to know that the library has a particular edition of a work. This information should be readily apparent from the bibliographic record. For serials, it is important to know that a library has a specific issue of a serial. U. S. MARC is developing a set of 800 fields that will contain information on holding, supplements, indexes, abstracts, etc., for the inputting library. This information would do a great deal to facilitate interlibrary transactions on both the national and international levels. To what extent this practice will be incorporated into the MARC records of other countries remains to be seen.

LANGUAGE BARRIERS AND NON-ROMAN ALPHABETS

As noted by Avram, one of the most obvious differences–language –can ". . . cause the greatest headaches."[47] Since the language used by the cataloging agency is the language of the country, subject headings and notes can cause difficulties. Unless thesauri used by the various cataloging agencies in other countries can be secured, subject searching will be virtually impossible. Even within one language, subject searching may be difficult. For example, within English-speaking countries, several types of subject schemes are used. Most libraries in the U. S. provide subject access through Sears or Library of Congress Subject Headings (LCSH), whereas the British use the PRECIS system.

Buckland and Lynch have suggested several scenarios that would circumvent the language barrier.[48] These suggestions relate to the use of expert systems to provide translations. Certainly this possibility should not be discounted. At the current level of development, however, the Linked Systems Protocol would require the individual searcher to understand enough about the foreign system to conduct a search in terms of that system. The LSP, of course, would allow the user interface to be in terms of the searcher's own system. Search terms, but not commands, would need to be entered in a form that is compatible with the foreign system.

Corresponding, the American Library Association (ALA) has established a standard set of characters to be used on all bibliographic records. Other countries have established similar protocols, the majority of which are very different from the character set established by ALA. As noted by Buckland and Lynch, "A searcher in the U. S. who tries a linked systems protocol connection to a library in Russia, Israel or Egypt can expect serious difficulties."[49] Even in countries where the same alphabet is used, small but significant differences in special characters can be problematic.

With serials, this problem will be compounded because a specific issue rather than the document described on the record will be the item of interest. Even if the use of 800 fields is adopted on an international scale, differences between countries in regard to volume and numbering designation, as well as just being able to read the volume and numbering designations of a non-roman alphabet, may prove to be problematic.

CONCLUSION AND RECOMMENDATIONS

Obviously the delivery of full-text documents internationally will entail a myriad array of problems additional to those involved in the vastly simpler intersystem exchange of bibliographic records within the United States. Unquestionably, international document delivery, particularly that of periodical articles, is a highly desirable goal to which to aspire. To an extent, it is already achieved through interlibrary loan. However, at this time, the international political situation is unstable, and it appears generally to remain so. Even within the United States, media coverage of international politics appears to be incomplete to the point of censorship, which should be particularly offensive to librarians, whose essential responsibility is the dissemination of information. Access to information is more important now than ever before because the world is at its most complex state in its history. By the same token, the databases of all three major American cataloging networks contain unique information which is needed by members of the other networks. Information in the form of serial records is particularly important because the construction of it is particularly complex and difficult. Absolutely no question exists that, if all the information contained in all the databases were made available to all members of all three networks, many members and many individuals would benefit. Before those in the library profession become overly concerned with international document delivery, we need to provide for a freer and more unified exchange of bibliographic information within the United States through a unified bibliographic database. Surely this need for information and the responsibility of the library community to provide it are significant enough to transcend any problems regarding the governance of three networks which have never been intended for profit in the first place.

Auspiciously, some recent developments with RLIN and OCLC appear to have very positive implications for a move in the direction of a unified database. At its meeting on March 7-8, 1991, the RLG board of governors discussed the possibility of the suspension of cataloging, acquisitions, and interlibrary loan activities on RLIN and the migration of those activities to OCLC, leaving RLG freer to concentrate on providing other information products and services. Plans were made for RLG President James Michalko to meet with OCLC officers to discuss a possible link between the two databases. The time frame for these possible changes is indefinite, as are the actual plans themselves.[50]

Meanwhile, OCLC has begun changing its pricing structure in a gradually increasing move toward contribution pricing, whereby charges for searching will increase and cataloging will be rewarded with credits. OCLC Vice-President Tom Sanville stated that this change is consistent with the promotion of a national database.[51] It is hoped that the change and RLG's plans will indeed lead at least to a merger of the OCLC and

RLIN databases, preferably to a merger of all bibliographic databases in the United States, including that of the Library of Congress, and finally to the fullest possible level of online cooperation. To quote Barbara Markuson and Henriette Avram regarding the development of a nationwide network, "Can we get on with it?"[52]

REFERENCES

1. Carolyn Havens, "The Networks Merger and Serials Control," *The Serials Librarian* 14, nos. 1/2 (1988): 33-40.

2. Henriette D. Avram, "The Linked Systems Project: Its Implications for Resource Sharing," *Collection Management* 9, no. 1/2 (summer/fall, 1987): 39.

3. Richard F. McCoy, "RLG in a Nationwide Network," *Toward a Common Vision of Library Networking: Proceedings of the Library of Congress Network Advisory Committee Meeting, December 9-11, 1985. Network Planning Paper* no. 13. (Washington, D.C.: Network Development MARC Standards Office, Library of Congress, 1986): 31-33.

4. Avram, "The Linked Systems Project," p. 39-54.

5. Ibid., p. 39-40.

6. Ibid., p. 42.

7. Sally H. McCallum, "Linked Systems Project in the United States," *IFLA Journal* 11, no. 4 (1985): 313-323.

8. S. Michael Malinconico, "Bibliographic Data Base Organization and Authority File Control," in *Authority Control: The Key to Tommorrow's Catalog; Proceedings of the 1979 Library and Information Technology Association Institutes.* (New York: Oryx Press, 1982): 1-18.

9. Henriette D. Avram, "Authority Control and Its Place," *Journal of Academic Librarianship* 9, no. 6 (Jan. 1984): 331-335.

10. Larry Auld, "Authority Control: An Eighty Year Review," *Library Resources & Technical Services* 26, no. 4 (Oct./Dec. 1982): 319-330.

11. Arlene G. Taylor, "Authority Files in Online Catalogs: An Investigation of Their Value," *Cataloging & Classification Quarterly* 4, no. 3 (spring 1984): 1-17.

12. Avram, "The Linked Systems Project," p. 47.

13. McCallum, "Linked Systems Project in the United States," p. 314.

14. Doris H. Clack, "Authority Control and Linked Bibliographic Databases," *Cataloging & Classification Quarterly* 8, no. 3/4 (1988): 35-46.

15. Avram, "The Linked Systems Project," p. 44.

16. Michael J. McGill, Larry L. Learn, and Thomas K.G. Lydon, "A Technical Evaluation of the Linked Systems Project Protocols in the Name Authority Distribution Application," *Information Technology and Libraries* 6, no. 4 (Dec. 1987): 253-265.

17. Wayne E. Davison, "The WLN/RLG/LC Linked Systems Project," *Information Technology and Libraries* 2, no. 1 (Mar. 1983): 34-46.

18. Henriette D. Avram, "Toward a Nationwide Library Network," *Journal of Library Administration* 8, no. 3/4 (1987): 95-116.

19. Avram, "The Linked Systems Project," p. 47.

20. Sally H. McCallum, "Linked Systems Project, Part 1: Authorities Implementation," *Library Hi Tech* 3, no. 2 (1985): 66.

21. Sally H. McCallum, "Linked Systems Project in the United States," p. 319.

22. Ibid.

23. Henriette D. Avram, "Retrospective Conversion: A National Viewpoint," *IFLA Journal* 16, no. 1 (1990): 55.

24. Avram, "Toward a Nationwide Library Network," p. 111.

25. Virginia Gillham and Margaret Beckman, "Individual Autonomy and Successful Networking: A Canadian Experience," in *New Horizons for Academic Libraries* (New York: K. G. Saur, 1979): 291-295.

26. Barbara E. Markuson, "Revolution and Evolution: Critical Issues in Library Network Development," in *Networks for Networkers*, Blanche Woods and Barbara Markuson (eds.). (New York: Neal Schuman Press, 1980): 3-28.

27. McGill, Learn, and Lydon, "A Technical Evaluation of the Linked Systems Project Protocols in the Name Authority Distribution Application," p. 255.

28. Susan K. Martin, "Balancing Needs: The Ideal Network of the Future," *Journal of Library Administration* 8, no.3/4 (fall/winter 1987): 131-141.

29. Ibid., p. 132.

30. "OCLC to Acquire LSP Computer Equipment," *Wilson Library Bulletin* (Nov. 1984): 171.

31. S. Michael Malinconico, "The National Bibliographic Network: A Patrician Pursuit," *Library Journal* 105, no. 15 (Sept. 15, 1980): 1791-1792.

32. Ibid.

33. Ronald Segal, "Technical Considerations in Planning for a Nationwide Library Network," *Bulletin of the American Society for Information Science* 6, no. 5 (June 1980): 14.

34. Ibid., p. 15.

35. "OCLC to Acquire LSP Computer Equipment," p. 171.

36. Henriette D. Avram, "Toward a Nationwide Library Network," p. 104.

37. Michael K. Buckland and Clifford A. Lynch, "National and International Implications of the Linked Systems Protocol for Online Bibliographic Systems," *Cataloging & Classification Quarterly* 8, no. 3/4 (1988): 26.

38. McCallum, "Linked Systems Project in the United States," p. 322.

39. Segal, "Technical Considerations in Planning for a Nationwide Library Network," p. 14.

40. K.W. Humphreys, "The Principles of the Relationship between National and University Library Collections as a Basis for a Network," *IFLA Journal* 9, no. 1 (1983): 20-27.

41. Ibid., p. 21.

42. Buckland and Lynch, "National and International Implications of the Linked Systems Protocol for Online Bibliographic Systems," p. 26.

43. Ibid., p. 26-28.
44. Avram, "Toward a Nationwide Library Network," p. 106-107.
45. Buckland and Lynch, "National and International Implications of the Linked Systems Protocol for Online Bibliographic Systems," p. 26.
46. Ibid.
47. Avram, "Toward a Nationwide Library Network," p. 105.
48. Buckland and Lynch, "National and International Implications of the Linked Systems Protocol for Online Bibliographic Systems," p. 26.
49. Ibid.
50. "News Fronts: Governing Board Directors RLG to Consider Big Changes," *American Libraries* 22, no. 4 (Apr. 1991): 278.
51. "News Fronts: Changes in OCLC Use Accelerate Changes in Pricing," *American Libraries* 22, no. 4 (Apr. 1991): 278.
52. Barbara E. Markuson, "Issues in National Library Network Development: An Overview" (paper presented to the Library of Congress Network Advisory Committee, May 1985), quoted by Avram, "Toward a Nationwide Library Network," p. 100.

ADDITIONAL SELECTIVE BIBLIOGRAPHY

"Agreement is Reached on LSP Priorities and Issues," *Library of Congress Information Bulletin.* 45 (Dec. 15, 1986), p. 403.

Avram, H.D. "Building a Unified Information Network," *EDUCOM Bulletin (US).* 23:4 (winter, 1988), pp. 11-14.

Besemer, S. "Criteria for the Evaluation of Library Networks," *Resource Sharing and Information Networks.* 4:1 (1987), pp. 17-38.

Billings, H. "Governing Library Networks: The Quick and the Dead for the 1990's," *Library Journal.* 114:18 (Nov. 1, 1989), pp. 49-54.

Boss, R.W. "Linked Systems and the Online Catalog: The Role of the OSI," *Library Resources and Technical Services.* 34 (Apr. 1990), pp. 217-228.

Brown, R.C.W. "Achievement, Potentialities and Limitations for Library Networking in Europe and North America," *Libri.* 39:3 (Sept. 1989). pp. 192-200.

Brown, R.C.W. "The Nationwide Network and OCLC: A Vision and a Role," *Toward a Common Vision of Library Networking: Proceedings of the Library of Congress Network Advisory Committee Meeting, December 9-11, 1985. Network Planning Paper* no. 13. Washington, D.C.: Network Development MARC Standards Office Library of Congress (1986), pp. 19-28.

Bruntjen, S. "The Political, Economic and Technological Roots of Some Legal Issues in Library Networking," *Journal of Library Administration.* 3:2 (summer, 1983), pp. 15-28.

Coyne, F.H. "Automated Authorities Maintenance at the Western Library Network," *Technical Services Quarterly,* 5:1 (1987), pp. 33-48.

Cugnet, C. "Networking in Transition: Current and Future Issues," *Library Hi Tech.* 6:4 (1988), pp. 101-118.

DeGennaro, R. "Library Automation and Networking: Perspectives on 3 Decades," *Library Journal.* 108:7 (Apr. 1, 1983), pp. 629-635.

Denenberg, R. "Open Systems Interconnection: The Linked Systems Project and Linking Libraries in New York State," *Bookmark.* 46 (winter, 1988), pp. 104-108.

Denenberg, R. "Linked Systems Project, Part 2: Standard Network Interconnection, *Library Hi Tech.* no. 2 (1985), pp. 71-79.

Denenberg, R. "The LSP/SNI Test Facility," *Library Hi Tech.* 13:4,1 (spring 1986), pp. 41-49.

Gapen, D.K. "Strategies for Networking in the Next 10 Years," *Journal of Library Administration.* 8:3-4 (fall-winter, 1987), pp. 117-130.

Gregor, D. "LSP: Implications for Our Libraries," in *ARL Conference Proceedings* (112th: 1988), ARL: Setting the Agenda for the 1990s. Washington, D.C. : Association of Research Libraries, (1989), pp. 33-37.

Hildreth, C. "Library Networks and Bibliographic Utilities: Major Organizations, Systems and Participants," in *Library Automation in North America: A Reassessment of the New Technologies on Networking.* New York: K.G. Saur (1987), pp. 35-123.

Hildreth, C. "Library Networking in North American in the 1980's Part I: The Dreams, the Realities," *Electronic Library* 5:4 (Aug. 1987), pp. 222-228.

Hoadley, I.B. "The Future of Networks and OCLC," *Journal of Library Administration.* 8:3-4 (fall-winter 1987), pp. 85-91.

"Implementation of the Linked Systems Project: A Technical Report," *Library Hi Tech.* 11 (1985), pp. 87-107.

Jacob, M.E.L. "Networking Priorities for Standards Development," *Information Technology and Libraries.* 4:4 (Dec. 1985), pp. 361-362.

Library of Congress. "Nationwide Network: Which Scenario is Best? *ASIS Bulletin.* 7 (Aug. 1981), pp. 17-19.

"Library of Congress and Research Libraries Group get Linked Systems Project Up and Running," *Library of Congress Information Bulletin.* 44 (Oct. 28, 1985), pp. 305-306.

McCoy, R.W. "The Linked Systems Project: Progress, Promise, Reality," *Library Journal.* 111:16 (Oct. 1, 1986), pp. 33-39.

Martin, S.K. "Library Networks: Trends and Issues," *Journal of Library Administration.* 8:2 (summer, 1987), pp. 27-34.

Martin, S.K. "Technology and Cooperation: The Behaviors of Networking," *Library Journal.* 112:16 (Oct. 1987), pp. 42-44.

Maruyama, L.S. "Nationwide Networking and Network Advisory Committee," in *The Management of Serials Automation: Current Technology and Strategies for Future Planning*, edited by Peter Gellatly. New York: The Haworth Press, Inc. (1984), pp. 245-256.

Morris, L.R. "Network Prices: Let the Buyer Beware," *Technical Services Quarterly.* 4:4 (summer, 1987), pp. 57-66.

"NACO is Enhanced by OCLC Implementation of the LSP," *Library of Congress Information Bulletin.* 46 (June 15, 1987), p. 254+

"NACO/LSP Contribution Begins at Yale," *Library of Congress Information Bulletin.* 46 (Oct. 12, 1987), pp. 438-439.

"NACO/LSP Success Continues: OCLC Contribution Begins," *Library of Congress Information Bulletin.* 47 (Jul. 11, 1988), p. 290.

"Online Contribution of Authority Records Expands via Linked Systems Project," *Library of Congress Information Bulletin.* 48 (Oct. 2, 1989), pp. 346-347.

Preston, W.R. "Library Networking: Regional, National, International: A Selected Bibliography," *Educational Libraries.* 14:3 (fall, 1989), pp. 118-120.

Rogers, J.V. "Networking: Selected Research Studies, 1979-1983," *Library and Information Science Research.* 6:2 (Apr. 1984), pp. 111-132.

Rosenberg, V. "Potential National Library Networks," in *The Transfer of Scholarly, Scientific and Technical Information Between North and South America.* Metuchen, N.J: Scarecrow Press (1986), pp. 489-530.

Schuman, P.G. "Library Networks: A Means, Not an End," *Library Journal* 112:2 (Feb. 1,1987), pp. 33-37.

Segal, J.A.S. "Networking and Decentralization," *Annual Review of Information Science & Technology.* 20 (1985), pp. 203-232.

Selig, G. "Planning Strategies for a Brave New World of Networks," *Data Communications (U.S.)* (Mar. 1984), pp. 139-148.

"Serial Record Division Celebrates 1st Anniversary as LSP Participant," *Library of Congress Information Bulletin.* 48 (Oct. 23, 1989), pp. 376-377.

Stozik, T. "The Linked Systems Project," *Bookmark.* 46 (winter, 1988), pp. 113-119.

Wood, J.L. "Factors Influencing the Use of Technical Standards in a Nationwide Library and Information Service Network," *Library Trends.* 31 (fall, 1982), pp. 343-358.

Ziegman, B.N. "WLN's Database: New Directions," *Cataloging & Classification Quarterly.* 8:3-4 (1988), pp. 101-109.

The Role of the Name Main-Entry Heading in the Online Environment

Olivia M. A. Madison

SUMMARY. The name main-entry heading has been a source of controversy throughout the history of Anglo-American cataloging with debate being closely tied to author identification. It is not surprising that debate has gained momentum as the functionality of online library catalogs and the costs of cataloging are under increasing close scrutiny. Following an historical overview of the name or author main-entry heading, this article discusses the finding and identifying functions of online catalogs as they relate to authorship. The article concludes that the name main-entry heading is an essential component of online catalog citation displays through which catalog users decide the usefulness of retrieved cataloging records.

INTRODUCTION

The controversy surrounding the name main-entry heading (coupled with the concept of authorship) has a long history in Anglo-American cataloging. During the twentieth century the debate relating to the necessity and value of the cataloging main-entry heading has been intertwined with the purposes of the cataloging record as expressed through the main entry. Respected leaders in the international cataloging community have participated within these debates, culminating in the publication and

---

Olivia M. A. Madison is an Associate Professor, Assistant Director for Public Services and formerly Head of the Cataloging Department at Iowa State University Library, Ames, IA 50011-2140. She currently represents the United States on the Standing Committee on Cataloguing, International Federation of Library Associations and Institutions.

acceptance of the *Anglo-American Cataloguing Rules*, Second Edition (*AACR2*). There was substantial and heated national debate over the main-entry heading during *AACR2*'s evolution, centering on the abandonment of the name main-entry heading. The corporate body main-entry heading was particularly targeted. The debate has again emerged, now within the new environment of online public catalogs with its democratization of access.

While the Preface of *AACR2* states that "the single most important contribution of this edition to meet the needs of machine processing resides . . . in . . . systematic description of all library materials, as presented in Part I," *AACR2*'s critics state that it pays little attention to entry access in machine processing and, in particular, the practical need for the main-entry heading within the online environment.[1] While the debate over the need for the main-entry heading has now been coupled with the democratization of access through the online automation of our local card catalogs, the arguments supporting its discontinuance are just as applicable to card catalogs, book catalogs, and microform/microfiche catalogs. Quite simply, the ultimate question was and still remains: what is the purpose of the name main-entry heading and is it worth the cataloging effort and expense?

The purpose of this article is to explore the issues relating to the name main-entry heading in the powerful environment of online library catalogs. This article will begin by defining the terms main entry, main-entry heading and author. Next, it will review the historical background of the concept of authorship within the main-entry heading and the criticism it provoked during the mid- and late-twentieth century. The functionality of online catalogs as it relates to finding and identifying specific library holdings will then be examined as those two functions relate to the name main-entry heading. The article will then assert that the name main-entry heading is an essential component of online catalog record displays by which catalog users determine the usefulness of retrieved records and will conclude with recommendations as to its continuing role within the online environment.

DEFINITIONS

Often the main-entry heading is casually referred to as the main entry. However, the term "main-entry heading" has a distinct definition to that of the main entry. Within the *Anglo-American Cataloging Rules*, Second Edition Revised (*AACR2 Revised*), the term "main entry" refers to the "complete catalogue record of an item, presented in the form by which the entity is to be uniformly identified and cited. The main entry may include the tracing(s) . . .'[2] In terms of online catalog displays, the main entry is often the same as what is referred to as the full public display, although usually call numbers, subject headings and library holdings are also included in such displays. The term "main-entry heading" is used when *AACR2 Revised* differentiates between the main-entry heading and all other entry headings, which are referred to as added entry headings.[3] A main-entry heading may consist of a title main-entry heading, uniform-title main-entry heading, personal name main-entry heading or a corporate-body name main-entry heading. When one refers to a personal-name main entry or a corporate-body name main entry, the underlying assumption is that this entry is generally considered the "author" of the work. Obviously, this is not the case for the title main entry or a uniform-title main entry, where the implication is that any entry for a personal name, corporate-body name or additional title would be relegated to the status of an added or secondary entry. The *Anglo-American Cataloging Rules* (*AACR*) states that an author could be either a person or corporate body and is "chiefly responsible for the creation of the intellectual or artistic content of a work . . .'[4] *AACR2*, by retaining the concepts of personal and corporate body name main entries, retained in general terms the notion of authorship. However, *AACR2* abandoned the concept of a corporate body author, and instead stated that corporate bodies emanate works, they do not author them. Its "Glossary" only has one author entry, that for personal author, which reads:

> The person chiefly responsible for the creation of the intellectual or artistic content of a work.[5]

AACR2 limited occurrences of personal authorship by eliminating certain classes of authors, such as editors and compilers, which were mandated in *AACR*. *AACR2*'s definition of corporate-body name main entry now only resides in Chapter 21:

> A corporate body is an organization or group of persons that is identified by a particular name and that acts, or may act, as an entity . . . Some corporate bodies are subordinate to other bodies . . . . Consider ad hoc events . . . and vessels . . . to be corporate bodies. . . . Consider a work to emanate from a corporate body if it is issued by that body or has been caused to be issued by that body or if it originated with that body.[6]

AACR2 Revised's Chapter 21 goes on to state those specific circumstances when a work may be entered under a corporate body name main entry, and instances of such entry are greatly restricted from the criteria found in *AACR*.

For the purposes of this article, the term name main-entry heading refers to both personal name and corporate-body name main-entry headings. In addition, the terms "author" and "authorship" will refer to both personal authorship and corporate body emanation (my apologies to the strict interpreters of *AACR2 Revised*). By these definitions then, the discontinuance of the name main-entry heading would then mean the discontinuance of the fundamental concept of general authorship contained within the Anglo-American cataloging tradition. Without a personal author or corporate body emanator, the remaining descriptive "title" heading would become the initial component of the title main entry or what Elizabeth L. Tate and others have referred to as the "Title Unit Entry."[7]

HISTORICAL BACKGROUND

Over the centuries, "library catalogs" have evolved from inventory lists (functionally analogous to libraries' shelf list files) to finding lists that recognize personal corporate body authorship. Ultimately, catalogs have served as finding lists as well as provided what has been termed a literary function. As the library profession debates the continuance of the name main-entry heading, ultimately it is debating whether or not to continue the concept of authorship as it is clearly identified within the cataloging record and used within the citation process.

AACR2 took a controversial position by limiting the instances of when authorship may be recognized. With its qualified definition that personal authors must be "chiefly responsible," it relegated individuals serving as editors and compilers to the status of added entries.[8] As mentioned above, the occurrence of corporate body authors, now emanators, is severely limited, which has had a major impact on the entry of serials and led to the increased use of serial uniform titles. In the future, will *AACR2 Revised* be remembered as merely the transition leading to powerful online catalogs, which will provide access to a vast array of equal access points? Was the early term "OPAC" (i.e., online public access catalog) a prophecy of what was to become a strict functional description of their evolution?

Dorothy Gregor and Carol Mandel, in their recent article on why and how cataloging must change (published in the April 1991 issue of *Li-*

brary Journal), state "it is no doubt valuable to have an easy way of ordering bibliographic records on the online catalog screen or in printouts for bibliographies, but it is not necessary to invest time in the choice of which access point will serve the "main" function of entry that will be used. For access purposes, it does not matter.'[9] Gregor's and Mandel's recommendation to discontinue the use of the main-entry headings in favor of reliance on equal access entry points is not new. Under the leadership of Charles Coffin Jewett and the influential Charles Ammi Cutter, author main-entry headings gained widespread acceptance in the United States in the last century. Internationally, this was not always the case. The unquestioned acceptance of authorship was not necessarily the norm in early twentieth-century Europe, particularly in Germany and in Scandinavia, nor in Japan or the Middle East. In 1935 in the United States, J. C. M. Hanson questioned the widespread usage of corporate body main-entry headings.[10] Julia Pettee's landmark 1936 article, "The Development of Authorship Entry and the Formulation of Authorship Rules As Found in the Anglo-American Code," strongly supported the primacy of the authorship concept.[11] In this article she suggests that two fundamental principles of the Anglo-American code bear upon the discussion of the authorship entry:

1. The book in hand is "a representative of a literary unit" and the catalog's function is to "assemble these literary units, issued in various forms, under a single caption" and therefore
2. The "attribution of authorship, or the substitution of a conventional form in lieu of author, is the quickest and surest way to assemble those units."[12]

Pettee concluded that while these two principles had not obtained international acceptance, library catalogs evolved from finding lists to that of incorporating the functions of assembling "under convenient headings all issues or forms of the same literary unit."[13] The convenient headings, Pettee goes on to state, are most satisfactorily created through the "attribution of authorship, using as the heading the name of the person, or corporate body responsible for the work, or using as a substitute for author heading, a conventional name not derived from the title-page but from the literary source of the book or document."[14] Furthermore, she urged the adherence to a narrow interpretation of authorship and advocated the cessation of form headings such as Congregationalists, Baptists and Mormons, Liturgy and Ritual as authors. Ultimately, the historical functions of library catalogs that Ms. Pettee identified defined the fundamental debate over the theoretical purposes of library catalogs and, in particular, the function of and need for the main-entry heading as the initial component of the main entry.

As Tate so carefully describes in her article "Examining the "Main" in Main Entry Headings," both international and national debate concerning the main-entry heading continued through the 1940s, 1950s and 1960s.[15] In 1961, the now famous International Conference on Cataloguing Principles was held in Paris at which a set of internationally-accepted cataloging principles were approved. These principles, commonly referred to as the "Paris Principles of 1961," represented a monumental international achievement, and they provided the theoretical foundation of two subsequent Anglo-American cataloging codes. Of particular interest to the purposes of this article are the principles' stated two functions of the catalog:

> The catalogue should be an efficient instrument for ascertaining
> 2.1 whether the library contains a particular book specified by
> (a) its author and title, or
> (b) if the author is not named in the book, its title alone, or
> (c) if author and title are inappropriate or insufficient for identification, a suitable substitute for the title; and
> 2.2 (a) which works by a particular author and
> (b) which editions of a particular work are in the library.[16]

With these internationally-accepted principles came the reinforcement of the concept of author, albeit with no definition or required placement within the descriptive record. However, the necessity of author identification continued to be questioned routinely within library literature. In 1964, Wesley Simonton advocated dropping the distinction between main and added entries and depending on the computer to assist the user in identification.[17] A decade later, in 1973, M. Nabil Hamdy advocated dropping the main-entry heading and establishing a title-unit entry to which would be attached name and title access points and subject headings.[18] At a conference held in 1976, Doralyn J. Hickey recommended that "the concept of 'main entry' and 'author entry' versus 'secondary entries' should give way to a sophisticated analysis of desirable access points to the bibliographic record. Common inquiry patterns of users should be investigated in order to design systems which will respond to those inquiries effectively."[19] In 1979, at an international conference on *AACR2*, Michael Gorman questioned the necessity of the main entry and stated that "the important functions of the main entry can be carried out in a non-main-entry catalog or data base.''[20] Then in 1983, Patrick Wilson challenged the need for identification of authorship and stated: ''A bibliographical record might now simply contain a title-page transcription, and the proper names contained in that transcription made searchable; this might easily be done without taking any position on the question of whether a name is the name of the author.''[21] He then queried ''what difference would it make'' if the identification of authorship was abandoned.[22] Michael Carpenter in 1989 promoted the general usefulness of the main entry, however in a different context. He suggested that displays could show any variant citation and should be dependent on the forms of headings searched and not on the authenticated or ''controlled'' forms.[23] Also in 1989 Arnold Wajenberg proposed maintaining the concept of authorship but with a limited definition. He preferred not to regard corporate bodies as authors.[24] Thus the debate has continued, with strongly-voiced positions taken on both sides of the authorship question. The question remains the same, although recast in the online environment: What purpose does the name main-heading entry serve?

ROLE OF THE NAME MAIN-ENTRY HEADING IN AN ONLINE ENVIRONMENT

As did their time-honored predecessors, the online library catalog has the same two primary functions as those identified in both the Paris Principles of 1961 and those stated by Charles A. Cutter nearly sixty years before.[25] First, the access provided by an online catalog enables a person to find a book held by a library of which the author, title, and/or subject is known. Second, the online catalog should identify all works by a given author, as well as which editions of a given work are held. At the time of *AACR2*'s publication in 1978, it would have been difficult to appreciate fully the future capabilities of online library catalogs. While I contend that these two functions remain central to the role of the online catalog, the implications of what they mean in today's automated environment have been expanded extensively.

1. Finding or Access Function

First, the definition of what is meant by ''held by the library'' has been transformed to include not only what is physically held within the library, but also what the library may be able to obtain through resource sharing. Through a single computer terminal, a library may now provide access not only to its collections but to the collections of other libraries, using the searching capabilities of one's local online catalog or local online union catalog. Access may also be provided by searching the database of a bibliographic utility, such as OCLC, or another library's online catalog through dial access capabilities. The material found through this expanded access may be another library's copy of a monograph that is sent through the U. S. Mail, or a "fax" of an article contained in a journal held by another library. In the near future, it will be common to obtain material contained in full-text online data bases. As a result, online catalogs now have the capacity to employ a dazzling array of methods to "find" a book by author, title or subject. Boolean operators and keyword searching can provide unbelievably precise strategies to find materials. Using the information stored in the fixed fields of the MARC communications format, retrieved data may far exceed that found through traditional access points. Catalog searches qualified by language, format (such as serial or computer file), government publication, etc., are now commonplace. The searching capabilities of the descriptive areas of cataloging records, such as content or summary notes, author statements, and publisher statements have been greatly expanded.

Within many online catalogs the distinction between bibliographic description and controlled name, title and subject access has evaporated, particularly in keyword searching. Unfortunately, as competitors rush to "bring up" keyword searching capabilities, searches may yield a frustrating assortment of unrelated and unexpected results, the outcome of poorly-conceived system index structures. For example, if the entire 245 title field is included in a keyword title index, the information contained in the statement of responsibility will then be indexed within keyword title searches because that information is contained in the "245" title field. Another problematic descriptive variable field is the contents note, represented in the 505 variable field. This note may contain both author and title information, and when it is indexed as part of the keyword title searching structure similar confusing results may occur when author information is indexed as well as the title information.

Clearly the access capabilities of online library systems are extremely powerful and exciting, particularly because descriptive information never before indexed is now capable of being searched. When general keyword indexes are constructed for purely descriptive information mixed blessings occur. For example, a card catalog user interested in finding films starring Rita Hayworth would have been frustrated had the actress' name not appeared as an added name entry. In an online search, if Hayworth's name appeared only in the credits notes of these film records, the user could retrieve them, provided these notes were indexed. However this extensive access capability may also result in "information overload," with thousands of search results listed in arbitrary group list displays. When individual records are examined, it can be baffling to understand why some records have been retrieved.

2. Collocation Function

The results of such powerful access may have the inevitable potential of creating havoc with the second function of online catalogs, that of collocation: defining what a library holds or may obtain from other libraries. While *AACR2 Revised* does not mandate that all works of a given author be entered under one form of heading (particularly because it calls for separate headings for those authors having separate bibliographic identities or for authors who publish under more than one name), it does mandate that reference structures be created to link related headings. Collocation provides organization to what might otherwise be random bibliographic chaos. Indexing "uncontrolled" bibliographic description as described above also produces chaos. Quite simply, the forms of names and series appearing in bibliographic descriptions do not always correlate with the controlled headings. The results of such conflicts are the unintentional creation of separate index files for the same individuals or corporate bodies and increased dependency on authority control systems to create bibliographic order.

Given the described implications of automated library holdings catalogs, what is the role of the name main-entry heading? The name main-entry heading serves two important functions: first, as a controlled access point and, second, as a primary component of the identifying citation of an individual work.

Controlled Access Point

One major role of the name main-entry heading is to serve as one of a group of controlled entry points. Those individuals who support discontinuance of the name main-entry heading believe it to be unnecessary because most online catalogs have indexing structures which treat all controlled access points equally, whether they are tagged as MARC 100/110/111/130 or 700/710/711/730 variable fields. The effect of this democratization of access infers that all access points are equal. In essence, there are no major or minor entries in terms of online retrieval. Gorman stated it straightforwardly: "for general purposes, all entries will be main entries.''[26] He could have also referred to all entries as added entries, or simply access points. By discontinuing the implicit identification of the main-entry heading, the process of descriptive cataloging could be simplified and thus made less expensive. While the unique tagging of the main-entry heading within the MARC formats allows this heading to be stored in a different online catalog index pointer than it would as an added-entry heading, for the purposes of strict access there does not appear to be any compelling reason to differentiate the two.

Author Within Cataloging Citation Practices

A second and unique role of the main-entry heading is to indicate within the main entry whether or not there is an ''author.'' In doing so, the main-entry heading provides an important component of formal bibliographic identification for the work, or its citation.[27] The rules for identifying name main-entry headings are complex and equally so are those rules surrounding forms of entry and reference structures. If no ''author'' is identified, then *AACR2 Revised* dictates that the main-entry heading becomes either the title proper (the ''descriptive'' title) or a uniform title heading. While a portion of the library community may be ready to discontinue the traditional citation practice of author/title as expressed through the main entry, I do not believe the users of library catalogs are quite ready. Cataloging citation practices of library catalogs provide the crucial identification of works and the means by which those works may be bibliographically linked. In addition, this citation methodology mirrors, sometimes imperfectly, the citation practices of commercial bibliographic agencies and general citation practices used within academic and popular literature.

Within descriptive cataloging practices, what are often referred to as linking notes to other editions and the resulting access points are crucial to the function of identifying other editions a library may hold of a given work. In addition, they are essential in describing and providing access between related works. Without the author component of many such free text citations and resulting entry points, the bibliographic displays may be quite useless in enabling the user to identify the relevance of individual linking works. Moreover, additional successful searches based upon title-based linking notes may be equally difficult to construct. There are many ways to construct access points based upon linking notes that enable unique search results. For example, if title-unit entry were to be used, one could qualify the title with a unique identifier such as a system record number, an OCLC record number, an ISSN or an ISBN. However, a displayed title qualified by an ISBN number is certainly unique as an access point, but it does not provide an intellectually recognizable citation. If a work is clearly a product of personal author or corporate body, is this the most identifiable citation within a linking note? Again, as stated above, access is not at issue, but rather how catalogers should provide intellectually recognizable linking notes and citation-based access points.

The users of our libraries do not work in a bibliographic vacuum composed of solely library online holdings catalogs. Commercial indexing and abstracting agencies and the commercial acquisitions community provide critically-needed citations, which then may become the citation forms used to search for library holdings. In addition, citation practices for scholarly and popular literature provide the basis for a large number of other known searches. While the majority of these agencies and literary citation practices agree on general concepts for the desirability of authorship, they do not necessarily agree on the detailed criteria for its recognition. However, it is now common for library catalog users to refer back and forth among these bibliographic sources and some general common practices should be expected.

The expectations of compatibility are growing exponentially between indexing and abstracting agencies and their cataloging rule counterparts as users are now independently searching these data bases, whether on CD-ROM or as data bases accessed through local library online systems. Sophisticated linking between online data bases will become commonplace in the future, with some libraries already in the process of implementing holdings linkages between locally-loaded indexing and abstracting databases and local library holdings. The task for complete compatibility is impossible among the services, much less between citation standards and current cataloging practices. It is not uncommon for an indexing agency to use different criteria to determine serial entry changes from cataloging rules, thus making linkages difficult. As Anne B. Piternick noted in her article dealing with the subject of authorship and responsibility in indexing and abstracting services, authorship practices differ among the services.[28] This is in part due to their differing biases toward the role of titles and subject access, but also to citation practices for diffuse authorship. Piternick also states that there appears to be a growing interest within the academic editorial community to define authorship more closely. She cites an editorial published in 1982 which suggests that:

4. An author should have taken part in the writing of the paper.
5. An author should have read the entire contents of a paper and assented to its publication before it is sent to a journal (*Annals of Internal Medicine* 97 (Oct.1982) 613-614.[29]

This call for more narrowly defined authorship echoes Pettee's earlier advice to the cataloging code revisers and parallels the general intent of *AACR2*.

Last, but perhaps most importantly, is the use of the main entry citation within the various index displays and cataloging record displays in online catalogs. Given the dramatic increase in records retrieved from the myriad of access points in online catalogs, citation displays based upon main entries must be as forthright and descriptively useful as possible. It is vital that the various displays provide adequate information for the user to quickly and easily decide on the usefulness of the records retrieved. In what has been its strength as well as its weakness, the MARC Format's variable fields closely mirror the card print format. Within the format, the main-entry heading is uniquely identified as opposed to other access points and description. Consequently, displays generated from the format allow authors to be associated with their respective titles. If more than one record is retrieved with any given search, a truncated display of all retrieved records is often provided. Two common display formats are: a brief one- or two-line listing of all matching entries with some additional identifier, or a brief record citation containing such information as author, title, edition, call number and holdings information. The order of arrangement of displays also varies: alphabetical by the matched entry, by publication date, or even in order of addition to the data base. Whatever the display order, it is important for each citation to provide appropriate information so that the user may quickly and competently identify it. In particular, the user should not have to routinely switch to full displays of numerous records to ascertain what is of interest. In addition, once a single bibliographic record is retrieved, whether in brief or full display, the display of the cataloging record with its corresponding call number and holdings information must be arranged so as to quickly provide identification of the work. In the card catalog format, the access point is often printed over a copy of the main entry card. It is just as important, if not more so, within the online environment, to provide brief cataloging displays which can quickly identify the work. Once a full record is retrieved, all access points should be displayed in order to help the user understand why the specific record was retrieved. The listing of all access points is particularly critical with keyword searching because of the unpredictability of searching results.

In addition to the various cataloging displays, automated library systems now provide numerous inter-dependent functions, which often display brief citations obtained from the cataloging records. Staff and library users accessing acquisitions, serials control, holdings, and circulation records must be able to quickly decide whether or not a given record's citation display represents the record needed. While access to these types of system records is often through standard number searches and machine-readable data such as barcodes, displays help mere humans verify records. Without a clear abbreviated identification of the work, the user must return to the full cataloging record.

The majority of the above-mentioned problems related to display and collation of a main-entry heading free catalog have been addressed by the critics of the name main-entry heading. The alternatives the critics suggest involve either using the statement of responsibility, or giving what would have been the name main-entry heading as the first access point and coupling it with the title. The use of the title page's statement of responsibility is problematic: layout of the author's name is not always straightforward. Publishers are not consistent in terms of order of layout of such information. In addition there is no guarantee that the "author" will even appear on the title page. Surely library users should be assured of consistency of such information in online catalog's displays. The solution most often discussed is that of placing the "author" as the first tracing, and using that entry in the needed displays as well as for the construction of book numbering in call numbers. By indiscriminately using the first access point in such a primary function gives that access point two different functions: one of authorship and the other of access. In many cases there would only be one heading tracing that would represent the author. There are other cases when the only name access point would not correspond to the author, thus causing confusion within the identification process. When there are multiple name access points, one heading would have to be chosen as the first, thereby constituting nothing more than a selection of a main-entry heading.

There is no doubt that cataloging costs are high and rising, and represent a major percentage of processing costs within technical services. Therefore, concerns over justifying the amount of the time spent in the cataloging process are legitimate. Certainly the value of the effort expended in determining main-entry headings must and should be questioned. However, the author coupled with title continues to serve as the most recognizable method of identifying cataloged works through the varying displays generated from online library catalog systems. There is no doubt that many problems surround the attribution of personal and corporate body authorship, but deleting authorship as a prominent part of the citation process would only create greater confusion with catalog organization. Below are given a few random observations relating to authorship and citation display.

Personal Authorship

The vast majority of decisions over personal name main-entry headings are straightforward and require little more effort than transcribing title page information. Generally there are one or two authors given in a simple arrangement on the title page following the title. This is assuming there is a title page on a printed page, or that it is reproduced or represented in some capacity in microfiche, microfilm, a computer file, etc. These bibliographic situations parallel the general assumptions regarding authorship. However, as any cataloger knows, there are many ambiguous situations, some of which the cataloging rules cover and others which they do not. There are indeed cataloging situations in which significant time and effort may be expended on behalf of the main-entry heading. They usually involve situations of unknown responsibility, shared responsibility, and mixed or diffuse responsibility. Depending on the material involved, different solutions regarding authorship become appropriate. Arnold Wajenberg[30] and Michael Carpenter[31] have done excellent work in describing such situations. Wajenberg noted specifically the difficulties associated with translations and those works, such as technical reports, motion pictures and operas, where usually there are many different bibliographical "functionaries."[32] He also included an example of a new authorship problem, works "written" by a computer program named Racter, which had been brought to the cataloging community's attention by Meredith Merritt.[33]

There is no doubt that once one leaves the bibliographic world of one personal author, complexities abound. The major issue for the future rests with whether or not *AACR2 Revised*, with its definition of personal name main-entry heading, achieves the goal of creating online catalog displays that clearly identify and cite works as expected by the catalog users. Alternately, would title entry based displays provide adequate identification? Below are a few examples involving the various types of responsibility indicated in *AACR2 Revised* which require a personal name main-entry heading. The title entry or entries are first given followed by the *AACR2 Revised* citation(s).

A. Old English furniture.
Old English furniture.

AACR2 Revised's entries:
Fenn, Frederick. Old English furniture.
Hughes, Therle. Old English furniture.

Note: These two works with the same title are not different editions of the same work. Without the personal name main-entry headings it would be impossible to identify the appropriate work through this display. Even if the publication date or publisher were added, the display would be problematic.

B. Boutell's manual of heraldry.

AACR2 Revised

Wheeler-Holohan, V. Boutell's manual of heraldry.

Note: While Charles Boutell wrote the original manual of heraldry, following his death, Mr. Wheeler-Holohan wrote a later edition. By entering the work under Wheeler-Holohan the work is differentiated from the edition that Boutell actually wrote. Without the personal name main-entry heading, the display would leave one to conclude that the displayed work was the original edition written by Boutell.

C. The Secret garden.

AACR2 Revised

Howe, James. The secret garden.

Note: James Howe rewrote Frances Hodgson Burnett's *The secret garden* for young readers. Without the personal name main-entry heading, the user might assume the display indicates the original work.

Corporate Authorship

AACR2 Revised certainly took major steps by discontinuing the strict notion of corporate authorship and severely restricting those instances when works emanate from them. Therefore far fewer main-entry headings are created. The six categories which allow a corporate body main-entry heading briefly include: (1) those of an administrative nature dealing with the corporate body itself; (2) some legal, governmental, and religious works; (3) those that record the collective thought of the body; (4) those that report the collective activity of a conference; (5) those that result from the collective activity of a performing group as a whole where the responsibility of the group goes beyond that of mere performance, execution, etc.; and (6) cartographic materials emanating from a corporate body other than a publisher or distributor.[34] Thus, *AACR2 Revised* bases the decision on whether or not to create a main-entry heading for a corporate body on the form of publication, not on any particular theoretical basis. Practically, the categories generally represent those instances of corporate body responsibility in which a heading would be linked to a generic title to provide adequate identification. For the sake of example, two such potentially generic title situations are annual reports and conference proceedings. While some conference proceedings include the name of the conference as part of the title proper or within the statement of responsibility, others do not and only contain the title "Proceedings." Also problematic are annual reports for the same reasons.

Examples of a title entry without the corporate body main-entry heading as opposed to the *AACR2* form of entry would be:

A. Institute report for . . .

AACR2 Revised:
Glasshouse Crops Research Institute (Littlehampton, England)
Institute report for . . .

B. Autumn statement.

AACR2 Revised:
Great Britain. Treasury.
Autumn statement.

C. Operations research proceedings.

AACR2 Revised:
Deutsche Gesellschaft fur Operations Research.
Jahrestagung.
Operations research proceedings.

D. Presentations at the . . . annual meeting.

AACR2 Revised:
National Association of Tax Administrators (U.S.).
Motor Fuel Tax Section. Meeting.
Presentations at the . . . annual meeting.

Without these personal and corporate body main-entry headings displayed in connection with their titles, all would be unidentifiable to users in short and brief displays. For the title entry displays, which would have contained personal name main-entry headings, to be in any way identifiable alone, the dates of publication would be necessary. However, for this type of title entry to be useful, the user must know the publication date. For the serial titles to be most meaningful they would need uniform heading titles containing corporate body headings. There is an obvious solution for both these inadequate monograph and serial displays: what would have been the personal or corporate body main-entry headings would serve as the first added entry of each record and be displayed in conjunction with the title. As stated above, for either solution, the cataloger would still need to spend the time and effort to decide on which name access point to use.

In light of the above, I suggest that the issue is not to discard the notion of main-entry heading, but rather to more closely understand and define what authorship should be. That is, tie the definition and use of authorship more closely to what would be "expected" within the confines of bibliographic identification, both for personal authorship and corporate body entries. While Chapter 21 is lengthy, the Anglo-American cataloging rules have organized the chapter into sections for the various general types of responsibilities, art, musical works, sound recordings, legal publications and religious publications. By doing so, the rules recognize variant conventions associated with these different types of materials, and have based solutions on the way individuals and corporate bodies are presented within the chief source of information.

Authorship in online catalogs should be tied to the usefulness of its organizational and identification functions. How is any work to be cited and identified? Furthermore, I believe that this is the practical "road" that *AACR2 Revised* built. Within all types of materials or fields of learning there are variances in how authorship is defined, and it has been historically important for catalogers to understand these conditions. For example, in motion pictures, titles are the generally accepted form of identification. There are no "authors." While an academician of film history may be particularly interested in the director, the public refers to films by title. In music, the uniform title coupled with composer provides the most pragmatic organization possible. However, an obvious area of variance between *AACR2 Revised* and some standard citation tools concerns editorship. Many of the standard citation practices suggest edited works be entered under the editors' names while *AACR2* mandates a title main-entry heading.

Within the context of material-based displays, I concur with Arnold Wajenberg's definition of authorship:

> An author of a work is a person identified as an author in items containing the work, and/or in secondary literature that mentions the work.[35]

Wajenberg's definition of authorship embodies the concept of attribution, a concept that *AACR2 Revised* embraced more fully with its revised rules for Chapter 21. These rules provide for entry under pseudonyms (e.g., Jean Plaidy, Victoria Holt, and Philippa Carr), bibliographic identities (e.g., Lewis Carroll and Charles L. Dodgson), and authors of revised works that still retain the original author's name in their titles. Wajenberg goes one step beyond using the work in hand as the sole source of information in establishing the "author" by advocating the use of secondary literature to attribute authorship when the work does not provide sufficient information.

CONCLUSION

Charles Cutter stated in 1904 that "the convenience of the public is always to be set before the ease of the cataloger," and thus provided the philosophical framework around which cataloging has grown.[36] To find materials conveniently the user of an online catalog must easily identify the displayed and cited works within cataloging records so as to judge their value to the user. It is becoming increasingly apparent that catalog users are quite content to use the most minimal displays imaginable to decide whether or not a displayed work fits the framework of the search completed. The results of a 1982 library catalog use study done at Bath University indicated that over 97% of the bibliographic needs of library staff and public catalog users are satisfied with what would be defined as a minimal-level record.[37] It is therefore paramount that before any decisions are made to change the name main-entry heading, it is vital to understand their consequences. Quite simply, the discontinuance of the name main-entry heading could result in dramatically abbreviated or confusing displays of cataloging records. It is crucial to the interests of catalog users that both catalog designers and catalogers study the impact of such a step carefully. There is no doubt that automation has created the most powerful access tool imaginable. Not only is the speed by which catalog users can search and find materials thousands of times quicker, but also users can create searching strategies that had been heretofore impossible. Probably such a leap in access functionally from our former catalogs (e.g., card catalogs, book catalogs, microfiche catalogs, etc.) to online catalogs will never again be matched. However, in twenty years library automated catalogs will no doubt contain new functions just as difficult to appreciate as those changes that have occurred during the past twenty years. No doubt the future of library automated systems is wondrous. The emphases will be on delivery of material, broader access to abstracting data and full-text data, and audio-driven access systems complementing key-stroke driven technology. However, ease of access coupled with precision and quick identification will grow in importance as the bibliographic universe increases.

The success of any library automated system depends on both its methods of access and also on its ability for system users to decide quickly if what they've found is useful. When searches are based on known items or authors, no matter how incomplete the search structure, it is mandatory that the information retrieved is easily understood and matched with what is wanted. The reasons for abandoning the name main-entry heading have everything to do with reducing cataloging costs and very little to do with improving the usefulness of online catalogs. Helen Schmierer has stated that "the library catalog is not a rude inventory of items; it is an organization of records designed to provide access to knowledge."[38] The loss of the name main-entry heading would affect the organization of our catalog records as well as the physical arrangement of library materials. The often-mentioned substitute for this identification is that of the first-named access point. If this change were made, decisions parallel to what are currently made regarding name main-entry heading would still need to be made. I concur with Wajenberg and Pettee that due to the central nature of authorship within citation practices, its definition needs to be continually refined. The issue is not whether an individual or a corporate body authored a work, but rather whether the presence or absence of the individual or corporate body seriously jeopardizes the identification of the work. Librarians must recognize that cataloging records do not reside in a bibliographic vacuum. Other bibliographic structures surround these records and now inhabit library automated systems. Librarians must not and should not abandon the principal of name main-entry heading, but rather continue to understand, and when necessary, modify how the name main-entry heading should be used within the universe of bibliographic control and its bibliographic underpinnings.[39]

NOTES

1. *Anglo-American Cataloguing Rules.* 2nd ed. (Chicago : American Library Association, 1978), p. viii.

2. *Anglo-American Cataloguing Rules.* 2nd ed., 1988 Revision. (Chicago : American Library Association, 1988), p. 619.

3. Ibid., p. 311.

4. *Anglo-American Cataloging Rules*. North American text. (Chicago : American Library Association, 1967), p. 343.

5. *Anglo-American Cataloguing Rules*. 2nd ed., 1988 Revision, p. 620.

6. Ibid., p. 312-313.

7. Elizabeth L. Tate, "Examining the "Main" in Main Entry Heading." In *The Making of a Code: The Issues Underlying AACR2*. Ed. Doris H. Clack. (Chicago : American Library Association, 1980), p. 109-140.

8. *Anglo-American Cataloguing Rules*. 2nd ed., 1988 Revision, p. 620.

9. Dorothy Gregor and Carol Mandel, "Cataloging Must Change!." *Library Journal* 116, no. 6 (April 1, 1991):45.

10. J.C.M. Hanson, "Corporate Authorship Versus Title Entry," *Library Quarterly* 5 no. 4 (Oct. 1935):457-466.

11. Julia Pettee, "The Development of Authorship Entry and the Formulation of Authorship Rules as Found in the Anglo-American Code." *Library Quarterly* 6 (July 1936):270-90.

12. Ibid., p. 270-271.

13. Ibid., p. 285.

14. Ibid.

15. Elizabeth L. Tate, "Examining the "Main" in Main Entry Headings," p. 113-115.

16. *Report: International Conference on Cataloguing Principles, Paris, 9th-18th October, 1961*. (London : Organizing Committee of the International Conference on Cataloguing Principles, 1963), p. 91-96.

17. Wesley Simonton, "The Computerized Catalog: Possible, Feasible, Desirable?" *Library Resources & Technical Services* 8 (Fall 1964):399-407.

18. M. Nabil Hamdy, *The Concept of Main Entry as Represented in the Anglo-American Cataloging Rules: A Critical Appraisal and Some Suggestions–Author Main Entry vs. Title Main Entry*. (Littleton, Colo. : Libraries Unlimited, 1973), p. 132.

19. Doralyn J. Hickey, "Theory of Bibliographic Control." In *Prospects for Change in Bibliographic Control: Proceedings of the Thirty-eighth Annual Conference of the Graduate Library School, November 8-9, 1976*. (Chicago : University of Chicago Press, 1977), p. 37.

20. Michael Gorman, "AACR2: Main Themes." In *Making of a Code: The Issues Underlying AACR2: Proceedings of International Conference on AACR2 Held in Tallahassee 11-14 March 1979*. Ed. Doris H. Clack (Chicago : American Library Association, 1980), p. 45.

21. Patrick Wilson, "The Catalog as Access Mechanism: Background and Concepts." *Library Resources & Technical Services* 27:1 (Jan-Mar. 1983):4-17.

22. Ibid.

23. Michael Carpenter, "Main Entry." In *The Conceptual Foundations of Descriptive Cataloging*. Ed. Elaine Svenonius. (San Diego : Academic Press, 1989), p. 88.

24. Arnold S. Wajenberg, "A Cataloger's View of Authorship." In *Conceptu-*

al Foundations of Descriptive Cataloging. Ed. Elaine Svenonius. (San Diego : Academic Press, 1989), p. 25.

25. Charles A. Cutter, *Rules for a Dictionary Catalog*, 4th ed., rewritten (Washington, D.C. : Government Printing Office, 1904), p. 11-12.

26. Michael Gorman, "AACR2: Main Themes," p. 46.

27. *Anglo-American Cataloguing Rules*. 2nd ed., 1988 Revision, p. 313.

28. Anne B. Piternick, "Authors Online: A Searcher's Approach to the Online Catalog." In *The Conceptual Foundations of Descriptive Cataloging*. Ed. Elaine Svenonius. (San Diego : Academic Press, 1989), p. 29-40.

29. Ibid., p. 31.

30. Arnold S. Wajenberg, "A Cataloger's View of Authorship," p. 21-27.

31. Michael Carpenter, "Main Entry," p. 73-95.

32. Arnold S. Wajenberg, "A Cataloger's View of Authorship," p. 22-23.

33. Meredith Merritt, "Racter the Author," *Library Journal* 110 (Nov. 1, 1985):160.

34. *Anglo-American Cataloguing Rules*. 2nd ed., 1988 Revision, p. 313-314.

35. Arnold S. Wajenberg, "A Cataloger's View of Authorship," p. 24.

36. Charles A. Cutter, *Rules for a Dictionary Catalog*, 4th ed., rewritten. In *Foundations of Cataloging: A Sourcebook*. Ed. Michael Carpenter and Elaine Svenonius. (Littleton, CO : Libraries Unlimited, 1988), p. 666-67.

37. Alan Seal and others, *Full and Short Entry Catalogues: Library Needs and Uses*. (Aldershot : Gower, 1982), p. 2.

38. Helen F. Schmierer, "The Impact of Technology on Cataloging Rules." In *The Conceptual Foundations of Descriptive Cataloging*. Ed. Elaine Svenonius. (San Diego : Academic Press, 1989), p. 115.

39. The author wishes to acknowledge the editorial assistance of Beth R. Barrett

Index

